Russian and Post-Soviet Organized Crime

The International Library of Criminology, Criminal Justice and Penology
Series Editors: Gerald Mars and David Nelken

Titles in the Series:

Russian and Post-Soviet Organized Crime

Edited by

Mark Galeotti

Keele University, UK

Published by
Dartmouth Publishing Company
Ashgate Publishing Limited
Gower House
Croft Road
Aldershot
Hants GU11 3HR
England

Ashgate Publishing Company
131 Main Street
Burlington, VT 05401-5600 USA

Ashgate website: http://www.ashgate.com

British Library Cataloguing in Publication Data
Galeotti, Mark
    Russian and post-Soviet organized crime. – (The
    international library of criminology, criminal justice and
    penology)
    1. Organized crime – Russia (Federation). 2. Organized crime –
    Former Soviet republics
    I. Title
    364.1'06'0947

Library of Congress Cataloging-in-Publication Data
Russian and post-Soviet organized crime / edited by Mark Galeotti.
        p. cm. — (International library of criminology, criminal justice, and peneology (sic!))
    Includes bibliographical references.
    ISBN 0-7546-2176-6
        1. Organized crime—Russia (Federation) 2. Organized crime—Soviet Union. 3.
Organized crime—Former Soviet republics. 4. Transnational crime—Russia (Federation)
5. Criminal law—Russia (Federation) 6. Political corruption—Russia (Federation) I.
Title: Russian and post-Soviet organized crime edited by Mark Galeotti. II. Galeotti,
Mark. III. International library of criminology, criminal justice & penology

    HV6453.R8 R86 2001
    364.1'06'0947—dc21
                                                                                00-069003

ISBN 0 7546 2176 6

Printed in Great Britain by The Cromwell Press, Trowbridge, Wiltshire

Contents

PART III ASSESSMENTS

PART IV RUSSIAN ORGANIZED CRIME AND THE RUSSIAN ECONOMY

PART V GLOBAL RUSSIAN ORGANIZED CRIME?

Acknowledgements

The editor and publishers wish to thank the following for permission to use copyright material.

Archives Européenes de Sociologie for the essay: Federico Varese (1994), 'Is Sicily the Future of Russia? Private Protection and the Rise of the Russian Mafia', *Archives européenes de sociologie*, **XXXV**, pp. 224–58. Copyright © 1994 AES. The text of the above article has been previously printed in *European Journal of Sociology*, **XXXV** (1994), pp. 224–58. Reprinted with permission.

Blackwell Publishers Limited for the essay: Mark Galeotti (1998), 'The *Mafiya* and the New Russia', *Australian Journal of Politics and History*, **44**, pp. 415–29. Copyright © 1998 Departments of Government and History, University of Queensland and Blackwell Publishers.

Demokratizatsiya for the essays: Louise I. Shelley (1994), 'Post-Soviet Organized Crime: Implications for Economic, Social and Political Development', *Demokratizatsiya*, **2**, pp. 341–58; Svetlana P. Glinkina (1994), 'Privatizatsiya and Kriminalizatsiya: How Organized Crime Is Hijacking Privatization', *Demokratizatsiya*, **2**, pp. 385–91. Reprinted with permission of the Helen Dwight Reid Education Foundation. Published by Heldref Publications, 1319 Eighteenth St, NW, Washington, DC 20036-1802.

Éditions de L'École des Hautes Études en Science Sociales for the essay: Federico Varese (1998), 'The Society of the *Vory-v-Zakone*, 1930s–1950s', *Cahiers du Monde russe*, **39**, pp. 515–38.

Foreign Affairs for the essay: Stephen Handelman (1994), 'The Russian "Mafiya" ', *Foreign Affairs*, **73**, pp. 83–96. Copyright © 1994 Council on Foreign Relations, Inc.

Frank Cass & Co. Ltd for the essays: Joseph D. Serio and Vyacheslav Razinkin (1995), 'Thieves Professing the Code: The Traditional Role of *Vory v Zakone* in Russia's Criminal World and Adaptations to a New Social Reality', *Low Intensity Conflict & Law Enforcement*, **4**, pp. 72–88; James Finckenauer and Elin Waring (1994), 'Russian Emigré Crime in the United States: Organized Crime or Crime that is Organized?', *Transnational Organized Crime*, **2**, pp. 139–55.

History Today Limited for the essay: Mark Galeotti (1994), 'Criminal Russia: The Traditions Behind the Headlines', *History Today*, pp. 12–14.

International Association for the Study of Organized Crime for the essay: Lydia S. Rosner (1995), 'The Sexy Russian Mafia', *Criminal Organizations*, **10**, pp. 28–32.

Jane's Information Group Limited for the essay: Mark Galeotti (2000), 'Inside the Russian Mafiya', *Jane's Intelligence Review*, March, pp. 8–9. Reproduced with permission from Jane's Information Group.

Alena V. Ledeneva (1998), 'Organized Crime in Russia Today', *Jamestown Foundation Prism*, 17 April, pp. 3, 7, 14, 15. Copyright © 1998 Alena V. Ledeneva.

Alena V. Ledeneva (1999), 'Practices of Exchange and Networking in Russia', *Journal of Financial Crime*, **6**, pp. 218–33. Copyright © 1999 Alena V. Ledeneva.

Oxford University Press for the essay: W.E. Butler (1992), 'Crime in the Soviet Union: Early Glimpses of the True Story', *British Journal of Criminology*, **32**, pp. 144–59.

Royal Institute of International Affairs for the essay: Phil Williams (1996), 'Hysteria, Complacency and Russian Organized Crime', *PSBF Briefing* (Royal Institute of International Affairs), **8**, pp. 1–6.

Sage Publications, Inc. for the essays: Robert J. Kelly, Rufus Schatzberg and Patrick J. Ryan (1995), 'Primitive Capitalist Accumulation: Russia as a Racket', *Journal of Contemporary Criminal Justice*, **11**, pp. 257–75; Joseph L. Albini, R.E. Rogers, Victor Shabalin, Valery Kutushev, Vladimir Moiseev and Julie Anderson (1995), 'Russian Organized Crime: Its History, Structure and Function', *Journal of Contemporary Criminal Justice*, **11**, pp. 213–43; Alexander S. Nikiforov (1993), 'Organized Crime in the West and in the Former USSR: An Attempted Comparison', *International Journal of Offender Therapy and Comparative Criminology*, **37**, pp. 5–15. Reprinted by permission of Sage Publications, Inc.

M.E. Sharpe Inc. for the essay: Steven J. Staats (1972), 'Corruption in the Soviet System', *Problems of Communism*, **21**, pp. 40-47. Reprinted with permission from M.E. Sharpe, Inc., Armonk, NY 10504.

Taylor & Francis Ltd for the essays: Gerald Mars and Yochanan Altman (1983), 'The Cultural Bases of Soviet Georgia's Second Economy', *Soviet Studies*, **XXXV**, pp. 546–60; Vadim Volkov (1999), 'Violent Entrepreneurship in Post-Communist Russia', *Europe-Asia Studies*, **51**, pp. 741–54.

Every effort has been made to trace all the copyright holders, but if any have been inadvertently overlooked the publishers will be pleased to make the necessary arrangement at the first opportunity.

Series Preface

The International Library of Criminology, Criminal Justice and Penology, represents an important publishing initiative to bring together the most significant journal essays in contemporary criminology, criminal justice and penology. The series makes available to researchers, teachers and students an extensive range of essays which are indispensable for obtaining an overview of the latest theories and findings in this fast changing subject.

This series consists of volumes dealing with criminological schools and theories as well as with approaches to particular areas of crime, criminal justice and penology. Each volume is edited by a recognised authority who has selected twenty or so of the best journal articles in the field of their special competence and provided an informative introduction giving a summary of the field and the relevance of the articles chosen. The original pagination is retained for ease of reference.

The difficulties of keeping on top of the steadily growing literature in criminology are complicated by the many disciplines from which its theories and findings are drawn (sociology, law, sociology of law, psychology, psychiatry, philosophy and economics are the most obvious). The development of new specialisms with their own journals (policing, victimology, mediation) as well as the debates between rival schools of thought (feminist criminology, left realism, critical criminology, abolitionism etc.) make necessary overviews that offer syntheses of the state of the art. These problems are addressed by the INTERNATIONAL LIBRARY in making available for research and teaching the key essays from specialist journals.

GERALD MARS
*Professor in Applied Anthropology, Universities of North London
and Northumbria Business Schools*

DAVID NELKEN
*Distinguished Research Professor, Cardiff Law Schoool,
University of Wales, Cardiff*

Introduction

Criminal Foundations

Crime holds up a mirror to its world, albeit a dark and distorted one. Increasingly, organized societies beget increasingly organized underworlds, just as globalization has led to transnational crime. So, too, does geopolitics have its own impact, from the reverberations of Hong Kong's return to mainland Chinese control on the global triad network to the collapse of Yugoslavia on the Balkan heroin routes into Europe. Undoubtedly the most dramatic political event of the late twentieth century was the collapse of the Soviet Union and its political empire, and this has also unleashed on the world a new and distinctive form of organized crime.

This distinctive, even postmodernist, form of organized crime is dominated by extremely loose and flexible networks of autonomous criminal entrepreneurs and is characterized by an especially keen awareness of the political environment in which it operates. To a large extent, this reflects its history: what may be new and disquieting to the rest of the world turns out, in its essentials, to have a long and shadowy tradition. Russia and the former USSR had, after all, thriving underworlds, shaped by the weaknesses of the regular police,[1] the corruption of the élites and an underground economy, which was at times tacitly accepted by the state as a means to bypassing the bottlenecks of the official, planned economy. My short essay, 'Criminal Russia: The Traditions Behind the Headlines' (Chapter 1) is precisely aimed at drawing links between the relatively primitive forms of crime in the tsarist era and their contemporary counterparts. The pre-revolutionary antecedents of today's *mafiya* were organized gangs of horse thieves, who were integrated into a nation-spanning network of brokers and dealers, as well as loose urban 'thieves' guilds', the *vorovskoi mir* – 'thieves' world' – dominated by the fraudsters, who were their arbitrators and bankers.[2] Already the criminals had their own criminal argot, known as *fenya* and a visual language of tattoos which united criminals whose native dialects of Russian might well be mutually incomprehensible. However, these essentially primordial structures were to be transformed during the Soviet era. Although, to an extent, this was an inevitable byproduct of modernization and urbanization, it was the politics of the Soviet era which were to give it the key stimulus to develop into a coherent criminal society.

The criminal world would be broken in two, and plunged into a revolution of its own. After all, organized crime within the USSR had to emerge within an authoritarian state and prospered when it was able to build alliances with it, or at least with elements within it. Under Stalin, the Gulag prison camps swelled as millions were sentenced – many but by no means all for trumped-up political offences. These prisons created a critical mass of criminals and the rise of a new élite, the *vory v zakone*, or thieves-within-code (as Serio and Razinkin discuss in Chapter 7, this literally means 'thieves-within-the-law', but it is best translated thus).

More to the point, with the camps expanding beyond the state's ability to police them, criminals were recruited to keep the political inmates in line. As unruly farmers, dissident intellectuals, out-of-favour communists and other political prisoners were sent in their millions into the 'Gulag Archipelago', a minority of the truly criminal inmates were successfully co-opted into helping their authorities control them. In Stalinist terms, these thieves, murderers, rapists and bandits were 'socially near', merely workers who had fallen from grace, and thus to be preferred to those imprisoned for political offences.

These collaborators – *suki*, 'bitches' – were sometimes despised and attacked, but there was a general acceptance within the underworld that preying on the hapless 'politicals' was often simply an extension of their criminal activities outside the camps. The real conflict was created by the massive expansion in the numbers of the *suki* and the change in their activities following the Nazi invasion in 1941. Many inmates volunteered to fight or were press-ganged into doing so. By fighting, they may have felt that they were simply doing their patriotic duty but, strictly speaking, they had broken the code of the *Vorovskoi mir*. When the war ended and they returned to the camps, along with many other ex-soldiers (such as those taken prisoner by the Germans), then the scene was set for a major confrontation between traditionalists and 'collaborators'. The 'Scab's War' (*such'ya voina* – more accurately, 'Bitches' War'), raged from the mid-1940s to the early 1950s[3] and not only helped render the 'Gulag Archipelago' effectively ungovernable, but also, as Varese explains (Chapter 2), reshaped the *Vorovskoi mir*. His essay draws upon as yet unique research within archives only opened after the Soviet collapse to explain how the Gulags created this new type of criminal, with rules, traditions and social structures all their own. In this, he builds on Glazov's ground-breaking essay of 1972 (Chapter 3), but also explains how the culture of the *vory v zakone* was, on the one hand, destroyed in the 1950s by the Soviet state and its *suki*, but at the same time elevated to mythic status. For it was the *suki* who won, and the new code no longer proscribed collaboration with the authorities. The way would now be open for a new generation of criminals to collaborate with dishonest Party functionaries and build the foundations for the true Soviet *mafiya*.

However, as Glazov explains, they would draw on the language, culture and traditions of the *vory*, appropriating even the name to themselves. An underground alliance between organized crime and elements of the state blossomed with the corruption of the 1970s and early 1980s, although the criminals were still the junior partner. Whatever the propaganda, this was, after all, a society with crime problems of its own. The streets were relatively safer than their Western counterparts but, as Staats demonstrates in Chapter 4, corruption underpinned the whole economic system.[4] His essay, 'Corruption in the Soviet System', was one of the first to place corruption at the centre of the Soviet social contract and remains perhaps the most powerful. By presenting corruption not solely as a malignant byproduct of Soviet rule but as a central element of the Party's social contract, Staats made an extremely important and acute contribution to understanding this regime. To an extent a tolerance of – and, at times, even encouragement of – corruption and black marketeering was part of a deliberate government policy to use underground resources to compensate for the shortcomings of the state-controlled economy. However, Mars and Altman (Chapter 5) were also able conclusively to illustrate the extent to which this also had a strong cultural and regional dimension (see also Amir, 1986; Critchlow, 1988). Not only did different cultures within this multi-ethnic land empire have different understandings of corruption, its acceptable uses and limitations, but many also regarded it as part of a covert struggle with the centre. Corrupting centrally-appointed élites and using corruption to embezzle government funds could thus be not only a source of mercenary gain but also a blow struck against imperial domination. Similarly, corruption to shield and support one's family and friends might have been illegal but was accepted as moral. In such gaps between the official legal and political system and public perceptions of right and necessity, organized crime in the non-Russian republics was able to flourish.

Largely by preying on the black marketeers and acting as their middlemen with corrupt elements within the national and local élites, the members of the *Vorovskoi mir* were undoubtedly beneficiaries of the relative stability and affluence of the early 1970s. Ironically, their services were even more in demand as shortages began to bite in the latter half of the decade. It was, however, with Gorbachev's reforms that they were able to move from the shadows. It was also only with his campaign of *perestroika* that more than the narrowest of debates on this question became possible. Before the mid-1980s, crime was largely a taboo topic within the USSR and – partly because of a total lack of data – was also largely absent from Western analyses, beyond the literature on corruption and the underground economy. Those rare exceptions tended either to be written by émigrés able to draw on their own experiences (for example, Brokhin, 1975; Chalidze, 1977; Simis, 1982; Zeldes, 1981) or by academics working closely with émigrés (such as Connor, 1972; Rosner, 1986). In 1982, former KGB chief Yuri Andropov, aware of the widening gap between real and published crime figures, had taken the first step towards openness by ordering that gap closed, and as a result 1983 saw an increase in the official crime figures of almost 23 per cent. However, it was under Gorbachev, with his campaign for *glasnost* ('openness') that wider debates about the problem were allowed, galvanizing Soviet and Western debates alike.

What is the *Mafiya*?

Butler's essay (Chapter 6), aptly subtitled 'Early Glimpses of the True Story', draws on the data which began to be released after six decades of propaganda and secrecy. As a concise summary of changing crime rates through the 1960s to the 1980s, and especially in the latter decade, it is still unsurpassed. His analysis reveals that the official figures – not that they should be regarded as telling the whole story – show a steady, if not uninterrupted, rise in reported crimes until the 1980s. Then, whether because of the growing crisis within the Soviet economy, the reforms which were introduced in a vain attempt to reverse it or, most likely, a combination of the two, the 1980s witnessed a rapid growth in crime rates. In particular, Butler discusses the explosion in group and organized crimes. After all, this was the era in which Soviet citizens started talking about their *mafiya*, although, initially, the term was very broadly defined – usually having more to do with corrupt Communist Party functionaries than organized crime as such.

But this was also the period when Soviet citizens were actually beginning to encounter their *mafiya* in the flesh. Gorbachev's anti-alcohol campaign proved as invigorating for organized crime as Prohibition in the United States. Not only did it, for the first time, give the criminals a new, mass market, it did so in such circumstances that they were widely regarded as allies rather than enemies of the public. His partial economic liberalization, creating private cooperatives, then proceeded to give the criminals new targets for their protection rackets and legitimate front organizations. The police, sharing the general public's suspicion of the cooperatives, proved unwilling to protect them against these predators and, by the end of the Gorbachev era, a majority were either criminal fronts or were having to pay protection money. Subsequently, attempts at political liberalization led to an attempted conservative coup and ultimately the collapse of the Soviet state in 1991, creating new states born bankrupt and in crisis.

Many therefore explain today's *mafiya* in terms of its recent and not-so-recent history. In an effective alliance of US and Russian analysts, Serio and Razinkin put the emphasis on the evolution of the old *Vorovskoi mir* and its traditions (Chapter 7). They see the *vory* as successfully evolving to meet the new conditions, acting as arbitrators and middlemen amongst the more operationally active, younger generation of *avtoritety* ('authorities'). While the above authors continue to put the main focus on the criminals, relegating the corrupt politicians and functionaries to the roles of clients and allies, Handelman's essay (Chapter 8) puts the emphasis more squarely on the corruption of the Party élite and its growing integration with organized crime. To Handelman, the dominant figure within this new underworld is the 'comrade criminal', the corrupt functionary who converts his political power into economic power with the active assistance of the criminal. Of course, the two are complementary – one of the most striking aspects of the criminalization of post-Soviet Russia has precisely been the integration of these two criminal milieus.

This integration helps explain organized crime's ability quickly to subvert and suborn local and national political structures (Boshkolov, 1995; Coulloudon, 1997; Shelley, 1997; Waller, 1994; Waller and Yasmann, 1997). In Chapter 10 Albini *et al.* see the key change as being the rise of syndicated organized crime since the late 1950s – structures which seek direct economic gain by providing illicit goods and services through threat, violence and obtaining protection from political and police actors. These syndicates, based on loose patron–client associations, proved effective in operating within the corrupted Soviet state of the Brezhnev era and surviving and thriving within the chaos of *perestroika* and post-Soviet Russian reform. In Chapter 9, Kelly, Schatzberg and Ryan go beyond this, conceptualizing this as a form of 'primitive capitalist accumulation', and arguing that all that is happening is that a centralized criminal empire is fragmenting into local ones which are using their existing coercive, political and economic resources to acquire more in the midst of this fragmentation.

Of course, there is a danger of overstating the power and unity of the *mafiya* and the extent to which it is an external parasite on society rather than part of it and the transition it is undergoing. In his second essay in this volume, Federico Varese takes a more conceptual view (Chapter 11), adopting Diego Gambetta's elegant, if not uncontroversial, notion that a mafia is essentially an illegal provider of non-state security (Gambetta, 1993). Varese thus explores the extent to which organized crime has prospered precisely because the state has proved unable or unwilling to meet its citizens' needs for security, whether personal security or the ability to recover debts. Drawing comparisons with Sicily, he concludes that its rise can be explained in terms of filling this vacuum, but that it also now has a vested interest in maintaining its role and thus ensuring that the state does not begin to meet its citizens' needs.

Assessments

In Chapter 12 Nikiforov seeks to draw a direct comparison with Western experiences – a valiant undertaking considering the near-unique conditions of the 1990s, with the confluence of post-imperialism, political and economic transformation, military collapse and local civil war.[5] Yet, perhaps the whole point is that this is something new. To Louise Shelley, one of the first

Western scholars to address the problem, organized crime has even become 'a new form of authoritarianism', on a par with the authoritarianism of the Soviet order in terms of its impact on civil society (Shelley, 1996). In her essay in this volume (Chapter 13), she looks broadly at the implications of post-Soviet organized crime and concludes that its pervasiveness may drag Russia and the other former Soviet states from the road to democracy and the free market. Instead, political clientelism and controlled markets may lead to a 'banana republic' model, displaying the forms of democracy but with true power in the hands of an entrenched and interconnected political–economic–military–criminal élite.

With the collapse of the USSR, though, organized crime was able to use its wealth, contacts and, ultimately, coercive power to full effect. In Chapter 14 Alena Ledeneva, one of the sharpest of the new generation of scholars hailing from Russia, outlines five key processes at work: economization, detraditionalization, professionalization, globalization and legalization. As organized crime develops, it is evolving away from its rough-and-ready roots and culture and is becoming instead a transnational business run by effective criminal entrepreneurs. Also, like organized crime elsewhere in the world, it has created a variety of enclaves outside government control. These tend to be geographically defined. In Chechnya, for example, a tradition of freewheeling banditry, the opportunities provided by organized crime and the promise of freedom from bitterly resented Russian rule served to turn it into a veritable 'free criminal zone' (Jennings, 1993; Lieven, 1998; Smith, 1988). The subsequent Russian invasions of 1994 and 1999 were essentially products of politics and imperialism rather than police actions, and did little to quell a criminal phenomenon which, by then, had largely outgrown the Chechen highlands (Galeotti, 2000a). Similarly, opium-producing regions such as Uzbekistan's Fergana Valley and Tajikistan's Gorny Badakhshan district are largely out of government control. Less overt has been the penetration of organized crime into local power structures. Regions such as Sverdlovsk and the Russian Far East are notorious for their criminalization, and efforts by Moscow to bring them to heel have largely been foiled by a dangerous alliance of gangsters and corrupt élites (Galeotti, 1998; Nomokonov and Shulga, 1998; Repetskaya, 1999). Serio's essay 'Shunning Tradition' (Chapter 15) is one of the very few to consider non-Russian organized crime (see also Galeotti, 2000; Lieven, 1998, ch. 10; Shelley, 1999b; Smith, 1998, Part 4).

Russian Organized Crime and the Russian Economy

Organized crime need not be defined by ethnic, geographic or political identifiers, though. In particular, organized crime has been able to assume a powerful role within a new economy which is largely based on either privatized elements of the Party-controlled economy or legalized aspects of the former underground economy. In Chapter 16 Svetlana Glinkina demonstrates the extent to which its combination of wealth, contacts and coercive muscle has allowed it to benefit from a rushed privatization, carried out by young reformers who genuinely believed that their main danger came from a Communist resurgence. Thus, they wanted to remove assets from state control, even if through an imperfect privatization which would allow huge portions of the economy to end up in criminal hands. Some industries – notably aluminium and car production – have become infamous for their criminalization and the periodic turf wars which explode over certain factories. Glinkina's essay is important for the links it draws between political change, economic reform and organized crime in this 'hijacking of privatization'.

Of course, organized crime does not 'own' Russia. The Interior Ministry routinely claims that it controls 40 per cent of the Russian economy, but this figure must be treated with considerable caution since not only has it remained suspiciously static for the period 1992–2001, but the 40 per cent figure also seems interchangeably applied to the proportion of firms under criminal control, proportion of GDP and proportion of the economy operating in the 'shadow sector'. However, what organized crime does not control outright it can influence. Alena Ledeneva has pioneered research into the informal economic linkages and exchanges known as *blat* (roughly translated as 'pull' or 'contacts'). Her studies, summarized in her second contribution to this volume (Chapter 17), not only underline the role of the criminals in this alternative economic system (see also Berliner, 1998; Ledeneva, 1998; Ledeneva and Kurkchiyan, 2000; Lovell *et al.*, 2001; Mars and Altman, 1983), but also attest to the scale and pervasiveness of the 'favour economy'. In its own terms this works effectively, but it also leaves much of the Russian economy outside the reach of the laws and the courts so that it becomes not only vulnerable to organized crime but also an active and enthusiastic customer and partner.

Volkov's thoughtful and penetrating dissection of 'violent entrepreneurship' – the process of translating coercive muscle into economic power – offers an invaluable additional perspective on the role of organized crime as an economic actor (Chapter 18). Drawing from primary research sources, Volkov is able to demonstrate not only that organized crime is a predator, but also that, as Varese suggests, it occupies distinct functional niches within the half-underground Russian economy. Central is the notion of a *krysha*, a 'roof' or 'protection', a very important but also complex and sometimes ambiguous concept. This term is used for a whole range of separate activities, from the simple – and parasitic – extortion of protection money to rather more positive services. A 'minimal' *krysha* simply means that the criminals will not victimize or rob you. A more advanced one would probably also extend to protecting you from other criminals. The 'best' sort, though, also provides a range of other services, from cheap loans (often as money-laundering ventures) to an inside track on whom to bribe within the local authorities to get things done. In the words of one young Russian entrepreneur, 'your first and most important business decision when setting up a new venture is who your *krysha* will be'. He is not alone: an estimated 70–80 per cent of firms pay an average of 10–20 per cent of their profits for this 'roof'.

However, despite superficial comparisons with the 'robber baron' period of US history, which lend themselves to a complacent assumption that market forces will eventually dispense with the *mafiya*, or even a romantic notion of the criminal as cutting-edge capitalist,[6] ultimately this is an economically and politically destructive phenomenon. Organized crime may cut red tape and cycle money into the economy in the short term, but it also creates and protects uneconomic monopolies and undermines the necessary faith in the level playing field of the law. As I discuss in my essay in the *Australian Journal of Politics and History* (Chapter 19) this has serious implications for the new Russian polity because it is weakening central authority in Russia, diluting the state's monopoly of coercion, discrediting the market economy and, in the final analysis, usurping and distorting the very functions of the state.

Global Russian Organized Crime?

Of course, what happens to a nuclear power spanning eleven time zones matters to the rest of the world. Post-Soviet organized crime has become a fully-fledged international security problem (Lallemand, 1997; Webster *et al.*, 1997). It has contributed to the corruption of the Russian military and the haemorrhage of weapons to the world's criminals and war zones (Vallance, 1994; Turbiville, 1995; Galeotti, 1999a). It brokers a huge and growing trade in narcotics to Europe and the Americas (Lee and MacDonald, 1993; Knabe, 1993; Lee, 1995; Galeotti, 1999b). The *mafiya* is also fervently internationalist and active in at least 26 foreign countries by mid-1998 (*Itar-Tass*, 1998).

To some, it was important – especially in the early years after the Soviet collapse – to adopt an overdelicate approach, seemingly unwilling to admit to the criminalization of the former Soviet states because it was politically inexpedient or implied some criticism of the transition from the Soviet model. To others, post-Soviet organized crime represented a potential Russian 'fifth column' abroad (Sherr, 1995). Indeed, initial assessments represented it as some monolithic criminal conspiracy. Claire Sterling (1994) saw the very real international cooperation taking place between criminal organizations – a natural product of globalization and the criminals' desire to maximize their profits while minimizing their risks – and characterized this as part of a growing 'Pax Mafiosa', a behind-the-scenes partitioning of the world between the godfathers. This scenario, more reminiscent of the machinations of SPECTRE in James Bond films, found favour with some, not least those within intelligence communities and their allies bereft of ideological foes since the end of the Cold War (see, Lupsha, 1996; Naylor, 1995; Williams, 1995). Lydia Rosner, herself a pioneer of the study of crime in the socialist bloc (see Rosner, 1986), issued a stern warning of the dangers in this 'sexy Russian mafia' myth (Chapter 20). Although she may underplay the nature of the challenge, her essay is a useful counter to the inevitable media myths surrounding this phenomenon.

This rather sterile debate, aptly characterized by Phil Williams (Chapter 21) as one between 'the hawks and the doves' has, fortunately, largely given way to more accurate assessments based on genuine research. His essay, originally published by the Royal Institute of International Affairs, offers not only a perceptive snapshot of the situation in 1996 but also identifies these two, equally misleading, schools of thought. The first, that of the worst-case assessment (the 'hawks') simply substitutes Russian *mafiya* for Soviet communism as a threat to the West, regarding it as a coherent and conspiratorial menace. The best-case assessment (the 'doves'), by contrast, denies that post-Soviet organized crime poses any real threat at all, regarding it as nothing more than a temporary and transitional byproduct of economic and political reform.

The market has not 'tamed' the *mafiya* – if anything, the previous studies have shown conclusively the degree to which organized crime has shaped the market in Russia. However, this is not to say that the 'hawks' have been vindicated. The threat to the West, as explored by Finckenauer and Waring in Chapter 22, is not directed and ideological but entrepreneurial and opportunistic. Their detailed study of Russian organized crime operating in the Tri-State Area (New York, New York State and New Jersey), in cooperation with a law enforcement task force – the first such major academic study of their operations outside Russia – refutes suggestions that post-Soviet organized crime in the USA has a traditional pyramidal structure, with strong hierarchies and chains of command stretching from top to bottom.[7] This essay draws uniquely on a major law-enforcement operation – and it is worth stressing how good investigation and good academic research can often seem very similar – as well as important debate on precisely what 'organized crime' really is. After all, the days of assuming that all gangs were tightly structured and disciplined hierarchies are over; many are much looser structures. Finckenauer and Waring's essay summarizes many of the key issues in their subsequent monograph, in which they conclude that this is not really 'organized crime' or even a 'mafia', so much as a network of criminals engaged in long-term cooperation (Finckenauer and Waring, 1998).

This is precisely what constitutes the *mafiya*. The Russian term is worth adopting because this is a distinctive form of organized crime. As I discuss in my short study for *Jane's Intelligence Review* (Chapter 23), even within Russia the pattern is of networks of semi-autonomous individuals and crews with a loose pecking order rather than the classic pyramids of organized crime. Indeed, this is the very strength of the *mafiya* model, a thoroughly modern, post-industrial form of organized crime – the product of the mobile telephone, the cashless bank transfer and air travel (Galeotti, 2000b). What it may lack in the security and economies of scale of the more rigidly structured traditional organized crime grouping, it makes up for with its flexibility and its resistance to 'decapitation' – there is no 'boss' to take out, no grand plan to foil. As such, there are several forms of *mafiya* penetration outside the former Soviet Union, ranging from the 'hard' penetration of direct incursion to the indirect influence acquired by providing 'criminal services' to indigenous organized criminal groupings.[8]

Conclusion

These, then, are the broad outlines of this evolving and emerging problem. It is undoubtedly a serious and growing transnational criminal challenge. Yet at the same time, the young field of the study of Russian and post-Soviet organized crime is proving equally dynamic and transnational.[9] For the first time, Western scholarship and research and data from the post-Soviet states is coming together, thanks as much to the new communication possibilities offered by the Internet as the opportunities to collaborate provided by the end of the Cold War. Free debate, a new cohort of young scholars and empirical research in places closed to foreigners until recently and on topics even Russians themselves could not discuss are making this not only a lively and impressive field of study, but one that is making an immediate and effective contribution to policy and law-enforcement responses to the problem.

Notes

1   This has been a recurring theme: as notional 'police states' go, Russia and the USSR have actually been strikingly underpoliced. See Conquest (1968); Galeotti (1993, 1997); Pustintsev (2000); Shelley (1990); Shelley (1996a); Thurston (1980); and Weissman (1985).

2   For further exploration of pre-revolutionary Russian 'organized crime', see also Chalidze (1977); Frank (1999, especially Chapter 4); and Frierson (1987).

3   Although official Soviet sources are now coming to light, and were used by Varese for his ground-breaking study of the *vory v zakone*, otherwise the main sources have been autobiographical accounts of Gulag survivors, typically political prisoners. The accounts with the greatest to say on the 'Scab's War' are Buca (1976); Kuznetsov (1975); Panin (1976); Scholner (1954); Shalamov (1990); and Solzhenitsyn (1973).

4   Other good studies of Soviet-era corruption and this informal social contract are Clark (1993); Holmes (1993); Holmes (1997); Jowitt (1983); Lampert (1984); Lovell *et al.* (2000); Millar (1985); Schwartz (1979); Simis (1982); and Vaksberg (1991).

5   For other attempts at comparisons (and discussion as to the limitations of such parallels) see Anderson (1995).
6   See, for example, Luttwak (1995). For an effective rebuttal of these comfortable assumptions, see Anderson (1995).
7   See, for example, the report on Russian penetration of California, by the Office of the Attorney General, State of California at http://tarens.ns.net/ag/gangs/rusorg1.htm.
8   For a more detailed discussion of this, see Galeotti (2000c).
9   For a comprehensive bibliography of works on crime, corruption and policing in Russia, from the nineteenth to the twenty-first centuries, see Galeotti (2000d).

References

Amir, M. (1986), 'Organized Crime and Organized Criminality Among Georgian Jews in Israel', in R. Kelly (ed.), *Organized Crime: A Global Perspective*, Totowa, New Jersey: Rowman and Littlefield.

Anderson, A. (1995), 'The Red Mafia: A Legacy of Communism', in E. Lazear (ed.), *Economic Transition in Eastern Europe and Russia*, Washington DC: Hoover Institute Press; also at http://www.andrsn.stanford.edu/Other/redmaf.html.

Berliner, J. (1954), 'Blat is Higher than Stalin', *Problems of Communism*, **3**(1).

Boshkholov, S. (1995), 'Organized Crime and Corruption in Russia', *Demokratizatsiya*, **3**(3).

Brokhin, Y. (1975), *Hustling on Gorky Street*, New York: Doubleday.

Buca, E. (1976), *Vorkuta*, London: Constable.

Chalidze, V. (1977), *Criminal Russia*, New York: Random House.

Clark, W.A. (1993), *Crime and Punishment in Soviet Officialdom*, London: ME Sharpe.

Connor, W. (1972), *Deviance in Soviet Society*, New York: Columbia University Press.

Conquest, R. (1968), *The Soviet Police System*, London: Bodley Head.

Coulloudon, V. (1997), 'Crime and Corruption after Communism', *East European Constitutional Review*, **6**(4).

Critchlow, J. (1988), 'Corruption, Nationalism and the Native Elites in Soviet Central Asia', *Journal of Communist Studies*, **4**(2).

Finckenauer, J. and Waring, E. (1998), *Russian Mafia in America*, Boston MA: Northeastern University Press.

Frank, S. (1999), *Crime, Cultural Conflict and Justice in Rural Russia*, Berkeley CA: University of California Press.

Frierson, C. (1987), 'Crime and Punishment in the Russian Village', *Slavic Review*, **46**(1).

Galeotti, M. (1993), 'Perestroika, Perestrelka, Pereborka: Policing Russia in a Time of Change', *Europe-Asia Studies*, **45**(5).

Galeotti, M. (1997), *Policing Russia*, Jane's Intelligence Review Special Report, Coulsdon: Jane's Publishing Group.

Galeotti, M. (1998), 'The Russian Wild East: A Complex Criminal Threat', *Jane's Intelligence Review*, **10**(9).

Galeotti, M. (1999a), 'Russia's Criminal Army', *Jane's Intelligence Review*, June.

Galeotti, M. (1999b), 'The "Russian Mafiya" and Europe's Narcotics Problem', *Interpol and Technology in Partnership: Fighting Drug Trafficking*, Lyon: Interpol.

Galeotti, M. (2000a), 'Chechen Crime Alive and Well', *Jane's Intelligence Review*, **12**(3).

Galeotti, M. (2000b), 'Globalising Crime', *Cross-Border Control*, **14**.

Galeotti, M. (2000c), 'The Russian Mafiya: Economic Penetration at Home and Abroad', in A. Ledeneva and M. Kurkchiyan (eds), *Economic Crime in Russia*.

Galeotti, M. (2000d), *Criminal Russia: A Sourcebook and Coursebook on 150 Years of Crime, Corruption and Policing*, (2nd edn), Keele: ORECRU.

Gambetta, D. (1993), *The Sicilian Mafia: The Business of Private Protection*, Cambridge MA: Harvard University Press.

Holmes, L. (1997), 'Corruption and the Crisis of the Post-Communist State', *Crime, Law and Social Change*, **27**(3–4).

Itar-Tass News Agency, 21 July 1998.

Jennings, A. (1993), 'From Marx to the Mafia', *New Statesman and Society*, 14 May.

Jowitt, K. (1983), 'Soviet Neotraditionalism: The Political Corruption of a Leninist Regime', *Soviet Studies*, **35**(3).

Knabe, B. (1993), 'Das Drogenproblem und die drogenmafia in den GUS-Staten', *Osteuropa*, **43**(11).

Kuznetsov, E. (1975), *Prison Diaries*, New York: Stein & Day.

Lallemand, A. (1997), *L'Organizatsiya, la mafia russe à l'assaut du monde*, Paris: Calmann Lâevy.

Lampert, N. (1984), 'Law and Order in the USSR: The Case of Economic and Political Crime', *Soviet Studies*, **36**(1).

Ledeneva, A. (1998), *Russia's Economy of Favours*, Cambridge: Cambridge University Press.

Ledeneva, A. and Kurkchiyan, M. (eds) (2000), *Economic Crime in Russia*, Dordrecht: Kluwer.

Lee, R. (1995), 'Drugs in Communist States and Former Communist States', *Transnational Organized Crime*, **1**.

Lee, R. and MacDonald, S. (1993), 'Drugs in the East', *Foreign Policy*, **90**.

Lieven, A. (1998), *Chechnya*, New Haven: Yale University Press.

Lovell, S., Ledeneva, A. and Rogatchevskii, A. (eds) (2001), *Bribery and Blat in Russia*, Basingstoke: Palgrave.

Lupsha, P. (1996), 'Transnational Organized Crime versus the Nation-state', *Transnational Organized Crime*, **2**(1).

Luttwak, E. (1995), 'The Good Bad Guys', *The Guardian*, 31 July.

Mars, G. and Altman, Y. (1983), 'How a Soviet Economy Really Works', in M. Clarke (ed.), *Corruption*, Basingstoke: Palgrave.

Millar, J. (1985), 'The Little Deal: Brezhnev's Contribution to Acquisitive Socialism', *Slavic Review*, **44**(4).

Naylor, T. (1995), 'From Cold War to Crime War. The Search for a New National Security Threat', *Transnational Organized Crime*, **1**(4).

Nomokonov, V.A. and Shulga, V.I. (1998), 'Murder for Hire as a Manifestation of Organized Crime', *Demokratizatsiya*, **6**(4).

Panin, D. (1976), *The Notebooks of Sologdin*, London: Hutchinson.

Pustintsev, B. (2000), 'Police Reform in Russia', *Policing and Society*, **10**(1).

Repetskaya, A. (1999), 'Regionalization and Organized Crime in Eastern Siberia', in E. Viano (ed.), *Global Organized Crime and International Security*, Aldershot: Ashgate.

Rosner, L. (1986), *The Soviet Way of Crime*, New York: Bergin and Garvey.

Scholner, J. (1954), *Vorkuta*, London: Weidenfeld & Nicholson.

Schwartz, C. (1979), 'Corruption and Political Development in the USSR', *Comparative Politics*, **11**(4).

Shalamov, V. (1990), *Kolyma Tales*, London: Penguin.

Shelley, L. (1990), 'Soviet Militia', *Policing and Society*, **1**(1).

Shelley, L. (1996a), *Policing Soviet Society*.

Shelley, L. (1996b), 'Post-Soviet Organized Crime: A New Form of Authoritarianism', *Transnational Organized Crime*, **2**(2–3).

Shelley, L. (1997), 'The Criminal-Political Nexus: The Russian Case Study', *NSIC Conference* at http://www.american.edu/transcrime/work/shelleyarticles.html.

Shelley, L. (1999), 'Organised Crime in the Former Soviet Union: The Distinctiveness of Georgia', *Legal Aspects of the Struggle Against Organised Crime in Georgia*, Tblisi: Institute of Legal Reforms [Georgia].

Sherr, J. (1995), 'Russia: Geopolitics and Crime', *The World Today*, **51**(2).

Simis, K. (1982), *The Corrupt Society* (also published as *USSR: Secrets of a Corrupt Society*), New York: Simon and Schuster.

Smith, A. (1988), *Allah's Mountains*, London: Tauris.

Solzhenitsyn, A. (1973), *Gulag Archipelago*, New York: Harper & Row.

Sterling, C. (1994), *Crime Without Frontiers*, Boston: Little Brown.

Thurston, R. (1980), 'Police and People in Moscow', *Russian Review*, **39**(3).

Turbiville, G. (1995), 'Organized Crime and the Russian Armed Forces', *Transnational Organized Crime*, **1**(4).

Vaksberg, A. (1991), *The Soviet Mafia*, trans. J. and E. Roberts, New York: St Martin's Press.

Vallance, B. (1994), 'Corruption and Reform in the Soviet Military', *Journal of Slavic Military Studies*, **7**(4).

Waller, J.M. (1994), 'Organized Crime and the Russian State', *Demokratizatsiya*, **2**(3).

Waller, J.M. and Yasmann, V. (1997), 'Russia's Great Criminal Revolution', in P. Ryan and G. Rush (eds), *Understanding Organized Crime in Global Perspective*.

Webster, W. *et al.* (eds) (1997), *Russian Organized Crime*.

Weissman, N. (1985), 'Regular Police in Tsarist Russia', *Russian Review*, **44**(1).

Williams, P. (1995), 'The New Threat: Transnational Criminal Organizations and International Security', *Criminal Organizations*, **9**(3–4).

Zeldes, I. (1981), *The Problem of Crime in the USSR*.

Part I
Criminal Foundations

[1]

Criminal Russia: the Traditions Behind the Headlines
Mark Galeotti

Suspects rounded up by President Yeltsin's interior ministry police in Moscow, October 1993: part of a co-ordinated crackdown on organised crime.

■ At the beginning of this year, the patience of market traders in the southern Russian town of Saratov broke. When local gangsters came as usual to collect their protection dues, they were beaten unconscious, then beaten some more, and then one of them was impaled upon a piece of metal scaffolding. This was an especially brutal and graphic example of the resistance of ordinary Russians to the new criminal class the collapse of the Soviet Union has liberated, but it harkens back to another age.

In 1873, a peasant by the name of Kuz'ma Rudchenko was found near a village called Brusovka, having been accused of stealing from the community. His hands had been chopped off, his head crushed and his body impaled upon a wooden plank. Far from an unusual and horrific crime, this was just an extreme instance of peasant *samosud* literally, 'judging for oneself' – the rough justice of the village community. Saratov today has its police force, but the market traders could not or would not trust them. Instead they took the law into their own hands, just as the peasants of imperial Russia had put their faith in samosud, rather than the Tsar's courts or the rural police.

Although both Tsarist Russia and the USSR were seen as police states, it is actually striking just how unruly they really were. The relatively few police officers at work were thinly distributed across this huge country. As a result, communities were encouraged or forced by necessity to

12

Self-policing? A village council or *mir* depicted in this 1803 engraving.

police themselves. Perhaps more importantly, though, policing remained a crudely political affair. The legal codes, concerns and priorities of the government seemed alien to most Russians, while the state's own agents seemed to break the laws openly with impunity.

The initial pattern had been set in Tsarist times. Until 1903, a mere 8,400 rural constables and sergeants were faced with the task not only of policing a countryside of over 124 million souls, but also collecting taxes, inspecting sanitation and carrying out a multitude of other administrative duties. The cities of Moscow and St Petersburg were exceptions. In 1905, Moscow had 4,843 policemen, meaning one for every 278 inhabitants, a ratio that compared favourably with those of Berlin (325) or Paris (336). Yet even where they were present in sufficient numbers, their training and methods left much to be desired. Whereas British constables would patrol a beat, their Russian counterparts were simply assigned places to stand within earshot of each other and waited for trouble to come their way.

Most importantly, they never really managed to win the trust and support of the commoners, not least because of their notoriously lax morals and their powerlessness in bringing the law to bear on the crimes of the rich and powerful. Tsarist Russia was a corrupt and lawless nation. Civil servants were even expected to survive by *kormlenie*, 'feeding', supplementing inadequate wages with back-handers and private scams. A government commission in 1856 even concluded that a bribe of less than 500 rubles – perhaps five times a policeman's entire annual salary – should not even be thought of as a bribe at all. No wonder that the Russian proverb had it that 'law and money flow from the same spring'.

In practice, the peasant community – the *mir* – looked after itself. Cutting wood illegally in forests owned by the Tsar or a landowner was regarded as perfectly acceptable. Crimes against other members of the mir, though, were punished accordingly, but usually through samosud rather than the state's legal system. In 1884 alone one district medical officer found himself carrying out autopsies on 200 victims of the lynch mob, in a province of only a quarter of a million inhabitants. As another peasant proverb had it, 'the vengeance of the village is nearer than the mercy of a Tsar'.

The 1917 revolution and the subsequent consolidation of Bolshevik power thus took place in a country already accustomed to think in terms of two sets of laws. There were those of the people, which addressed matters of day-to-day life and the community, and which were enforced by the community. Those of the state, by contrast, as often broken by the state's own agents as enforced, seemed very far from the concerns of the common man or woman. Although the Bolsheviks had expected to bridge this gap, the state of the nation they inherited forced them to think first of survival. The First World War cost Russia some 16 million deaths. The *besprizornye*, homeless, rootless, orphaned children, came to number seven million. Millions of homeless peasants, jobless workers and hungry deserters had no stake in this new world of famine, revolution and civil war. Many turned to brigandage and street crime to survive. The newly established Bolshevik state, though, could not and would not tolerate such anarchy. In the period 1826-1905, the Tsarist regime had shot 894 criminals and revolutionaries. Even in 1906, the peak of late Tsarist repression, the gallows and the firing squads had accounted for some 1,310 victims. But in contrast in eighteen months over 1918-1919, the Bolshevik secret police, the *Cheka*, killed over 8,300 'enemies of the people'.

When, after all, did Soviet Russia ever have a chance to build a stable, law-based state? The 1920s saw a process of re-urbanisation which unsettled traditional patterns of life, even before the whirlwind of industrialisation, forced labour and political terror which was Stalinism destroyed them. Then came the Second World War, and a post-war era characterised by yet more problems of displaced populations and lawlessness. Having defeated the Nazis, the forces of the state were forced in effect to reconquer the USSR, fighting daily battles against deserters and bandits. Rail travellers lived in fear of the *koshki*, 'cats', grappling hooks which bandits would hurl through train windows to snag plunder, which would then be pulled out off the train, whether a bag or even a person.

Crime still prospered under the Bolsheviks, while many of the old ways simply adopted new guises. Denunciation to the secret police, often on the most ridiculous charges, replaced cruder and more physical ways of settling old scores. Corrupt bureaucrats revived the practices of

Photographing a criminal in Siberia, 1894.

Life in a Tsarist gulag: peasant women selling provisions to prisoners in Siberia, 1891.

kormlenie and corruption. The Cheka had not only adopted many of the methods of its Tsarist counterpart, but hired many of its agents. Stalin's regime was able to impose some form of law and order, but through the use of police state techniques, and the massive and arbitrary use of terror and imprisonment. Perhaps it is more accurate to say that Stalin restored order, but at the cost of making a mockery of any notion of law in the Soviet Union. Ironically, he also created a new type of Soviet criminal.

Criminals may be outside the law, but they are never outside society. Tsarist Russia's criminals mirrored the rest of society: broken into mutually supportive communities, strongly conscious of pecking orders and fiercely protective of their livelihood. The structure and attitudes of the mir and the urban guilds were reflected in those of the gangs of the *vory v zakone*, 'thieves in law'. They had their own distinctions, a whole hierarchy of illegal trades, from petty bandits to some twenty-five different thieves' 'professions' (from horse thief to burglar) to the frauds, the aristocracy of the *vorovskoi mir*, the 'thieves' world'. They had their own language, a thieves' cant full of borrowed words from Romany, Yiddish and a dozen European tongues (English gave them *shop*, while the German 'guten morgen' became the slang for a morning burglary). They even developed a code of tattoos, different patterns and pictures recording everything from gang rank to whether or not the criminal had killed.

All this survived the Revolution, especially the code of the thieves in law, which emphasised style, skill and above all loyalty. They were meant never to co-operate with the authorities under any circumstances, and it was to be the collapse of this taboo which led to the next stage in the black evolution of Russian criminality. Stalin's mass purges saw the labour camps expand at an extraordinary rate. From a prison population of 198,000 in 1927, by 1939 the figure was closer to three million. Many of these newcomers were innocents or political prisoners who knew nothing of the codes of the vorovskoi mir and the authorities did all they could to play on this division. Criminals began to be offered more opportunities to gain power within the camps by acting as trustees and keeping the 'politicals' in line. Then the Second World War saw many others volunteer to join the army as a way of getting out of the camps.

After the war, they returned to prison and, like the trustees, were labelled 'dogs', collaborators, by the other thieves in law. The late 1940s and early 1950s saw the whole prison system torn by the so-called 'scab wars', as these 'dogs' took on the traditionalists and eventually won, a hidden war in which thousands died, and which the government either let happen or simply could not prevent. The prisons thus became dominated by criminals who had come to see the advantages in co-operating with the authorities. When the camps began to be opened after Stalin's death in 1953, criminals, as well as political prisoners were to benefit. Massive opportunities beckoned to ambitious men, and the victors of the 'scab wars' also won this new battle for underground power. By 1956 they had consolidated their power so much that they held a gang bosses' gathering to divide up the country between them. They even called it a 'Congress', in mockery of the Communist Party's assemblies. What was the secret of their power? The 'dogs', unlike the traditionalists, looked to buy out and cultivate alliances with members of the political élite and the structures of the state, from the KGB and police to the Party civil servants.

From then, the worlds of Soviet organised crime and politics became increasingly close. The lax Brezhnev years of the late 1960s and 1970s represented its heyday, and were characterised by the almost open flaunting of such alliances. The entire Party leadership of the Uzbek Soviet Socialist Republic defrauded Moscow of billions of rubles, paid in return for cotton which existed only on paper. Even Brezhnev's family was implicated. His son-in-law helped cover up the Uzbek scandal, while his daughter's love for diamonds led to her involvement with a dubious adventurer called Boris the Gypsy and a dozen scams and smuggling operations.

Thus when Gorbachev and then Yeltsin began liberalising Russia, they were freeing a country already riddled with corruption, dominated by organised crime. The near collapse of the government and the economy has left them almost the only powers in the land and a people who never learned to trust the state. Once this meant samosud. Now it means arming private security guards, turning to lynch law or accepting the gangs' terms. Russians are, after all, used to being ruled by criminals.

Mark Galeotti is Lecturer in History at the University of Keele and author of The Age of Anxiety: Security and Politics in Soviet and Post Soviet Russia *to be published this November by Longman.*

Women convicts at work near Nerschinsk, 1898.

[2]

FEDERICO VARESE

THE SOCIETY OF THE *VORY-V-ZAKONE*, 1930s-1950s[1]

Vory-v-zakone (thieves-in-law) were a peculiar type of criminal that emerged in the Soviet labour camps in the late 1920s. Many dissidents encountered the *vory* in the camps and described their behaviour. Dmitrii Likhachev, later to become one of the most prominent scholars of medieval Russian language and literature, met the *vory* while he was a convict at the Belomorsko-Baltiiskii canal construction site in the early 1930s.[2] After his release, Likhachev wrote a fascinating yet generally ignored essay on the language of the "thieves." He observed that the *vorovskoi mir* (the world of thieves) at the Belomorsko-Baltiiskii canal construction site was far from anarchical: "Despite thieves' apparent lack of discipline, their lives are governed by a network of strict regulations that extend to the most minute matters and ultimately by a system of 'collective beliefs' that is remarkably uniform among criminals with different ethnic roots."[3] The *vory* spent most of their lives in the labour camps, consistently refusing to work. They developed an ideology of monastic purity, a ritual for the initiation into the fraternity and achieved a leading role over the *blatnye*, professional criminals who aspired to become *vory*, the highest possible honour in the criminal world. The fraternity survived until the 1950s, when it was virtually destroyed by a new generation of criminals who rejected the rules of the fraternity and clashed and eventually killed almost all of its members. Camp authorities likely encouraged the "war" against the *vory*, known as *such'ia voina* (1948-1953).

Before their destruction, the *vory* formed a society of criminals comparable to more famous secret fraternities, such as the Neapolitan Camorra, the Sicilian Mafia and the Japanese Yakuza. A number of dimensions could be identified for detailed comparison, yet the basic facts concerning the *vory* must first be established. The aim of this paper is thus to present a preliminary exploration of a fascinating yet little-known chapter in Soviet history.[4] Although a great deal of uncertainty still surrounds the life of *vory*,[5] the memoirs of dissidents published in the sixties and seventies can now be supplemented with unpublished recollections by convicts and official documentation emerging from the Russian archives.[6] Drawing upon some of that evidence, the first part of the paper sketches the main features of the *vory* society, while the second and the third consider its origin and fall.

Cahiers du Monde russe, 39 (4), octobre-décembre 1998, pp. 515-538.

The vory-v-zakone, *1930s-1950s*

Maximilien de Santerre, a French-Russian "spy" born in 1924 and confined to the Gulag in 1946 for 12 years, observed that some criminals in the camp followed a peculiar dress code and mannerism.[7] They wore "home-made aluminium crosses round their necks" and waistcoats.[8] Santerre came to understand that these were "symbolic attribute[s] of a *vor-v-zakone*. Senior *vory* (the so-called *pakhany*) often were bearded and almost always wore their shirts outside the trousers with one or several waistcoats above."[9]

The *vory* also had tattoos covering their bodies. The iconography of the tattoos varied. According to Santerre, "their chests are often tattooed with a picture of praying angels on each side of the crucifix; underneath are the words: 'O Lord, save thy slave!' or 'I believe in God,'" indicating some respect for religion.[10] Gamaiunov reports that, until the fifties, a typical *vory* tattoo depicted a heart, pierced by a dagger.[11] Gurov writes of a *vory* tattoo picturing the suits of aces inside a cross and symbolising membership into the society. In his view, criminals had tattoos "to prove their strength. The tattoo also had a 'communication function'. It helped the recidivists recognise each other." Accordingly, the *vory* sought to maintain exclusive use of their tattoo designs; non-*vory* found wearing them were punished by death.[12]

The *vory* spoke a language of their own (*fenia*), its grammatical structure being Russian, but with a different vocabulary. This idiom attracted the interest of Dmitrii Likhachev, who stressed the "magical nature" of the word for these criminals and drew a parallel between primitive people and *vory*. He also noticed that knowledge of the jargon enabled a *vor* to fully assert his position among other criminals.[13] Chalidze provides a brief discussion of the origin of this language. He maintains that it emerged out of nineteenth-century criminal slang, which in turn was a combination of peddlers' speech, sailors' slang as well as Yiddish and Romany. He concludes that the jargon was greatly influenced by the advent of the Gulag camp system: "Today [...] there is a great deal of overlapping between prison speech and thieves' slang."[14]

A dress code, tattoos and even a language of their own would not distinguish the *vory* from any other human group that lives in a closed space, such as sailors, soldiers and ordinary convicts. The *vory* stand out among such groups because they formed a secret criminal fraternity, with its own code of behaviour and ritual for initiation of new members.[15] Furthermore, the *vory* created rudimentary yet effective "courts" where members' misbehaviour was judged and wrongdoers punished.

An early observer of the society, V.I. Monakhov, describes the gathering which would "crown" a *vor*, known as *skhodka* (meeting). Upon the recommendation of the members, the meeting accepted the novice into the society and the new *vor* swore an acceptance oath: "As a young lad, I set foot on the road of a thieves' life. I swear before the thieves who are at this meeting to be a worthy thief, and not to fall for any trick of the members of the CheKa."[16] Monakhov's version of the initiation ritual is supported by the account given by a *vor* called Ch. of his own crowning in 1951 at the age of 18.[17] After swearing the oath, Ch. was warned by his mentors of the punishment he would incur if he failed to abide by the oath. A *vor* who did so became, in the eyes of the fraternity, a *legavyi*, the *vory* equivalent of *sbirro* (cop) and *infame* (traitor) for the Sicilian Mafia and the most vicious insult a *vor* could have thrown at him.[18]

A police document from the early fifties describes an initiation ceremony that took place in rather unusual circumstances, in a transit-prison in the Krasnoiarskii *krai*, where 10 cells had been set aside to house hardened criminals. Confined to isolation cells, the criminals were forced to conduct the ceremony in writing, by pen and paper.[19] The pieces of paper were later confiscated by police, who then wrote a report of the incident. According to the report, a note (*ksiva*) recommending a novice (*maliutka*) was sent from one cell to the others.[20] It praised the "baby," said to possess the right qualities to be admitted into the family of *vory*. In particular, his mentors wrote, "his behaviour and aspirations are totally in accordance with the *vory*'s world-view"; he "defied camp discipline for a long period of time and is practically never let out of the punishment cell"; he, "at the request of the members, collected money for several months from other prisoners in one of the camp's sub-units" (the money was called "thieves' blessing" — *blago vorovskoe* — and amounted to the payment of "protection" money to the *vory*); and "even though still young, his mind is remarkable and in accordance with our world-view. We are glad to welcome new thieves into our family." The first cell that received the note was unambiguously positive in its response: "This guy will be a *vor-v-zakone*. God bless him." The second cell was also in favour, although rather less enthusiastic: "If his soul is pure, let him in." Apparently, without any objections from other *vory*, the novice became a new member of the fraternity.[21]

The *vory* were the inner circle of a wider criminal milieu. Those who aspired to become *vory*, or, in Sicilian Mafia jargon, to be "made" members, belonged to the same environment and abided by the same rules of behaviour as the "made" members. Thus to an external observer the *blatnye* and *vory* might have seem indistinguishable. Indeed, some sources use the two terms interchangeably. Within the *vory* itself, a distinction could be identified between junior and senior *vory*. For example, Ch. refers to senior members, the *pakhany*, who could have objected to his young age. Although the fraternity was a society of equals, the *pakhany* were older *vory* with a particular moral authority.[22]

Nicknames were formally given in the course of the initiation ritual. The name the *vor* acquired at the ritual arguably was quite distinct from an ordinary nickname (*klichka*). It marked the new life the criminal was about to enter. Thus, following a practice common in other secret societies and religious orders (such as the Catholic Church), nicknaming amounted for the *vory* to a re-christening, as observed by Likhachev: "the adoption of a nickname is a necessary act of transition to the *vory*'s sphere (it amounts to a peculiar 'taking of monastic vows')."[23] Ch. recollects that at his crowning he could finally dispose of his "childish nickname *malysh* (the young one), and get an adult nickname, which I chose myself." Reportedly, Ch. chose the nickname *likhoi* (dashing).[24]

A *vor* might spend many years of his life in prison. "To them, prison is their native home," writes Solzhenitsyn.[25] The length of time spent in prison was a source of prestige and a sign of distinction among the criminals who aspired to become *vory*. In this sense, the *vory* were a peculiar brand of criminal produced by prison culture, a feature that distinguishes them from Sicilian Mafiosi. Each *vor*, when out of prison, joined thieves' communes known as *kodla*.[26] Santerre reports that *kodla* could reach the size of 20-30 people. Up to ten different specialties, such as pickpocketing, burglary, and motor vehicle theft, were often represented in a single commune. The communes were supposed to be united by ties of solidarity, fraternity and relatively equal rights:[27] "In such groups (the *vory*'s communes), no direct leader exists. The *vory*'s *skhodka* is the organ of representation and control. Any member of the society could ask for a *skhodka* to be held."[28] While regional and local meetings were held, the regional *skhodki*, where general problems concerning the society were addressed, rarely were. This is not surprising, given the limitation on movement for ordinary citizens of the Soviet Union, let alone former convicts.

The *vory* were required to follow a strict code of behaviour in their interaction with each other. Members of the brotherhood were supposed to be honest and helpful to one another and always tell the truth to fellow members.[29] Thieves-in-law were supposed to avoid conflict among themselves and not to undermine each other's authority.[30]

> "All *vory* are honest and helpful in their dealings with one another, but the paracriminal population practice deceit and theft on one another and are chary with assistance. Observers of these classes have sometimes been misled into imagining that their behaviour is typical of the *vory*. However, the solidarity of the latter is well attested, and political prisoners in Stalin's camps are often surprised at the co-operation that developed between *vory* who had not known each other before."[31]

Vory were supposed to share all they had with fellow *vory*. Those who deviated from this norm would have been punished: a *vor* could have been brought to trial and consequently deprived of his thief's privileges for concealing cigarettes from fellow members.[32] A thief had no right to insult or raise his hand against another thief.[33] Violence, without sanction from a proper *vory* "court," was prohibited.[34]

A professional code of conduct regulated the interactions between the *vory* and the outside world. The *vory* considered the code to be part of their trade, as Likhachev notes in his 1935 essay on the thieves' language. Some elements of the code can be partially inferred from the notes exchanged at the transit prison in the Krasnoiarskii *krai*. Prior to and following initiation, a *vor* was supposed to have acted as a social outcast. Activities that suggested the state had power over the criminal, whether serving in the Red Army, paying taxes or working in the camps, were strictly forbidden.

In the camps, the *vory* thus systematically refused to work.[35] In particular, they refused to "take part in the construction of a prison, disciplinary barracks, stretch a barbed wire or clean the prohibited zone."[36] Systematic refusal to work was punished by camp authorities and Soviet courts.[37] Nevertheless, camp authorities generally avoided direct confrontation with the *vory*.[38]

A proper *vor* should not, prior to initiation, have been involved in political activities and, upon entering the fraternity, should have severed all links with society, including familial ties. His family was the *vory* brotherhood.[39] Professional criminals who remained attached to their families were called *domashniki* and on that basis could be refused entry into the brotherhood.[40]

Despite this prohibition against family ties, the *vory* exhibited an outward cult of motherhood, as seen in the tattoo born by many *vory* with the words "I won't forget my own mother." Varlam Shalamov, who spent a total of fifteen years in the camps (1937-1953) and is one of the most important writers of camp literature, identified a puzzling contrast between that professed cult of motherhood and the actual indifference shown by *vory* towards their natural mothers.[41] As Shalamov observes, "there is one woman who is romanticised by the criminal world, one woman who has become the subject of criminal lyrics and the folklore heroine of many generations of criminals. This woman is the criminal's mother." At the same time, however, "no criminal has ever sent so much as a kopeck to his mother or made any attempt to help her on his own." Shalamov thus concludes that the cult of the mother, although surrounded by a poetic haze, was "nothing but a pack of lies and theatrical pretence. The mother cult [was] a peculiar smoke-screen used to conceal the hideous criminal world."[42] Gurov provides a different explanation of the same phenomenon. The "mother" invoked by the *vory*, Gurov argues, was not the natural mother but rather a metaphor for the *vory* brotherhood, their new family.[43]

Women had no place in the hierarchy of thieves. "A third- or fourth-generation criminal learns contempt for women from childhood," writes Shalamov. "[...] Woman, an inferior being, has been created only to satisfy the criminal's animal craving, to be the butt of his crude jokes and the victim of public beatings."[44] A *vor* might have had a wife, but any real attachment to her was viewed as detrimental to the member's dedication to the society.[45] The *vory* code did not preclude monogamy, yet such faithfulness to one's wife was seen as a sign of weakness and "seldom lasting."[46]

Chalidze points out that the wife of a thief was allowed practically no social relations with others from outside the criminal world; she was the property of her husband. If he went to prison, she generally would have cohabited with one of his fellow thieves, while continuing to take an interest in his welfare. Although wives were not despised as much as prostitutes and female citizens not connected with the criminal world, they had no special rights: "the relation of a thief to his wife is that of a master to his slave, except that the slave has voluntarily chosen her lot."[47] While the wife may have chosen voluntarily to join the criminal community, she was unable to secede from it. If the criminal's wife failed to meet her obligations, she was warned; if she failed again she was punished.[48] According to Shalamov, there were no *ménages à trois* involving either lawful wives or prostitutes. Both prostitutes and legal wives could have been told to satisfy the needs of others, but the understanding was that there was always only one "owner."[49]

Women criminals — their bodies, like the men's, covered with tattoos[50] — existed and were referred to with a variety of words, including *vorovka*, *blatnaia*, *blatniachka* and *vorovaika*.[51] Like the men, they refused to work and occasionally took part in crimes committed by the *vory*. They were not, however, allowed to enter the male fraternity.[52] It remains unclear whether they formed a separate fraternity of their own.[53]

Thieves did not cultivate paternal feelings or care much about children. The *vory* took for granted that "a thief's son will become a thief and his daughter a companion of thieves, although this does not always happen, especially nowadays."[54] The son of a thief could therefore benefit from the reputation of his father, even though he was subject to the same initiation ritual as everybody else.[55]

Although passive homosexuality was strictly forbidden, active homosexuality was allowed.[56] Drugs also were allowed and could be freely taken: "thieves often suffer from epilepsy and drug addiction. In the prison drug stores they get ether, luminal, drugs mixed with cocaine, morphine and opium."[57]

The attitude of the *vory* towards property seems to have derived from the prohibition against entering into obligations with the non-criminal world. Property bound criminals to the material world, reducing their commitment to the *vorovskoi mir*. The *vory* were supposed to show contempt towards the accumulation of assets. Only short-term use of stolen cash or goods was allowed. The *vory* could use property that was at the disposal of their group but were not to own anything on a long-term basis.[58] A related rule of behaviour concerned stolen property: a *vor* who had found another *vor*'s property was not obliged to return the find to its owner.[59]

As a matter of course, detachment from the outside world included detachment from the most despised officials, law enforcers. A recruit was to have had no connections with law-enforcement agents in his past in order to be eligible for admittance into the society. Even the most insignificant act of camaraderie towards officials would have been sufficient cause for expulsion from the fraternity: "the laws of *blatnye* prevent one to offer any help to a chekist, and to accept presents or tips from them. For instance, one old *blatnoi* was deprived of his rights as *vor* only because he accepted a pack of tea from one camp guard."[60] The rumour that a criminal had contacts with police officers was considered enough to infer that he was bargaining for a softer sentence and intended to betray fellow criminals.[61] The prohibition against contacts with law-enforcement officials thus extended to a prohibition against holding the position of headman or foreman in the camp: "the *vor* who occupies such a position ceases to be a *vor*. He steps outside the law (*zakon*)."[62]

Professional killers were not allowed to enter the fraternity. The *vor* allegedly had a strong code against murder.[63] During his activities he was supposed to refrain from using violence. He was supposed to steal and rob without bloodshed. It was acceptable to kill only in order to defend one's honour or one's life.[64] Still, any thief who committed murder had to justify the act to the society.[65]

A *vor* was allowed to leave the fraternity, but under no condition was he allowed to betray old fellows.[66] In this regard, *vor* Ch. challenges the plot of the Soviet film *Kalina krasnaia* (1974) by Vasilii Shukshin. The protagonist in the film, Egor Prokudin, is killed by *vory* because he decided to leave the fraternity and lead an honest life. To this Ch. responds that, "I respect Shukshin, but he was wrong. This rule never existed. If a thief assassinated another thief because of this, he would himself be accused of unruly behaviour and killed."[67]

The *vory* were supposed to acquire a leading role in the camps, to rule over criminals "according to the *vory* rules" and to search for recruits. "Candidate members" (usually referred to, in camp jargon, as *patsany*) were asked to perform tasks on behalf of the *vory*, mainly connected with raising funds for *obshchak*, the communal fund to support group activities, bribe officials and care for the families of the imprisoned. The *obshchak* was financed both by extortion from inmates and contributions from the outside. The gang members operating outside collected money and goods and gave them to *vory* inmates, who in turn distributed them in the prison.[68] Once free, the *vor* was supposed to earn his living only through illegal activities and never to work. Because the *obshchak* was supposed exclusively to serve the *vory* in prison, the free *vor* could not rely upon it for support. In fact, the free *vor* was obliged to contribute to the *obshchak*.[69]

An acceptable way to earn money for all *vory*, besides stealing, was by winning at card games. Card playing was widespread in the camps. Shalamov recollects that "every night the criminal element in the camp gathered [...] to play cards."[70] Likhachev writes that winning a game was considered a good omen and "good omens may impel a thief to commit a daring theft, a bad omen stops him from carrying out his plans."[71] Card playing was also a vicarious form of fortune telling: "usually the thieves carry one or two packs of cards with them, which they use to tell fortunes, playing *shtos* [...] He will use the cards to decide his future and his next enterprise. If he wins, he is sure to complete his criminal plan in a lucky way. If he loses, he loses self-confidence as well."[72] Being good at cards was a sign of good fortune and capacity to bring good fortune to the gang: "a lucky card player will be taken by a thief as a companion for his gang in the hope that he will bring them luck (even if the card player uses sharp practices, since they are acceptable among thieves ...)."[73]

A thief could put at stake in a card game anything he had, including his finger, an arm, the promise to carry out a daring act or even his own life. If he lost his stake, it had to be redeemed immediately, no matter what it was. The penalty for defaulting was expulsion from the fraternity or, in some cases, death.[74]

Questions concerning the brotherhood were discussed, including "crimes" and punishments, at the *skhodka*, the *vory* meeting. Likhachev refers to courts managed by criminals. These courts dealt with any breach of the *vory* code of conduct: "behaviour among thieves is regulated and circumscribed by innumerable rules, standards and notions of propriety and good manners, all interrelated in an intricate hierarchy. Any violation of these rules is punished by a thieves' court, which has its own procedure. The penalty is always severe and is inflicted without delay."[75]

Shalamov confirms Likhachev's early findings that thieves' courts operated in the camps.[76] For instance, disputes over a woman (usually a prostitute) would be settled at a *skhodka*: "there are instances when hot tempers and the hysteria characteristic of all criminals will make him defend 'his woman.' On such occasions the question is taken up in a criminal court, and the criminal prosecutors will cite age-old traditions, demanding that the guilty man be punished."[77]

Santerre refers to these meetings as *tolkovishcha*, where the *vory* "discuss all questions concerning them. All the most important solutions are taken there." As a rule, the meetings were closed, with women and non-members not allowed to attend.[78]

"Once his honesty is put into question, the fate of a *vor* is decided at the *tolkovishcha*. [...] A *tolkovishcha* may often go on for several days, during which hot arguments are voiced, the slightest details are remembered, even of things and events that happened many years ago. Depending on the crime, a *vor* is sentenced."[79]

Data gathered by Monakhov testifies that major criminal *skhodki* took place in Moscow in 1947, Kazan in 1955 and Krasnodar in 1956. Monakhov reports an estimated attendance of 200 to 400 people.[80]

From the various accounts of such meetings, four types of punishment handed down by the *vory* "courts" can be identified. First was a prohibition against boasting in public, described by Likhachev. Boasting and story telling were common among *vory*.[81] According to Likhachev, the purpose of the story was less to convey truth than to portray the characters, especially the victims, in humorous ways and to demonstrate the smartness, shrewdness and boldness of the *vor* telling it.[82] Likhachev notes that "to stop and expose the lies of a story-teller is a deep insult. It is considered an infringement of the thieves' force and dignity." It was an open challenge. Only when the *vor* infringed the code, may have he been stopped:

"It is possible to object to the story teller only in one case: if he has somehow broken the thieves' ethics, the thieves' rules (laws). One punishment, although not severe, is to be forbidden boasting, which is considered as bad as exile from the [thieves'] sphere. In this case the thief no longer has the right to tell stories about his heroic deeds. Everyone has the right to stop him, even if what he says is true."[83]

A second punishment was a public slap in the face, inflicted for minor offences, such as having insulted another *vor*. To slap a *vor* in the face in front of everybody was a severe blow to his reputation.[84] A third and more serious punishment, especially for those living in the camp, was permanent expulsion from the brotherhood. The expelled *vory* would join the caste of the *muzhiki*, the common convicts. The criminal elite in the camps could freely victimise the *muzhiki* and steal their belongings without asking permission from anyone.[85]

A fourth possibility was corporal punishment, usually 50 hits with a stick, according to Santerre. In one such case, a *vor* who had been insulted by another and was supposed to carry out the punishment failed to perform the ritual properly: before starting the execution he should have said, "I'm not taking responsibility for bruises and blood!" He did not and was himself punished in place of the original perpetrator.[86]

The death penalty was inflicted for grave breaches of the *vory* code of behaviour, such as informing on fellow *vory* or repeatedly cheating on them.[87] Santerre reports that the sentence was carried out according to the following ritual: first the guilty person was "rotated," thereby taking away his soul: the victim would then be given the chance to die as a *vor* by standing with his back to the wall, tearing his shirt open, and addressing his several executioners armed with knives, saying: "take my soul."[88]

The *vory-v-zakone* exhibited a distinct style of dress, had their bodies covered with tattoos and spoke a peculiar slang. What made the society of the *vory* a peculiar and significant criminal phenomenon however was their secret initiation ritual and the abidance to a set of rules of behaviour. "Courts" existed to make sure members followed them and punished wrongdoers. Although an individual *vor* might have had an interest in punishing a fellow member, that task was the exclusive responsibility and prerogative of the *vory* meeting.

The origin of the vory

The evidence presented thus far refers mainly to the *vory* in places of confinement from the early 1930s to the early 1950s. It is also a static picture, depicting the society as it would have appeared to other convicts. Data from the 1930s testifies to the existence of the society of *vory-v-zakone*. Gurov, drawing on classified Ministry of Internal Affairs (MVD) material, concludes that "the *vory-v-zakone* were firmly established by the beginning of the 1930s."[89] According to MVD data, in the 1950s the vast majority of the *vory*, 80%, were professional pickpockets. The percentage of thieves-in-law did not exceed 6 to 7% of the total number of professional criminals and recidivists.[90] Precise geographic and ethnic details of the phenomenon are more difficult to provide. Gurov writes that *vory* operated within the territory of the Russian Soviet Republic and were of Slavic origin. *Vory* of Central Asia, Georgia or the Baltic were few and had been in prison in Russia.[91] Drawing on some of the available evidence, this section attempts a preliminary account of when and where the society and the term associated with it emerged.

Rossi maintains that the society existed in tsarist Russia. He writes that *staryi blagorodnyi vorovskoi mir* "is the old noble thieves world, the world of real thieves.

Many legends tell of the heroics of the old noble thieves' world that existed in tsarist Russia and even into the 1930s."[92] Santerre believes that "the *vory* existed in Russia long before the revolution." He adds, however, that "the Soviet reality, and especially its social and economic system, created the specific conditions, in which a criminal world with its completely peculiar features was born and flourished."[93] Gurov takes an opposing view, noting that pre-revolutionary criminologists (such as B.S. Utevskii, S.N. Krenev and I. N. Iakimov) refer neither to the phenomenon nor to the term *vory-v-zakone*. He comes to the conclusion that the *vory-v-zakone* did not exist in tsarist Russia and emerged only after the revolution.[94]

As far as the origin of the term is concerned, Gurov seems to be correct. V.F. Trakhtenberg records in 1908 the terms *urka* ("big, daring thief") and *oreburka* ("petty thief") in his celebrated dictionary of criminal slang.[95] Popov in 1912 has the words *blatnoi* ("criminal"), *urka* and *vozhak* (leader).[96] A dictionary published in 1927 contains the word *zakonnyi*, meaning "real, of good quality," and *vozhak*.[97] Likhachev, writing in a Soviet academic journal in 1935, calls criminal leaders *vozhaki* and *golovki* (heads), common words with no specific connotation. However, Likhachev uses the adjective *vorovskoi* to refer to the sector of the underworld these leaders control: *vorovskoi prestupnyi mir* (thieves' criminal world) and *vorovskaia sreda* (milieu).[98] Official documents refer in the late 1940s to "*vory-retsidivisty*"[99] and, by 1953, to "so-called *vory*."

Shalamov, writing at the end of the 1950s and referring to the "war" against the *vory* that began in the 1940s (the *such'ia voina*, see below), uses the form *zakonnyi vor* and *vor-v-zakone*.[100] Ivan P. Vorida, the author of a Soviet *sbornik* of criminal expressions published in 1971, records the terms *vor-v-zakone* and *vor-zakonnik* and notes that such criminals ceased to exist in the fifties.[101] The *vor* Ch., giving his testimony in the late 1980s and referring to the early 1950s, discusses the *bratstvo* (fraternity) of the *vory-v-zakone*. Only at the time when the society was about to disappear, was the form "*vory-v-zakone*" recorded.

The origin of the phenomenon thus must be searched under a different name or names. Prison life during the tsarist period has been described by a number of sources, including Dostoyevsky's *Notes from the house of the dead*, based on the author's experience as a convict in Omsk from 1850 to 1854.[102] Dostoyevsky portrays the criminals' passion for card playing, boasting and vanity.[103] He also describes the practice of swapping places: one convict would pay another to take his place and serve his sentence. Once the prisoner had agreed to swap and had already spent the money, he could not change his mind. If he tried to, he would be punished by the other convicts for not keeping his promise.[104] The fact that other prisoners took upon themselves the burden of punishing somebody with whom they had not been dealing testifies to the existence of norms of behaviour ("keep thy word") and collective punishment. Rossi also mentions that professional criminals in tsarist Russia would "keep their word."[105]

Vlas Mikhailovich Doroshevich (1864-1922), who visited Sakhalin penal colony at the end of the nineteenth century, writes of a type of prisoner "who wanted to gain the respect of his comrades and become an 'Ivan', the hero of the colony." Such prisoners would do so by defying prison rules and bravely enduring the ensuing punishment.[106]

There is also evidence that senior prisoners forced newly-arrived convicts to pay them a tribute. In 1900, prisoners Averkiev, Utkin and Bashmakov were terrorising new convicts, extorted food and money from them in the Nikolaevskaia corrective prison in Ekaterinburg, as detailed in a report dated 24 October 1901 of the prison head to the prison inspector of the Perm' region.[107]

Individual and sporadic defying of prison rules and forcing newly-arrived convicts to pay a tribute are near-universal features of prison life. Neither the writings of Dostoyevsky, Doroshevich nor the archival evidence I have been able to consult refer to organised groups of convicts that systematically refused to work or collaborate with the authorities and, most importantly, that possessed an initiation ritual, strict rules of behaviour and criminal "courts" to enforce such rules across different prisons.

Outside camp walls, however, a fraternity more similar to the *vory* may have existed at that time. Russian juridical literature refers to *arteli* (guilds) of ordinary thieves, including horse thieves, from the middle of the nineteenth century onwards.[108] Iakushkin, the author of a reference book on customary law published in 1896, describes a beggars' *artel'* as follows:

> "All the beggars here and for some distance beyond make up a regularly organised association known as the 'beggars' guild', with an elected guild-master and its own laws, custom and language. New members are nominated by their comrades and must accept the obligations of the guild. A person entitled to practise as a beggar by reason of physical deformity or disablement is apprenticed for a time to a fellow beggar, after which he is enrolled on a list and has to pay a subscription. As a rule, the term of apprenticeship is six years and the subscription 60 kopecks; but an apprentice may elect to serve a shorter term and pay a higher subscription. Membership in the guild is effected by a special ceremony. The aspiring member is brought into the assembly, and after mutual greetings, the guild-master tests his knowledge of the prayers, beggars' songs, and the special language of the fraternity. The apprentice bows and kisses the hand of each person present and is then admitted as member and assigned an area where he can beg. A feast is given in his honour, and, on this occasion, he is allowed to sit with the others for the first time. The guild-master is elected for an indefinite period and is generally a blind beggar; he convokes the guild for necessary business, including the punishment of transgressors. This used to take the form of a beating but is now usually a fine for the purchase of church candles. The most ignominious punishment consists of slitting the offender's wallet, signifying that he is no longer entitled to practise as a beggar. A steward is elected to look after funds and expenses. Both extraordinary and annual assemblies are held, the latter on the first Monday of Lent or on Whitsunday, when a new candle is placed in the Church on behalf of the fraternity. The funds accumulated by the guild are generally devoted to church purposes [...] The beggars have a language of their own, which they endeavour to keep secret from outsiders."[109]

The *artel'* described by Iakushkin was a group operating independently, in competition with other groups. This does not exclude the possibility that *arteli* at times joined forces or maintained relations with one another. Sergei Maksimov, for example, reported a case in his *Fatherland notes* in which some beggars' *arteli* joined together to exclude a rival group from a fairground.[110]

The *arteli* resemble the *kodla*, the thieves' communes described above. Yet, four significant differences can be identified between the *vory* communes and the nineteenth century *arteli*. First, the *artel'* was a group of people involved in the same business, who organised and accepted the leadership of a fellow-member. It exercised a localised monopoly over a certain sector of the underworld. The members of a *kodlo*, by contrast, were not all specialised in one sector of the underworld. Different professions were represented in a single *kodlo*. This means that a *kodlo* was not an association that aspired to obtain a monopoly over a specific sector of the underworld and in a specific territory, as was the *artel'*.

Second, no one could "buy" the title of *vor*, although it might have been the case that young criminals worked under the protection of a *vor* in a *kodlo*, and entered a sort of apprenticeship relation. Third, the *kodla* apparently were associations of *primi inter pares*, meaning no recognised hierarchy existed above the *vory*. The *skhodka* was the collegial organ that discussed matters and settled disputes among *vory*. The fourth and most significant difference relates to the national scale of the fraternity of the *vory*, which far exceeded that ever achieved by *artel*i. There is no evidence that pre-revolutionary *artel*i had created a systematically-organised structure with the purpose of co-ordinating their activities. Nor is there evidence that the *artel*i merged into a single national organisation or that entry into one *artel'* meant automatic recognition by other *artel*i. Likhachev, Shalamov, Santerre and many others met organised criminals in camps that were as far apart as the Belomorsko-Baltiiskii canal construction site in European Russia and Kolyma in the Arctic, facing Alaska. This is a formidable achievement for a criminal fraternity, considering the vastness of the country and the scope of its activities: devising rituals, policing behaviours, settling disputes among members and protecting insiders from outside challengers.

A question follows from the above: how could such a society succeed where the *artel*i failed, namely in forming a national network? In order to answer this question, one must consider the nature of both the *artel*i and the *vory*. Both aimed to supply members with a valued "good": those who joined would benefit from a privileged position in their trade or in the camps. The crucial condition for such an organisation to exist would therefore be a possibility to distinguish members from non-members and to punish both those who faked membership and those who misused the organisation's privileges or violated its code of behaviour. This in turn would require close proximity, potential for repeated interaction among members and the presence of information channels. The localised nature of the *artel'* provided these conditions and enabled the *artel'*s leadership to levy a fee on entrants, distinguish members from non-members and punish wrongdoers. Despite appearances to the contrary, these conditions were also well provided by the Gulag system. Furthermore, the scale of the Gulag archipelago allowed for the spread of the fraternity's rules and punishments, enabling the society to reach a national dimension.

The camp system was a fairly integrated system: it supplied a source of contacts for criminals and an opportunity to share their experiences and devise ways of promoting their common interests. By the middle of the 1930s, the network of corrective labour camps was already fairly extensive. The northern camps, situated in the former Komi-Zyrianskaia *oblast'*, held some 41,000 prisoners. In the far eastern camps, some 15,000 people were engaged in the building of the Boguchinskaia railway, as well as fishing and forestry. The Visherskie camps, which were chiefly involved in chemical, paper and timber production, held a further 20,000 prisoners. There were 24,000 prisoners in the Siberian camps and 40,000 in the oldest of the Solovetskie camps, building the road from Kem' to Ukhta.[111] A recent estimate suggests the total number of those repressed in Gulag camps and colonies in the period 1934-1952 reached over 18 million.[112] Prison numbers were not static within and between camps: inmates entered the camps, left the camps and were transferred around the camps. Recently disclosed data places the number of intra-Gulag camp transfers for the period 1934-1947 at around 3 million.[113]

Intra-Gulag transfers allowed not only repeated interaction but also the spread of information, another crucial requirement for the group to persist. The sharing of precise information was necessary in order to inform the prison population about new entries into the *vory* brotherhood, check reputations, expose frauds and monitor convicts' transfers. In fact, news spread quickly among the different camps, as in the following story taken from the memoirs of General A.V. Gorbatov, a Soviet Army general detained in 1939 in a camp in Maldiak, Kolyma region, containing 400 political prisoners and some 50 criminals:

> "Boris is nicknamed 'The Careerist.' He got his name in one of the northern camps because he made himself out to be a big criminal, with six murders and five major robberies to his credit. He is believed and is appointed a senior prisoner. Then it turned out that he is simply an independent, petty thief. There is a great fuss and he is demoted and given his nickname."[114]

In a similar incident, Iadviga Iosifovna Verzhenskaia learned the fate of her husband through the criminals' information network. Arrested in 1938 as a member of the family of a traitor of the Motherland, she was very anxious to know the fate of her husband, arrested the year before. While discharging her duties in the camp hospital, she befriended some criminals, who offered to help her find information about her husband. After some time, she received "a tiny piece of paper" with news about his fate (he had been executed immediately after arrest).[115] Apparently, a sophisticated system for transmitting coded information between different camps existed, perfected by many generations of criminals. The system attracted the attention of the police, who claimed that they had broken the code and that it consisted of a cryptographic language.[116]

Transfer was not a sure escape from a "sentence" passed by a *skhodka*. Convicts could arrange for a criminal to be punished by fellow criminal authorities in the destination camp. In one case, a criminal (*urkagan*) lost his left hand at playing cards but could not bring himself to cut it and tried to run away. The authorities re-captured him and transferred him to another camp, but his fate was sealed. The criminals found out where he had been sent and arranged for the sentence to be carried out there. He was killed.[117]

As the population of the camps grew in size, the Gulag became an even more significant source of contact between criminals scattered across the Soviet Union. The camps quickly became the best possible medium for the swift dissemination and maintenance of *vory* rituals and traditions.[118] While the fraternity surely drew upon the rich pre-revolutionary underworld culture, such a milieu never produced a national organisation. A crucial factor for the existence and the endurance of the *vory* was the Gulag system, as it developed from the 1920s onwards. This by itself does not answer fully the question of the emergence of the *vory*; rather it points to the presence of a crucial and necessary condition.

The fall of the vory

The *vory* society did not survive for long. It was almost entirely destroyed by the end of the 1950s during what came to be known as *such'ia voina* (bitches' war).[119] Various sources evidence their downfall: Gurov writes that by the mid-fifties, 300 *vory* were known to reside in Soviet prisons; by the end of the 1950s, the *vory* had "virtually disappeared."[120] According to Bukovskii, a political dissident who served his sentence in a camp in the Perm' region in 1973-1974, only a "few dozen" survived in the entire Soviet Union.[121] Perushkin uses a similar figure: "the number of thieves-in-law who survived the bitches' war did not exceed two dozen."[122] We shall now turn to this specific event of Soviet camp history.

With the onset of the Second World War and the seemingly unstoppable progress of the German Army into Soviet territory, a number of Soviet convicts were granted early release on the condition that they join the army. Roughly one million inmates left the Gulag during the war to enter the armed forces.[123] Although most of the people who had been granted early release in order to fight the Nazis were serving sentences for absenteeism and "insignificant work-related or economic crimes," some hardened criminals and even *vory* may have ended up at the front. In that vein, Shalamov maintains that during the war "many *vory*-recidivists and *urki*" were sent to the front and that, in particular, the army headed by Marshal Rokossovskii was comprised of former inmates.[124]

The outflow of the camp population did not last long. The system experienced an influx of convicts from 1944 onward. The total number of prisoners in corrective labour camps and colonies rose from 1.2 million in January 1944 to 1.7 million in 1946, more than a 40% increase.[125] In 1947, a total of 626,987 new inmates entered the Gulag. This trend continued until 1953, when it reached its peak of 2.45 million inmates. In this period, the prison population also changed in character. In the years 1939-1940, the Soviet Union annexed the Baltic republics, western Belorussia, Moldavia and western Ukraine. Especially in western Ukraine and the Baltic republics, hostile nationalist movements resisted annexation (for instance, annexation was fiercely opposed by the Organisation of Ukrainian nationalists, the OUN). Soviet authorities repressed these nationalist organisations and, as a consequence, the percentage of inmates from the Ukraine and the Baltic regions increased in the years 1944-1946 by 140 and 120%, respectively.[126]

The camp system saw also the arrival of the Soviet soldiers and officers who had allowed themselves to be captured by the enemy, some 360,000 individuals.[127] To this number should be added the survivors of the army put together by general Vlasov, who had fought with the Nazis in order to free his country from the Bolshevik regime. Ordinary citizens, starving peasants and criminals also entered the Gulag in great numbers, mainly as a consequence of the newly-adopted strict laws on the protection of property.[128]

The new inmates were not the political dissidents, intellectuals, party officials, clerks and peasants of the 1930s. They formed a pool of people trained in the use of violence who were able to pose a serious threat to the traditional criminal world.[129] Even those who had been convicted for crimes unrelated to nationalist activities and surrendering to the enemy were likely to have served in the war and therefore to have combat experience. For instance, Grigorii Antonov had been demobilised from the army and was working at the Groznyi Oil Institute when, in the summer of 1951, he was arrested. He recalls how in the Pechorskaia transit prison, "we found ourselves in a barrack where most of the inmates are criminal offenders and one of them took a fancy to my high collared naval jacket. Since I did not want to give it up voluntarily, a fight broke out." Antonov managed to hold on to his jacket but at the cost of being stabbed in the chest:

"I have told this story in some detail because it is my 'camp baptism.' It is then that I decided how I would act and react and this enabled me thereafter to keep my head above water, earn the respect of those around me, and win friendship and loyalty of my comrades in captivity. I became, in camp jargon, an 'experienced pigeon.' Life had almost no value for me, and I was afraid of nothing and of no one. No one could insult or offend me or my comrade without answering for it."[130]

Convicts like Antonov were "not at all the shy type," as a political convict in the Kengir camp in 1953-1954 put it; they were "a united mass of people, ready to repel [the criminals]."[131] This is in sharp contrast to the past, when criminals — whether *vory* or ordinary criminals — could easily terrorise the political prisoners and ordinary citizens caught up in the repression.

Official documents record tensions between the new "working prisoners" and "criminal-bandit elements," like the traditional *vory*. For the first time, the "working prisoners" managed to fend off the criminals. "In Obskii MVD corrective labour camp, construction site no. 501, a group of bandits entered the barrack and tried to seize a parcel and money from two prisoners on 10 January 1951. The two convicts resisted, and one of them was wounded by the bandits. Other prisoners rose to defend them, with nearly 400 people taking part in the assault against the bandits. As a result, 4 people were killed and 9 wounded."[132] In the Vanino transit camp in September 1953, a large-scale fight broke out between ordinary prisoners and a small group of 10-15 criminals who were trying systematically to rob and steal from other inmates. The guards had to use firearms to separate them.[133] In November 1953, the "working contingent of prisoners" put up an "organised rebuff of the bandit elements" in the camp unit no. 19 of the sixth department of Pechorskii corrective labour camp.[134]

A special report on the Burminskii department of the Karagandiskii camp gives details of a fight between the two groups:

"Working prisoners organised themselves in order to drive out of the zone those prisoners who belong to a group of criminal-bandits. With this aim in mind, they disassembled plank-beds in the living quarters of the barracks, armed themselves with boards, canes and some of them with knives and other objects and attacked the prisoners '*vory*', who lived in separate barracks, and beat them."[135]

The following extract, recounting another episode that occurred in 1953, again refers openly to the *vory*:

"In the camp unit no. 6 of the Suslovskii department 21 prisoners belonging to the *vory* grouping organised a mass robbery of prisoners who honestly perform their working duties. [...] After the arrest and isolation of the above-mentioned group, in the same camp unit a remaining group of 40 prisoners, who rotate around the group of *vory*, headed by bandit Nikolaev, tried to organise a reprisal of the victims-prisoners, but were rebuffed. As a result, some *vory* were beaten with canes and fists. The *vory* were isolated and transferred to the other camp units. Instigators of the attempted execution were punished."[136]

Life for the criminals had certainly become harder in these new times. Some criminals and even some *vory* must have realised early on that they could now maintain their position in the camps only with the direct support of the authorities. To seek such support, however, would have violated the *vory* code of behaviour and required an open break with past practices.

THE SOCIETY OF THE *VORY-V-ZAKONE*, 1930s-1950s 529

Even without the challenges from the new inmates, the fraternity already was under strain. Reportedly, some *vory* had served in the Second World War. According to the thieves' laws, all the *vory* who fought for their country during the war stepped outside the "law." Their "crime" was to have put on uniforms and carried rifles, two symbols of a prison warden's authority.[137] Upon their return to the camps, they were nicknamed *voenshchina* (soldiery) and expelled from the brotherhood.[138] Shalamov maintains that, as a form of retaliation, the leaders of the *voenshchina* announced a "new law" in a transit prison in Vanino bay in 1948. This new "law" allowed criminals to work as prison trustees, headmen and foremen, and to occupy various other positions of responsibility within the camp.

General Serov, deputy minister of Interior Affairs, acknowledged that "signs of repentance" appeared among "criminal-bandit elements," in an order sent to Republican governments and the Gulag administration in February 1950. He instructed the administration to identify roughly 15-20 prisoners of this type in each camp and to transfer each one of them from strict regime to ordinary regime camps. Informants for the camp administration were to be recruited from this pool of people.[139]

At the same time, criminals in camps of strict regime also were collaborating with the authorities. For instance, a report sent to G. M. Malenkov, the Secretary of the Central Committee, dated 14 May 1952, indicates that "in some camp sub-units of the strict regime the administration of Dal'stroi camp recruited dangerous criminals-recidivists in the camp service. Although they had been sentenced several times, some of these criminals were appointed prisoner representatives."[140] Similarly, in Viatlag, "a group of recidivists, headed by a camp clerk,[141] prisoner Kurochkin, and some foremen occupied all the most important positions in the camp."[142] In the Viatskii labour corrective camp, "criminal-bandit elements have been recruited as camp service staff and lower level production supervisors," recites a report dated 10 May 1954.[143] In a far-away forestry unit in Kolyma, "deep in the taiga," criminals took over and were running the plant, terrorising the local population, until the criminals were liquidated in 1953 by the authorities.[144]

The *suki* not only worked for prison authorities and harassed working prisoners, with negative consequences for camp life and productivity,[145] but they also directly targeted unrepentant *vory*, with the support of local camp authorities. According to Shalamov, Korol', the leader of the *voenshchina* responsible for the "new law," was used by the prison authorities to expose *vory*. In 1948, all the prisoners of the Vanino bay transit prison were lined up and forced to strip. The *vory* were recognised by their tattoos. If they wanted to save their lives, they had to reject the old law and go through a new ritual that would mark their entrance into the group of the *suki*.[146] If they refused, they were killed. Many *vory* refused and, apparently, a massacre ensued. News spread quickly through the camps and reached Kolyma, where Shalamov was a convict. There, the *vory* prepared themselves to face this formidable challenge. A fully-fledged "war" broke out when Korol' and his assistants were given permission by camp authorities to visit other transit prisons. They went as far as Irkutsk (Solzhenitsyn arrived in the Gulag when the conflict was under way and was informed of it on his journey there).[147]

Santerre recounts a clash between *suki* and *vory* in the summer of 1948 in a camp in the Inta region involving 100 *vory* and 150 *suki*. The authorities allowed the two sides to come into contact, but only the *suki* were allowed to carry their weapons. Few *vory* survived.[148] In another instance, in 1949, a captain Kobets personally armed a group of *suki* and encouraged them to attack the *vory* being held in a disciplinary barrack.[149]

Official documents confirm that mass disturbances were taking place in various camps. In the Voronezh region in August 1952, a prisoner was killed. The report of this incident adds that this murder was part of a grander plan of the "criminal-bandit elements" to carry out "physical execution of prisoners, foremen and their assistants."[150] In a different instance, "on 4 September 1952 group disturbances took place and 4 prisoners were killed in department no. 10, the Peschanyi MVD camp, as a result of the fact that groups of prisoners who are at enmity with each other are kept together."[151]

Inspectors cited camp authorities and their failure to keep the different criminals separate as the cause of two other serious incidents. On 4 December 1952, at construction site no. 508, fifty-one "*byvshie* (former) *vory*" came into contact with 42 prisoners that "were hostile to them." A "mass disturbance" broke out, with the camp guards firing at the convicts that were trying to find refuge in the prohibited zone. Six people were killed and 29 severely wounded.[152] On 10 November 1953, in the Pechorskii corrective labour camp, 24 prisoners were killed and 29 wounded when "hostile attitudes between different groups of prisoners had not been taken into consideration" and the groups had been allowed to mix.[153]

New groupings formed, and some of their labels are recorded. Gurov refers to the *krasnaia shapochka* gang and *bespredel'shchina* gang.[154] A report of 14 October 1953 refers to "a group of bandit-prisoners who call themselves '*bespredel'niki*' and includes 40 people."[155] In the Sibirskii corrective labour camp, a report notes, there were four groups that were hostile to each other: "two of them are bigger and are at enmity with each other. The first group calls itself '*vory*' and includes more than 800 people. The second calls itself in the camp jargon '*piatiblochniki*' and it consists of nearly 600 people."[156] Officials were at pain to discover who belonged to which group. On 28 January 1953, in a Kizellag sub-unit, criminal proceedings were instituted against two camp supervisors for having beaten a convict almost to death. They had been trying to compel the convict to disclose "to which one of the groups that are at enmity with each other he belongs."[157]

At least at a certain point in time, a camp would either be under the control of *suki* or *vory*. Reportedly, the prison camps in the Vorkuta area were under the control of bitches,[158] whereas the Aleksandrovskaia transit prison and "the prison camps of Pot'ma and the Ust'-Vymlag were under the control of *blatnye*."[159] In the Aleksandrovskaia transit prison, in fact, an expedition of bitches "met with misfortune."[160] In July 1953, a group of 218 prisoners arriving in the Pevek settlement of the Chaun-Chukotskii camp were greeted with the following words: "Hurrah to *vory*! We'll kill *suki*!"[161] To end up in the camp where the enemy group was in control could have been dangerous. A report notes that prisoners who belong to the group that happens to be losing in a certain camp seek refuge "in the isolation wards and penalty isolation wards [...] in order to escape reprisal."[162]

A report on the "state of affairs in the corrective labour camps and colonies," sent to the Central Committee of the Communist Party, gives a rather alarming yet partial total of the camp disturbances: "During January, February and March [1954], 129 murders were committed in the camps and colonies, due to gangsterism, personal reckoning, revenge, and *enmity between groups of criminals-recidivists*."[163] Among those who died over the years of this "war," there were Korol' himself, who was blown up with explosive smuggled from a mining site, and some prominent *vory*, such as Poltora Ivana Balabanov and Poltora Ivana the Greek.[164]

Conclusion

The *vory-v-zakone* bore tattoos and spoke a language of their own. They also followed well-defined rules that regulated interaction among members and between *vory* and outsiders, such as family, strangers and officials. Most importantly, a ritual marked entry into the brotherhood. "Made" members who did not follow the rules were summoned to a rudimentary tribunal, where their crimes would be discussed and, if the defendant was found guilty, a sentence passed. The sentence was carried on behalf of the society as a whole, not of the single member who had been insulted or put in danger by the lawbreaker. These features place the *vory* alongside more famous criminal fraternities, such as the Sicilian Mafia, the Neapolitan Camorra and the Japanese Yakuza.

When then did the society form? A definite answer has not been given so far. Surely the *vory* emerged from the rich Russian underworld, which had developed a culture of its own over the centuries. I have, however, pointed out to crucial differences between the *vory-v-zakone* on the one hand and professional guilds of criminals and prisoners that lived in the tsarist period on the other. The Soviet Gulag system seems to have provided some crucial conditions for the society to exist, but other elements must also have been at work. We might speculate that when unemployment and rising crime rates followed the Russian Revolution, professional criminals faced formidable competition from a new breed of individuals who had entered the criminal world, such as the *besprizornye* and impoverished middle class. The relative strength of each traditional criminal *artel'* in fencing off penetration from unorganised criminals was surely put to test and new loyalties forged in hardship. An incentive to distinguish professional criminals and new entrants might have emerged at that point. A national-level organisation able to intervene and settle disputes among its members as well as with other organisations and independent criminals operating in the country might have emerged at this point in history, although further research is necessary to confirm this hypothesis.

We know that the traditional *vory* were almost decimated in the early 1950s. The *such'ia voina* was the last episode in the history of the original fraternity. A peculiar phenomenon occurred at that time: ordinary convicts started to sympathise with the *vory*, who were heavily harassed by a new class of criminals and by the authorities. The myth of the *vory*, the dashing heroes of the criminal world who preferred to die not to betray their "ideals" was born at this moment. A new fraternity appeared in the 1980s and, as every observer of things criminal in Russia knows, the new *vory-v-zakone* became a worrying feature of post-communist Russia.

Nuffield College
Oxford, OX1 1NF, UK

email: varese@sable.ox.ac.uk

532   FEDERICO VARESE

1. During my stay in Russia, I greatly benefited from the help of the staff of the State Archive of the Russian Federation, in particular Ms. Dina Nikolaevna Nokhotovich, the staff of the Memorial Archive in Moscow and the staff of Perm' State Archive. I am grateful to Andrea Graziosi and Diego Gambetta for their valuable comments on an earlier version of this paper, Oleg Podvintsev and Andrei Suslov for their help in Perm' and Sergio and Marina Rossi for their hospitality in Moscow. This study would not have been completed without the assistance of Galina Varese. The Department of Applied Social Studies and Social Research (Oxford University) has given me a grant that covered some of my expenses. A version of this paper is chapter 9 of my Ph.D. dissertation, *The emergence of the Russian Mafia* (Nuffield College, Oxford, 1996). The usual disclaimers apply.

2. On this episode of Russian history, see M. Gorky, L. Averbakh, S.G. Firin, A. Williams-Ellis, *The White Sea Canal. Being an account of the construction of the new canal between the White Sea and the Baltic Sea* (London: John Lane, 1935).

3. D.S. Likhachev, "Cherty pervobytnogo primitivizma vorovskoi rechi,"*Iazyk i myshlenie*, Proceedings of the USSR Academy of Science, III-IV (1935): 47-100, here p. 55.

4. On the *vory* in English, see J. Serio, V.S. Razinkin, "Thieves professing the code," *Low Intensity Conflict & Law Enforcement*, 4, 1 (1995): 72-88 and M. Galeotti, "Criminal Russia: The traditions behind the headlines," *History Today*, 44, 8 (1994): 12-14.

5. A.I. Gurov has aptly remarked: "Literary sources as well as USSR Ministry of Interior data dealing with norms of behaviour (the so-called 'laws') and the criminal activities of this criminal association are extremely poor and often rather contradictory." *Professional'naia prestupnost'* (Moskva: Iuridicheskaia literatura, 1990): 108.

6. I have collected evidence in the State Archive of the Russian Federation (GARF, mainly the Gulag fund no. 9414, the MVD fund no. 9401, and the Procurator fund no. 8131 and the Khrushchev personal files, OPKh), the State Archive of the Perm' Region (GAPO) and the Memorial Archive of repressed people (Memorial). Hereafter I will cite the relevant archive followed by numbers that refer, respectively, to the fund (*fond*) , the list (*opis'*), the file (*delo*) and the sheet numbers (*list*).

7. Maximilien de Santerre, *Sovetskie poslevoennye kontslageri i ikh obitateli* (Munich: Institut po izucheniiu SSSR, 1960): 88. The Soviet government abducted the author in 1945. Because of his unruly behaviour and escape attempts he was put among prisoners, usually criminals, "refusing labour and discipline" (*otritsalovka*). This gave Santerre an opportunity to mix mainly with criminals (p. 3). On *otritsalovka*, see J. Rossi, *The Gulag handbook* (New York: Paragon House, 1989): 286.

8. M. de Santerre, *op. cit.*: 92, see also D.S. Likhachev, *art. cit.*: 62.

9. M. de Santerre, *op. cit.*: 63. In some instances, *vory* showed compassion and respect towards men of the church, as they showed high spirituality (*ibid.*: 80); see also Y. Glazov, "'Thieves' in the USSR as a social phenomenon" [1976], in Id., *The Russian mind since Stalin's death* (Dordrecht–Boston–Lancaster: D.Reidel Publishing Company, 1985): 39.

10. M. de Santerre, *op.cit.*: 89; Y. Glazov, *art. cit.*: 39.

11. I. Gamayunov, "*Thieves-in-law*: Devils dressed as Robin Hood," *The Moscow Times* (11 January 1995): 9.

12. A.I. Gurov, *op. cit.*: 111. Prisoners' tattoos would require a separate study. See A.G. Bronnikov, *Tatuirovki u prestupnikov v Rossii* (Perm': mimeo, 1996).

13. See especially D.S. Likhachev, *art. cit.* : 63.

14. V. Chalidze, *Criminal Russia. Essays on crime in the Soviet Union* (New York: Random House, 1977): 57.

15. Rituals also mark the entry in other organised criminal groups, such as the Japanese Yakuza, the Hong Kong Triads, the Sicilian Mafia and American Cosa Nostra. The extent to which individual members do actually follow the code of conduct is a different issue.

16. Quoted in A.I. Gurov, *op. cit.*: 110. V.I. Monakhov, an investigator at the USSR Ministry of Internal Affairs (MVD) published a book for internal circulation in the mid-fifties that explored the features of organised crime. Gurov extensively draws on Monakhov's work for his treatment of criminality in the period 1930-1950.

17. Ch. was arrested in 1981 and, in the 1980s, was serving his sentence in the Voronezh region. His criminal career includes 7 convictions and 25 years behind bars. He agreed to reveal the traditions and rules of the *vory* and completed 13 notebooks. A.I. Gurov collected this evidence and relied on this material for the treatment of the *vory* in his book, *Professional'naia prestupnost'*.

Later, A.I. Gurov and V. Riabinin published extracts of the notebooks in A.I Gurov, V. Riabinin, "Ispoved' vora v zakone," *Na boevom postu*, 12 (1990): 50-62; 1(1991): 75-84; Id., *Ispoved' vora v zakone* (Moskva: Rosagropromizdat, 1991).

18. See G. Falcone, M. Padovani, *Cose di Cosa Nostra* (Milano: Rizzoli, 1991): 100. For the meaning of *legavyi*, see Iu. Dubiagin and E. Teplitskii, *Kratkii slovar' ugolovnogo zhargona* (Moscow: Terra, 1993).

19. Discipline in the Krasnoiarskii *krai* prisons had been the subject of some concern. According to a report dated August 8, 1939, "there is practically no cell isolation between prisoners in Krasnoiarskii common prison. By use of threads, cords, ropes and even planks, prisoners systematically pass correspondence, objects and products from one cell to another. Meetings between prisoners from different cells during transfers became a common practice." GARF, 9401/1a/0252/10-11. For a similar report for prison 1 in the Saratovskii region see GARF, 9401/1a/0251/6-7.

20. M. de Santerre also refers to *ksivy*. "*Blatnye* refer to their letters as *ksivy* and attach them the importance of a document [...] Such letters are always written by a collectivity and signed *bratsy vory* or *bratsy urki*" (*op. cit.*: 90).

21. A.I. Gurov, *op. cit.*: 110-111.

22. A.I. Gurov and V. Riabinin, *art. cit.*: 82. "According to the law, there is a complete democracy among *blatnye*, however a scarcely noticeable yet very strong gradation of hierarchy exists. At the top there are the so called *pakhany* (*pakhan* means father in the *vory* jargon)." M. de Santerre, *op. cit.* : 64, see also 63.

23. D.S. Likhachev, *art. cit.*: 61.

24. See Appendix A in F. Varese, *op. cit.*, where I have analysed 254 *vory* aliases.

25. A. Solzhenitsyn, *The Gulag archipelago 1918-1956* (Glasgow: Collins–Fontana, 1974): 516. See also Id., *Sobranie sochinenii*, vol. 5: *Arkhipelag GULag, 1918-1956* (Vermont-Paris: YMCA-Press, 1980): 492 and M. de Santerre, *op. cit .*: 68, 86.

26. M. de Santerre, *op. cit.*: 55.

27. M. de Santerre, op. cit.: 55, Y. Glazov, *art. cit.*: 39, and A.I. Gurov, *op. cit.*: 115. V. Bukovskii wrote of the *vory* of the fifties: "Thieves traditionally lived in 'families' and regarded one another as 'brothers.'" V. Bukovskii, *To build a castle. My life as a dissenter* (London: Andre Deutsch, 1978): 245.

28. A.I. Gurov, *op. cit.*: 115.

29. A.I. Gurov, *op. cit.*: 113. A related rule, reported by D.S. Likhachev (*art. cit.*: 58), is that a *vor* is not supposed to ask a direct question to another *vor*. "We must note that the rules of proper *vory* behaviour do not allow a thief to ask questions." Likhachev continued: "This is not only a precautionary measure in order to keep secrets. This rule lies deep in the language consciousness of thieves and is connected with their subconscious belief in the magic power of the word." These rules should be evaluated in the context of camp life, where a well-oiled network of informers operated (A. Graziosi, "The great strikes of 1953 in Soviet labor camps in the accounts of their participants. A review," *Cahiers du Monde russe et soviétique*, 33, 4 (1992): 428.)

30. A.I. Gurov, *op. cit.*: 111. The rule prohibiting quarrelling with other members is the fourth rule (out of eight) recited during the Sicilian initiation ritual. See P. Arlacchi, *Gli uomini del disonore. La Mafia siciliana nel racconto del pentito Antonio Calderone* (Milano: Mondadori, 1992): 57.

31. V. Chalidze, *op. cit.*: 54. V. Shalamov, *Kolyma tales* (London: Penguin Books, 1994): 413, noticed that newly-acquainted *vory* supported each other.

32. M. de Santerre, *op. cit.*: 92.

33. *Ibid.*: 62.

34. The rule prohibiting the use of violence between members of the society is shared by the Japanese Yakuza, the Hong Kong Triads, the Sicilian Mafia and American Cosa Nostra.

35. See M. de Santerre, *op. cit.*: 51, 64, 111 and Y. Glazov, *art. cit.*: 54, 239.

36. M. de Santerre, *op. cit.*: 63. Refusal to work put the *vory* in the same position as radical Christians, the so-called *Krestiki*, who categorically refused to obey any order coming from the Soviet regime. *Ibid.*: 53.

37. Official documents refer to hardened criminals who "systematically refused to work" (GAPO, R-1461/28/2, date: 1940) and went as far as mutilating themselves (e.g. GARF, 9401/1a/179/48-49, date: 08 April 1943).

38. "It is strange, but the camp administration almost always takes into consideration what the *blatnye* are supposed and not supposed to do, thus avoiding sure troubles." M. de Santerre, *op. cit.*: 63.

39. A.I. Gurov, *op. cit.*: 108.

40. M. de Santerre, *op. cit.*: 56.

41. V. Shalamov is well known in the West as a literary figure for his book *Kolyma tales*. He is also the author of eight essays on the criminal world written in the late fifties and now printed in the Russian edition of his completed works: V. Shalamov, *Kolymskie rasskazy*, vol. 2: *Ocherki prestupnogo mira* (Moskva: Sovetskaia Rossiia, 1992): 5-96. Hereafter, we shall refer in particular to his "Such'ia voina" and "Zhenshchina blatnogo mira" (the latter is translated as "Women of the Criminal World" in V. Shalamov, *Kolyma tales, op. cit.*: 415-31).

42. V. Shalamov, *Kolyma tales, op. cit.*: 428-429. V. Chalidze, on the contrary, takes the cult of motherhood at face value and adds: "Cases are known in which a thief who is hard pressed by the police risked arrest in order to visit and help his mother." V. Chalidze, *op. cit.*: 53.

43. A.I. Gurov, *op. cit.*: 111.

44. V. Shalamov, *Kolyma tales, op. cit.*: 419. See also M. de Santerre, *op. cit.*: 92.

45. It appears that indifference to the natural family is greater among the traditional *vory* than in other criminal organisations, such as the American Mafia, Cosa Nostra and the Yakuza. Commitment to the "family" should be the criminal's primary concern, but attachment to one's own natural family is considered acceptable. See O. Demaris, *The last Mafioso* (New York: Bantam Books, 1981): 4; P. Arlacchi, *op. cit.*: 58 and D.H. Stark, *The Yakuza: Japanese crime incorporated*, Ph.D. Thesis (Ann Arbor: University of Michigan, 1981): 89-90.

46. V. Chalidze, *op. cit.*: 52.

47. *Ibid.*

48. *Ibid.*: 51-52.

49. V. Shalamov, *Kolyma tales, op. cit.*: 420.

50. M. de Santerre, *op. cit.*: 89.

51. *Ibid.*: 92; Ia. A. Tregubov, *Vosem' let vo vlasti Lubianki* (Munich: Possev-Verlag, 1959): 147, quoted in Y. Glazov, *art. cit.*: 238.

52. "According to the law, a woman cannot enjoy the rights of *blatnye*, even less has she the right to interfere with the affairs of *vory* or discuss their behaviour. There are no *blatnye* women as such. There are the so-called *vorovaiki*. Most often they, even taking part in thefts, are reckoned as transitional wives of *vory*." M. de Santerre, *op. cit.*: 92.

53. This would be the subject of a separate study.

54. V. Chalidze, *op. cit.*: 53.

55. Cosa Nostra in Sicily operates according to a similar logic: "One becomes a Man of honour mainly as a family inheritance, but not as straightforwardly as in the aristocracy (where the succession is automatic from father to son)." The candidate is under scrutiny for years, before being finally admitted into the organisation (P. Arlacchi, *op. cit.*: 7).

56. A. Vardi, *Podkonvoinyi mir* (Munich: Possev-Verlag, 1971): 31, quoted by Y. Glazov, *art. cit.*: 238.

57. Y. Glazov, *art. cit.*: 44; A. Solzhenitsyn, *Arkhipelag GULag, 1918-1956, op. cit.*, III-IV: 429.

58. V. Chalidze, *op. cit.*: 47. Soviet citizens were entitled to own items of personal property, as stated by art. 10 of the 1936 Soviet constitution. See F. Varese, "Is Sicily the future of Russia? Private protection and the rise of the Russian Mafia," *Archives européennes de Sociologie*, 35 (1994): 235.

59. M. de Santerre, *op. cit.*: 95.

60. *Ibid.*: 62.

61. Both the Yakuza and Cosa Nostra have rules against appealing to the police or law. See D.H. Stark, op. cit.: 240 and P. Arlacchi, *op. cit.*: 57.

62. V. Shalamov, *Ocherki prestupnogo mira, op. cit.*: 61.

63. A letter published in Perm's weekly magazine devoted to criminal matters *Dos'e 02* (14 September 1994) also testifies to this. The author, a convict, regrets that the criminals of the 1990s who claim to be the heirs of the traditional society have betrayed the old rules. As an indicator of such betrayal is the fact that new *vory* are murderers. "Thieves-in-Law [...] do not exist any more. If they are thieves, they are not *in-laws*, but rather *in-pen*. Thieves in the old times despised

murderers, but now every second thief is a murderer. The thieves' law exists no more." Though a restrain on the use of violence is typical of other organised criminal groups, an explicit rule against murder is peculiar to the *vory*.

64. M. de Santerre, *op. cit.*: 56.

65. *Ibid.*; Y. Glazov, *art. cit.*: 45.

66. Y. Glazov, *art. cit.*: 43. V. Chalidze, *op. cit.*: 52, seems to take the opposing view on this issue.

67. A.I. Gurov and V. Riabinin, "Ispoved' vora v zakone," *Na boevom postu*, 1 (1991): 78. *Kalina krasnaia* (The red snowball tree, USSR, 1974, 100 mins), directed by Vasilii Shukshin, starring V. Shukshin, and Lydia Fedoseeva. After Egor is killed, a woman from the gang regrets his death. The gang's boss says: "He was just a *muzhik*. There are a lot of them in Russia."

68. This fund was also called *chernaia kassa*, the black fund. See A.I. Gurov, *op. cit.*: 231.

69. *Ibid.*: 115.

70. V. Shalamov, *Kolyma tales, op. cit.*: 5. See also V. Shalamov, *Ocherki prestupnogo mira, op. cit.*: 60.

71. D.S. Likhachev, *art. cit.*: 56.

72. *Ibid.* On vory playing *shtos*, see also V.P. Artem'ev, *Regim i okhrana ispravitel'no-trudovykh lagerei MVD* (Munich: Institute for the Study of the USSR, 1956): 96.

73. D.S. Likhachev, *art. cit.*: 56.

74. V.P. Artemev, *op. cit.*: 96-97; Y. Glazov, *art. cit.*: 44. "On August 14, prisoners of the camp sub-department no. 7 UITLK Karpov, Foteev, Mitrakov, Makushin (all of them are *vory*-recidivists, sentenced many times, serving their sentence according to decree dated 04 June 1947) were playing cards. Karpov lost 12,000 roubles to Mitrakov. They agreed that Karpov could redeem his debt by killing prisoner Perchikov. Karpov and his accomplice Foteev both hit Perchikov three times with a brick on the head on 16 August 1948. Perchikov was sent to the hospital in serious condition. Makushin knew of the murder's plans and didn't inform the camp administration. All of them were sentenced to different terms." GAPO, R-1366/3/177/14. Women had similar rules. In March 1948, three hardened female criminals were charged for the killing of another female inmate in the Kus'inlag camp. By playing cards the four of them had decided who should carry out a "sentence" they had passed on the deputy head of the camp. The designated murderer refused and was punished accordingly. See GAPO, R-1366/3/177/3-4.

75. D.S. Likhachev, *art. cit.*: 55.

76. V. Shalamov, *Ocherki prestupnogo mira, op. cit.*: 60.

77. V. Shalamov, *Kolyma tales, op. cit.*: 420.

78. "Only in rare cases, when a *tolkovishcha* takes place in a prison cell with other convicts, strangers may witness similar meetings." M. de Santerre, *op. cit.*: 57.

79. *Ibid.*: 58.

80. A.I. Gurov, *op. cit.*: 115.

81. *Vory* were very sensitive to their public performance. D.S. Likhachev (*art. cit.*: 59) notes that a popular motto of the *vory* was: "In public, even death is beautiful." By contrast, "bragging and showing off" are prohibited among members of Cosa Nostra. See P. Arlacchi, *op. cit.*: 57.

82. D.S. Likhachev interprets *vory* boasting as a shamans' practice. "Boasting among thieves shares characteristics of the shamans' practice. They are boasting in order to strengthen their own power, self-control, self-confidence and at the same time to consolidate their power over their subordinates. The majority of thieves' songs also bear an imprint of this boasting. The thieves' song is usually the story of a thief and his heroic deeds, often it is in the first person, singular or plural" (*art. cit.*: 59-60).

83. *Ibid.*: 59.

84. *Ibid.*; A.I. Gurov, *op. cit.*: 113.

85. According to M. de Santerre, *op. cit.*: 58, this penalty was called "earthing" (*zemlenie*).

86. *Ibid.*: 62-63.

87. For such cases, see e.g. A.I. Gurov, *op. cit.*: 114.

88. M. de Santerre, *op. cit.*: 58 and Y. Glazov, *art. cit.*: 40. It might have been the case that the meeting decreed that a lawbreaker was unworthy of being killed as *vor*, and ordered to "strangle or kill him with logs." Nevertheless, he would never have been killed while asleep. M. de Santerre, *op. cit.*: 58.

89. A.I. Gurov, *op. cit.*: 108; see also Id., *Krasnaia mafiia* (Moskva: Miko Kommercheskii Vestnik, 1995): 104.

90. Quoted in A.I. Gurov, *op. cit.*: 115.

91. *Ibid.*: 116.

92. J. Rossi, *op. cit.*: 23.

93. M. de Santerre, *op. cit.*: 60-61.

94. A.I. Gurov, *op. cit.*: 108.

95. V.F. Trakhtenberg, *Blatnaia muzyka (zhargon tiurmy)* (St. Petersburg, 1908).

96. *Slovar' vorovskogo i arestantskogo iazyka*, compiled by V.M. Popov (Kiev, 1912).

97. *Slovar' zhargona prestupnikov (blatnaia muzyka)*, compiled by S.M. Potapov (Moscow, 1927).

98. D.S. Likhachev, *art. cit.*: 47, 49, 55, 58.

99. GAPO, R-1366/3/177/14, date: 1948.

100. See V. Shalamov, *Ocherki prestupnogo mira, op. cit.*: 64, 66, 68, 69, 70.

101. Ivan P. Vorida, *Sbornik zhargonnykh slov i vyrazhenii, upotrebliaemykh v ustnoi i pis'mennoi rechi prestupnym elementom* (Alma-Ata, 1971): 1, 5.

102. *Zapiski iz mertvogo doma* is based on the author's Siberian notebook, a series of 522 entries that he was able to write down while still in prison.

103. See respectively F.M. Dostoyevsky, *Notes from the house of the dead* (London: Penguin Books, 1985): 41, 32, 84, 87.

104. *Ibid.*: 101.

105. J. Rossi himself however refers to this as a "legend." "Legend has it that, during tsarist times, the chief of a prison, without vacillating, would release even the most inveterate thief or killer, if the latter gave his word to come back ..." J. Rossi, *op. cit.*: 55.

106. V. M. Doroshevich, *Sakhalin: Katorga* [1903] (Parizh: Biblioteka "Illiustrirovannoi Rossii," 1935): 37-38.

107. GAPO, 164/1/19/314.

108. See C. Frierson, "Crime and punishment in the Russian village: rural concepts of criminality at the end of the nineteenth century," *Slavic Review*, 46, 1 (1987): 62. *Arteli* were of course not a feature of the criminal world only. For instance, Russian hunters in eastern Siberia in the seventeenth century organised themselves in *arteli*. See O.V. Bychkov, "Russian hunters in eastern Siberia in the seventeeth-century life-style and economy," *Arctic Anthropology*, 31, 1 (1994): 72-85.

109. E. Iakushkin, *Obychnoe pravo* (Iaroslavl': Tipo-Litografiia Gubernskoi Zemskoi Upravy, 1896), quoted by V. Chalidze, *Criminal Russia, op. cit.*: 40-41.

110. S. Maksimov, *Otechestvennye zapiski*, 12 (1869).

111. E. Bacon, *The Gulag at war* (London: Macmillan, 1994): 47. In order to have the full picture of forced labour in the Soviet Union between 1932 and 1947, one should add roughly two million forced to reside in labour settlements.

112. E. Bacon, *op. cit.*: 37; see also pp. 27 and 11.

113. V.N. Zemskov, "Arkhipelag GULag: glazami pisatelia i statistika,"*Argumenty i fakty*, 45 (1989): 6-7.

114. A.V. Gorbatov, *Years off my life* (London: Constable, 1964): 141.

115. Memorial, 2/1/33/1-109.

116. See A.G. Bronnikov, *Tainye sposoby sviazi prestupnikov* (Perm': UVD Permskoi Oblasti, 1994) and A. Gurov, "Tradizioni e tipologie della criminalità russa,"*Modernizzazione e Sviluppo*, 4, 1-2 (1993): 38.

117. V.P. Artemev, *op. cit.*: 97.

118. The importance of prison as a source of contacts and as a vehicle for the dissemination of information is noted by Reuter in connection to the American Cosa Nostra. See P. Reuter, *Disorganised crime. The economics of the visible hand* (Cambridge-London: MIT Press, 1983): 158. Having been a prisoner provides an inexpensive signal of reliability to other Mafiosi. Once out of prison, interactions are less risky.

119. The use of "*suka*" to mean "turncoat thief" appears to date from the late 1920s. During the tsarist period, "*suka*" was used to describe policemen (see, e.g., *Slovar' vorovskogo i arestantskogo iazyka, op. cit.*: 83). J. Rossi (*op. cit.*: 441) points out that the meaning of "turncoat thief" is not

recorded in the *Slovar' solovetskogo uslovnogo iazika* by N. Vinogradov (1927). I have found it used by Leonid Leonov in his novel *Vor* (Moskva–Leningrad: Gosudarstevnnoe Izdatel'stvo, 1928: 313). M. de Santerre offers a rather imaginative etymology: supposedly, it refers to special she-wolves trained to bring a wolf over to the hunters (*op. cit.*: 77).

120. A.I. Gurov, *op. cit.*: 119-120.

121. "In short, there are no thieves 'under the law' nowadays, except perhaps for a few dozen living out their lives in various jails (I managed to meet a few in Vladimir)." V. Bukovskii, *op. cit.*: 246.

122. V. Perushkin, "Vory i avtoritety," *Argumenty i fakty*, 6, 747 (February 1995): 5.

123. See decrees of the Supreme Soviet adopted on 12 July and 24 December 1941, E. Bacon, *op. cit.*: 105 and N. Werth, "Violenza, repressioni, terrori nell'Unione Sovietica," in S. Courtois, ed., *Il libro nero del comunismo* (Milano: Mondadori, 1998 : 213), transl. of *Le livre noir du communisme* (Paris: Robert Laffont, 1997). It should be noted that the *Livre noir* gives a very partial view of *communisme*. Although Werth's contribution lends credibility to this overall view, it provides an outstanding investigation of the Soviet camp history.

124. V. Shalamov, *Ocherki prestupnogo mira, op. cit.*: 57. Moreover, convicts who had served their sentence were also sent to the front.

125. A.N. Dugin, "Gulag: otkryvaia arkhivy," *Na boevom postu* (27 December 1989): 3-4 (quoted in E. Bacon, *op. cit.*: 91); E. Bacon, *op. cit.*: 38 and N. Werth, *art. cit.*: 214.

126. N. Werth, *art. cit.*: 215. See also M. Craveri, "Krizis GULaga. Kengirskoe vosstanie 1954 goda v dokumentakh MVD," *Cahiers du Monde russe*, 36, 3 (1995): 320.

127. See Stalin's order no. 270 (16 August 1941), E. Bacon, *op. cit.*: 93.

128. See the decree adopted in 1946 "on the protection of state corn crops" and the two decrees adopted in 1947 "on the protection of socialist property" and "on the protection of personal property of citizens." In application of the 1947 decrees, 300,000 people were convicted in the period 1947-1952. V. Zemskov, "GULag," *Sociologicheskie issledovaniia*, 6 (1991): 10-11; N. Werth, *art. cit.*: 220.

129. A. Graziosi, *art. cit.*: 423: "The decisive change [in the composition of the camp population], however, came about during, and immediately after, World War II, with the arrival of prisoners many of whom had military and organisational experience, including many officers: men used to fighting and difficult to handle."

130. Grigorii Antonov, Letter to Vladimir Murav'ev, July 1989, reprinted in S. Vilenskii, ed., *Resistance in the Gulag 1923-56. Memoirs. Letters. Documents* (Moscow: Vozvrashchenie, 1992): 122. On the Kengir revolt of 1954, see M. Craveri, *art. cit.*

131. Varashak Batoyan, "My recollections of Kengir," in *Resistance in the Gulag, op. cit.*: 103.

132. GARF, 8131/ 32-III/ 3027/79.

133. GARF, 8131/32/3030/61.

134. GARF, 8131/32/3030/40.

135. GARF, R8131/32/3025/139, date: 08 November 1953.

136. GARF, 8131/32/3030/137. For a similar case, see GARF, 8131/32/3030/177.

137. D.S. Chalidze, *op. cit.*: 49.

138. According to V. Shalamov (*Ocherki prestupnogo mira, op. cit.*: 63), the *vory* explained their actions as follows: " — You have been in the war? That means that you are a bitch, and should be punished according to the law. You are also a coward. You had no will-power to refuse to serve; you should have taken a new sentence or even died, but you should not have gone to the front." Shalamov maintains that these renegades ended up in Magadan and Ust'-Tsil'ma camps. Gurov records *otoshedshie* as another word for the *suki*. A.I. Gurov, *op. cit.*: 117.

139. GARF, 9401c/12/145/55, date: 25 February 1950.

140. GARF, 8131/32-III/3027/164.

141. The *nariadchik* was a person working in the Accounting and Distribution section of the camp. See J. Rossi, *op. cit.*: 246.

142. GARF, 8131/32/3030/18, date: 06 December 1953.

143. GARF, 9401/12/02681/373.

144. GARF, R-8131/ 32-III/3033/155.

145. Invariably, the above quoted reports castigated local executives for using dangerous recidivists in official positions. The authorities had tried to cope with the growing unrest in the

Gulag by creating special camps for political prisoners (order dated 16 March 1948) and for especially dangerous criminals (order dated 31 December 1948), and rewarding those who repented. It should be added that this period of camp history (1947-1956) was also marked by the first uprisings in the Gulag. At least 14 incidents have been recorded. On these events, see at least A. Graziosi, *art. cit.*, M. Craveri, *art. cit.*, and S. Vilenskii, ed., *op. cit.*

146. According to V. Shalamov, the ritual consisted in kissing a knife that would knight them as "new *vory*." Shalamov suggested that the new ritual is taken from a Walter Scott novel, a popular author in the camps (*Ocherki prestupnogo mira, op. cit.*: 65).

147. When the group of prisoners Solzhenitsyn was part of encountered the *suki*, a convict explained to the newly arrested captain: "These are the *bitches* — the ones who work for the prison. They are enemies of the *honest thieves*. And the honest thieves are the ones imprisoned in cells." A. Solzhenitsyn, *The Gulag archipelago, op. cit.*: 544. See also *Arkhipelag GULag, 1918-1956, op. cit.*: 517.

148. M. de Santerre, *op. cit.*: 59.

149. *Ibid.*: 60.

150. GARF, 9401c/12/851/239, date: 12 December 1952.

151. "Contrary to orders of MVD of the USSR no. 00840-1951 and no. 0043-1952 those groups of prisoners that are at enmity with each other aren't isolated, continue to be kept together and terrorise the camp population." GARF, 9401c/12/791/223, date: 10 October 1952.

152. GARF, R8131/32-III/3025/225-227.

153. GARF, 8131/32/3030/25.

154. See J. Rossi, *op. cit.*: 181; A.I. Gurov, *op. cit.*: 118.

155. GARF, R8131/32/3025/230.

156. GARF, 8131/32/3030/129. The 800-people estimate is either an exaggeration or, more likely, it refers to the entire milieu of individuals who rotated around the *vory* proper.

157. GARF, R8131/ 32-III/3025/7.

158. M. de Santerre, *op. cit.*: 71.

159. *Ibid.*

160. A. Solzhenitsyn, *The Gulag archipelago, op. cit.*: 581; see also V. Shalamov, *Ocherki prestupnogo mira, op. cit.*: 68.

161. GARF, R-8131/ 32-III/3033/175.

162. GARF, 8131/32/3030/263.

163. GARF, OPKh/2/450/472 (emphasis added), date : 26 May 1954.

164. V. Shalamov, *Ocherki prestupnogo mira, op. cit.*: 69. It should not come as a surprise that criminals could come in possession of explosives. According to one report, 7 kilos of explosives and 810 knives had been found in the possession of convicts in the Bodaibinskii MVD corrective labour camp in the first half of 1951. GARF, 8131/ 32 (III)/ 3027 (vol.1)/76.

[3]

"Thieves" in the USSR—
a Social Phenomenon

Yuri Glazov

A MONG the many problems of post-revolutionary Russia, the so-called
" thieves " (*vory*), their behaviour and psychology, might constitute
an important subject of scholarly interest. " Thieves " means here not so
much ordinary pick-pockets and robbers (which these persons could
indeed be) as, rather, honoured members of a powerful underground
crime institution. In the prison-camp empire which flourished in Russia
until Stalin's death in 1953 and a number of years thereafter, thieves were
actually permitted by the authorities to establish their supremacy in the
camps over millions of *muzhiki*, common workers and peasants, and
"fascists," as the intelligentsia were often called in prison-camp slang.
The authority and influence of the thieves' brotherhood outside the
prison-camp walls was too important to be disregarded.

The thieves' associations are not specifically Russian. Sicilian-born
mafia and organized crime institutions in America are typologically
related social phenomena, although in many respects the function and
structure of the thieves' institution in Russia seem to constitute a quite
different picture. The Russian institution of the thieves is an esoteric
order of professional outlaws, whose behaviour is based on strictly
defined rules. Although it is difficult to trace here the historical traditions
of this institution, a list of the notables of pre-revolutionary Russia,
including such heroes as Yermak, a conqueror of Siberia in the sixteenth
century, Razin and Pugachov, prominent leaders of two peasant revolts,
might help us in understanding the thieves' historical roots.[1]

T HE Soviet system inherited some features of what might be called
the past grandeur of the Russian Robin Hood tradition. The new
power came into existence in 1917, using at least a few questionable
methods. The party leadership was fully aware, for instance, of the bank
hold-ups carried out by Lenin's party members.[2] The behaviour of the
revolutionaries in the Winter Palace, where priceless vases were used as
chamber pots, aroused the indignation of Maxim Gorky in 1917.[3]

---

[1] The glorious traditions of robbers in Russia date from the time of the Tartar yoke.
In 1375 Kostroma was attacked by robbers. *Entsiklopedicheskii slovar*, Vol. 51, p. 115.
A number of famous robbers of ancient Russia were lauded in folklore, like Solovei—
robber, Vasili Buslaiev, Ivan Cain, and the Cossacks. Writers of the highest calibre wrote
about them, such figures in classical Russian literature as Pushkin, Dostoyevsky, Tolstoy
and Chekhov, as well as the Soviet authors Gorky, Mayakovsky, Leonov, Seyfullina,
Makarenko, Tendryakov, Maksimov, Solzhenitsyn, and many others.

[2] Leonard Schapiro, *The Communist Party of the Soviet Union*, p. 88; David Shub,
Lenin, p. 61.

[3] Bertram D. Wolfe, *The Bridge and the Abyss*, Praeger, p. 87, Maxim Gorky,
Nesvoyevremyennye Mysli (Paris, 1971), pp. 118, 122.

From the 1917 Revolution to the end of the 1950s the underground
world of professional criminals played an important role in the history
of Soviet society. As a result of years of war and the succeeding transformation in Russia, millions of youngsters lost their parents and homes.
Streets became their playground, robbery a life-long profession, prison
and prison-camps their real homes and places of recreation. While on the
upper levels of the society the activity of building socialism was in full
swing, on its lower levels, embracing millions of common people, the
whole country was terrorized on a day-to-day basis by this underground
force.

Stalin himself used to boast of his close relations with the underground
milieu of pre-revolutionary Russia. The changes in prison conditions and
climate after the middle of the 1930s might be explained by Stalin's
personal instructions.[4] Stalin obviously understood criminal psychology;
and the behaviour of the NKVD leaders and some Red Army chiefs
might be better understood if the impact of prison-camp psychology and
the underground were traced in more detail.[5]

In the four decades after the Revolution of 1917 a specifically prison-
camp subculture came to life. This subculture had clear space boundaries,
time dimensions and life-values. The prison-camp world had its own dialect
of Russian, grammar and vocabulary. The population of the prison-camp
empire numbered up to fifteen million until 1939, and included as a rule
the most active and temperamental citizens of post-revolutionary society.
The prison-camp kingdom had its own uniformity, prescribed on the one
hand by State Security directives and on the other by the well-established
organized crime institutions. Prison-camp culture was characterized by
its peculiar philosophy and interrelations (including sexual) between
members of that highly stratified society.

ALTHOUGH dozens of books have been written in various languages
about prison-camps in Russia, there is still no book or article about
the "thieves," this peculiar tribe of Soviet society which could be considered as an aristocracy of the prison world. The society of the thieves
is an esoteric sect, with its own religion, and an extremely rigid code of
secular behaviour. Most writers, however, who describe their prison-

---

[4] September, 1936 brought the NKVD Stalin's rebuke that it was "four years behind
in this matter." Adam Ulam, *Stalin*, p. 419.

[5] Marshall K. Rokossovsky was a former prisoner, well-known for his relations with
the former convicts, who were glad to serve in his army. One of the great heroes during
World War Two, Alexandr Matrosov was a daring man, whose mentality was shaped by
the prison-camp atmosphere. P. Yakir in his *Childhood in Prison* eloquently describes
the atmosphere producing young criminals. "Misha talked of the mood in the com-
pound. The likely lads who had come from Moscow were setting the tone, criticizing
the activists for collaborating with the camp security officers; friers (who do not belong
to the underworld fraternity) made escapes while they, who had once had real rogue's
blood in their veins, actually narked for authorities." Pyotr Yakir, *A Childhood in Prison*
London 1972), p. 103.

"THIEVES" AS A SOCIAL PHENOMENON 143

camp experiences (independently of each other) emphasize the phenomenon of the prison-camp aristocracy as the most important, and most unpleasant, feature of life in their incarceration.[6] "Twenty per cent of criminals keep in terror 80 per cent of morally pure prisoners. Three per cent of criminals (*blatars*) keep in blind obedience all the rest of the criminal world."[7]

For these people, having to live side-by-side with professional robbers and murderers was more unpleasant than the sadism of camp personnel, or the knowledge that as a political prisoner one was condemned to decades of incarceration, enforced, exhausting manual labour, starvation and complete separation from relatives and friends. These criminals were little short of omnipotent within the camp, well-informed by spies, and proud of being incorrigible.

In fact, the whole of the USSR was at one time covered by a network of well-organized and professionally-trained outlaws. The hierarchy of these outlaws is shaped like a pyramid, broadly based and tapering towards the top. But at the top there is no single man like the American

---

[6] Alexander Solzhenitsyn, *Arkhipelag Gulag* I–II Paris, 1973, p. 415; Aurel Von Juchen, "Was die Hunde heulen," Deutsche Verlags Anstalt, Stuttgart, 1958, p. 124; Lev Ginzburg, "Dudka krysolova," Moscow, 1960, p. 166; Ivan Solonevich, "Rossiya v lageriakh *Golos Rossii*, 1938, p. 253; V. I. Yukshinski, "Sovetskie kontsentrationnye lageri v 1945–1955," Institute for the Study of the USSR, München, 1958, p. 29; Gustav Herling, *A World Apart*, New York, trans. from the Polish by Joseph Mark, 1951, p. 27.
    It is worthwhile to give here a passage from the work of a foreign lady who found herself in the post-war prison-camp empire and found out about this phenomenon.
    " ' Who is Zagriskin? ' I asked.
    ' The king of Vorkuta ' Anne explained. ' He owns the whole darn railroad system we are building. Well he does not actually own it, but he behaves as though he did. Imagine, that dog got out of the camp two years ago, and now he practically runs the country. Has the confidence of Moscow—a criminal, a former convict, a murderer, and now he exploits the prisoners worse than any free man. He was one of the worst criminals up here; only sat for eight years though; they let him out on good behaviour. He was a Blatnoy and became a 'Suka.'
    I did not understand, ' What are Blatnie? What are Suki? '
    ' The Blatnie are a very tight criminal group ' Ruth explained. ' They have extremely strict rules by which they live, one of them being that they must never work for anyone, especially not for the government. They live entirely from theft and murder, but usually take from the rich and give to the poor. When one of them disobeys the rules or does anything unworthy of a Blatnoy, such as getting a job, he is called Suka—female dog—and is liquidated by his former gang members. He is a traitor, see, and is considered worse than a government official.'
    I tried to find out more about this interesting subject later by asking my Russian colleagues. But they knew very little about it. In fact, most of them had never heard of the Blatnie (thieves) before they became prisoners and were brought in contact with them. It seemed a phenomenon so far outside normal society that an ordinary citizen never suspected its presence. And yet it was an enormous organization, covering the whole territory of the Soviet Union. It was in no way formalized, simply a loose fraternity with an iron code." Erica Wallach, *Light at Midnight* (New York, 1967), pp. 229–30. What Erica Wallach writes about the thieves' habits and customs should be carefully checked and corrected, but her first impression about this tribe of thieves and bitches is of great interest for us.
    [7] Mikhail Rozanov, Zavoevateli belykh piaten/*Conquerors of the White Spots*, Possev-Verlag, Limbourg, 1951, p. 255. Regarding domination of the thieves in prison-camps, see A. Solzhenitsyn, *Gulag Arkhipelag,* III–IV, p. 424. Cf. also L. Kopelev in *Khranit vechno*, Ardis, 1975, pp. 447, 605.

" Godfather." The society is composed of many families (*kodlo*), who are supposed to be united by ties of solidarity, fraternity and relatively equal rights. To become a fully fledged member of the thieves' fraternity, many years of training and tests are necessary. While young, the *maloletka* (teenager) is considered a novice; only later can he call himself a *vor* or true thief, a name which has a respectful connotation among many Russians.[8]

IN a country where the law as an embodiment of justice became the target of wit and cynical remarks, thieves do not fail to live by their own law, based on their own ideals of justice. This law is, naturally, unwritten, but it nonetheless prescribes every aspect of the thief's life. Spiritual life, language, prison-camp *mores*, evaluation of human beings, relations with other thieves in the framework of their own community, judgment and punishment for infraction of thieves' rules, work and leisure, eating and drinking, treatment of their own bodies, attitudes towards sex and women, towards renegades from the thieves' society, relations with common people outside and state officials inside the camps —all these aspects of life are treated in their laws.

FOR the thieves, the basis of their standards is their own spirit (*dukh*), and those who possess it, the thieves, are *dukhariki*. The notion of the spirit is particularly important under the exhausting conditions of the camps which the thieves call their " native home." Given the starvation diet and hard labour there, a person's ability to survive depends almost entirely on keeping his spirit alive. The thieves wear home-made aluminium crosses round their necks, and their chests are often tattooed with a picture of praying angels on each side of a crucifix; underneath are the words: " O Lord, save thy slave! " or " I believe in God." An appeal to God will be found even on their legs, such as: " O Lord, save me from the Cheka." [9] This does not mean that the thieves are religious in the generally accepted sense. Although in rare cases the thieves are known to have been compassionate and helpful towards " saints," as religious people are called in the prisons,[10] there are no facts confirming the existence of any purely religious rituals among thieves.[11]

---

[8] " Thief " is also a self-definition among the members of this underground body. Other self-definitions among them are : honest thief (*chestnyi vor*), lawful thief (*zakonnyi vor*), thief-in-law (*vor v zakone*), lawyer (*zakonnik*), vagabond (*blatnoy, bosiak, brodiaga*), *zhigan, urka, urkach, urkagan, chesniaga*. See M. de Santerr " Sovetskie poslevoennye kontslageri i ikh obitateli," Munchen, 1960, Institute for the Study of the USSR, p. 55.

[9] M. de Santerr, op. cit. p. 89.

[10] Ibid. p. 80. Good attitudes towards religious people were seen in cases when the religious person showed examples of very high spirituality.

[11] Songs and tap-dancing (*chechetka*) among thieves constituted a kind of religious ritual.

"THIEVES" AS A SOCIAL PHENOMENON   145

Since thieves worship spirit and spirituality, its level is what determines a thief's status in his fraternity. They have various methods of determining whether a newcomer belongs to the thieves or not.[12] If a newcomer shows obvious signs of being a member of their clan, the thieves of the cell or of the camp invite him to their secret meeting (*tolkovishche* or *pravilka*) in order to establish his credentials and spirit in the thieves' society. Like their trials, such meetings are well-guarded, and include some features of religious rituals.

The thieves laws are extremely rigid, and if they find out that one of their number has deviated from the laws, he is usually summoned to a secret trial. If found guilty he may lose his status as a thief and his spirit, a penalty which is termed " earthing." In the case of the death verdict the thieves execute their condemned fellow: they do so by first " rotating " the guilty person, thereby taking away his soul.[13] The death verdict having been announced, the victim stands with his back to the wall, tears his shirt open in front, and addressing his several (never one) executioners, who are armed with knives, says: " Take my soul! "

THE thieves' law declares complete contempt towards females. Under no conditions may women become members of their privileged clan on any level whatsover. Within the society of thieves neither permanent families nor wives are allowed.[14] Fraternal life within the society of thieves is a matter of fierce pride and does not leave the individual any chance for privacy or personal preferences, which might jeopardize his devotion or weaken his ties to the brotherhood, and so endanger his fellows' security as well as his own. A thief is entitled to take only a temporary wife or girlfriend, and the higher the thief's status, the better are his chances of receiving a more desirable girlfriend, whether within the prison-camp or elsewhere.

As far as their sexual life is concerned, the thieves know almost no limits. All pretty female prisoners are considered their property, and the right of the first night belongs to the head of the thieves' family. But a thief has no commitments towards the women he has relations with, whether they are female thieves or not.[15] The female thieves, although

[12] A common trick to identify their own members was to spread on the floor at the entrance of a prison-cell a new silk shirt or clean towel. A newcomer to the cell might be perplexed even to touch the expensive stuff with his shoes and is thus immediately identified as a person alien to the clan. A thief entering the cell for the first time puts his feet on the shirt or towel and quietly cleans them, revealing his membership in the thieves' fraternity.

[13] M. de Santerr, op. cit. p. 58. Solzhenitsyn, op. cit. p. 433.

[14] Varlam Shalamov writes about possible exceptions, but he confirms the point of view according to which the thieves could have their families and wives only in the past, and never in the present. Varlam Shalamov, " A Woman of the Underground World," *Grani*, October 1970, Possev Verlag, No. 77, p. 41.

[15] In Russian, *vorovka* a she-thief, *blatnaia* a woman belonging to the world of the thieves, *blatniachka*, *vorovaika* she who belongs to the thieves' world. A good description of a queen of the women thieves is given by Y. A. Tregubov, " Vosem' let vo vlasti Lubianki," Possev-Verlag, 1959, p. 147 (Eight Years in Lubianki Prison).

lacking equal rights with male thieves, are forbidden to have intercourse
with any men who are not members of the thieves' family. A female thief
may well kill a non-thief if he attempts to make love to her or rape her.[16]
A female thief feels proud to be the property, although temporary, of an
elder thief (*pakhan*). There are no love triangles among them or cases
of rivalry because mutual girlfriends are forbidden. But close ties of
solidarity and fraternity allow them in a time of sexual hunger to share
the same girl for one night.[17] The majority of thieves suffer from venereal
diseases, which do not worry them at all. Thieves generally do not live
long anyway: they tend to die in their twenties or thirties.

Homosexuality is not banned by their laws, and in fact all thieves
know this practice.[18] But passive homosexuality is entirely forbidden;
passive homosexuals are not even considered human beings. Men in the
prison camps who have been raped are regarded as outcasts. They are
not allowed to sit at the same table with the others, or to eat from the
same plate or with the same spoon. They are called " roosters " (*petukhi*)
and are permitted to keep company only with other prison-camp male
prostitutes. A thief would consider it below his dignity to associate in
any way with a " rooster." Should a thief himself be raped by his foes,
honour dictates that he murder his rapers and then take his own life.

In spite of this contempt for relationships with women, the thief's
feelings for the mother figure are extraordinarily strong.[19]

The mother-cult, very widespread, demands that each thief bear
tattooed on his breast: " I won't forget my own mother! " The mother-
cult among thieves is of foremost importance for understanding the nature
of their society because of its obvious relation to the traditional Russian
mother–cult and to the cult of the Mother Goddess of India (e.g. the
South Indian war-goddess Kotravai, who danced among the slain on the
battlefield and demanded that her worshippers rob and kill).[20] The
mother–cult demands neither respect toward females generally nor the
worshipping of one's own mother in particular. Nevertheless, in thieves'
circles harsh words about anybody's mother are at once cut off and
suppressed.

In the dark life of thieves the notion of the mother remains a bright
spot. In their songs, functionally replacing prayer, they sing about mother
not without feeling:

> Mammy worked hard to support our family.
> While I softly started stealing,

---

[16] Varlam Shalamov, Woman of the Thieves' World, *Grani*, 1970, p. 32.

[17] Shalamov, ibid. p. 34. In times of sexual emergency the criminals deprived of
female society used to arrange what was known in the prison-camp as a " streetcar,"
(*tramvai*) a rape squad.

[18] An outline of their sexual behaviour is given by A. Vardi, *Podkonvoinyi mir*,
Possev Verlag, 1971, p. 31.

[19] Ibid. p. 39; A. Solzhenitsyn, *Arkhipelag Gulag*, III–IV, p. 429.

[20] A. L. Basham, *The Wonder that Was India*, New York, 1959, p. 312.

"THIEVES" AS A SOCIAL PHENOMENON   147

" You will become a thief just like your daddy! "
Shedding tears mummy kept saying.[21]

This subject runs through numerous thieves' songs. In the above-quoted couplet the real meaning is probably that the thief's own mother had given her blessing, however painful and reluctant, to her dear son's professional début. The Mother who is praised so lovingly in these songs might be not the thief's own mother, but the reflection of a general cult of motherhood, so frequently found among primitive tribes.

THE thieves' knowledge about the life outside prison walls and prison-camp barbed wire is at best vague. The distance between prison-camp life and the so-called free life of Soviet Russia as viewed by the thieves is not much less than the distance between the Soviet " free world " and Western European or American life. It is only the camp life which is seen by the thieves as real and, perhaps, even natural. Their excursions beyond the prison areas never last for long. To the thieves, the life of the western world is even more fabulous. Stories about American gangsters are heard with incredulity. Those from the West who find themselves in Soviet prison camps are called simply " spies " and " westerners."

Various segments of the population, both outside the prison camps and within, originally received their names and nicknames from the thieves. Persons belonging to that outside world are " friers," from the German frei or free. The chiefs and guardians of the camps are called " vermin " (*gady*). Those thieves who become renegades are called " bitches " (*suki*). The bitches are the worst foes of the thieves. Common prisoners working under the vermin's supervision are called " workmen " (*rabotiagi*), which in Russian slang has the connotation of draught animals. Those of the camp population who occupy relatively easy and profitable positions are " fools " (*pridurki*). Thieves are considered to be the privileged layer of the population, and like patricians in ancient Rome or the aristocracy of mediaeval Europe, they set the standard of behaviour in the prison camps.[22]

A central concept in the thieves' philosophy is the sense of their own exclusive rights to being considered human. It is only " honest thieves " of their brotherhood who are " human beings " or " men." There have been frequent cases when if three thieves were sitting in a cell, inhabited by over a hundred other prisoners, they might exchange loud remarks with their fellow thieves in adjacent cells: " Hey, how many human beings have you got there? We are three! " [23] The thieves' self-confidence and strength are based on solidarity within the framework of their fraternity, shrewdness in matters of survival and endurance of the exhausting conditions around them.

[21] Shalamov, op. cit. p. 40.
[22] Alexandr Vardi, op. cit. p. 121.
[23] M. de Santerr, op. cit. p. 23.

THEIR fearlessness and undisguised contempt for death is an important part of their self-discipline.[24] Except perhaps for a group of highly religious people who would often prefer torture and death to yielding to the authorities' pressure,[25] the thieves represent a rare group within the Soviet population who seem to have overcome all fear. And it is fear that has been exploited so succesfully by the organs of state security to " keep order." But a thief has nothing to lose; he has no property. He himself is the property of his own order. On pain of death he is forbidden to have any collaboration with officials and must avoid even minor infractions of the clear-cut prescriptions of the fraternity. A thief is allowed to leave his order (which is called " to tie the knot "), but under no conditions may the rules be transgressed while he is still a member.[26]

The thief's criminal career becomes progressively more involved in professional intricacies; the ups and downs of such an adventurous life and endless imprisonments mean the loss of almost all chances to get back to an ordinary life, in which with his poor education he could in any case play only a miserable and insignificant role. Yet within his community a thief has enormous importance and respect; his life is a great adventure, marked by extraordinary dangers and tests; and he finds deep satisfaction and pride in his ability to ignore pain and death. These and some other considerations can explain the phenomenon of almost unprecedented intrepidity shown by the thieves.

Under Stalin and for years after, hardly anybody had any security. The thieves had no difficulty observing in their prison life endless scenes of human degradation, which occurred not without their assistance. Moreover, their own dignity was contrasted to the willing and flattering servility of younger aides as well as to the obedience of many other prisoners living in fear and trembling. It was, therefore, their fearlessness as thieves which brought them to the seat of power and pleasure. Since only fellow thieves were human beings feelings of guilt and compassion for others were to be carefully avoided. The more scrupulously the thief took pains to strengthen his spirit, the less the likelihood of unworthy fears reappearing.[27]

---

[24] The nature of fear in Soviet Russia is still an unexplored subject, which however might explain important aspects of the human psychology in the country. Nadezhda Mandelstam treats this subject as a landslide disease in her second book of memoirs, *Vtoraia kniga*, Paris, 1972, p. 187 ff.

[25] E.g. a scene of the treatment of nuns in a Vorkuta prison-camp depicted by Erica Wallach, op. cit. p. 374–5.

[26] In an Inta prison-camp in the forties the thieves beheaded one of their fellows for the following misdeed: he had been seen eating fat just at the time when a few members of his fraternity were confined to a frozen lock-up and were not given either tobacco or rye bread for a few days by the guard. M. de Santerr, op. cit. p. 67.

[27] The thieves do not worry about either the next day or their future. Their rules demand that they not keep any food for the next day, but rather give it away to others. M. de Santerr, op. cit. p. 25. Words from *Matthew*, 6.25 may be recalled here in order. to understand better their style of life: " Therefore I tell you, do not be anxious about your life, what you shall eat or what you shall drink, nor about your body, what you shall put on." One should not much wonder at this. Traditions of flagellants and castrates in Russia offer many examples of rather peculiar interpretations of the Bible.

"THIEVES" AS A SOCIAL PHENOMENON   149

While thieves' spirits are to be safeguarded with constant vigilance (amidst the daily feuds and knife fights), their bodies seem to be trifles which can be almost entirely neglected. Scars and burns cover each thief's body, and the thief's dignity increases in direct proportion to the number of wounds and burns. This capacity to endure physical pain is incredible. Severe frost tortures them no more than burning heat.[28] They are able to live many days without any food at all. To write a number of protesting words on a wooden log with his own blood is something that a thief does without a second's hesitation. In order to get around a chief's orders or just to be sent to a hospital (a place of relative leisure), a thief readily swallows a dozen pieces of broken glass or sharp metal sticks. Or he might swallow a fishing hook tied to a thin rope, the other end of which is stretched to the cell's door in such a way that opening the door causes the thief's stomach and throat to be ripped by the sharply pointed hook.[29] Nailing the scrotal sac to a wooden bench is commonplace protest among thieves and their tribesmen.[30] They can cut off a finger or all five at once without a second thought. Having lost all his money at cards, a thief may stake his finger, or an arm or even his own life. If he happens to lose, he quickly cuts off the finger and keeps playing.[31] When he loses his stake, whatever it may be, the item must be redeemed immediately. There can be no reneging. Otherwise he will be proclaimed a bitch (*suka*) and knifed.[32] In the Northern forests, where prisoners were forced to saw wood, there were cases when thieves cut off their left hands and nailed them to a log which was then left to drift down the river to the south.[33] In a grave situation, a thief might publicly stab himself, much like the samurai ritual of harakiri; in these cases the thief makes strong and deep strokes upon his bare belly.[34] Thieves and their girlfriends view such ceremonies with the understanding that such an action proved the thief's high spirit and courage.

The communal spirit of thieves' life means that even food and tobacco are not personal property. A thief must not only give away the leftovers of his daily meals to those who serve him, but also, if he receives any food packet, he must put it on the table and say: " Come up and take, whoever is entitled to! " For concealing cigarettes from his friends, he

[28] A naked thief is able to sit for hours in frosty weather just on snow to express his indignation or protest regarding the chief's order. Viacheslav P. Artemyev, *Rezhim i Okhrana Ispavitelnotrudovych ragere i MVD*. Institute for the Study of the USSR, Munich, 1956, p. 96. Solonevich tells a well-known story about a young thief who having been put into a stove with consuming flame shouts angrily at those outside who forgot to shut the stove's door and thus had hurt him with a chilling draft. Ivan Solonevich, Rossiya v kontslageriakh / " Golos Rossii," 1938, p. 53.

[29] Anatoly Marchenko, *Moi pokazania*, Paris, 1969, p. 129.

[30] Dimitrii, Panin, " *Zapiski Sologdina*," Possev Verlag, Frankfurt/Main, 1973, p. 245.

[31] Am Marchenko, *My Testimony*, London, 1969, p. 141. Artemyev, op. cit. p. 97.

[32] Viacheslav Artemyev brings into his book a story about a thief who, having played away his left hand, tried to escape to another prison-camp, but ultimately was stabbed. Artemyev, op. cit. p. 97.

[33] M. de Santerr, op. cit. pp. 94, 97.

[34] Sergei Maximov, *Taiga* (New York, 1952), pp. 132–40.

may be brought to trial and consequently deprived of his thief's privileges.[35] Thieves' abilities to endure starvation are equalled by their enormous ingenuity in making drugs, spirits, etc. Spirits are prepared out of practically anything, including tooth powder and brake fluid. Thieves often suffer from epilepsy and drug addiction. In the prison-camp drugstores they get ether, luminal, drugs mixed with cocaine, morphine and opium.[36] A two-ounce tea packet boiled in a cup of water produces a hard drug called " chifir."

Their instinct for survival, paradoxically, rivals their utter contempt for death. If there is no limit to a thief's self-mutilation in the defence of his dignity, there is also no limit to his mutilation of others when his survival is actually endangered. In this case, thieves' laws extend their freedom of action even to cannibalism. In order to survive the escape from a prison-camp located in Siberia or Northern Russia, which involves running across thousands of miles of " tayga " forests without food or villages, they bring along " meat " or " walking cans." [37] These are common prisoners who must accompany the thieves in their escape and who may be stabbed by them and eaten in case of starvation. The thieves' laws demand at the same time that a murder can be committed only in emergency, and should be justified later by the person who did it.

IN a country whose first rule runs, " He who does not work, neither shall he eat," and in the prison-camp institutions called " correctional labour camps," the thieves obey a rigid rule of their own constitution: not to work for the state. Work of any form, if enforced by state officials, means collaboration with the authorities, which is forbidden by the thieves' own rules. Whatever the punishment inflicted for non-working: beating, starvation, a freezing cell, the thieves are ready to endure it. They are usually well-informed about the state and prison-camp laws, particularly the one which prescribes the death penalty for a prisoner who has refused work three times. A thief will never reject three demands to work in a row. Finding himself under the menace of the third order to work, he will provoke a fight, perhaps wound or kill somebody, or hurt himelf and wind up in a punishment cell or hospital for a week or two.

Thieves' philosophy of manual labour seems simple, as in their proverb-like sayings: " Working makes horses kick the bucket," " Work is not a wolf—it won't escape to the forest," " Keep your lousy porridge, and keep your job too!," " Do not do today what you can put off until

35 M. de Santerr, op. cit. pp. 92–93.

36 Solzhenitsyn, op. cit. p. 429.

37 Varlam Shalamov writes about this phenomenon in his stories about Kolyma. The author of this paper read this story while in Russia in one of the *samizdat* editions. Among those of his stories which had already been published outside Russia, this one has not yet been found, as well as other stories depicting the thieves' world with a scholarly accuracy. M. de Santerr brings these facts of cannibalism up in his matter-of-fact notes. M. de Santerr, op. cit. p. 65.

tomorrow," "Do not save for tomorrow what you can eat today," "One day rest—one year of life." If summoned to work by their chiefs, the thieves try to avoid blunt and harsh negative answers, but will speak in a manner reminiscent of Zen wisdom or Sufis: "Boss, I have two left hands," "We'll go down to the coal mine when they cut windows through there," "I didn't put the coal there—why should I dig it out?," "You, dear boss, will not be able to heat the hut with this coal—you had better dig it out yourself."[38]

The fact that they do not want to work, or in their terms "to plough," does not mean that they are unable to work. In rare cases, when common prisoners show their inability to cope with a difficult assignment or to finish it on time, thieves might agree to try their hands at manual work, although usually after delicate negotiations through a go-between trustworthy to the robbers' brotherhood. Their agreement to work is usually conditional upon the fulfilment of their several demands, such as the release of one of their fellows from a punishment cell. As soon as the job has been started, 20 or 30 thieves can do in one or two days what a 100 other prisoners could not do in a week or more.[39]

While the thieves are behind barbed wire, they are supposed to coexist with the authorities. The thieves must never serve the state security officials who govern the prison-camp empire from without. They lose their status if they participate in building a prison-camp or installing barbed-wire around the prison. They treat the prison-camp heads with a certain contempt. They "thou" their chiefs, while the latter generally address them in a very polite manner, using their first names and patronymics. Relations with the prison-camp authorities make the thieves always vigilant. They jeopardize status not only by "leaving for a corridor," which includes not just washing the floor or stoking the prison stove, but even by doing a minor favour for a chief. So if a thief even holds the guards' keys for a single moment, he may be put on trial for moral turpitude.[40] Among the thieves' proverbs, one says: "There are only two varieties of Chekist, those who are bad and those who are very bad."[41]

[38] Thieves are masters of short succinct speech. See M. de Santerr, pp. 64, 111. The list of examples might be very long, e.g.: "Whether you work or not, you will not be praised." "It's me who does not work and it's myself who is not praised." "This forest was not planted by me—I am not entitled to saw it." "Everybody knows on Saturday we don't go to work, but for us any day is a Saturday." Eugenia Ginzburg, *Journey through the Whirlwind* (New York, 1967), p. 402.

[39] V. Artemyev, op. cit. p. 96. The author does not go into detail about the conditions under which the thieves would agree to work without becoming bitches.

[40] M. de Santerr, op. cit. pp. 64, 77. In the forties the thief Agayev, called Gypsy, while arguing with an officer of the State Security Police outside the prison-camp wire, kicked the officer, whose military cap fell to the ground. Facing the officer's gun and repeated command to pick up the cap, the thief did not and paid on the spot with his life. M. de Santerr, op. cit. p. 64.

[41] In secret instructions of the Gulag authorities was the following: "Criminals—socially akin to the Soviet power, and they should be paid attention in the struggle with the prison-camp counter-revolution." V. Artemyev, op. cit. p. 98.

152   Y U R I   G L A Z O V

UNTIL the late 1930s, the thieves' domination of the prison-camp empire had no serious limitations. The authorities did not worry much about the thieves' spreading throughout the country. Indeed, once they had uprooted the entire life of the country, the authorities began to consider the thieves' establishment to be rather useful. To be sure, the thieves were the products of all the years of revolution, industrialization and collectivization. But they also served an important function in making the population more dependent on the authorities. The mere presence of thieves in large numbers aroused in the population feelings of almost sacred fear towards prison-camp life, and discouraged any thought of opposing authority. Moreover, the thieves took special care to punish those persons who tried to rescue their friends in time of danger.[42] Prisoners often found themselves helpless facing the thieves and their well-organized power under something close to official approval.

The authorities tried to tame the thieves instead of liquidating them. Gradually they succeeded in creating a new layer among the thieves, persons harshly described as " bitches." The wolf-like strength of the thieves could be defeated and disorganized only with the help of the specially trained and state-supported army of bitches, former thieves cooperating with the state.[43] The authorities tried to re-orient some of the thieves, and Anton Makarenko's much-praised autobiographical book *Educational Epic* describes his painful efforts to turn young thieves into bitches.[44] A good number of young thieves yielded to the shrewd and intelligent pressure. However, until 1941 when the Soviet Union was led into the second world war, the bitches had no serious impact on the thieves' society and they lived under the constant menace of being stabbed by their own former brethren.[45]

The war, especially its second half, brought deep changes in the thieves' position. On pain of execution, they were drafted into the army at the beginning of the war; but they knew the tricks for being arrested and returned to their " native house " before they ever reached the front lines.[46] When the Soviet Army entered the Eastern European countries, the thieves saw their chance and joined the army, creating the Fifth

[42] A. Solzhenitsyn, *Arkhipelag Gulag*, III–IV, Paris, 1974, p. 418.

[43] Leonid Leonov wrote about " bitches " in 1926 in his *The Thief*. Cf. Leonov, *Sobranie Sochinennii*, Vol. 3, 1970, p. 585, " ssuchilsia paren', pravda tvoia. . . ." One of the interpretations of the " bitch " etymology was connected with a habit of hunters who train special she-wolves (bitches) to bring a wolf over to the hunters. M. de Santerr, op. cit. p. 77.

[44] Anton S. Makarenko, *Pedagogicheskaya poema*, Moscow, 1935; Peter Yakir in his " Childhood in Prison " shows some of the difficulties of such a reduction, Pyotr Yakir, *Detstvo v tiurme*, London, 1972, p. 108.

[45] Solzhenitsyn writes about execution of the top thieves in 1937, op. cit. p. 428. M. de Santerr writes about the supremacy of the thieves before World War Two, op. cit. p. 108. Panin writes about non-execution of criminals in the early forties: " they were used to coping with counter-revolutionaries," Zapiski Sologdina, p. 250.

[46] Solzhenitsyn, op. cit. p. 430.

"THIEVES" AS A SOCIAL PHENOMENON 153

Ukrainian Front.[47] Having robbed and murdered and having been praised for it by their officers, they returned home after the war to practise their professional occupation, which again led to quick arrest and camps.

But the thieves who remained behind considered these former colleagues to have broken the laws of the brotherhood by their participation in the war on the side of the authorities, which was seen as collaboration with the state security forces. The victorious newcomers still boasting of their war adventures were greeted as " bitches " by those " honest thieves " who had remained confined, subject to starvation and unbelievable hardships. In 1946–48 in the Soviet prison-camps another war took place, " a war of thieves and bitches, which shook down the Archipelago in the post-war years." [48] This was a war of life and death, a ruthless battle or "chopping" (*rubka*) in which thousands of criminals participated on both sides.

Before the " Great Fatherland War " of 1941–1945, the thieves seemed to enjoy a rather privileged position; they had been given free rein with the political prisoners ("incorrigible enemies of the people "), while for the most part the " bitches " were planted outside the prison-camp area at that time. In the post-war period prison-camp policy was directed to increase the bitches' role. In the prison-camp thieves and bitches had now acquired separate spheres of influence. The prison-camp authorities, time and again, were recruited from the bitches; they would set thousands of bitches against the thieves, men whose mutual solidarity had been tested by the fire and dangers of the recent war.[49]

The phenomenon of bitches is not new in Russia. There has been a tradition of recruiting criminals by the Tsarist police and the Tsarist authorities, at least since Ivan Cain of the seventeenth century and continuing up to the last days of the Romanov dynasty, as exemplified by figures like Malinovsky, Father Gapon and Azev.[50] One of the earliest post-revolutionary examples of " bitch-making " might be ascribed to the development of the Russian Orthodox Church headed by the stubborn Patriarch Tikhon. In the early twenties the authorities sponsored the creation of the Russian Living Church (which lasted for two decades).

The laws of the thieves and the bitches were directly opposed. According to the former, bitches could not be rehabilitated; they must be exterminated. By contrast, the bitches wanted not so much the death of

[47] Ibid. pp. 430–31. A common citizen in Russia knew of four Ukrainian Fronts.

[48] Solzhenitsyn, op. cit. p. 412. In 1948 in Inta " Shargolino summer house " 150 armed bitches were mixed together—naturally, as the result of a special decision of the authorities—with about 100 thieves. A battle immediately took place, and almost 90 thieves were killed in battle, while about 10 thieves made up their minds to yield and agreed to become bitches. De Santerr, op. cit. pp. 59–60.

[49] The prison-camps of Mordovia-Pot'ma and Ust'-Vym were under the thieves' control, while the Vorkuta prison-camps fell under the dominion of the bitches. M. de Santerr, op. cit. p. 71. The top positions in prison-camps were kept now by former thieves. Wallach, op. cit. p. 229. Bitches could be used now as heads of working teams. Solzhenitsyn, op. cit. p. 427, And they usually showed the best examples of leadership over the prisoners.

[50] Adam Ulam, *Stalin*, pp. 66–67, 73, 125.

the thieves as their agreement to take the bitches' oath and join their reformed fraternity. As soon as a thief expressed a desire to join the bitches' ranks, he was immediately acknowledged a full-fledged member of the new fraternity. Transformation of the thieves into bitches was actually an adaptation of the thieves' community to a new social environment, which required a splitting of the personality. The supremacy of the ego gives way to the supremacy of state interests.

The process of bitch-making should be understood against the general social background. In the post-war period, the wars between thieves and bitches coincided with the party-sponsored campaigns of 1946–50 in the fields of literature, music, cinema, biology, arts and sciences. As a common rule, bitches treated prisoners even more harshly than the thieves had done. They were not bound by any laws. Their greed and lust had no limits. When the bitches transgressed all limits of " decent behaviour," the local camp authorities would " allow " the thieves to put an end to these extremes rather than resort to legal processes.[51] The late 40s and the 50s were a hard period in the history of Russian thieves. The first two years of bloody wars with the bitches were followed by prison-camp uprisings of Ukrainians. This became a general signal for a furious settling of accounts. Both thieves and bitches were ruthlessly murdered in what was called the " Massacres of St. Bartholomew." [52] In the 50s, a number of desperate uprisings of prisoners occurred from one end of the prison-camp empire to the other.[53]

THE state security brains-trust made a number of new attempts to stir up the criminals against the common prisoners and the Soviet population in general. After Stalin's death the Soviet Government announced the so-called Voroshilov Amnesty. The result was violent: " All the country was submerged by a wave of murderers, bandits and thieves, who had been caught not without difficulties soon after the War." [54] Robbery and stabbing, as well as violent " entertainment " took place daily in the streets and overcrowded trains. A month after Stalin's death the whole population of the country was terror-stricken, and the hidden intentions of the authorities to increase the dependence of the population on the government were perhaps realized. The thieves and bitches, having had their fun, could be sent back to their permanent prison residences.

[51] M. de Santerr, op. cit. pp. 72, 73, 76.

[52] Ibid. p. 182. The usual method of execution used on common prisoners—the thieves called them " angry friers belted with scrap-iron "—was to hold them by the legs and smash their brains on a rock or stone wall.

[53] Dimitry Panin, op. cit. p. 506.

[54] Solzhenitsyn, op. cit. p. 420. A description of what took place was given by Vardi, op. cit. pp. 248–50. A thief who tells about his adventures in the country in those days expressed his amazement that their coded language (*phenia*) was understood in many official places he had visited during his short-term vacations after years of being confined in his " native home."

"THIEVES" AS A SOCIAL PHENOMENON   155

Since 1953 the thieves' attitude towards common prisoners "friers belted with scrap-iron" (*frier lomom podpoiasannyi*) has, however, undergone some shifts. Solzhenitsyn writes that it was during Stalin's time that the thieves were sent to isolated cells and even isolated prisons.[55] M. de Santerr and other authors do not talk about such changes in Stalin's camps. Radical changes in the situation of the thieves were made by the authorities, according to our information, only in the late 1950s, mainly under Khrushchev.[56] Prisoners who had resisted the thieves' attempts to rob them were sometimes left undisturbed.[57] Since 1953 the thieves have not done much to political prisoners. In the Norilsk and Dzhezkazgan uprisings against the authorities, which took place in 1954 and 1955, thieves participated side-by-side with political prisoners. Thieves began respecting "friers" who imitated their behaviour and language. In some cases, they welcomed them as fellows.[58]

Perhaps such an unexpected evolution of the thieves' psychology inspired the authorities to launch a more frightening campaign against them. In the second half of the 1950s, the prison-camp empire was gradually reduced to a fraction of its former size. It was at this time that these "stubborn recidivists," as they were called by the authorities, were given their last chance. Either they must "tie the knot" (*zaviazat*), put an end to their professional activities, or be isolated from the rest of the population and prisoners. Most were put in solitary confinement.[59]

SEVERAL aspects of the history of the thieves in post-revolutionary Russia are interesting. On the bottom of the ladder, there were a few other underground institutions which persisted in challenging the authorities and resisting their pressure. The thieves can be approached as a socio-religious sect within the mainstream of the Russian sectarian tradition. Indeed, their strict separation of spirit and body is reminiscent of the teaching of the Russian flagellants (*khlysty*).[60]

The sizeable membership of the thieves' society is living proof of the failure of the state ideology. While the common people react passively to that ideology, the thieves reject it root and branch. Scrupulous in their mutual relationships, the thieves looked upon the whole society as devilish and its common people as "devils" (*cherti*). Men who had been

---

[55] Solzhenitsyn, ibid. p. 433.

[56] Among persons to whom I acknowledge my gratitude for information about this matter, I should express my gratitude to Viktor Balashov, a post-graduate student from New York University at Albany.

[57] Yu. B. Margolin, *Puteshestviie v stranu ze-ka* (New York, 1953), pp. 354–56.

[58] M. de Santerr, op. cit. pp. 83–84.

[59] It was about them that Marchenko wrote in *My Testimony*, p. 141 ff.

[60] See K. Kutepov, *Sekty khlystov i skoptsov*, Kazan, 1882, p. 63. A number of features like separation of spirit and body, mortification of the body and freedom from the flesh, division of all people into us and them, non-marriage and non-caring about children, cult of the mother (among the Khlysts, of the god-mother), and general contempt towards women, night as a time for rituals, as well as other features tell us about the kinship of these systems.

YURI GLAZOV

engaged in building the new society were " non-beings " (*néliudi*), who could be robbed, threatened, or stabbed without any remorse whatsoever. To associate with that official society in any way could involve loss of membership in the thieves' society or even death.

For at least three decades the Soviet authorities treated this tribe fairly mildly, and used the thieves' clan shrewdly in their dealings with real revolutionaries, with what remained of the Russian intelligentsia, and with millions of common people undergoing hardships in the course of wide-scale industrialization and collectivization. Paradoxically enough, the extremes of the new society produced a layer of people who, with all their wild nature and unbelievable cruelty, helped stabilize the new social structure. Moreover, the phenomenon of thieves gave support to the notion that honour and dignity can survive, albeit in peculiar forms, under the most horrible circumstances.

Without exterminating the thieves physically, the authorities did their best to develop the institution of bitches in order to cope ultimately with the thieves and more successfully tame the stubborn population of the prison-camp empire. Bitch-making exposes the methods used by the highest officials of Soviet Russia to liquidate or to re-educate the " thieves " in their own party, in the arts and sciences, as well as in various religious institutions of Soviet Russia. If the thieves' institutions are evidence of the depth of anarchist traits in the Russian mind, the phenomenon of bitches perhaps demonstrates the ultimate strength of the state which seems capable of gathering under its command all layers of the society, even the most stubborn and independent.

Corruption in the Soviet System

By Steven J. Staats

Corruption is present in varying degrees and forms in all but the most primitive societies. Certainly, the Soviet Union has not been immune. The national, regional and local press of the USSR contains myriad accounts of bribery, falsification of reports, party-state complicity in concealing corruption, misuse of public office and state funds, and patronage and nepotism in personnel appointments. The persistence with which the various forms of corruption have appeared as objects of criticism throughout the postwar period attests to the deep roots of this phenomenon in the Soviet political soil.

It is surprising that this enduring aspect of Soviet society has been subjected to so little scholarly examination—that its incidence, scale, and functions have not been rigorously investigated by Western scholars.[1] A primary obstacle to such examination is the fragmentary and indirect nature of the evidence provided by the official Soviet newspapers, magazines, and specialized journals. In the first place, most public accounts of corruption deal with misdeeds at regional or local levels and studiously avoid mention of wrongdoing at higher echelons—a result of the near-absolute power of high bureaucratic officials and their ability to suppress criticism of themselves in the Soviet Union's controlled press. Furthermore, sporadic campaigns of corruption-reporting may be consciously-designed efforts by the party leadership to discredit minority groups (e.g., the Jews)[2] or political opponents, or else to single out a particularly undesirable or harmful form of corruption and to impress local officials with the necessity of combating it.[3] Thus, we encounter what might be termed the "corruption" of Soviet corruption-reporting. For this reason, it is obviously impossible to arrive at comprehensive statistics concerning the incidence of given types of corrupt practices or their scale (i.e., the amounts of money involved).

Despite the inadequacies of the source materials and the selectivity of Soviet exposés of corruption, a systematic analysis of the available evidence—taking into account the acknowledged shortcomings of this material—can nevertheless shed considerable light on the nature and functions of corruption in the Soviet Union, as well as on the administrative and political system which breeds it. At the outset, however, we must devise a suitable definition of corruption—which is itself a risky matter, for the

---

[1] There are some exceptions: e.g., Leonard Schapiro notes that 9 percent of the 140,000 Communist Party members purged in 1921-22 were ousted for engaging in bribery, extortion, and other such corrupt acts (The Communist Party of the Soviet Union, rev. and enl. ed., New York, Random House, 1971, p. 236), and Sir John Maynard wrote of the succeeding NEP period as a "saturnalia of corruption, . . . with Soviet authorities horrified at the corruption which they found among the heads of state trusts and party members" (The Russian Peasant, New York, Collier, 1962, p. 194).

[2] For example, I. Leibler notes that 55 to 60 percent of all those shot for bribery, embezzlement, and speculation under 1961 Soviet legislation were Jews, with the figure running as high as 90 percent in the Ukraine. Soviet Jewry and Human Rights, Melbourne, Ramsay Ware Publishing, Ltd., 1965, pp. 30-35.

[3] For a discussion of how the CPSU Central-Committee selects and controls what is to be published, see Alfred G. Meyer, The Soviet Political System, New York, Random House, 1965, pp. 343-44.

Mr. Staats is currently a James B. Duke Commonwealth Fellow at Duke University (Durham, N.C.). He has contributed to Melbourne Journal of Politics and is currently working on a book examining corruption in modern societies.

definition can easily become so all-encompassing as to lose its capacity to serve as a principle of differentiation. Samuel P. Huntington perhaps comes closest to a workable definition of corruption for our purposes:

Corruption is behavior of public officials which deviates from accepted norms in order to serve private ends.[4]

Such a definition does, of course, introduce a relativistic note,[5] for corruption thus depends as much on the existence of a rule or norm as on the occurrence of a deviant act, and the rules and norms may change over time. The value of a concept such as "deviation" for defining corruption is that it emphasizes the fact that corruption need not be a property *inherent* in certain forms of behavior, but rather that it is a property *conferred upon* such behavior by the audiences which indirectly or directly witness them and reprove them by laws, regulations, and decrees.

Thus, for an act to fit our definition of corruption in the Soviet context, it must, first, violate some stipulation of the legal, political, or administrative codes of the USSR. The violation may be either active or passive (as in a failure to act when a certain act or procedure is required). The second distinguishing characteristic is that the act must be committed in relative secrecy, an indication that the perpetrator(s) recognize that the act is objectionable in the eyes of Soviet society. Third, there must be a transaction of some kind whereby inducement is involved. The inducement may be positive, as in the case of bribery or drawing upon bonds of friendship or kinship in order to influence decisions of government, or it may be negative, as in a threat to withdraw a benefit or impose a penalty. Beyond a certain point, negative inducement clearly ceases to be corruption and becomes coercion.

So much for a definition of corruption. More important is the question of why corruption exists in the Soviet Union, of the functions it performs in Soviet society and politics. Students of corruption have suggested that it is intimately related to a

society undergoing social change. They argue that corruption is particularly prevalent in a society that is in transition from traditional, ascriptive, particularistic, and diffuse patterns of organization to more modern, achievement-oriented, universalistic, and specific patterns.[6] While, as we shall see below, it is true that certain types of corruption in the Soviet Union owe their existence to such a transitional situation in the more backward areas of the country, this hardly explains the persistence of corruption throughout what is basically a modern bureaucratic state.

The Soviet state bureaucracy, like most modern bureaucracies, is marked by both limited scope (the range of matters it can affect) and limited weight (the degree to which it can participate in rule-making). This would also seem to indicate that Soviet conditions are not favorable for corruption, since corruption, as F. W. Riggs has suggested,[7] is more likely where bureaucracies engage in a wide scope of activities and are relatively unlimited by the central political authorities. The Soviet state bureaucracy is limited because each department tends to be functionally specific and responsible for the implementation of a narrow range of policies. And although the bureaucracy as a whole plays a significant role in rule-making through *rule-application*, its weight is severely limited by the tight political control and interpenetration of its structure by the Soviet Communist Party. Such a fusion of party and state authority—with the intensive system of cross-checks and monitoring that it entails—might normally be expected to discourage, if not preclude, administrative corruption.

The Functionality of Corruption

What then explains the prevalence of bureaucratic and political corruption in the USSR? In examining the problem, the author has erected several theoretical models to explain the ubiquity and importance of various forms of corruption and to demonstrate that

---

[4] *Political Order in Changing Societies*, New Haven, Yale University Press, 1968, p. 59.

[5] Although one might desire a definition permitting comparative analysis of corruption in diverse societies, there is also the danger of introducing Western or non-Marxist biases. For example, it is doubtful whether the expediting activity of industrial managers considered corrupt by USSR legal standards would be considered corrupt in the West.

[6] Representative examples of this approach may be found in Ronald Wraith and Edgar Simpkins, *Corruption in Developing Countries*, London, G. Allen and Unwin, 1963; W. F. Wertheim, *East-West Parallels: Sociological Approaches to Modern Asia*, Chicago, Quadrangle Books, 1965, pp. 103-31; and Huntington, *op. cit.*, pp. 59-71. The model of transitional society is drawn from Max Black, Ed., *The Social Theories of Talcott Parsons*, Englewood Cliffs, N.J., Prentice-Hall, 1961, p. 350.

[7] *Administration in Developing Countries*, Boston, Houghton and Mifflin, 1964, pp. 226-27 and 246-47.

Corruption in the Soviet Union

corruption—in addition to serving private ends—performs certain necessary functions in terms of the Soviet political system as a whole.[8] By examining the functionality of corruption, one may discover that the phenomenon is, in fact, an important feature of the system rather than an aberration.

The first hypothesis to be tested is that corruption may be a method of adjusting a poorly-articulated administrative structure. As Soviet spokesmen openly admit, many areas of administration still suffer from chronic inefficiency, poor staffing and organization, and lack of coordination among agencies that are interdependent. A particularly persistent problem is the inability of the bureaucracy to deliver industrial raw material supplies on time and in the required quantities and quality. As a representative of one knitting enterprise recently complained,

. . . Year in and year out the association is allotted only enough yarn for its production program, and we have no chance to build stable inventories. Hence the downtime of knitting machinery. Because of interruptions in raw material deliveries, it is frequently necessary to have materials delivered by airplane.[9]

Faced with the imperatives of surmounting such problems in order to fulfill production targets, managers resort to *blat* or the intermediation of the *tolkach.*

The Soviet expression *blat* refers to the use of personal influence to obtain favors to which a certain department, enterprise, or official is not legally or formally entitled. It can refer to such actions as procuring materials in contravention of the provisions of the state plan, or persuading ministry officials to relieve one's own firm of a difficult production task. The influence exerted may be based on friendship, but there is often an implication of a reciprocation of favors *quid pro quo.* The institution of the *tolkach* (or expediter) is also resorted to when the manager chooses to operate indirectly in achieving his ends. One Soviet commentator, A. Frolov, observed in *Pravda* of January 21, 1971, that the *tolkach*

remains very much a part of contemporary Soviet society, a fact which, he patently admits, "is attributable to violation of production cooperation plans by enterprises and supply agencies, to frequent changes by ministries in enterprise plans, to lateness in supplying technical documentation, and to carelessness and substandard work. . . ." Yet, as interviews with Soviet émigrés reveal, such widespread informal mechanisms are not sanctioned by the rules or ideology of the system[10]—*i.e.,* they are corrupt.

What one discovers is that in certain circumstances, corruption on a limited scale may make an important contribution to organizational efficiency and goal-fulfillment. The motivation to perform corrupt acts in such instances may stem from identification with and concern for the interests and goals of the larger organization. In a word, such corruption may be functional in terms of the standards of performance set down by central agencies. Significantly, a study of the reasons for the continuance of *blat*

[10] See John A. Armstrong, "Sources of Administrative Behavior: Some Soviet and Western European Comparisons," *American Political Science Review* (Menasha, Wisconsin), September 1965, p. 655, fn. 10.

EXPEDITIOUS MEASURES

Before me sits a typical "expediter" (*tolkach*) who wishes to remain unnamed. The "expediter" works for a bus factory. In the first quarter of last year alone, he was on official travel more than two months. [He asks:] "Are my enterprise and I really to blame for these travels? Do you think it is enjoyable to go knocking on doors with a briefcase full of letters and orders and to have to beg and plead for supplies and equipment? But everything has to be done to avoid paralysis of the enterprise's work. . . ."

We read in a document of the USSR People's Control Committee: "Travel expenses related to supply matters accounted for more than 70 percent of all money spent on official travel by the four furniture factories of the Omsk Lumber (Omskies) Trust."

The increase in travel of so-called "expediters" is attributable to the fact that while factory supply personnel are [held] fully responsible for securing the necessary materials for their enterprises, the various subdivisions of the USSR State Supply Committee—the territorial administrations, depots, and other supply installations—are not [held] responsible for supplying plants and factories with supplies, raw materials, and parts.

—A. Frolov, in *Izvestia*, Jan. 21, 1971.

---

[8] One must avoid the extreme of ascribing only positive functions to corruption and failing to trace undesirable side effects. This shortcoming is present with some representatives of the structural-functional school of sociology; see for example Jose Veloso Abueva's "The Contribution of Nepotism, Spoils and Graft to Political Development," in *East-West Center Review* (Honolulu), No. 3, 1966, pp. 45-54.

[9] *Pravda* (Moscow), Dec. 16, 1969. For other accounts of bureaucratic bottlenecks see *ibid.,* Oct. 23, 1969, Jan. 9 and March 6, 1970, and *Izvestia* (Moscow), Oct. 29, 1969, and Dec. 5, 1970.

and bribery in the Soviet system carried out by researchers of the Soviet prosecutor's office in 1961 arrived at essentially the same conclusion.[11]

This is not to suggest that corruption of the above order does not create its own problems. Failure of an organization to honor a delivery contract (because the item was sent elsewhere as a result of some corrupt arrangement) may, for example, disrupt another organized economic or administrative activity. In other words, because of their particularistic nature, there is no guarantee that such corrupt relationships will produce a final result conforming to true or stated national interests or priorities. Consequently, the regime officially proscribes such behavior, presumably winking at it when favored activities benefit and prosecuting it when the overall effects prove harmful.[12]

This first model of corruption stresses relationships *within* the administrative bureaucracy. A second model concentrates more on the role of corruption in mediating between the interests of the Soviet citizen as a private consumer of goods and services and the administrative bureaucracy which is the ultimate purveyor of these goods and services. Because of the rigidities of the Soviet command economy, there is a continual imbalance between supply and demand. To the extent that corruption works to equilibrate these two forces—*i.e.*, to introduce market (albeit, black-market) attributes into the command system—it can be seen to be functional.

Thus, black markets have thrived in numerous fields—the private manufacture of consumer goods in short supply, currency speculation, sale of grain and other primary food commodities that have been diverted from state supplies by illegal means or grown by persons spending excessive time in cultivating private plots, and the construction of private houses or dachas. *Izvestia* of August 21, 1968, devoted a whole section to discussion of speculation and profiteering on "deficit" goods smuggled out of factories and warehouses for sale on the black market.[13]

There is also what has been termed "black-market bureaucracy,"[14] a form of corruption resulting from the fact that the Soviet government is equally unable to satisfy popular demand for services. That is, prices on government services often are set according to supply and demand (through the mechanism of bribes) rather than remaining fixed impartially for all comers, as would be the case in an ideal bureaucratic system. Thus, a construction official in Pskov was found guilty of accepting a 200-ruble bribe (approximately 222 dollars) in order to assign company housing space to an individual out of turn.[15] In his time, Khrushchev attacked the prevalence of such corruption:

Bribes are given for selling off state resources, for granting permits for apartments, for allotting plots of land, for granting pensions, for admission to higher educational establishments, and even for the awarding of diplomas. . . . This disease, this bribery, has infected some of the central departments and institutions, including many leading officials with a party card in their pocket.[16]

Bribe-taking continues to concern Soviet leadership, as evidenced by Brezhnev's comments at the 24th CPSU Congress last year.[17]

In its "ideal" form, black-market corruption is universalistic and impersonal—the goods or services go to the highest bidder. More frequently, however, the model is impure: the bureaucrat performs illegal favors for relatives, members of his ethnic group, or close friends (nonetheless extracting from them what he can in cash, goods, or services). The particular type of black-market corruption which predominates varies widely from area to area in the Soviet Union. The first is more likely to occur in modern urban, industrialized areas, whereas personal links presumably prevail in the many rural and minority areas where traditional norms persist.[18] While the latter

[11] *Sotsialisticheskaia zakonnost* (Moscow), August 1961.

[12] Decrees of May 1961 and February 1962 established the death penalty for repeated or serious bribery, embezzlement, black-market operations, pilfering, etc. The decrees did fail to single out illegal procurement activities by enterprises for such punishment, and a content analysis of the Soviet press since then has failed to turn up any executions for this particular sort of activity. For texts of the decrees see *Izvestia*, May 7, 1961, and *Vedomosti Verkhovnovo Soveta SSSR* (Moscow), Feb. 21, 1962, pp. 221-22.

[13] For details on the various Soviet black markets see *Message from Moscow*, London, Jonathon Cape Ltd. 1969, pp. 151-62.

[14] The author has adopted, with significant alterations, this theoretical framework from R.O. Tilman, "Emergence of Black-Market Bureaucracy: Administration, Development, and Corruption in the New States," *Public Administration Review* (Washington, DC), September-October 1968, pp. 440-42.

[15] *Pravda*, Aug. 13, 1969.

[16] *Ibid.*, Nov. 20, 1962.

[17] The General Secretary called for continued struggle against such vestiges of the past as "money-grubbing, bribe-taking, parasitism, slander, anonymous letters, drunkenness, etc." *Ibid.*, March 30, 1971.

[18] T. W. Shinn provides a detailed exposition of the persistence of traditional norms in outlying regions of the USSR in "The Law of the Russian Peasant Household," *Slavic Review* (New York), October 1961, pp. 80-85.

Corruption in the Soviet Union

cases support the contention that corruption is closely identified with transitional societies, the former type is very much part of the Soviet Union's version of a modern bureaucratic state. Whenever the centralized allocative mechanism breaks down in the face of serious disequilibrium between supply and demand —regardless of whether one is talking about baby carriages or apartment permits—corruption is likely to result, introducing market features in the command economy.

Having examined two models which demonstrate the functions that corruption performs in the Soviet system, we can turn to a brief analysis of who it is that participates in corrupt practices. There is little information to suggest what there may be in the Soviet cultural learning process that conditions a person to accept illegal inducements in order to perform illegal acts. However, it is possible to detect certain groups in the Soviet Union that tend more than others to become involved in corruption. The first such group, though not necessarily the most important, consists of the natives of Central Asia and other relatively backward areas of the Soviet Union. Here, the loyalties of citizens are fragmented, centering more on family, caste, ethnic, and religious ties, or even a shared local dialect, rather than on allegiance to broader communities. In many respects, corruption in such areas is indeed linked to the transition of the given area to a more modern social structure. A report from the December 1969 plenary session of the Central Committee of the Azerbaidzhan Communist Party typifies this situation:

Many instances of unscrupulousness in the selection and promotion of cadres were discovered in Kirovabad; this has led to large-scale embezzlement and theft. There is speculation in private homes and automobiles in the city; individual homes are being constructed by people who cannot afford them, and large plots of land were illegally taken from the state. Taking advantage of his official position [as First Secretary of the Kirovabad City Party Committee], Comrade Alizade promoted his relatives and close friends to responsible posts, though they were not entitled to such posts by personal, professional, or political qualifications.[19]

The most common participant in corrupt activities is the administrator or bureaucrat who is in a position

[19] "Communique on the Plenary Session of the Azerbaidzhan Communist Party Central Committee," *Bakinskii rabochii* (Baku), March 2, 1970.

to expedite a shipment or shunt goods and services off to the private consumer who is willing to pay the black-market price. As has been demonstrated above, such aspects of the Soviet system as poorly articulated bureaucratic channels and tautness in the supply of goods and services combine to encourage bureaucrats to accept bribes in return for performing illegal acts. Furthermore, the command economy places heavy pressures on managers and bureaucrats to fulfill plans. When a bonus, job tenure, or promotion is riding on successful fulfillment of a production assignment, a manager may well resort either to false reporting or to *blat*.

Party Involvement

A striking feature of most of the cases of Soviet corruption open to our scrutiny is that they involve members of the Communist Party. As noted above, most cases involve corruption in lower party echelons, although according to Soviet testimony, the phenomenon does reach into the highest party and government circles.[20] The fact that corruption persists within the very institution which is supposed to monitor and control all aspects of Soviet life suggests the existence of a common interest impelling party members as well as other social groups to collude in the perpetration and/or concealment of corrupt acts.

We are dealing here with what is referred to in the USSR as *krugovaia poruka* (mutual guarantee)—*i.e.*, the rendering of mutual aid among members of a group who feel a sense of solidarity, mutual responsibility and dependence, particularly when the aid occurs outside of or in direct violation of the formal rules of the organization.[21] For *blat*, bribery, misappropriation, and other forms of corruption to be successful, there must be the active assistance or ac-

[20] See Khruschev's comment in this regard (p. 43 above). G. M. Malenkov in his *Report to the 19th Party Congress*, Moscow, Foreign Languages Publishing House, 1952, p. 124, castigated many high-level officials for corrupt practices. More recently, Oleg Penkovsky observed: ". . . The sons, daughters, sons-in-law of all our important party and government officials finish higher educational institutions and get good jobs . . . everything is done by pull, through friends and family connections. The newspapers scream that nepotism must be stamped out, but what happens? They punish some factory director for giving a job to his niece. But we must look higher and see what is happening at the top." *The Penkovsky Papers*, London, Fontana Books, 1967, pp. 211-12.

[21] The pioneering work in the study of *krugovaia poruka* was performed by J. S. Berliner in *Factory and Manager in the USSR*, Cambridge, Massachusetts, Harvard University Press, 1957, pp. 320-29.

quiescence of others in its execution and in the evasion of detection or punishment. Motivation for such behavior is likely to exist when a number of persons depend upon one another in important ways, such as in the proper completion of their respective tasks in the society's division of labor; when, at a given time, several of them have burdens that could be lightened or problems that could be solved by violating the rules; or when it is possible that, sooner or later, any of the persons involved might find himself faced with similar burdens. *Krugovaia poruka* implies reciprocity, but not necessarily on a *quid pro quo* basis.

Krugovaia poruka comes to embrace those very individuals whose duty it is to prevent and expose collusion and corruption. By the very nature of their job, the controllers are thrown into close contact and interaction with those whom they are assigned to supervise, and in the process the controllers often become dependent upon the controlled. Such collusion may result in *semeistvennost*—i.e., the establishment between government agencies of strong and viable protective alliances that cut across the lines of command and supervision meticulously constructed by the CPSU to exercise control over the state structure. Here, the close relationship between party and state, designed to ensure compliance with central party directives, may actually work to impede compliance by making it difficult to properly assign credit or culpability in a given sphere of activity.

The Soviet party has consistently attempted to prevent corruption and collusion among party and government officials by maintaining close control over key personnel appointment through the *nomenklatura* system. The Soviets define *nomenklatura* as "a list, whose incumbents are approved by a higher party, governmental, or professional organization."[22] However, the evidence of collusion and "mutual protection societies" refutes such judgments of Soviet institutions as ". . . the scope for local officials to manipulate party membership policies for their own purposes is likely to be narrow."[23] Once the power to appoint key local officials has been diverted to promote private ends, the *nomenklatura* system can

---

[22] *Entsiklopedicheskii slovar v dvukh tomakh* (Two-Volume Encyclopedic Dictionary), Moscow, 1964, Vol. II, p. 107. L. G. Churchward has estimated that some 400,000 positions in the local government of the USSR and an additional 200,000 positions in central and republic governments are filled from the *nomenklatura* lists. "Bureaucracy in the USA-USSR," *Coexistence* (London), No. 5, 1968, pp. 205-06.

[23] T. H. Rigby, *Communist Party Membership in the USSR, 1917-67*, Princeton, Princeton University Press, 1968, p. 62.

BATTLING BRIBERY

In a special decree of February 20, 1962, the Presidium of the USSR Supreme Soviet increased the criminal responsibility for bribery. The decree specifies as aggravating circumstances the acceptance of bribes by officials in responsible positions, repeated acceptance of bribes, or the use of extortion. In such cases, the guilty are subject to deprivation of freedom for terms of eight to 15 years and confiscation of personal property; under especially aggravating circumstances, the penalty is death. The responsibility for giving a bribe or acting as a go-between was also raised.

—From article by N. Zhogin, USSR Deputy Prosecutor General, *Izvestia* (Moscow), March 14, 1970.

A regular plenary session of the USSR Supreme Court was held a few days ago with A. F. Gorkin presiding. The plenary session heard reports by V. I. Maisuradze, Chairman of the Georgian Republic Supreme Court; B. A. Azan, Chairman of the Latvian Republic Supreme Court; and V. I. Terebilov, Vice-Chairman of the USSR Supreme Court, on the fulfillment of the July 31, 1962, resolution of the plenary session of the USSR Supreme Court "On Judicial Practice in Cases of Bribe-Taking." The plenary session noted that the above-mentioned crimes, as judicial practice corroborates, are *not widespread* in the country, *but nonetheless represent a major social danger* and require decisive measures to eradicate them. Meanwhile, available data indicate that although judicial bodies have conducted a certain amount of work in recent years in intensifying the fight against bribe-taking, in a number of places courts are not yet taking appropriate measures to mobilize every effort to liquidate this shameful vestige of the past.

—From an *Izvestia* report, July 10, 1970. (Emphasis added—Ed.)

---

actually operate to protect corrupt officials. No criminal proceedings can be initiated against an official without the consent of the party organs to whose *nomenklatura* list he belongs.[24] An incident reported in *Pravda* of January 28, 1970, is revealing in this regard. A collective farm chairman in Orenburg Province was relieved of his duties by the party for embezzlement, nepotism, and corruption. Instead of facing legal prosecution for his misdeeds, the faithful comrade next turned up as manager of the district government's communal enterprises—in other words, he was promoted. There are numerous complaints in the Soviet press that local party bodies not only fail to discipline malfeasants in their ranks

---

[24] Churchward, *op. cit.*, p. 205.

Corruption in the Soviet Union

AN OUNCE OF PREVENTION . . .

Caption: "Laying in a Supply." Commentary in upper right corner states: "The warehouses of many enterprises are overloaded with excessive inventories of raw and semifinished materials."

—From *Krokodil* (Moscow), No. 5, February 1969.

adequately,[25] but also suppress criticism and persecute those who attempt to disclose corrupt practices.[26] As a result, party members often ignore their solemn obligation to

develop criticism and self-criticism . . ., to come out against all actions which inflict damage on the party and the state, and to report them to party organs, up to and including the Central Committee of the CPSU.[27]

In saying this, one must not overestimate the extent of corruption or overlook other factors which might reduce collusion between party and other agencies. For instance, a party secretary who be-

[25] *Pravda*, Jan. 2, 1970. See also *ibid.*, Aug. 11, 1969, and Jan. 11, 1970, and *Izvestia*, Nov. 1, 1969, and Nov. 11, 1970.
[26] See *Pravda* of Jan. 28, Feb. 8, May 22, Oct. 7, and Nov. 31, 1970.
[27] *XXII sezd Kommunisticheskoi Partii Sovetskovo Soiuza: stenograficheskii otchiot* (22nd CPSU Congress: Stenographic Report), Moscow, Foreign Languages Publishing House, 1962, Vol. III, p. 338.

comes too involved in the fortunes of a factory manager whom he was assigned to control clearly loses his usefulness in the eyes of his party superiors and will likely be removed if the relationship is discovered. And there is nothing to guarantee that the party will protect its appointees from government prosecution under the stringent anticorruption legislation enacted in May 1961 and February 1962.[28]

Corruption in Perspective

What general conclusions can one draw from this examination of corruption in Soviet society? First, it is clear that corruption, while not necessarily institutionalized, is an important systemic feature of contemporary Soviet life and not just a transient phenomenon. One might say that the only thing worse than a society with a rigid, overcentralized bureaucracy is one with a rigid, overcentralized, and *honest* bureaucracy. Our examination has demonstrated that in the Soviet case it is often as much for organizational ends as for personal gain that the Soviet administrator hoards materials, conceals resources, participates in the black market, and breaks countless other rules imposed on him.

While unlimited corruption can obviously be destructive of organizational goals, the current situation in the USSR displays none of the symptoms of those societies (described by Samuel P. Huntington[29]) in which corruption is most evident among national leaders, which suffer from a low level of political institutionalization, and which are therefore susceptible to violent overthrow. From the admittedly impressionistic picture afforded by Soviet evidence, it would seem that corruption is most frequently encountered at the lower levels of the CPSU and government apparatuses, and that the incidence of corruption does not increase the higher the rank of the officials examined.

One way of looking at the role of corruption in Soviet politics is from the perspective of interest articulation. As we have already noted, lower party and government officials often find considerable common interest in moderating output goals, procuring resources, and collaborating to insulate one another from the pressures exerted by their superiors. Interestingly enough, this provides evidence of strong interest articulation at the *output* or *imple-*

[28] See footnote 12.
[29] *Op. cit.*, p. 61.

mentation stage of Soviet politics.[30] One might suggest that it is at this point, rather than at the input stage, that particular interests are most effective in amending concrete Soviet policies.

This insight, incidentally, introduces new perspectives on the autonomy and unity of party organizations and on the differentiation of the government and party hierarchies. Normally one might assume that the presence of corruption in a Soviet-type system would serve to differentiate the two hierarchies, *i.e.*, that corruption would be symptomatic of the government bureaucracy's efforts to escape from the controlling policies of the party. Instead, at least at the local level, corruption actually leads to consolidation and unity of the two hierarchies, albeit through patronage, nepotism, and incorrect selection of leading cadres. In well-organized protective alliances between local party and state officials, there may be an elaborate conspiracy to cut corners, break laws and regulations, defraud higher supervisory organizations, and engage in other illegal practices. This suggests a distinct conflict between *official* and *real* roles. It also illustrates the relative independence of many lower officials from control by higher echelons and refutes the oversimplified notion of Soviet bureaucratic politics as represented in the pure totalitarian model—in which an omnipotent elite issues commands which subordinate elements blindly execute.

The fact that party and government functionaries are intimately involved in Soviet corruption differentiates this phenomenon from the situation in certain Asian countries where corruption seems centered among groups that are denied access to formal political channels (*e.g.*, minority groups or foreign companies). The subjects examined in our study were not out-groups denied access to membership in the CPSU.

Some forms of corruption in the Soviet Union are linked to the social transformations taking place in a modernizing USSR. In outlying locales the various forms of corruption help to "humanize" social change and the harshness of elite-conceived plans for social and economic modernization. People caught in the throes of change may have more faith in a system that they can influence to some degree, through personal action, than one they do not know how to manipulate or are unable to manipulate. The

human element provided through nepotism and kinship ties may thus be an important means of ensuring loyalty on the part of a tradition-bound people to new social structures. In Myron McMullan's words, a degree of low-level corruption can "soften relations of officials and people,"[31] or as Edward Shils stated, it "humanizes government and makes it less awesome."[32]

Collusion, concealment, and cooperation in corrupt activities by certain party officials and state employees may even directly enhance their feeling of having a stake in the system and give them a vested interest in retaining its general form. Thus, the CPSU ceases to be a remote abstraction or oppressor; gradually, by action and deed rather than by propaganda, it becomes a helpful and tangible organization worthy of support. Involvement engenders a sense of belonging, and a sense of comradely solidarity based on friendship replaces the rigid and elaborate rules of personnel selection by the party.

Finally, even the periodic exposure of corruption scandals and the efforts to combat corruption may, in fact, serve to strengthen overall values, to follow Max Gluckman's argument.[33] Social norms usually emerge as an abstract synthesis of the repeatedly expressed sentiments of the community regarding a given type of behavior. Reiterated group censure of a given act of deviation sharpens the authority of the violated norms and defines more clearly the boundaries of acceptable behavior. There have been numerous antiparasite and anticorruption drives in the Soviet Union (apart from the normal operations of control agencies).[34] The masses have been mobilized into "people's control" organizations, people's militia squads, and "young Komsomol" groups to assist in combating black marketeering, currency speculation, and parasitism (living on private sources of income). Through such devices, the elite groups attempt to resuscitate citizen support for the norms of the regime and to suppress any deviant behavior.

From all this, it emerges that corruption is unlikely to be eradicated tomorrow in the Soviet Union, if only because of the important functions it continues to perform. It appears that corruption may be as integral to Soviet life as vodka and kasha.

---

[30] J. C. Scott suggested this process of group influence and described the groups most likely to benefit from it in developing Asian countries. "The Analysis of Corruption in Developing Nations," *Comparative Studies in Society and History* (London), June 1969.

[31] "A Theory of Corruption," *Sociological Review* (Keele, England), June 1961, pp. 181-200.
[32] *Political Development in the New States*, Mouton, 1962, p. 385.
[33] See Gluckman's *Custom and Conflict*, Blackwell, 1955, p. 135.
[34] See P. Juviler and H. W. Morton, Eds., *Soviet Policy Making*, London, Pall Mall Press, 1967, pp. 168 ff.

[5]

SOVIET STUDIES, vol. XXXV, no. 4, October 1983, pp. 546–560

THE CULTURAL BASES OF SOVIET GEORGIA'S SECOND ECONOMY

By Gerald Mars and Yochanan Altman*

1. *Introduction*

THE primary purpose of this paper is to demonstrate, with the aid of illustrative cases, the link between the core values of Georgian culture and the working principles of its second economy. We aim to show that only by first understanding underlying cultural forces can we begin to grasp the reasons why Georgia, of all the Soviet Republics, should possess such a dynamic and deeply entrenched second economy (Grossman, 1977)—estimated by some scholars at over 25% of the Republic's GNP (Wiles, 1981).

The method we have adopted to obtain our data is a unique variant of anthropological fieldwork and a methodological note is therefore in order.

2. *A Note on the Sample and on our Method*

The method we adopted to delineate the core cultural features of Georgian society and which was also used to obtain our case material is what we term 'retrospective reconstruction'. Its mode is primarily anthropological. This is to say, it depends for its primary data upon anthropological fieldwork within a living bounded community—in this case among a community of 5,000 recently arrived immigrants from Soviet Georgia to Israel. Our method was to use this community as a data base to allow a reconstruction of institutional features as these existed—and still exist—in Soviet Georgia. It involved residence and social participation among the community for a period of over sixteen months by at least one and for some periods by both of us. This has been supplemented by a visit by one of us to Soviet Georgia, by continuous searches into the Georgian and Soviet press and by regular contact with specialists on Georgia including native Georgians in the UK.

(i) *The sample*

We are aware that Georgian Jews are in some respects not culturally synonymous with the Georgian majority and we have been particularly concerned in checking our data to ensure the applicability and relevance of our findings to the wider Georgian scene.

It is believed that Georgian Jews have a history of settlement at least since the eighth century and that they have consistently enjoyed a freedom of residence and worship unusual in the history of the Jewish diaspora. We have found that our informants, though following Jewish food taboos and maintaining a ban on marriage outside their faith, were nonetheless more integrated into their host society than Jews in other Soviet Republics (Ben Zvi, 1963; Ben Ami, 1965). Their lingua franca was Georgian and, as Mark Plisetsky, a Soviet ethnographer, has observed:

Generally speaking Georgian Jews live the same way as their Gentile neighbours . . . have the same customs, furniture, domestic equipment and dress. Wedding ceremonies too are the same, the only differences are a few songs in Hebrew of a religious or ceremonial nature . . . Jews and Georgians have the same names. (Plisetsky, 1931, p. 36)

In their economic activities Georgian Jews did not operate in any sense as an ethnic or sub-economy. The majority of our informants, though over-represented in trading occupations, were nonetheless widely spread in the lower and middle levels of the economy and in their economic relationships predominantly worked alongside non-Jews and were involved with them in a wide range of social and leisure activities. This extensive integration into the wider Georgian society did not, however, preclude a massive exodus to Israel in the early 1970s—a phenomenon more fully explored elsewhere.

The majority of our sample are from the rural areas of Georgia which, according to the 1979 Soviet census, contain half of the total population. However, according to Dragadze (1976) there are close links between town and country while Parsons (1982) argues that 'Georgians consider rural Georgia as the repository of the nation's cultural heritage'. We feel justified, therefore, in regarding our sample of Georgian Jews as a suitable source of effective data on the wider Georgian scene.

(ii) *The Method*

Since our method depended primarily upon the anthropological mode of participant observation we were thereby able to cross-check information received from different informants. We made intensive use of key informants, used structured interviews, and collected life histories. The principal language used in fieldwork was Ivrit—modern Hebrew. We came to recognise three fieldwork phases that are conceptually, though were not necessarily chronologically, separate.

Phase I involved straight anthropological fieldwork: the focus was to collect data on our migrants *in* Israel; to chart their social relations, to identify their principal social institutions and their basic cultural postulates. A further aim was to identify the differences as well as the similarities between our sample and that of the indigenous peoples of Georgia. As well as providing useful data on settlement in Israel this phase allowed the growth of trust by enquiring into relatively unworrying aspects of their social life as it unfolded at the time, *i.e.* 'How are marriages arranged *here*?' 'How are economic relationships organised *here*?'

Phase II then attempted to translate the understanding of observed social process retrospectively to Georgia. 'How were marriages arranged over there?' 'How were economic relationships organised over there?'

Phase III was directly concerned with second economy relationships in Georgia which can only really be understood when one has prior understanding of social institutions derived from Phases I and II. The questions here dealt with how people participated in or had experience of second economy activity in Georgia. The emphasis was on building up detailed cross-checkable case studies which then provided our basic resource for secondary analysis. Attention was constantly paid to the typicality of our data.

We believe that the unique contribution of anthropological fieldwork as a primary tool to an enquiry such as ours is two-fold: first, the core of its methodology depends on building rapport over time within the context of a close-knit community—which thus allows the build-up of good will and trust. At the same time it offers the opportunity to cross-check and validate the data obtained. It can therefore look in depth into questions which other methods of data collection may only hope to scratch on the surface. Second, anthropology's principal claim to academic specialism is that it concentrates on culture, that is, on the transmission of shared values and attitudes and on the characteristic ways by which people confront their everyday existential issues. In doing so it applies a conceptual approach to data that is holistic and which therefore encourages a linkage across the main institutional areas of social life. The operation of informal economies can thus more readily be considered within their social and cultural milieu.

3. *Georgian Society's Core Values*

(a) *General*

Our delineation of Georgian core values is primarily derived from our involved anthropological participation within our sample community in Israel. They conform, however, with our expectations derived from anthropologists who have made a speciality of other Mediterranean and Latin cultures. Peristiany (1966) and Davis (1977)—to mention just two—agree on the basic cultural homogeneity of this region.

While the pre-revolutionary Caucasus enjoyed considerable attention, the extent and quality of later work, however, are much more limited. The standard Soviet ethnography, *Narody Kavkaza* (Kardanov, 1962) devotes its overwhelming attention to the material culture of past generations. We attempted to monitor existing material from the West (*e.g.* Grigolia, 1939) and more recent journalistic impressions (*e.g.* Dragadze, 1976) which broadly conform with our own systematic findings.

To be accepted in Georgian society involves descent and membership in families where both sides are noted for respectability. This is a feature found not only in Georgia but also elsewhere, all along the shores of the Mediterranean (Peristiany, 1966). Georgian families are bilateral: they trace descent on both sides but stress the male line and within it an emphasis on agnates—on the solidarity and mutual obligations of brothers. When an individual's acts are evaluated this is done in the context of an assessment—and of continual reassessment—of his family and its honour. The same assessments, though less pronounced, apply also to associates and to friends.

Women are important in Georgian society as the articulation points between groups of males and the ensurers of male descent. Whereas the honour of men is achieved by assertion and dominance, the honour of women is passive and mainly associated with sexual modesty. As with manly honour, their passivity reflects also on the wider honour of their family and therefore of their menfolk, and to a lesser extent on that of their associates.

Honour, and its corollary shame, are constant preoccupations in Georgia. Within family groups spheres of action are well defined; they do not overlap and they are non-competitive—everyone knows their place. Beyond the family, however, these limitations are reversed. Insecurity and instability in the perpetual ranking and re-ranking of personal relationships is the norm. Males have therefore constantly to prove themselves as men. They are, in this respect, perpetually 'on show'. They need constantly to demonstrate their worthiness to public opinion in general and to their peers in particular. This requires the demonstration of 'manliness' and use of goods in display and consumption.

In this kind of 'honour and shame' society where peer approval is so important hierarchical official relations are resented and resisted and are the source of perpetual conflict. The individual Georgian sees honour accruing to families and sees families linked by a common honour. In such a context there is little role for the state or for any centrally-organised hierarchy. Relationships need always to be personalised and abstraction has no place.

(b) *Competition*

Competition involves conspicuous display and the necessary involvement of one's peers in relationships of obligation. Feasts and bouts of excessive and competitive drinking are extensive in Georgia, whilst sitting rooms, which are the essential preserve of men, are the physical base for the demonstration of display items. Dressing up is important, as is eating out with friends in cafes and restaurants. All of these activities will affect a man's standing and influence the formation of his own network (discussed later) including the ranges of choice he will have in selecting spouses for himself and later for his children. So the Georgian is pushed to obtain resources which are practically non-existent in the formal economy. It is this which provides the underlying personal motivation and the dynamic force which boosts the republic's second economy.

(c) *Trust*

Trust is the basis of honour. A man who is not trusted has no honour: a man without honour cannot be trusted. Of course trust is a fundamental requirement in the operation of the second economy. When deals are illegal one cannot make contracts nor ask for the help of the law. Therefore a man's word has to be his bond. An illegal financier who used to give loans solely on a man's word of honour told us that a person who abused the trust given to him would be socially excommunicated. In this kind of society to be dishonoured is to face social discredit, but it is discredit that goes beyond the individual, since the whole family is contaminated; and not only the core family but the associated in-laws as well. One way to show the interchange between trust and honour is to look at the way loans are given at times of crisis. We will do this in the second part of this paper by presenting a case study.

(d) *Networks*

If trust is important to the second economy, networks—particularly those based on the family—are its backbone. In a highly personalised society, where a person is measured on his honour—and on the honour of his closest associates—the body of people to whom he can personally relate and through whom he can extend relations with others who might latently prove significant becomes an individual's major resource. The extent and weight of a person's network are the primary determinors for the type of occupation he will be able to enter. And when he is in a post he can use his network to facilitate the gaining of honour, whilst the gaining of honour will facilitate the further growth of his network. Networks are thus crucial in the obtaining and distribution of resources and are central to understanding the second economy. While the paper focusses upon the role of family and kinship as the basis of personal support networks, what we call 'network cores', we would emphasise that such cores are supplemented by peer group membership. This is why the possession of brothers is particularly valued: they are both kin and the source of same generation peer contacts.

(e) *Taking risks*

Reckless risk taking is a valued macho attribute in Georgia and the successful gain both in honour and in resources. Risk taking, however, is also a necessary attribute for business ventures and its high social valuation provides a necessary validation for activity that is the object of formal discrimination. This urge to gamble therefore goes some way to explain why people accept the constant pressure of daily risk taking when they engage in regular second economy work, and also why the entrepreneurial spirit should be so pronounced in Soviet Georgia despite Moscow's persistent attempts to control it. But these are entrepreneurs of a different mould from those traditionally associated with Western capitalism—with the development of thrift and with Weberian ideas of deferred gratification: these are gambling entrepreneurs concerned to spend and to display.

The taking of risks is essentially linked to the operation of networks as providing the basis of one's personal support in crises. Having a large and strong network means taking less risks, since networks are a major resource to take advantage of in times of need. The absence of an effective network, as we shall see, means either that a person is limited to less risky jobs or is involved in a greater chance of exposure and conviction.

We offer these core features of Georgian culture, not to present them as iron laws that formalise or rigidly channel conduct, but as ideals that are expected to be followed. Though the norms of ordinary life might fall short of expected behaviour the ideals nonetheless set the standard.

4. *Case Study: The Market Trader: How the Culture Underlies the Second Economy*

The following case is told by an informant who at the time was seventeen years old. The subject of the story is his father who was a small businessman, running a small shop in a typical Georgian small town market holding some forty shops and a few stalls. The events happened at the beginning of the 1970s. Such traders are particularly vulnerable to checks or raids because, in the nature of their occupation, they necessarily commit offences. The most common offences are overcharging, selling unlicensed items and selling lower class items as of higher quality.

On Monday the traders got warning of a possible raid sometime during the coming week. The warning arrived from a person who was not a trader but had much invested interest in the market. He was "a silent partner" to some of the shops there. This person had a link to somebody in Tbilisi who would be expected to know of such things. A check with the local officials failed to verify the warning. They did not know anything, but people in the market nonetheless took the warning seriously. After all it came from a highly regarded person. Some of them closed their shops for the whole week—most of these were the more established shopkeepers. Some said they were sick, others had family obligations. You don't need too much of an excuse. The rest, including my father, could not afford to close entirely. So they tried their luck.

A few stayed open all the week—others closed only on certain days. My dad closed on Tuesday and Wednesday and opened on the Thursday. Thursday, being market day, involved obviously a higher risk—but also a higher chance for earning, especially as some shops did not operate because of the scare. The special control committee arrived on Thursday. It was a central committee on an irregular check mission—and that is why the local officials were not told.

This is a rather common method of by-passing the local authorities. This was an *ad hoc* committee of eight persons working in two sub-groups, comprising persons from the commerce departments in some local governments and representatives from the central office of the *OBKhSS* (the economic police).

A local boy of fourteen was given some money to buy a few things at my dad's shop. The boy was probably a Komsomolnik (a member of the communist youth, who take on—among other civilian duties—help in controlling consumer prices). Three men, disguised as customers, watched him. He purchased a pair of trousers and was charged 4·4OR instead of 3·60R; a pair of socks for 3·20R instead of 1·20R and an elastic band for underwear of which he got 7m. instead of 9m. as charged. The control men identified themselves, charged my dad with speculation (which is a criminal offence) and ordered him to close his shop, which was thereafter sealed until a formal inquiry was set up. He was taken immediately to the town's police station.

The rumour spread immediately at the market place and details quickly reached our home—though we lived some two hours away by train from the market. At once all our relations and neighbours came in to share the tragedy with us. My father's brothers and my mother's cousin—who happened to be visiting the town at that time—started to plan how to get him out of the mess. First of all, all the goods we had at home were dispersed quickly to face a possible police raid on our home. They were put, for the time being, at my father's brother's place.

My uncles and my mother's cousin made contact with the head of the police station where my father was arrested. It seemed possible to release him for a considerable amount of money. My mother's cousin proved to be of crucial importance. He was much richer than our family—he ran a factory in Tbilisi and had many contacts with officials there and knew in person the man who had issued the warning to the market traders.

He asked this person to come urgently from Tbilisi and both went to see a senior policeman. Of course they took a lot of risk, since they demanded the release of my father as well as the dropping of the charges against him. The charges however could not be dropped though they were much reduced. This was arranged for 5,000R to be handed in in cash. [Comparing this account with other information and discussing this case with other informants revealed that this was not an excessive demand in the given circumstances.] How was the sum raised in a short time? 2,000R were given by my family. Part of it we held at home as a matter of regularity for emergencies. The rest was given as a loan by my relatives. 3,000R were raised by the traders in the market—both Jews and gentiles.

The loans were given under no guarantee, without any condition or specified time for their return. It was all done on the understanding that a person's honour commits him and his family to see to it that the loans are returned as soon as possible. In this particular case it took 18 months to return the lot.

On his release, father went together with a few others (including me) to empty his shop of the illegal goods he held there. [Instead of 34 items he was licensed to deal with, he stocked 240, which means simply that this state-owned shop was used to run a private business. If caught and convicted of this offence he would have been sentenced for 'sabotaging the state's economy', for which the minimum sentence is 15 years imprisonment.] Luckily, dad was clever enough to have left a window unlocked—through which we managed to get in with the help of the gatekeeper who was given 100R. We dispersed the goods among the other shops in the market—the traders had authorised the gatekeeper to open their shops to do it. But a considerable amount was loaded on a van we brought with us. On leaving, we phoned to our house from the gatekeeper's home, saying: "the birds are on their way" which was an agreed code meaning; "the goods are on the way—be ready to disperse them".

My mother's cousin was driving. He was a man in his thirties and very tough. Since it was early morning, we were easily detected by the police patrols and were ordered to stop. [Police patrols are a constant factor to consider when delivering illegally. There should be a bill of lading (*faktura*) specifying the source and destination of all goods in transit. This is why most illegal deliveries are carried out during daytime when the likelihood of raising suspicion is low.] Of course we could not stop and a chase developed. But we knew the roads very well and managed to get away. On arrival we unloaded at my mother's cousin's place, since our home could already have been under surveillance. Small traders were waiting with cash to buy the goods off us at purchase price [that is—not to take advantage of the person's difficulty]. Within 90 minutes all was gone.

In what sounds like an adventure story we can detect all the values which function both as instigators to action and as the necessary preconditions for a successful operation. Trust is an essential key factor in raising a large sum of money in a short time, as well as in exchanging goods only on word of honour. Networks are the skeleton on which this case successfully came to a (relatively) happy end. Without the help of his family, the tradesmen-colleagues and his neighbours, this trader would have been doomed. One can argue, however, that had his network been larger and stronger (to include for instance senior police) he would have been saved from troubles at the outset. But he took risks without having a strong enough backing and was lucky to escape, though at considerable monetary as well as other cost (he could not go on with his trade).

An example of such a powerful network in operation was told to us by the son of a powerful second economy financier whose brother had been arrested for an economic offence. The Attorney General of that region, who was on the monthly 'pay roll' of this person's father, was approached to help but sent a messenger to say that he could not help in this particular case. His father's reply was: 'Tell him who sent you, that if my son is not released this evening—he will have no job to return to tomorrow'. Within twenty four hours our informant's brother had been released and the charges quashed.

5. *The Social Correlates of Occupations*

If we look at some representative occupations in terms of their related networks and the risks involved in them, we find (see Table 1) that there is a close relationship between occupations and personal networks: a small and/or weak network enables an individual to operate only in a low-risk occupation. A strong and/or extended network allows for the taking of bigger risks and allows entry into more prestigious occupations. Earnings, as

GEORGIA'S SECOND ECONOMY

TABLE 1

REPRESENTATIVE OCCUPATIONS AND THEIR RELATED NETWORK CORES, RISKS AND INCOME

Occupations	Network Cores*		Risk Involved			Monthly Income Formal and informal
	Occupational weight	Total score	Low	Medium	High	
Group I Personal services and shopfloor workers						
(a) Barber	1+1	2	✓			400–600R
(b) Shoemaker/repairer	1+1+1+2	5	✓			400–600R
(c) Hatter	1+1+1+1	4	✓			300–500R
(d) Small snack-bar operator	2+1+1+1+1+1	8	✓			300–400R
(e) Blue-collar worker	1+2+1+1+1+1+1+1+2+1	11	✓			250R
Average		6·0				
Group II Middlemen and small business operators						
(f) Shop assistant	1+2+2+1+1+2+1	10		✓		300–500R
(g) Shoemaker: foreman and middleman	2+1+1+1+2+1+1+1+2+1	12	✓			600–900R
(h) Taxi driver	3+1+1+3+2+3+1+1	15		✓		800–1,000R
(i) Small shopkeeper	2+1+1+1+1+1+1	8		✓		500–800R
Average		11·25				

Group III
Professional and executives

(j) Supermarket manager	$3+3+3+3+3+3+1+1$	20	✓	2,000R–2,500R
(k) Small factory executive	$3+1+3+3+3+3$	16	✓	1,000–2,000R
(l) Medium factory executive	$2+2+3$	7	✓	1,000–1,500R
(m) Big factory executive	$3+3+1+3+3+3+3$	19	✓	2,000–10,000R
(n) Import warehouse executive	$3+2+1+1+1+1$	9	✓	3,000–5,000R Starter 1,000R
(o) Physician (GP)	$1+3+3+3+3+3$	16	✓	Specialist up to 15,000R
	Average	14·50		

*Network cores are computed here from males within the nuclear families of origin and marriage. We thus include father of ego, father of wife, brothers, sisters' husbands and wife's brothers. Their 'weight' is then calculated on the basis of a rating of their occupation, classified into: personal services/shop floor labour = 1 point; middlemen/small businessmen = 2 points; professional/executives = 3 points. Only socially active persons are considered. The deceased and young are excluded. Though network cores are kinship based their extension depends upon peer group contact.

TABLE 2

FORMAL SOVIET VALUES VS THE GEORGIAN VALUE SYSTEM

Principle	Formal Soviet Values	Georgian Values
1	Separation and insulation of private life from work life.	There is a fusion of work life and private life.
1 (a)	Since private and work lives are conceptually separate they are not rated vis-a-vis each other nor seen as competing for personal resources.	Since private and work lives are fused within one conceptual system the resources from one can be used in the service of the other. Since private concerns are dominant, work roles and resources are therefore subordinate to private concerns.
2	Recruitment on impartial universalistic merit.	Nepotism as a moral duty.
3	Hierarchical organisation: directives go down; information flows up.	Patron-client networks: directives come from where the real power is vested; information flows along network lines.
3 (a)	Officials are responsible to the official above them and for the work of subordinates.	Officials are primarily responsible to the claims of obligation and reciprocity imposed by network relationships.
3 (b)	Work roles and relationships are unambiguously defined.	Work roles and relationships are part of a total role set (work is not set apart from the rest of life).
4	Decisions are based on rules and analogies.	Decisions are submitted to honour commitments.
5	Every role is replaceable.	Every role holder is network-bounded.

would be expected, are linked to risk, and risks and earnings are both linked to honour—all derive from the effectiveness of network.

A barber (Case (a)) defined the risks in his job in these words:

To start with, people have their personal barbers, and they definitely would not give me in [report to the authorities for overcharging or supplying extra services]. They amount to 85% of our clients. For the rest, we [he and the other seven in his barbers' shop] run a quota. Everyone in his turn will take on outsiders, since you cannot charge them above the basic rate. But even, say, they catch you: what would they do? It's peanuts we're talking about. The most I would get is a warning from my cooperative headquarters. But it is different with a grocer because for him to make profit would mean to charge on some items at least 200% more and then when you are caught, either you pay every penny you've earned or you spend your life in jail.

This informant knew what he was talking about. He had tried for two years to be a grocer and had had to quit. The risk was too high: with a personal network score of only 2·0 (see

Table 1) he lacked adequate support—he could rely on no effective network either to prevent troubles or to mitigate them if they arose. Persons lacking effective networks can only make an adequate living by entering personal service occupations where their second economy activities are limited to regular clients. These they can charge more for that extra touch—the personal service—which is so highly considered in a macho society.

Of course it is not only low-status jobs which involve low risks. The qualified physician benefits from both high status *and* low risks. The physician (Case (o)), like the barber, the tailor, the hatter and the small cafe operator, makes his real money through strictly face-to-face interaction: the service giver and the client are the only parties to a transaction, thus minimising the chances of detection. But such professionals and their low-risk earnings are exceptional and the market accordingly recognises and adapts to the demand for places at medical school. Entrants must therefore be highly talented or able to command massive resources. In Tbilisi University's medical school, the only one in Georgia, competition for entrance is so rigorous that we were told that there were twenty applicants for each place and that a fee of 'up to 50,000R'[1] could be charged to ensure one's admittance. Here again a strong network is required to raise such large sums.

The medium risk occupations—those in Group II, middlemen and people in small business—are also mainly in contact with a regular circle of clients. But they also have more dealings with strangers, and the nature of their interaction is not always face-to-face as it is in personal service. This necessarily makes them more prone to detection if they break the rules and hence reinforces their need for strong backing from a good, reliable network. The average total score of those in Group II occupations is 11·25 compared with 6·0 in Group I.

In high-risk occupations the need for a strong network is paramount and here the average score is 14·50. Any small-town factory or supermarket has to obtain informal authority from the head of the local economic sector or from the *ispolkom* chairman himself. Usually too the head of the local police also has to be involved—at least passively. These officials are often placed on a monthly payroll and so too are their subordinates. As one factory executive explained: 'And what if the *ispolkom* chairman or the head of police is on leave? We have to pay their deputies, just in case they are in charge when some trouble occurs'.

Surprisingly, however, some high-status, high-earning, high-risk jobs are not backed with an influential network. Indeed, to take the case of one medium factory executive (1)—the production manager in a foodstuffs factory of several hundred workers—he made a deliberate choice to be extremely cautious. He used to practice only overproduction, that is, to make use of the state's machinery—but he would obtain raw material and labour at his own expense. He was careful not to reduce the standard of his products and he produced only the items he was licensed to. He was also careful about how he organised his factors of production—what Georgians call his 'combination'—so that many of his shop floor workers would not know too much about it.

When we compare this executive's situation with that of our big factory executive (m) we get a very different picture. He was considered one of the four most powerful people in his town. As production manager in a light furniture factory with a staff of 1,400 he had to have the backing of all the powerful job holders in his enterprise which involved a much higher order of necessary coordination. On his monthly payroll were the head of the enterprise, the *ispolkom* chairman and his deputy, the head of the police plus three of his staff. They required a combined monthly 'salary' bill of 1,500R.

This person not only used state machinery for production and the formal distribution chain to dispose of it—as did executive (I)—but he also reduced the product's standard, acquired raw material from his formal supply, produced with it products which were in high demand—not necessarily those he was licensed to—and finally distributed B quality products to meet his quota while A quality products found their way to the second economy. In this way he satisfies two aims. Firstly by skimping on the quality of his formal production he is able to obtain extra scarce materials for his informal production. Second, by ensuring a higher quality for his informal production he ensures that it obtains a head start in competiton for sales against the formal products.

However, the figures in Table 1 need care in interpretation. There can be cases where either a strong network would not necessarily be of benefit to a person or where a good and risky position is held without an adequate supporting network. The first position is highlighted by the blue-collar worker (e) who had an extensive familial network, but who could not benefit from it. He had eloped with his wife rather than submit to parental choices and vetoes and his network could therefore be regarded as damaged. Neither family was happy with the match. (This, by the way, brings out the role of women in the second economy—on which we have no space to elaborate here.) Without capital, without effective family, he had to enter blue-collar shop floor work where only occasionally was he offered extra work for second economy production—thus explaining his relatively high pay for manual work.

High pay alone does not however indicate high honour. In this culture, where individual autonomy is highly valued, the closeness of earnings between Groups I and II does not point up the essential differences between a job that allows one to take risks and a job that does not. Perhaps even more striking as an example of the care necessary in interpreting Table 1, is the case of the executive of a central warehouse (n) who was in control of imported consumer goods. These are of course in high demand. We believe this person was placed in that position *because* he possessed only a weak network and would thus not have been able to take full advantage of his highly sensitive job.

6. Conclusions

Having presented the core values of Georgian society and looked in some detail into their operation 'on the ground', we would now like to suggest some tentative conclusions concerning their articulation within the Georgian national economy. The most obvious conclusion from our data is the deep discrepancy they suggest between the formal, bureaucratic model of the Soviet economy—the way the economy is supposed to work—and the nepotistic, highly personalised entrepreneurial nature of Georgia's economy—the way that economy *really* works. Why, for instance, the key institutionalised function of the *tolkach*—the 'fixer'—in the Soviet economic system (Berliner, 1952) has no equivalent in the Georgian economy, nor in the Georgian language. The *tolkach* as such does not exist in Georgia. This is not because the system does not need this function but because the function has no need to be formalised and concentrated in a single role. It is a function that is dispersed and is always latently active within personal networks. Every Georgian is a potential *tolkach* in his own interest or in the interest of his network.

Since the formal system is predicated upon the idea of an individual's insulated occupancy of a role it follows that defective role performance should be curable by the replacement of the performer. This approach is always subject to some modification but the extent of its limitation in Georgia is almost finite in a culture so based upon personal networks. Here replacing one person by another cannot really change anything. The Moscow and (especially since 1973) some of the Tbilisi authorities have been concerned for years to bring an end to the Georgian way of running their republic. Their most serious attempt was the replacement of Mzhavanadze as first secretary of the Georgian Communist Party in the early 1970s. However, in its essentials the system has not changed, and the reasons are clear; in a network-based culture, though a person can be replaced, networks continue to exist. Persons will use personal support networks to try to find a lead to the new appointee, or if he proves too difficult to deal with, find a way to get rid of him or make his task impossible by limiting access to the social resources he needs.

We were told by an informant who was the personal chauffeur of an *ispolkom* chairman, and who thus had free access to much delicate information, that it was normal practice when a job changed hands to pass over the job's associated networks. Thus, in a 'casual conversation' the new appointee, if an outsider, would always ask: 'Are there any people around to count on?', and his predecessor would then reply: 'If you need anything—you can trust . . .'

In a similar way networks are used to mitigate penalties and to reduce disturbances on the occasions that exposure proves inevitable: criminal charges are reduced in scale; the honour code ensures that collaborators remain unrevealed to the authorities and evidence is removed or tampered with—all through the use of personal support networks.

But networks can also operate coercively—reciprocities and obligations have to be matched—not just in the immediate or short term but essentially because they become *part of a flow* that binds network members together. In such circumstances each network member finds that the network acts as a net; each member becomes a resource to others—a link in a chain upon which many others may depend. An informant who tried to stop fixing higher education entrance found himself trapped in this way by the demands of his network. He was not given the chance to leave his position. We thus can see that a network acts like a net in two senses: for some it can act as a safety net; for others it becomes an entanglement. 'A fence is built of wire and one man builds another' says a Georgian expression that neatly encapsulates this idea of linkages and networks. A factory executive explained it this way:

> You can't be innocent. Once you occupy a certain position, people expect you to pay them and if you don't—they will either see to it that you're replaced or that you're incriminated [and thus removed forcibly]. This is not difficult to fix. Everyone assumes there can be no genuine mistakes—a mistake would immediately incriminate you.

But normally such coercion is unnecessary. People remain in networks and conform to the social expectations these require because their *total* social situation demands it.

When the significance of network affiliation is considered alongside the macho virtue of risk taking, we can see how their combination is crucial to the idea of excess. In no way can the average—not the exceptional—Georgian male conform to the model of Soviet eco-

GEORGIA'S SECOND ECONOMY   559

nomic man. Formal income counts for only a proportion of total income, and it is extra income from the second economy that is vital to a full social role that requires excess in feasting and display. As our informants say 'if you are poor and the house is empty—then where is your pride?' Georgian men not only benefit economically from 'screwing the system'—their very honour as men demands that they should screw it excessively.

We believe we can now go some way in explaining why the Georgian second economy should be larger in real terms than the second economies of other Soviet-type republics. To be sure, other Soviet-type economies display the same kind of second economy practices (see for example the works of Staats, 1972; Berliner, 1957; Katzenelinboigen, 1977; 1978 (b); Simis, 1982). They too depend for much of their informal economic activity on 'friends of friends'. But it is the degree to which networks in Georgia are institutionalised as a means of linking individuals through trust-based honour commitments that form the cornerstone of Georgia's second economy. The difference may appear to be merely one of degree but it is based on a fundamental cultural distinction.

We hope we have demonstrated how a concern with the central interest of anthropology—the idea of culture, the application of the concept of personal support network and the alliance of these to the anthropological method of patient participant observation, can produce understanding of an economic system that would otherwise be unobtainable. Other Soviet-type economies based on different cultural core values may well display high levels of second economy activity. Ofer and Vinokur (1979), for instance, suggest that this is the case in the Central Asian Republics—well known to be second only to Georgia in this respect. It is not sufficient, however, to consider merely the overall outcome of second economy activity. If this phenomenon is to be understood it must be examined in the context of its cultural setting. Recourse to the methods and concepts of anthropology is we would argue, the only way that this can be achieved.

Middlesex Polytechnic

*This study was funded by The Nuffield Foundation (UK). An earlier version of this paper was delivered to the Western Slavic Association Conference at Honolulu, Hawaii, in March 1982.
[1] Simis (1982) states that the standard fee at the same time to which our information refers was 15,000R. We would however expect the price to be higher for Jews than for non-Jews.

References

Ben-Zvi, I. *Israel's Exiled,* Ministry of Defence Publications, Tel-Aviv 1963 (Hebrew).
Ben-Ami. *Between the Hammer and the Scythe,* Am-Oved, Tel-Aviv 1965 (Hebrew).
Berliner, J. S. 'The Informal Organisation of the Soviet Firm', *Quarterly Journal of Economics,* 1952, p. 342–365.
Davis, J. *People of the Mediterranean.* Routledge & Kegan Paul, London 1977.
Dragadze, T. 'Family Life in Georgia', *New Society* 19 August 1976, p. 393–5.
Grigolia, A. *Custom and Justice in the Caucasus: the Georgian Highlanders.* University of Pennsylvania, Philadelphia 1939.
Grossman, G. 'The Second Economy of the USSR', *Problems of Communism,* September/October 1977, pp. 25–40.
Katzenlinboigen, A, 'Coloured Markets in the Soviet Union', *Soviet Studies,* Vol. XXIX, No. 1, (January 1977) pp. 62–85. *Soviet Economic Planning,* M. E. Sharpe, NY 1978.
Kardanov, B. A. et al. *Caucasian Life* (Vol. 2) Publication of the Academy of Sciences, Moscow 1962 (Russian).

560

The Anthropology of Drinking. Cambridge University Press, 1983.

Parsons, R. 'National Integration in Soviet Georgia', *Soviet Studies,* Vol. XXXIV No. 4, (October 1982) pp. 547–69.

Peristiany, J. G. (ed). *Honour and Shame.* Weidenfeld and Nicolson, 1966.

Plisetsky, M. *Religion and Customs of Georgian Jews.* Moscow 1931 (Russian).

Ofer, G. & Vinokur, A. 'The Private Sources of Income of the Soviet Urban Household'. Research Paper. *Kennan Institute for Advanced Russian Studies.* Washington, DC, January 1980.

Simis, K. *USSR: Secrets of a Corrupt Society,* Dent, 1982.

Staats, S. S. 'Corruption in the Soviet System', *Problems of Communism,* January/February 1972.

Wiles, P. J. D. *Die Parallelwirtschaft.* Sonderveröffentlichung des Bundesinstituts für Ostwissenschaftliche und Internationale Studien, Cologne, 1981.

Part II
What is the *Mafiya*?

[6]

BRIT. J. CRIMINOL.   VOL. 32   NO. 2   SPRING 1992

CRIME IN THE SOVIET UNION

Early Glimpses of the True Story

W. E. BUTLER*

In late 1990 the Soviet Union published official statistics on crime for the first time in six decades. This article reports on the figures and trends against limited retrospective data and trends in criminal law reform.

The Soviet revolutionaries who swept to power in October 1917 believed they possessed the answer to crime in two senses: an exhaustive explanation as to why crime exists in society, and the creation of preventive and correctional schemes for reforming those whose behaviour strayed from the established canons.[1] The considerable implications of these convictions for Soviet criminology in the 1920s were translated, *inter alia*, into research designs that attracted international attention.[2]

From the late 1920s to the early 1930s, the statistical incidence of criminal phenomena disappeared from public view, having been classified as a state secret. The precise scenario of security classification and the relevant legislation are still not fully a matter of public record.[3] Thereafter the public was for some three decades given only ritualistic incantations that crime rates were dropping, occasional press reports of particularly pernicious crimes (and executions), and a criminological literature that dealt in abstract weeded percentages rather than hard empirical data on the incidence of crime.

In 1961 the national scheme for reporting crime was unified and tightened. Law students were introduced more systematically to the mysteries of forensic statistics through a course and textbooks bearing that name—but without actual figures, of course. Very occasionally hard figures on crime did appear, selectively and highly localized, in the professional literature. These snippets Western specialists assembled in valiant attempts to generalize about the incidence of crime,[4] especially the differences between so-called 'ordinary crime' and so-called 'political crime'. Informed Soviet emigrés who had worked professionally as criminologists and who presumably had access to the classified data either honoured their legal obligation not to disclose it or refrained from reconstructing from memory a complex data system.[5]

Within the Soviet Union the policy of classification grew progressively more absurd.

---

* Professor of Comparative Law in the University of London; Director, Centre for the Study of Socialist Legal Systems, University College London.

[1] See W. E. Butler, *Soviet Law*, 2nd edn. (London, 1988): 323–33; R. Makepeace, *Marxist Ideology and Soviet Criminal Law* (1980); H. J. Berman, *Justice in the USSR*, rev. edn. (1963): 363–82.

[2] P. H. Solomon, Jr., *Soviet Criminologists and Criminal Policy: Specialists in Policy-Making* (1978).

[3] What is probably a partial list of the information subject to state secrecy at the time is reproduced in H. J. Berman and P. B. Maggs, *Disarmament Inspection Under Soviet Law* (1967): 112–13. Criminal statistics are not mentioned in this version, which replaces a list adopted in 1947, and has since been replaced.

[4] The most ambitious extrapolations were undertaken with skill and imagination in G. P. van den Berg, *The Soviet System of Justice: Figures and Policy* (1985).

[5] I. Zeldes, *The Problems of Crime in the USSR* (1981).

CRIME IN THE SOVIET UNION

The persistence and pervasiveness of crime had discredited the easy axiomatic assertions of the 1920s and begged for serious comparative analysis. Professional Soviet criminologists were hamstrung in their efforts to analyse and evaluate the accumulated data on patterns of crime; many were cut off from the full data, and those with access were barred from debating candidly, and thereby disclosing, policy options founded on statistical revelations or patterns. Foreign colleagues met with disbelief and incomprehension reports couched in dogmas of the past and lacking the most elementary empirical foundations.

Perestroika has brought changes—two, in fact—but not as rapidly and easily as might have been supposed. The first was a relaxation in law (but not subordinate act) of the restrictions which barred disclosure and publication of criminal statistics.[6] Notwithstanding the change, it has apparently required two years and the issuance of a new list of items not subject to disclosure or publication to commence the process of dislodging full crime statistics with some retrospective coverage.[7] It cannot be asserted with complete certainty that crime statistics have been fully authorized for disclosure as the list of official secrets is itself classified,[8] and where *by law* data in the past have been deliberately falsified for publication[9] these are not matters to be taken for granted.

The second change is in crime itself. By all accounts the incidence of reported crime has increased alarmingly in the Soviet Union. The reasons are the subject of lively discussion in all Soviet media, fuelled by official monthly reports issued by the USSR Ministry of Internal Affairs. Perestroika is itself held partly to blame. How the phenomenon of law and order will be addressed under reform conditions remains to be seen. In the short term, however, the increase in crime has caused the postponement of criminal reform legislation whose leitmotif was humanization and decriminalization and provoked a lively debate about capital punishment.[10]

Crime Reporting and the Legacy of the Past

Statistics on criminality were among the data to be collected by the 'Moral Statistics Section' of the RSFSR Central Statistical Administration created in 1918,[11] a function replicated in the USSR Central Statistical Administration formed in 1923.[12] While the

---

[6] See the joint Decree of the Central Committee of the CPSU and the USSR Council of Ministers of 17 July 1987, no. 822, 'O merakh po korennomu uluchsheniiu dela statistiki v strane', *Svod zakonov SSSR*, V: 280–2. Some of the surviving absurdities of these policies are discussed in V. Lunev, 'Prestupnaia mifologiia', *Izvestiia*, 13 April 1991, p. 3, cols. 2–7.

[7] A. Illesh and V. Rudnev, 'Tsenzura otmenena, tsenzory ostaiutsia: popytka retsenzii na knigu o gosudarstvennykh tainakh', *Izvestiia*, 9 October 1990, p. 3, cols. 1–5.

[8] In December 1990 the USSR Constitutional Supervision Committee declared unconstitutional the practice of not publishing, or publishing only in part, the texts of normative acts which affect the rights and freedoms of citizens. For commentary on the Opinion, see Iu. Feofanov, 'Sposobna li vlast' byt' chestnoi', *Izvestiia*, 16 December 1990, p. 3, cols. 1–6.

[9] It was disclosed in 1988 that for decades Soviet maps had been deliberately falsified as a legal requirement, presumably for what were perceived to be security reasons.

[10] These matters have been discussed at length in an Anglo-Soviet symposium on criminal law and procedure held at University College London in March 1990. The papers and a translation of the draft Fundamental Principles of Criminal Legislation of the USSR and Union Republics, second version, have been published as a special issue of *Coexistence*, 28 (1991): 159–96.

[11] Adopted 25 July 1918. *SU RSFSR* (1918), no. 55, item 611; on the drafting history, see *Dekrety sovetskoi vlasti* (1964), 3: 87–93.

[12] *Vestnik SNK i TsIK* (1923), no. 1, item 26.

W. E. BUTLER

practices of the period deserve further study, it is certainly the case that data on the incidence of reported crime, criminal convictions, and sentencing policies were reported and discussed in the press and cumulated in annual statistical yearbooks. From the beginning of the early 1930s the reporting of this type of 'negative phenomena' was prohibited on grounds of official secrecy and the moral statistics sections were reportedly abolished. Apparently, however, the statistics on criminality continued to be gathered by the departments concerned (probably the respective police and procuracy agencies), and by the courts, but not released outside those agencies.

Why the Soviet authorities chose to make the incidence of crime a state secret remains the object of speculation. One reason widely adduced was the obvious ideological inconsistency between the declared achievement of socialism by Soviet society and the continued pervasiveness of criminality. Crime by definition was expected to die out, to disappear, under socialism and communism; on this argument, failing to disclose the incidence of criminality would be a cosmetic touch of self-deception that would enable ideological appearances to be maintained.

Perhaps. But another factor may have been the large-scale employment of state repression against perceived 'class enemies' in the course of forced collectivization of agriculture, the persecution of individuals and groups deemed to be hostile to those in power, and in due course the systematic elimination of elements of the populace on wholly contrived grounds. As these were treated at the time as ordinary criminal phenomena, the statistics of reported crime and convictions, if accurately kept, presumably would have disclosed massive increases in criminality and prosecutions even more difficult to reconcile with the ideological transition to socialism.

If those statistics were kept and are accurate, they have yet to be disclosed. Soviet journalists frequently cite Western sources for the period, and no Western source can be said with assurance to be accurate. Millions of those convicted have since been formally rehabilitated; that it, not pardoned, but the conviction reversed and expunged from the record. Usually the legal grounds are the absence of the constituent elements of a crime. If the statistical record was rigorously compiled under Stalin, how should the rehabilitation process be reflected? Should the original figures be reduced (no crime was committed, hence both the reported crime and conviction figures are erroneous)? Or should asterixed figures be inserted to offset the original figures with the rehabilitations? While the net result of either approach is to reduce criminality levels for the period, it takes no account of the criminality of those who perpetrated the wrongful accusations, convictions, and executions, and who now lie in the pages of history. At a minimum, it is to be hoped that full disclosure will be made of the retrospective data for the complete Soviet period.

In 1961, as mentioned above, the statistical procedures for reporting crime were revised and tightened, and two years later institutes within the USSR Ministry of Internal Affairs and the Procuracy of the USSR began to pioneer sociological–criminological analyses of criminality based on the statistical records; but they were unable, because the figures were state secrets, to publish them openly. For nearly a quarter of a century they laboured under those constraints, lending to discussions of criminal policy an Aesopian dimension based on hints 'between the lines' as to what the true situation was and how it might be rectified. The legislative changes enacted in 1987 allowed the disclosure and publication of statistical data relating to seven types of crime. The

CRIME IN THE SOVIET UNION

following year a Moral Statistics Department was re-created in the USSR State Committee for Statistics, and in 1989 the final decision was taken to remove all restrictions on the publication of composite data concerning registered crimes and the total numbers of convicted persons. Under way are major retrospective official publications and studies which promise a further account of criminality, convictions, and what the literature calls 'other negative phenomena'.[13]

It is clear that the statistical data accumulated since 1918 do not lend themselves to direct comparison from one period to another. The substance of the criminal law has been amended repeatedly, pre-trial investigative practices have changed, and so too have the procedures for recording reported crimes. Data issued by the Russian Republic in the 1920s disclosed a conviction rate per 100,000 population of 2,910 for 1924 and 1,774 for 1926.[14] Presumably excluding the early purges, the rate for 1935 had declined to 720 and continued to drop until the Second World War, excluding counter-revolutionary and labour crimes (shirking and leaving a job without permission). Criminality rose again during the war and early postwar years, but by the mid-1950s had again declined to 400 per 100,000 population. These are all convictions, of course, and will not fully reflect patterns of reported crime. The social discipline associated with Stalinist authoritarianism is credited for the decline in crime to 1955.[15]

With the amelioration of authoritarianism associated with de-Stalinization, accelerated by the Twentieth Congress of the Communist Party of the Soviet Union in 1956, reported crimes per capita began to rise sharply, from 187 per 100,000 population to four times that figure in 1989, although the growth was not uninterrupted.

The 'early glimpses' of data on criminality are drawn principally from the first statistical manual issued since the classification of such data as a state secret in the early 1930s. Three agencies have collaborated in providing the data: the USSR Ministry of Internal Affairs, the Procuracy of the USSR, and the USSR Ministry of Justice. While the data are fullest for the calendar year 1989, selected data are reported for the period 1961 onwards. For those nearly three decades the system for reporting crimes and convictions remained essentially uniform; the USSR and union republics adopted criminal legislation which was identical or similar in key respects for these purposes; and the territorial boundaries and court system remained essentially intact and comparable. While the compilers further argue that 'the repeated clarifications of, changes in, and additions to' Soviet criminal legislation did not exert 'material influence on the principal indicators of criminality',[16] this is less than persuasive. It is perhaps a point that the changes were highly synchronized and occurred in all or nearly all union republics more or less simultaneously. But campaigns in certain republics against certain types of crime are likely to have influenced the figures, and it may be that other factors need to be weighed too; for example, the influence of Guiding Explanations of the Plenum of the USSR Supreme Court, and the definition of 'conviction' under the Soviet appeals system. Moreover, there are the periods of decriminalization and criminalization to be considered, and the role of administrative penalties in the entire process.

---

[13] This is the chronology given in A. I. Smirnov (ed.), *Prestupnost' i pravonarusheniia v SSSR* (1990), p. 4.

[14] Ibid., citing *Statistika osuzhdennykh v RSFSR za 1926 g.* (1928); for an example of empirical studies of the period, see *Prestupnik i prestupnost'* (1926–7), 2 vols. (available on microfiche).

[15] V. V. Luneev, in Smirnov, *Prestupnost'*: 4–5.

[16] Ibid.: 6.

W. E. BUTLER

Criminality: An Overview from 1961 to 1989

The definition of criminality is not entirely straightforward. Reported crimes, for example, are apparently to be distinguished from 'registered crimes'. The latter are treated as the 'facts' of crimes with regard to which criminal cases are initiated, and it is these which are ordinarily recorded as crimes for statistical purposes. The numbers of persons who have committed crimes is a separate statistic calculated at the procedural stage of a criminal proceeding when the conclusion to indict is confirmed and the file of the case is referred to a court. Depending upon the outcome of the trial, a rectification is introduced in the records to take account of acquittals.[17]

For the purposes of criminological analysis, sixteen of the most common crimes whose constituent elements and registration procedures remain unaltered since 1961 are selected to provide a general picture of criminality trends. These fall into three groups:

1. Crimes committed with the use of force: intentional homicide, attempted homicide; intentional grave body injury; rape; attempted rape; malicious and especially malicious hooliganism.
2. Mercenary crimes: theft, assault with intent to rob, open stealing, swindling.
3. Economic mercenary crimes: stealing committed by way of appropriation, embezzlement, abuse of official position, bribery, speculation, deception of purchasers and customers.[18]

While it seems to be the case that from 1966 to 1980 the increase in registered crimes stabilized to approximately the annual population growth, there are other elements in the pattern which require explication. First, from 1961 to 1965 the rates decline each year, including nearly a 10 per cent drop in 1963 as compared with the preceding year. And 1966 reveals a remarkable 18 per cent increase over the preceding year; 1983 a 21 per cent increase over 1982; and 1989 a 31.8 per cent increase over 1988. Other major fluctuations are 1968 (8 per cent above 1967); 1974 (8.7 per cent above 1973); 1978 (8 per cent above 1977); 1979 (9.5 per cent above 1978), and 1987 (9.5 per cent decrease from 1986).[19]

The year 1989 by all accounts was a deplorable one. While registered crimes had increased by 31.8 per cent over 1988, the detection rate was up by only 1.4 per cent. Within those figures, the crimes least susceptible to non-detection, homicide and attempted homicide, had increased by 28.5 per cent. Property offences committed against citizens were up by 55.1 per cent, and against state and social ownership, 34.7 per cent. The crime rate in the cities increased, not surprisingly, much more rapidly than in the countryside. As part of the transition to the market economy, the numbers of economic crimes declined, mostly perhaps because the constituent elements of those offences were not consistent with the market economy ethos. Group and organized crime increased so sharply that law enforcement agencies created special detachments for crime of this type. Juvenile crime in 1989 showed a 21.2 per cent increase over 1988

---

[17] A. I. Dolgova and S. V. Tiurin, in Smirnov, *Prestupnost'*: 7.

[18] For the constituent elements of these crimes, see the translation of the 1960 RSFSR Criminal Code as amended in W. E. Butler, *Basic Documents on the Soviet Legal System* (London, 1983): 295–394.

[19] Unless otherwise indicated, all figures are drawn or extrapolated from Smirnov, *Prestupnost'*.

CRIME IN THE SOVIET UNION

TABLE 1   *Total Crime Statistics, 1980–1989*

	1980	1985	1988	1989
Total reported crimes	3,238,212	4,216,335	3,864,169	4,376,829
Total registered crimes	1,527,557	2,083,501	1,867,223	2,461,692
Total criminals elicited[a]	1,328,143	1,728,184	1,286,505	1,303,958
Total convicted persons	998,194	1,269,493	679,168	684,070
Total deaths from crimes	n.a.	n.a.	52,901	66,626

[a] Includes persons whose cases were referred to a court and those whose materials were sent to a comrades' court, commission for cases of minors, and the like.

and throughout the 1980s was roughly double the equivalent increase in population of that age.

Criminality in the Union Republics

The Union of Soviet Socialist Republics in the period under consideration was composed of fifteen union republics, each organized on an ethnic basis and containing the largest concentration of the nationality whose name it bears. As one would expect, the pattern of criminality varies from one republic to another. In 1989, as compared with 1988, all union republics experienced an increase in registered crime. The highest percentage increases were in Estonia (57.3 per cent) and Lithuania (46.3 per cent), and the lowest in Georgia (6.4 per cent) and Azerbaijan (6.9 per cent). Throughout the 1980s generally the highest average annual increases in registered crimes occurred in Moldavia, Lithuania, Kirgiz SSR, and Uzbekistan. Georgia and Azerbaijan actually experienced a decrease during the 1980s. Using the sixteen comparable crimes cited above, the highest registered crime rates occurred in Latvia, the RSFSR, and Estonia, and the lowest in Armenia and Azerbaijan. The incidence of economic crimes was lowest in Estonia and highest in Kazakhstan, Uzbekistan, and Georgia, but in all republics these crimes dropped in 1988–9. Juvenile delinquency was highest as a percentage of total crimes in Latvia, the RSFSR, and Belorussia, and lowest in Armenia and Azerbaijan.[20]

To Western eyes Armenia stands out in the tables as the union republic with consistently the lowest crime rate. For the period 1980–9, the highest figure for crimes registered was 8,548 (1983), and the lowest 6,324 (1988). These figures per capita are roughly comparable with Azerbaijan, and the two together are in a class of their own compared with all other union republics. Armenia, of course, has a Christian heritage, and Azerbaijan, an Islamic. They seem to be fertile ground for empirical criminological research in order to identify the reasons for the unusually low figures.

Some union republics contain chapters in their criminal codes devoted to 'crimes constituting survivals of local customs'.[21] Arranged marriages, bride-price, blood feud, polygamy, and the like are punished under the relevant articles when those customs are practised in certain parts of the Soviet Union. From time to time individual cases have

[20] Dolgova and E. M. Iutskova, in Smirnov, *Prestupnost'*: 23–5.
[21] See Articles 231–236 of the RSFSR Criminal Code, translated in Butler, *Basic Documents*.

W. E. BUTLER

been reported,[22] but in the absence of statistics there has been no indication of the extent to which the law has over several generations succeeded in eliminating these practices. Data for 1985–9 record the following numbers of registered crimes in this category: 1985: 900; 1986: 872; 1987: 832; 1988: 636; 1989: 615. There is no breakdown by union republic available.[23]

Individual Crimes

Intentional homicide

Under the RSFSR Criminal Code intentional homicide is divided into that committed under enumerated aggravating circumstances and that committed without aggravating circumstances. The figures for 1980–9 fluctuate widely. While the increase from 1988 to 1989 was a widely advertised 28.5 per cent (from 16,702 to 21,467), the total number of homicides in 1989 was virtually identical to the total for 1980. In 1987 the figure was roughly one-third the figures recorded for 1980 and 1989.

No explanation is offered for the fluctuations. In 1980 69.5 per cent of homicides (including attempts) occurred by reason of domestic grounds, jealousy and the like, whereas in 1989 homicides for those reasons amounted to 33.9 per cent of the total. The RSFSR and the Ukraine accounted for 75.3 per cent of all homicides. Areas where there have been ethnic disturbances (Uzbekistan, Azerbaijan, Armenia, Kazakh SSR) show increases, but not in sufficient numbers to account for the overall increase. The Ukraine, for example, recorded 573 more homicides in 1989 than the preceding year.

Of the 21,467 homicides (or attempts) committed in 1989, 1,326 were committed with the use of a weapon; 13,480 were committed in cities and urban-type settlements; 7,987 in rural localities; 523 by minors; 1,328 by groups of persons; 7,071 by persons previously convicted of a crime; 11,904 in a state of intoxication; and 19 by narcotics addicts. The reasons for the homicides require explication. For 1989, some 33.9 per cent are attributed to domestic reasons; 0.9 per cent to mothers killing a new-born child; 2.2 per cent to hooliganism; 0.8 per cent to rape; and 0.6 per cent to assault with intent to rob. Fully 61.6 per cent are attributed to 'other reasons and circumstances'.

Intentional grave bodily injury

Pursuant to the RSFSR Criminal Code, injuries in this category include life-threatening injuries; loss of vision, hearing, or any organ; loss of functions of any organ; mental illness or other impairment of health linked with loss of at least one-third labour capacity; miscarriage; and the like.

Except for 1983, when an increase was recorded, the numbers of registered crimes in this category declined every year from 1980 until 1988 and 1989, when spectacular increases of 31.6 per cent and 38.4 per cent respectively were recorded. The RSFSR and Ukraine accounted for 83.1 per cent of all such offences in 1989. As in the case of homicides, those union republics where ethnic disturbances have occurred show large

---

[22] See *Soviet Statutes and Decisions*, 1/4 (1965); J. N. Hazard, W. E. Butler, and P. B. Maggs, *The Soviet Legal System*, 3rd edn. (1977); idem, *The Soviet Legal System: Law for the 1980s* (1984).

[23] Insight into the persistence and in some cases transformation of these practices amongst the Buriats is to be found in C. Humphrey, *Karl Marx Collective: Economy, Society and Religion in a Siberian Collective Farm* (1983).

CRIME IN THE SOVIET UNION

percentage increases but small absolute increases. Between 1988 and 1989, for example, the absolute numbers of offences in Armenia rose from 156 to 230; in Azerbaijan from 281 to 387; in Uzbekistan from 834 to 1,159; but increases of this order were dwarfed by the RSFSR increment of 10,233 in the same period.

Rape

Although rape (including attempts) in 1989 showed a marked 23.5 per cent increase (21,873) over the preceding year (17,658), the total overall approximated the figures for 1980, 1981, 1983, and 1984. Seen as a percentage of total crime against the person, rape in 1988 and 1989 constituted about 20 per cent of the total. The RSFSR and Ukraine account for 79.3 per cent of rapes, and the Kazakh SSR a further 7.7 per cent; Belorussia 3.7 per cent, and the Uzbek SSR 2.6 per cent. Of the 21,873 rapes (or attempts) in 1989, 14,094 were committed in cities or urban-type settlements; 7,779 in rural localities; 2,689 by minors; 4,934 by groups of persons; 6,725 by persons previously convicted of a crime; 11,405 by persons in a state of intoxication; and 35 by narcotics addicts.

Hooliganism

Despite its use in the popular British press, the term in the Russian language has a highly specific definition laid down in Article 206 of the RSFSR Criminal Code: 'Intentional actions flagrantly violating public order and expressing a clear disrespect for society'.[24] The Criminal Code distinguishes among petty, ordinary, malicious, and especially malicious hooliganism. Petty hooliganism is now an administrative offence.

In the case of this crime, patterns of law enforcement are believed to account for fluctuations in the incidence of the offence, including the extent to which campaigns against drunkenness and alcoholism proved to be effective. In 1989 hooliganism (143,008) increased by 22.4 per cent over the previous year but was still markedly less than all years from 1980 to 1986. Of the 142,008 registered facts of hooliganism, 118,062 were classified as malicious or especially malicious hooliganism.

Assault with intent to rob

This crime is defined by Articles 91 and 146 of the RSFSR Criminal Code. The statistics for 1988 (42.8 per cent) and 1987 (71.7 per cent) show very large increases over each respective preceding year, although the overall incidence of this crime comprises less than 10 per cent of total registered crime in the USSR. The RSFSR and Ukraine account for 77.8 per cent of all instances of this crime, followed by the Kazakh (5.2 per cent), Uzbek (4.8 per cent), and Belorussian (2.8 per cent) republics. It is principally an urban crime. Of 22,174 instances recorded in 1989, 18,706 occurred in cities and urban-type settlements and 3,468 in rural localities; 1,857 were committed by minors, 7,359 by groups of persons, and 7,869 by persons who had previously committed crimes.

[24] See Butler, *Basic Documents*: 371.

W. E. BUTLER

Open stealing

In 1988 this crime showed a 44 per cent increase over 1987 but replicated levels reached in 1983, 1984, and 1985. For 1989 the percentage increase was 66.3 per cent (111,601 instances) over 1988, which for the first time placed this crime into a new category of incidence. The RSFSR and the Ukraine accounted for 80.5 per cent of open stealing in 1989, and the Kazakh SSR for a further 7 per cent. About 90 per cent of all such crimes (101,529) occurred in cities or urban-type settlements; 12,779 were committed by minors, 15,914 by groups of persons, and 16,437 by persons who had previously committed a crime.

Theft of state, social, or personal property

Under the RSFSR Criminal Code, the secret stealing of property is theft. It is instructive to consider the incidence of the crime against state or social property, on one hand, and personal property, on the other.

Theft of state or social property   The year 1989 is the last for which property offences will be wholly comparable with the post-1961 era. The 1990 USSR Law on Ownership is the first in a series of enactments wholly reordering the forms of ownership and their respective roles in the Soviet economy.[25] In due course criminal legislation will have to be altered accordingly, but in fact major transformations are in progress as state property is removed from state ownership or privatized and citizens are allowed to own most types of means of production. The theft of state and social property in 1989 was valued at 72,200,000 roubles, of which 24,900,000 roubles represented theft from warehouses, depots, stores, and other trade centres.[26]

Although this crime showed sharp increases in 1988 and 1989, the total figure for 1988 was well below those for 1983–5; indeed, 1983 showed a 22.7 per cent increase over 1982. None the less, the 1989 total of 296,985 thefts represented a 61.5 per cent increase over 1988 and was virtually double the number of thefts registered in 1987 (which was the lowest figure in the entire 1980s). Three republics—the RSFSR, Ukraine, and Kazakh SSR—account for 85.7 per cent of all thefts. Compared with most crimes reviewed here, the rural component is unusually high: 104,566 out of 296,985. Minors committed 23,038 such thefts, groups of persons 42,675; and a relatively small percentage, 29,804, were committed by persons who had previously committed crimes. Throughout 1989, excluding July and November, the number of thefts committed increased from month to month.

Theft of personal property of citizens   Personal ownership, a term dating from the mid-1930s in the USSR, is being replaced in civil legislation by a new expression: 'ownership of citizens'. The 1990 RSFSR Law on Ownership in the RSFSR, in employing this expression, groups it under 'private ownership' together with the ownership of juridical persons. In due course the word 'personal' will be expunged from

---

[25] *Vedomosti SND SSSR* (1990), no. 11, item 164; translated in W. E. Butler, *Basic Documents on the Soviet Legal System*, 2nd edn. (1991): 269–81. The Law on Ownership in the RSFSR was adopted 24 December 1990. See *Ekonomika i zhizn'*, no. 3 (1991): 13–14.

[26] V. A. Serebriakova, in Smirnov, *Prestupnost'*: 57.

CRIME IN THE SOVIET UNION

criminal legislation. Thus the year 1989 will be the last comparable to the post-1961 data for this type of crime.

In 1989 some 845,157 thefts of personal property were committed, a percentage increase of 54.1 per cent over 1988 and 247.2 per cent over 1980. While the increase from 1988 to 1989 was substantial, a 60 per cent increase also occurred in 1983 as compared with 1982. The RSFSR, Ukraine, and Kazakh SSR accounted for 84.5 per cent of the registered crimes. Of the total number of thefts committed, 252,960 were from the flats of citizens (an increase of 43.9 per cent over 1988); 697,803 of the thefts occurred in cities or urban-type settlements; 79,685 were committed by minors; 96,891 were committed by a group of persons; and 92,812 were by persons who had previously committed a crime. July and November excepted, every month showed an increase, with October being the peak month.

Appropriation, embezzlement, or other abuse of official position

These actions fall under Article 92 of the RSFSR Criminal Code. From 1980 to 1986 the number of these crimes increased annually for the USSR as a whole, a result attributable to active law enforcement measures, and declined from 1987 to 1989. Soviet specialists, however, believe the real incidence of these crimes has increased, and that the statistical decrease merely means that a greater number of incidences are latent.[27] Of the 81,228 such crimes committed in 1989, 49,114 occurred in cities and urban-type settlements, 7,319 were committed by a group of persons, and 2,889 by persons who had previously committed a crime. The last figure, representing 3.5 per cent of such crimes, is evidence that persons with a previous criminal record are not commonly appointed to executive or economic posts.

Speculation

The offence of speculation likewise after 1989 joins the category of crimes not comparable with post-1961 data. In principle, it is not consistent with a market economy. During the transitional era, however, the offence has been recast in an all-union law of 3 November 1990 directed primarily against hoarding.[28] From 1980 to 1988, but for a small decrease in 1983, registered instances of speculation increased by 2,000–4,000 per year, amounting in 1989 to 45,140 (down 95 from 1988). About 80 per cent of the crimes occurred in cities or settlements of an urban type. Minors accounted for fewer than 1 per cent of offences, although data on administrative penalties for speculation may disclose a different pattern. Groups of persons accounted for about 5 per cent of the registered crimes, although difficulties of proof are believed to conceal a larger number of group offences. The number of persons previously convicted of a crime is only 4–6 per cent, some 1,874 in 1989.

The union republic distribution of this crime differs. The RSFSR and Ukraine in 1989 accounted for under 70 per cent. In the Uzbek SSR there were 3,828 registered crimes; 2,387 in the Kazakh SSR; 1,865 in Georgia; 1,252 in the Azerbaijan SSR; and

[27] E. F. Pogebailo and E. M. Iutskova, in ibid.: 68.
[28] *Izvestiia*, 4 November 1990, p. 1, cols. 6–7.

W. E. BUTLER

1,063 in Belorussia. Then the numbers drop sharply; Lithuania recorded 597 instances and Estonia only 93.

Bribery

This is a serious crime, encompassing the receiving or giving of, or acting as an intermediary in, a bribe. The number of registered crimes grew annually from 1980 to 1986, but dropped sharply (60 per cent) from 1987 to 1989. In 1989, 4,292 instances of bribery were registered. The incidence of offences to 1986 is attributed to active law enforcement measures; the reduction since 1987 is not regarded as a real reduction but rather as the concentration of law enforcement resources on other matters. The RSFSR in 1989 accounted for nearly 50 per cent of bribery cases (2,195) and the Ukraine for 25 per cent (1,049).

Narcotics

Before perestroika commenced, the Soviet Union denied the existence of a narcotics-related crime problem. Compared to most industrial countries, the Soviet statistics suggest not a non-existent problem but a rather negligible one. Only about 1–2 per cent of crimes in the USSR are classified as narcotics-related. For the Soviet Union as a whole in 1989 there were 28,471 such crimes, a drop of 20.6 per cent from 1985 (35,847). Much of the decrease can be attributed to the decriminalization in 1987 of the use of narcotics and the acquisition of narcotics in small amounts.

The pattern varies, however, from one republic to another. While the RSFSR, Ukraine, Georgia, Armenia, and Turkmenistan experienced declines, often substantial reductions, in narcotics-related crimes, others had considerable increases. Belorussia increased from 56 in 1985 to 323 in 1989; Estonia from 5 to 29; Lithuania from 23 to 125; and Latvia from 45 to 138. Azerbaijan, Uzbekistan, Moldavia, and the Kazakh republics recorded slight increases.

The per capita recorded use of narcotics also varied sharply, rising for the USSR as a whole from 30.1 to 41.4 per 100,000 population between 1985 and 1989. The highest recorded figure is 140.5 in the Turkmen SSR, which is more than twice as high as the other Central Asian union republics: then Kazakh SSR (63.6); Uzbek SSR (57.9); and Kirgiz SSR (55). The Ukraine shows a startlingly high figure (53.3) compared with the other European union republics: RSFSR (35); Belorussia (6.8); Estonia (19.3); Moldavia (11.6); Latvia (21.3); and Lithuania (19.5).

Narcotics-related crimes are to be distinguished from other crimes committed by drug addicts. The composite data are shown in Table 2.

The Perpetrators

The numbers of crimes, of course, are not identical to the numbers of persons who perpetrated them. In 1989, 1,303,958 persons who committed crimes were adjudged to have done so. Of these, 85.3 per cent were males and 14.7 per cent females. During the period 1985–9, the percentage of female minors who committed crimes grew from 4.1 per cent to 7 per cent.

Juvenile delinquency generally is growing. In 1989 212,457 minors committed

154

CRIME IN THE SOVIET UNION

TABLE 2   *Narcotics-related Crimes*

	1985	1986	1987	1988	1989
Total crimes	2,970	5,405	5,279	4,134	3,457
Intentional homicide	36	30	26	41	44
Intentional grave bodily injury	45	37	27	35	32
Rape	28	34	12	18	16
Assaults	16	37	26	58	46
Open stealing	72	88	50	84	69
Theft of personal property	381	479	474	720	571

Source: A. V. Gorkin, in A. I. Smirnov, ed., *Prestupnost' i pravonarusheniia v SSR* (1990).

crimes. The proportion of crimes perpetrated by minors jumped from 10 per cent in 1985 to 16.3 per cent in 1989. There is a general trend towards crimes being perpetrated by younger people, with the over-30s now committing 42.8 per cent of crimes in 1989 (as against 52.1 per cent in 1985). The distribution of perpetrators by basic occupation has remained stable: workers commit roughly 50–52 per cent of crimes; collective farmers 5.7 per cent; employees 8.7–13.2 per cent; students 8.3–10.6 per cent (of whom university students perpetrate about 11 per cent of crimes by students); and unemployed 11.8–16 per cent. From 19.1 to 23.9 per cent of the perpetrators were committing a second offence. About one-third of all criminals acted in a state of intoxication, whereas less than one-fifth of 1 per cent were on drugs. The latter figures represent a significant increase, having been as low as 24.3 per cent in 1986 at the height of the anti-alcohol campaign. Indeed, the effects of that campaign as measured by crime rates seem to be confined to 1986.

Of those committing a second offence, more than half had previously served a term of deprivation of freedom, and 29.2 per cent committed their second crime within a year of being released. Persons convicted for a first criminal offence in 1989 included 31,063 (3.1 per cent) who had committed several crimes but had not been apprehended. 5.7 per cent had committed homicide; 6.4 per cent rape; 6.2 per cent open stealing; and 6.9 per cent theft of personal property.[29]

Conviction figures for individual crimes were as shown in Table 3.

Profile of Convictions and Sentencing Policy

For statistical purposes convictions are the total number of court judgments which have entered into legal force. On the whole, the patterns and trends reflected in the volume of registered crimes are reproduced at the level of convictions, although there are deviations when the numbers of registered crimes rise and the numbers of convictions fall, and vice versa. The reasons vary: a campaign by internal affairs or procuracy agencies against certain activities; a fall in the detention rate; recourse to non-penal measures of social pressure; redefinitions of crimes; and others.

Particularly evident is the practice of preliminary investigation and inquiry agencies during 1985–9 to make extensive use of Article 5-1(2)-(4) of the Fundamental Principles of Criminal Procedure of the USSR and Union Republics. Those provisions

---

[29] M. A. Alekseeva, in Smirnov, *Prestupnost'*: 81–3.

W. E. BUTLER

TABLE 3   *Conviction Figures for Individual Crimes*

	1980	1985	1989
Intentional homicide	22,176	19,929	17,990
Intentional grave bodily injury	39,388	38,110	32,422
Rape	23,983	22,980	22,305
Open stealing	49,978	55,892	49,882
Assault with intent to rob	23,398	19,989	19,756
Stealing of state or social property	145,653	161,677	126,101
Theft of personal property	163,291	238,171	218.096
Appropriation, waste, abuse of official position	69,858	110,101	79,380
Speculation	29,057	38,459	42,796
Bribery	4,858	7,420	2,632
Narcotics-related crimes	12,763	32,223	18,872
Total crimes registered	1,328,143	1,728,184	1,303,958

enabled the investigative or inquiry agencies to relieve persons who have committed minor crimes from criminal responsibility and apply 'measures of social pressure' without referring the case to a court for trial. In 1985 16 per cent of persons who perpetrated a crime were so treated; in 1988, 37 per cent; and in 1989, 34.6 per cent. The trend is similar in all of the Union republics, and the lower rate of convictions in 1987–9 is partly attributable to this.[30]

In the period 1980–9 the peak year for numbers of convictions was 1984 (1,288,458); the figure for 1989 (684,070) was almost half that. The reduction in numbers of narcotics-related crimes since 1987 is attributed to the introduction of administrative responsibility, and the sharp reduction in female criminality in 1988–9 is to be explained by the decriminalization in 1987 of several constituent elements of crimes concerning the manufacture of strong alcoholic beverages (for which 80,000 women were convicted in 1986).[31]

The actions of investigative agencies in relieving large numbers of persons from criminal responsibility before trial were paralleled in the courts, where from 1985 to 1989 the number of persons sentenced to deprivation of freedom dropped from 45.2 per cent to 35.8 per cent. The courts increased the use of 'conditional punishments' and financial sanctions. For the gravest crimes—intentional homicide, grave bodily injury, rape, and assault with intent to rob—more than 90 per cent were sentenced to deprivation of freedom.

Measures of social pressure usually are assigned by courts to minors aged 14–17, but about half are relieved of criminal responsibility at the pre-judicial stage. In 1989 27,235 minors were sentenced to deprivation of freedom, about half of whom had committed a second offence; the remainder were sentenced for grave crimes committed with force.

Unemployed persons in 1988 accounted for 19.8 per cent of those convicted, down from 22.2 per cent in 1985 but up from 5.5 per cent in 1987. Those who committed a crime while intoxicated comprised 48.7 per cent of convicted persons, up from 37.4 per cent in 1986 and 38.2 per cent in 1987 (the height of the anti-alcohol campaign). In

---

[30] This is also noted in the statistics issued in the *Biulleten' verkhovnogo suda SSSR*, no. 3 (1990): 29–30, for the year 1989.
[31] Z. G. Iakoleva, in Smirnov, *Prestupnost'*: 91.

CRIME IN THE SOVIET UNION

TABLE 4   *Totals of Convicted Persons Sentenced for Various Crimes, 1985 and 1989*

	1985	1989
	1,269,493	684,070
Intentional homicide (and attempts)	18,670	13,178
Grave bodily injuries	34,802	25,208
Rape (and attempts)	22,614	17,199
Hooliganism	161,093	61,323
Stealing of state, social, and personal property	42,483	33,418
Assault with intent to rob	15,797	10,132
Theft of state and social property	132,600	72,581
Theft of personal property	178,218	124,490
Speculation	20,522	10,090
Bribery	5,723	964
Narcotics-related crimes	25,627	12,247
Total acquittals	2,909	5,022

1989, 38.1 per cent of persons convicted had been previously convicted and 27.4 per cent had a previous conviction not expunged from the record or quashed.[32]

The total acquittals figure given is at variance with that released by the USSR Supreme Court. In 1989, with regard to cases in which a preliminary investigation was conducted, the Supreme Court figures show 2,372 acquittals, as opposed to 2,395 in 1988. However, they note that courts sometimes declined to consider a case in substance instead of issuing a judgment of acquittal.[33]

Sentencing problems are reflected in Table 5. No statistics, it should be noted, are given for capital punishment. Presumably 'other punishments' includes that exceptional measure of punishment. The absolute figures for 'other punishments' were 23,105 in 1985 and 4,117 in 1989.

TABLE 5   *Sentences as Percentage of Total Convictions, 1985 and 1989*

	1985	1989
Total convicted (no.)	1,269,493	684,070
Deprivation of freedom	45.2	35.8
Correctional tasks	21.8	23.7
Conditionally	3.8	7.3
Conditionally with obligatory enlistment for labour	8.5	6.8
Specified execution of judgment	9.3	13.1
Fine	9.7	12.7
Other punishments	1.7	0.6

[32] Pursuant to Article 57 of the RSFSR Criminal Code, persons are deemed not to have a record of conviction if they meet the criteria laid down in the Article. This process of quashing a record of conviction, or removing it from the record, is of great importance in connection with definitions of recidivism, employment, and the like.

[33] *Biulleten' verkhovnogo suda SSSR*, no. 3 (1990): 30.

W. E. BUTLER

In a separate release of data, the USSR Ministry of Justice disclosed that in 1989 276 persons were sentenced to the death penalty and that the sentence was commuted for 23. A comparison was drawn with 1985, in which 770 persons were assigned capital punishment, which was commuted in 20 instances. In 1986 the respective figures were 526 (41 commuted); 344 in 1987 (47 commuted); and 271 in 1988 (72 commuted). The courts prescribed capital punishment principally in cases of homicide and rape.[34]

Road Traffic Offences

A car remains one of the prize purchases of every Soviet citizen. Although the waiting list is lengthy, each year more than a million vehicles are added to the stock privately owned in the USSR. By British consumer standards, they are of poor quality: heavy, poorly engineered, not manoeuvrable, and uneconomical. The regulations governing alcohol levels in the bloodstream are categorical—the admissible maximum is 0 per cent.

Road traffic accident statistics are recorded by the internal affairs agencies. The present rules stipulate that accidents in which people are killed or injured are to be recorded as part of state statistics. 'Killed' is defined as persons killed when the accident occurred or who die within seven days thereafter. 'Injured' means people who sustain bodily injuries which require either hospitalization or out-patient treatment. Between 1971, when the current registration procedure was introduced for road traffic accidents, and 1989 more than 900,000 persons have been killed and more than 4.6 million injured.[35]

In 1989 substantial increases in road traffic offences were recorded. The total of such offences increased by 16.9 per cent over 1988; the number killed by 24.3 per cent, and the number injured by 16.76 per cent. Increases were recorded in all union republics except Azerbaijan. Of all accidents where the driver was at fault, 39.8 per cent were not licensed to drive the vehicle they were operating and 22.1 per cent were intoxicated. About 20 per cent of pedestrians who were killed or injured were also intoxicated. In 1989 319,557 accidents were recorded, in which 58,651 persons were killed and 347,402 injured. Table 6 shows a breakdown of types of offences for 1989.

TABLE 6   *Types of Road Traffic Offences Occurring in 1989*

Drivers	
Exceeding speed limit	47,448
Failure to observe traffic signals	6,582
Violation of rules for turning and changing lanes	23,145
Violation of rules for intersections and right of way	24,206
Crossing opposite traffic lane, violating rules for overtaking	39,982
Following too close	7,552
Driving without licence	99,713
Pedestrians	
Jaywalking	32,457
Failure to observe traffic signals	3,895
Unexpected alighting	23,992
Children under age 7 crossing road unaccompanied	3,813

[34] See *The Times*, 18 January 1991, p. 12, cols. 4–6. For a recent discussion of capital punishment, see I. I. Karpets, 'Vysshaia mera. Za i protiv', *Sovetskoe gosudarstvo i pravo*, no. 7 (1991): 49–53.
[35] L. N. Ignatov, in Smirnov, *Prestupnost'*: 98–9.

CRIME IN THE SOVIET UNION

Fire, Safety, and Arson

During 1989, 157,118 fires were registered in the USSR (only fires causing damage of 50 roubles or more are registered). 9,135 persons died in those fires, an increase of 635 over the preceding year, but lower than 1986 when 11,066 persons died. In the USSR as a whole, 10,951 fires were classified as arson, an enormous increase over 1988 when 6,130 were so recorded and 1987 (4,851 so recorded).[36] No separate statistics are given for the number of convictions for arson.

Conclusions

These early glimpses of the official criminal statistics are a welcome exercise in glasnost. Even in this preliminary and incomplete form, they help explain what Soviet criminologists have been talking about in the abstract and why criminal law reforms have pursued their respective courses.

In the Soviet context their scholarly importance is potentially manifold. Since Marxism-Leninism has accepted axiomatically the pre-eminent role of social forms in shaping individual behaviour, the statistical data, especially since 1961 but probably also earlier, should have been the primary empirical base for policy dialogue about the course and efficacy of Soviet criminal policy. Presumably based at least partly on statistical evidence, Soviet criminal law reform, sentencing policies, and correctional labour policies have been adjusted to rectify or produce desired policy objectives. More perhaps than most modern penal systems, the Soviet Union has been well placed to experiment over the years with 'soft' and 'hard' penal policies and measure their respective 'results'. In retrospect, with full data, the findings of those 'experiments' may have general comparative applicability.

The data released require, of course, a great deal more filling out. It is not merely the retrospective statistics which are required. If meaningful comparative analysis is to be attempted, it is imperative that the basis for compiling the data over the years becomes a matter of public record. These will need to be evaluated against the background of law enforcement campaigns of various types launched over the years, and perhaps instructions to investigative and procuracy agencies regarding the disposition of certain types of cases.

The same applies to court statistics. Sentencing patterns may well reflect policy choices regarding deterrence, retribution, and the like. How these signals were communicated to the populace at large, however, without disclosing the data remains a mystery for the moment. The deterrent impact of capital punishment, if such there be, must have been nominal if the use of that exceptional measure was massively greater than the number of instances publicly reported.

Preliminary data released for 1990 showed a still-rising crime rate: 2,786,605 crimes were committed, a 13.2 per cent increase over 1989. Street crime increased by 5.9 per cent. The republics showing greatest rises were Armenia, Estonia, Latvia, Lithuania, and Kirgizstan.[37]

---

[36] A. V. Filatov, in ibid.: 105.
[37] *Izvestiia*, 20 February 1991, p. 6, cols. 1–3.

[7]

Thieves Professing the Code: The Traditional Role of *Vory v Zakone* in Russia's Criminal World and Adaptations to a New Social Reality[1]

JOSEPH D. SERIO and VYACHESLAV RAZINKIN

INTRODUCTION

Vor v zakone (Thief professing the code') occupied a place of great respect and authority in the former Soviet underworld.[2] He was the keeper of the thieves' code (*vorovskoi zakon*) which guided his behavior and that of his followers. Rarely committing crime, he was the organizer of criminal activity and ultimate arbiter of thieves' justice (*vorovskaia spravedlivost'*), settling disputes among groups and fixing sanctions against code violators. This 'godfather' proved himself sufficiently flexible to survive the many changes Soviet society underwent while maintaining the core of his code. Once again, in post-Soviet uncertainty, he is redefining the rules by which he lives in order to ensure his survival in an increasingly competitive atmosphere. Harnessing vast economic and political influence, he will play a major role in the future development of Russia. Internationally, top vory v zakone are becoming more ambitious, establishing extensive criminal networks among the United States, Europe and the former Soviet Union.

HISTORY

The ordinary thief has existed in Russia for centuries, becoming increasingly specialized over time. During the time of Peter the Great (1695–1725), the country was teeming with thieves. On the outskirts of Moscow alone, there were more than 30,000, though level of organization and mutual cooperation was insignificant. They lived apart and ran separate, isolated gangs. 'Thief' at that time simply meant he who takes another's property. During the eighteenth century, however, levels of

Low Intensity Conflict & Law Enforcement, Vol.4, No.1 (Summer 1995), pp.72–88
PUBLISHED BY FRANK CASS, LONDON

organization were increasing as indoctrination into criminal groups, financial contribution as a membership requirement, use of nicknames among criminals and a distinct argot (*fenia*) came into greater use. By the end of the nineteenth century, the criminal world had developed a professional nucleus (*iadro*) and specific divisions of labor with the first signs of a criminal 'boss' emerging.

Predecessors of the *vory v zakone* developed quickly after the Russian Revolution of 1917. In an effort to create instability, chaos and panic, the political enemies of the new state began to draw into their fold traditional professional criminals. However, it was impossible to unite the political and traditional criminals without some degree of assimilation of the former into the criminal world. As a result, the politicals frequently became heads of juvenile criminal groups and eventually took the name 'zhigani'. *Zhigani* borrowed the criminal traditions and customs and adapted them to the new conditions, giving ideological overtones in an effort to disseminate their message to the widest audience possible. This also helped avoid total assimilation into the criminal world. As the 'ideological' opposition to the new state, the *zhigani* developed the following laws, as the specialist S. Ia. Lebedev has noted:

1. Forbidden to work or take part in the work of society
2. Forbidden to have a family (*postoiannaia sem'ia*)
3. Forbidden to take up arms on behalf of the state
4. Forbidden to cooperate with authorities as a witness or victim
5. Obliged to contribute money for the common good.

This was the first stage in the formation of new regulative traditions and customs while traditional attributes (tattoos, jargon, nicknames, gestures) and emotional elements (songs, verses, sayings) of the criminal world remained more or less constant.

Failure to unite internally, however, resulted in conflicting philosophical viewpoints: one that defined 'profession' (traditional criminal) and one that leaned toward 'social status' (*zhigani*). Toward the end of the 1920s and into the 1930s, a leadership crisis developed. The lower rungs of the hierarchy began to disobey the *zhigani* and promoted their own leaders, *urki*. Constant conflict between *urki* and *zhigani* created the need to perfect the code of the underworld. Based on pre-Revolution criminal traditions and customs, a single 'law' was accepted to regulate the behavior of top representatives of the criminal world. By this code, the most authoritative criminals became known as '*vory v zakone*' or 'thieves professing the code'.[3]

Correctional labor camps acted as the medium for further development and swift dissemination of thieves' traditions and customs throughout prison. Having been released from prison, former inmates continued the propagation of the code, attracting greater number of adherents and thus strengthening the *vor*'s authority and promoting group cohesion.

By the time the opening salvos of World War II sounded, *vory v zakone* were a potent force in the Soviet criminal world. The war, however, had a profound effect on the criminal community. Part of the thieves' brotherhood responded to the call to defend the Motherland while others elected to remain in prison, true to their oath. At war's end, those who had violated the code by taking up arms in support of the state attempted to reintegrate into the criminal world. Because of their defection from the criminal ranks, however, they were now considered turncoats or 'bitches' (*suki*) and forbidden to reclaim their authority. This tension among the elite led to the 'bitches war'.

The 'bitches war' (*such'ya voina*) was a battle to the death in prison between criminals adhering to the thieves' law and those who betrayed the code by taking up arms in the name of the state. The 'bitches' introduced an alternative code at the end of World War II that allowed for collaboration with state authorities in an attempt to regain authority they had abandoned during the war. An eyewitness account relates the essence of the conflict: Word had been passed through the prison communication system that the *vor* Viktor 'Goose' Gusev had served at the front. His cell mates confront him.

'Sure I had 'em,' he said. 'Military decorations! They're all marks of the war. Big deal. Almost all of Rokossovsky's army was made out of prison camp convicts like me. No, brothers, I'm no bitch.'

'What's a bitch?' asked one of the petty thieves. He had a bald prominent forehead and they called him Vladimir — or Lenin for short. 'What's a bitch?''

'A bitch?' the Redhead grumbled. 'Anyone who renounces our faith and betrays his own kind.'

'But I didn't betray anyone,' the Goose shot back at him. 'I was in the army, that's all. I fought the enemy!'

'Whose enemy?' Lenin screwed up his eyes.

'What do you mean, whose? The enemies of the Motherland, of the State.'

'This State some friend of yours?'

'No, but there are times when —'

'You listen to me, you bastard,' said Lenin. 'You're a third-time loser already, thanks to that State of yours. You telling me you can't figure it out?'

'Figure what out?'

'The difference,' said Lenin. 'The difference between them and us. If you're in shoulder straps —'

'I haven't been in uniform in a long time!'

'Doesn't matter. I'm speaking generally. About the rules. If you're in shoulder straps, you're not one of us. You're under their rules, not ours. At any moment they could order you to guard the prisoners and you'd do it. If they ordered you to guard the storehouse, you'd guard it. And if, all of a sudden, some thieves decided to get into that storehouse and lift a thing or two, what then? You'd have to shoot them, right? That's the rules!'

'That's all theories,' the Goose muttered, looking around.

'It could happen in the real world.'

'Well, in the real world, I did my shooting at the front, in a war. I don't see what's wrong with that.'

'We do,' Lenin said firmly. 'A real thief doesn't have to serve the authorities. Any authorities!' He moved, raising his voice. 'Am I right?'

'Right!' they answered him.

'Right,' he repeated weightily. 'That's the law.'⁴

Soviet prison authorities attempted to use the 'bitches war' to systematically exterminate certain prisoners at the hands of their criminal colleagues. Warring groups were deliberately placed in the same facility, and the administration did not immediately suppress fights that erupted. The bloodletting became so great that the *vory* were forced to adapt their code to survive. After much debate, they settled on an exception to the rules: thieves had the right, in case of extreme need, to become team leaders and barbers in the camps. A team leader could always save and feed several friends at a time. Barbers had access to sharp-edged objects – razors and scissors – a distinct advantage during the period of intracamp bitch warfare.

In the 1950s some *vory* began to drift from criminal traditions. Prison administrations frequently supported those thought to be leaving the ranks of *vory*, considering their mutiny in a positive light. Using the cover provided by the officials, these criminal elite collected power in their own hands and began to establish their rule over the criminal world. They once again set down the 'law' and fashioned themselves the protectors of criminal tradition and custom. These *vory v zakone* who left the fold and then reclaimed power (known as *otkoloty*) formed new groups and continued to develop their criminal activity. The initial decline in the number of *vory* was misunderstood by law enforcement officials to be the *vor*'s final destruction, the disappearance of traditions, customs and the code.

Law enforcement organs were so convinced that the criminal leaders and their groups had disappeared forever that they practically ceased all work in this area by the 1960s. Despite this belief, there was no evidence that the draconian measures used by the state had been successful. Social and economic conditions of the time actually encouraged an increase in crime and created an ever more important role for the thief. Special meetings (*skhodki*) were held by the *vory v zakone* in various regions of the country – Moscow (1947), Kazan (1955), Krasnodar (1956) – to discuss the development of criminal activity. At the Moscow and Krasnodar meetings, several *vory* were convicted by their fellow Thieves and received the ultimate punishment. In 1979, a major meeting was held in Kislovodsk between *vory v zakone* and the so-called underground shopkeepers (*tsekhoviki*) at which it was decided that the *vory* would take 10 percent of the shopkeepers' illegal income.[5]

Vory – Georgian Style

In 1982 a *skhodka* was held in Tbilisi, Georgia, when *vory* gathered to discuss whether they would move more actively toward gaining political power. Because of the close relationship between the criminal world and state bureaucracy, there already existed ample opportunity for the *vory* to realize their ambitions. Regional government organs were already part of the so-called mafia structures (predominated by state officials). Four years later, the issue was raised again. Wanting to 'play by the rules' as understood at that time, the *vor*, Vaska Brilliant, insisted that his fellow criminal leaders not get involved in politics. Opposing him were *vory* from the Caucasus mountain region, particularly Georgians. The resulting difference of opinion among the *vory* paved the way for Djaby Ioseliani, one of the best known and influential *vory v zakone*, to become Georgian President Eduard Shevardnadze's right hand man, as written sources and an author interview with Volobuev in 1993 indicated. *Vory* have become so popular in Georgia that more than 25 per cent of school children surveyed said they aspired to be *vory v zakone*.

In 1985, the Central Committee of the Georgian Communist Party ordered the law enforcement organs to crack down on *vory v zakone*. To emphasize the importance of this mission, the Central Committee made it clear that officials failing to carry out the assignment would be treated as law breakers themselves and be dealt with accordingly. By the middle of 1986, 52 *vory v zakone* had been imprisoned. However, judges gave them the lightest sentences possible. Whether they saw the futility of the exercise, lacked legislative support (there was no law under which one could be punished for being a *vor v zakone*) or felt pressure from either the criminal world or perhaps from *vory* protectors in the party apparatus is not clear. Four *vory* were imprisoned for violating probation; 9 for being vagrants and leading other forms of 'parasitic lifestyles'; 14 for illegal possession or storage of arms and ammunition; 19 for drug dealing and 6 for various illegal activities. None was arrested for his organizational role in the commission of crime. In any case, it was difficult to effectively prevent *vory* from plying their trade since they could easily continue from their prison cells. Moreover, this particular operation caused even further dissemination of thieves' traditions as many Georgian *vory* went to work in other parts of the Soviet Union until pressure from law enforcement had subsided.

It is important to note certain differences between Russian and Georgian *vory*. Although the Russians have altered their code several times since World War II, they have tended to follow basic tenets such as no cooperation with state authorities, adherence to established procedure for 'crowning' new *vory*, dissemination of thieves' code to attract juveniles and make financial contributions to the support fund. Georgians, who make up 31.6 percent of the 'Soviet' *vory* population (to the Russian 33.1 percent), developed their position among *vory v zakone* in the 1970s. Theirs is not a deeply ingrained tradition, and, in general, they grew up according to societal norms vastly different from those of the Russians. Strongly rooted in extended family and clan relationships, Georgians are likely to derive support from and engage in crime with blood relations or lifelong friends rather than a criminal brotherhood of unrelated members.

In addition, money figures more prominently in the acquisition of the *vor*'s title among Georgians than Russians. Members of the Georgian criminal world are known to have bought their respected position rather than have lived according to the code. For this reason, some underworld figures and law enforcement officials do not consider them authentic *vory v zakone*. There was among Russians, until recently, a directly proportional relationship between prison time served and level of respect in the criminal community. With the proper amount of money, Georgians could avoid prison time and be counted among the *vory*. Thus, one may find a 20-year-old Georgian *vor*, but one would be hard pressed to find one among the Russians.

THE CODE

By tradition, *vory v zakone* scorned everything associated with 'normal' society, thus it was not surprising to find that prison had been the only place the thief called home; freedom was thought to be temporary, as 'the Georgian' indicated to one of the authors in a 1991 interview). Prison was not necessarily dishonorable or detrimental to criminal activities; it actually served to strengthen a thief's reputation. Sentence duration and respect seemed directly proportional. His code forbade him to engage in prison work under any circumstances, which still holds true should a *vor* be convicted. It is incumbent on the inmates to assume prison duties of the *vor* if necessary. For his part, the *vor* had to accept any punishment given by the prison administration for refusing to work. For the most influential of *vory*, the threat of punishment by the administration was not realistic for, in many cases, it was the *vor* who would control the prison facility. In this case, continuing criminal activity from a prison cell was not difficult. The thief could arrange a private room with a television and inter-prison telephone at his bedside. It was possible to arrange calls to virtually any part of the country or even overseas.

Some activities are looked upon as collaboration with the prison administration and thus forbidden by the code. These included informing on other inmates; accepting leadership positions in prison with the support of the administration; participating in the construction of isolation cells or compounds: taking up arms or any other activity that may be interpreted as cooperating with the government or prison administration. The *vor* was permitted contact with law enforcement officials only if such meetings furthered the *vor*'s interests without assisting law enforcement.

The dramatic events in the former Soviet Union have changed the *vor*'s attitude toward prison. If before it was a badge of honor and legitimacy to have spent most of one's life in prison, now the *vor* strives to stay out of prison, considering even a single day behind bars unacceptable. The traditional symbols of the *vor*, such as extensive body tattoos, are being forsaken. Clean-shaven, donning the finest clothes, driving foreign cars and owning three or four of the best apartments available, *vory* are openly enjoying the fruits of their labor. (One Georgian *vor* has suits flown in from Paris for his choosing.) This is in contrast to the traditional code according to which thieves were not permitted to have an apartment or house (a practice noted by 'the Georgian' in his 1991 interview).

One aspect of the traditional code that retains its weight is punishment for anyone who insults a *vor*. Assaults on the physical integrity or authority of the *vor* must be answered with a harsh and timely response. For example, if someone hits the *vor*, thus insulting his honor, the offender must be killed (author interview with 'the Georgian', 1991). In 1989, the *vor*, Sultan, and his associate, Avil, were at a Moscow restaurant when a crowd of young men at the next table became noisy. Sultan introduced himself and requested a quieter tone. Put out by the request, one of the men hit Sultan. The next day Avil, carrying out the proper punishment, returned to the restaurant and killed the offender. The *vor* 'Sasha', arrested for theft when he was sixteen years old, was still in prison eighteen years later for, among other things, murdering a fellow inmate who insulted his honor (author interview with 'Sasha' in prison, 1991).

Vory v zakone strive to attract as many juveniles as possible into their sphere of influence which has become easier with the breakdown of social institutions and rapidly rising inflation. A common mistake among researchers is to attribute the current instability among the criminal elite to up-and-coming juveniles who refuse to bow to traditions. While there certainly are young criminals who are in competition with the *vory*, the latter still control vast numbers of juveniles across the former Soviet Union.

Traditional code of vory v zakone

1. A thief must turn his back on his family – mother, father, brothers, sisters...the criminal community is family.
2. It is forbidden to have a family – wife, children.
3. It is forbidden to work; a thief must live off the fruits of criminal activity only.
4. A thief must give moral and material assistance to other thieves using the *obshchak* (money fund).
5. A thief must give information about accomplices and their whereabouts (e.g. locations of hideouts) only in the strictest confidentiality.
6. If a thief is under investigation, a petty thief must take responsibility upon himself to give the suspected thief time to flee.
7. When a conflict arises in a criminal group or among thieves, there must be a meeting (*skhodka*) to resolve the issue.
8. When necessary, a thief must attend a meeting (*skhodka*) to judge another thief if his conduct or behavior comes into question.
9. Punishment for a thief decided by the meeting must be carried out.
10. A thief must be proficient in criminals' jargon (*fenia*).
11. A thief must not enter a card game if he does not have the money to pay.
12. A thief must teach his craft to novice thieves.
13. A thief should keep a gofer (*shestiorka*) under his influence.
14. A thief must not lose his sense when drinking alcohol.
15. A thief must not in any way become involved with the authorities; a thief must not participate in social activities; a thief must not join social organizations;

16. A thief must not take up weapons from the hands of state authority; a thief must not serve in the army;

17. A thief must fulfill all promises made to other thieves.

BASIC FUNCTIONS OF *VORY V ZAKONE*

In general terms, *vory v zakone* must fulfill four basic functions in order to maintain effective leadership in the criminal world: the information function, organization function, normative-regulatory function, and a decision making function.

Information

Vory v zakone oversee the collection, analysis and evaluation of information on a wide range of topics including those regarding specific individuals, events, and rules of both the criminal world and those of law enforcement, including those developed by prison administrations. Like any good manager, the *vor* must stay apprised of changing conditions around him while making decisions that will affect the future of the groups under his influence. This is necessary for regulation of internal and inter-group relations and the successful execution of illegal activities by the groups.

Organization

While the information function of the *vor* can be critical to the success of his groups, no less important is the actual planning of the operation and delegation of responsibilities to group members, as well as control of their fulfillment. Given the idiosyncrasies of group dynamics and varying talent of members, it is reasonable to assume flexibility in the hierarchical structure and division of labor within groups, in contrast to the views of many scholars who assert that groups observe a 'strict' hierarchical arrangement and internal discipline. In any event, the *vor* must be competent enough to marshal his forces effectively in the execution of criminal activity. Successful acquisition of benefits – material or otherwise – for his groups is the ultimate measure of the *vor*'s talent. Failure in this can result in a loss of credibility.

Regulatory

An important aspect of the thief's functions is development and maintenance of a mechanism to perpetuate groups even if the head is in some manner unable to continue in his role. One method is the dissemination of criminal ideology and the romanticizing of criminal life, aimed particularly at juveniles and newly convicted individuals. This may prove easier within the confines of prison as the targets of the propaganda have few opportunities to avoid members of a given group or its leader. As social and economic conditions in the former Soviet Union worsen, the attractiveness of the criminal milieu will likely persuade increasing numbers of disaffected youth to choose a life of crime.

The *vor* is responsible for the maintenance of thieves' law among members of his groups. Rules and sanctions for their violation must be clearly stated and punishment decisive. Failure to maintain at least an appearance of control can be detrimental to the credibility of the *vor*. Insult to the *vor* or infringement on his authority can result in stiff penalties (as mentioned above).

Further, the *vor* is charged with regulating inter-group relations, holding the interests of the groups under his influence in the fore. In prison, this means providing protection for every convict who works to strengthen the leader's authority. In freedom, meeting with other *vory* is essential in attempt to avoid misunderstanding and conflict of interests.

Decision-Making

The decision-making function is fundamental and encompasses virtually all activities of the *vor*. As leader, he must bear responsibility for the 'correctness' of his decisions, and their accordance with norms and rules disseminated among criminals. The choice of correct decisions and the successful fulfillment of directives naturally serve to strengthen his authority.

Common Monetary Fund

One of the most important tasks assumed by the *vor* is maintenance of a monetary fund (*obshchaia kassa*, or *obshchak*) for the material well-being of the groups. The *obshchak* serves several purposes. First, the size of the fund gives corresponding authority to the particular *vor*, and, hence, to his groups, both within prison and in the wider criminal milieu. Second, within prison, *obshchak* funds are used in attempts to bribe administration officials; outside, the funds are used to buy state officials and others. Third, funds are used in the acquisition of foodstuffs as well as alcohol and narcotics for the prison community. Fourth, money is allocated for planning and perpetrating new crimes. Fifth, the *obshchak* makes possible financial assistance to families of imprisoned group members.

One Soviet scholar attempted to estimate the portion of *obshchak* moneys dedicated to each of these activities. Assistance to families of imprisoned group members, for example, consumed some 22 percent of the funds, 26 percent to the preparation of new crimes, and 30 percent went to loan sharking. This scholar, however, does not indicate how he reached these figures. Others estimate that from 30–50 percent of *obshchak* funds are used to bribe officials (according to G.F. Chebotarev in a 1992 interview).

The *obshchak* is maintained through three main avenues: profits from criminal activity, a 'tax' levied on criminals violating traditions and norms of the criminal world and contributions to the *obshchak* from associated groups.

THE STRUCTURE

Vory v zakone are believed to occupy the highest level of the criminal hierarchy, although there are opinions that they are found at lower rungs of the so-called criminal pyramid and answerable to a higher authority. This, however, does not seem likely as the *vor* is, in prison, essentially the master of his environment and, in freedom, influences hundreds of criminal groups over vast stretches of territory. Examples of the latter are Evgeny Petrovich Vasin ('Jam' – controlling the Russian Far East), Vyacheslav Kirillovich Ivankov ('Yaponchik' – the Soviet Union's most influential *vor*, based in New York, and recently arrested there), Otari Kvantrishvili (most powerful *vor* in Moscow until his murder in April 1994) and many others.

There is a distinction made in the Russian language between 'leaders' (*lideri*) and 'thieves professing the code' (*vory v zakone*). According to official statistics, there are approximately 20,000 leaders of criminal groups while *vory* currently number less than 400 in Russia (more than 700 in the former Soviet Union). Based on these figures and the overall role of the *vory*, it is reasonable to assume that in the criminal world it is the leaders who answer to the *vory*.[6] This is supported by A. I. Gurov when he refers to the *vory* as 'supermen...big-time mafiosi, leaders of criminal communities', a point he made in a 1991 interview with one of the authors.

The *vor* has a trusted advisor (*sovetnik*) who is adept at working the prison system. The advisor well knows the situation in the prison, its internal procedures and vulnerable points. He helps establish channels to 'import' forbidden goods into the prison, such as liquor, narcotics and women. one of the most important functions of the *vor*. His advice is important in the *vor*'s decision making regarding future group activities.

This holds true outside the prison environment as well.

The level below the *sovetnik* is the 'supply group' (*gruppa obespechenie*). Members of this level carry full responsibility for organization, storage and use of general supplies and the common monetary fund. As a rule, they enjoy close relations with the *vor*. In prison, group members attempt to protect members of the supply group from encroachment by surrounding convicts or the prison administration.

The next level is the 'security group' (*gruppa bezopasnosti*). These individuals are responsible for the more physically challenging administrative activities of the group. They extract debts and collect moneys for the support of the common fund as well as protect members of the group. In prison, they oversee punishment of non-productive convicts who are under the influence of the *vor*. Frequently, former athletes are used because of their strength and are referred to as 'pit bulls' or 'torpedoes'.

The next level is occupied by the *shestiorka*, the bag man, errand boy or other group 'gofer'. These members are usually recruited from among those convicts having a material or psychological dependence on the groups.

As in any organization, the criminal group demonstrates its hierarchy in part by the perquisites bestowed on its members. For example, in prison, group hierarchy is usually demonstrated in individual prison cells. The *vor* occupies the most comfortable space in the cell usually near the window, away from the door and the communal toilet (*parasha*). It is symbolically important for the *vor* to maintain his distance from the toilet as part of his efforts to maintain a base of authority. As 'the Georgian' indicated in a 1991 interview with one of the authors, the space near the communal toilet is reserved for the 'small fry' and homosexuals, 'for this is where shame resides'.

CURRENT DEVELOPMENTS IN THE THIEVES' WORLD

There are currently 387 *vory v zakone* based in Russia, 100 of whom are serving prison sentences. (There are an additional 339 from other republics of the former Soviet Union who frequently operate on Russian territory.) Two-thirds of this criminal elite are Russians (33.1%) and Georgians (31.6%); the remaining are Armenians (8.2%), Azerbaijanis (5.2%), Uzbeks, Ukrainians, Kazakhs, Abkhazi and others (21.9%). The highest concentrations of *vory* are found in Moscow region, where 10 were arrested in 1993.

That year the Russian Ministry of Internal Affairs (MVD) detained 45 *vory* for organizing and committing crimes. Of these, 20 were convicted.

Because *vory* act as organizers or 'inspiration' for crime rather than actually participating, lack of appropriate legislation hinders their prosecution.

Contrary to the belief that *vory v zakone* are a dying breed, this criminal elite is adapting its way of life to the vast changes that the former Soviet Union has undergone. First, they continue to welcome new *vory* into their ranks. In the first six months of 1994, 16 candidates were given the title as opposed to only 11 in all of 1993. For the past three years, some 35 new *vory* have been 'crowned'. Because of the highly secretive nature of coronation ceremonies, it is likely that law enforcement officials do not know the true extent of the criminal elite.

Second, their age range would indicate a fairly high vitality: 85.6 percent of the *vory* are between 30 and 40 years of age, while only three are known to be between 60 and 65 and one is 73. Several are between 22 and 25 years old. In February 1994 organized crime officers detained one Georgian *vor v zakone*, nicknamed 'Mishel', who was born in 1972.

Third, dissemination of so-called thieves' ideology, especially among juveniles, is continuing apace. Juveniles are a particularly vulnerable group given the breakdown of Russian social organizations, lack of law enforcement resources to counter juvenile crime and worsening economic conditions. The tremendous increase in the number and ambition of young criminals has led some researchers to conclude that the newcomers will not respect the role of the *vory* and thus cause a great decline in *vory* influence. While there are certainly juveniles who reject the authority of the thief, many take advantage of the protection and stability provided by the *vory*. In addition, *vory* will not simply allow their power to be usurped. The *vor v zakone* Abrek is reported to have said, 'Explain to the youngsters – they have no idea how to behave themselves. They have their own laws; there can be none of that. They live in our house where there is a single law.'

Fourth, *vory v zakone* are making impressive territorial gains. In the past decade, significant dissemination of thieves' traditions has been noted throughout Russia, particularly in the Far East, Siberia and in the Ural Mountain Region. In the 1990s other regions have fallen under the influence of *vory*: Pskov, Omsk, Smolensk, Buryatia and others. According to police officials, the St. Petersburg criminal world never acknowledged the traditions of the *vory v zakone*. In 1993 the *vor* Yakutyonok from Perm began to bring several major St. Petersburg criminal groups under his tutelage. The Georgian *vory* 'Tomaz', 'Avto' and 'Nugzara' were detained there for their role in the extortion of several million rubles from a wealthy Georgian businessman. Though there was previously thought to be one or two *vory* operating in St. Petersburg, as of

September 1994 the total known to law enforcement officials was nine.

Likewise, in 1992–93 *vory v zakone* successfully took control of criminal groups in Astrakhan, Yaroslavl, Kaluga, Kostroma, Tambov and several other regions. Traditionally, *vory* are very active in Krasnodar, Khabarovsk and Primorsky territories as well as Rostov, Irkutsk, Amur and Tiumen regions. One location that has attracted the attention of *vory v zakone* is Sakhalin. In the past two years, 30 *vory v zakone*, including the powerful 'Jam', 'Arsen' and 'Dato', have gone to inspect the island's usefulness as a transit point for narcotics trafficking and stolen automobiles as well as money laundering. Economically weak, Sakhalin is a prime location for investing *obshchak* moneys to develop real estate and industry. It has also been useful in establishing contacts with Japanese organized crime groups.

Fifth, *vory v zakone* are actively moving into the international realm. The legendary *vor*, Vyacheslav Kirillovich Ivankov ('Yaponchik'), known throughout the former Soviet Union as 'the father of extortion', until his arrest earlier this year operated out of New York, building networks between Russia and the United States. One of his close colleagues, 'Taiwanchik', who had been operating out of Germany, is said to have recently gone to the United States because of mounting pressure by German law enforcement. 'Macintosh', allegedly one of the founders of a major Moscow bank, is reported to be in the United States and intends to have several associates join him there. In addition, 50 *vory v zakone* are said to be based in Vienna from where they oversee operations back in Russia.

These gains have not been made without losses to the criminal elite. In the past two years, more than 20 *vory v zakone* have been murdered, including the most influential of the Soviet underworld: Otari Vitalievich Kvantrishvili ('Otarik') – a Georgian *vor v zakone* believed to have been the most powerful crime figure in Moscow who maintained a high profile and was becoming increasingly involved in politics; Sultan Daudov – said to have been the only *vor v zakone* recognized by the Chechen crime community; and Givi Mikhailovich Beradze ('Scarface') – an influential Georgian *vor* based in Moscow. Attempts have been made on many others as well. Andrei 'Signature' Isaev was shot in Moscow (and was said to have turned up at a New Jersey hospital to recuperate).

Some have claimed the wave of murders to be a concerted effort by the Ministry of Internal Affairs to wipe out the *vory* community. Understandably, top officials give no credence to this theory. Given the traditional role of the *vory* in maintaining order over the criminal world, such a policy would not seem to be in law enforcement's interests. More likely the reasons vary widely: revenge motive, disputes over money,

86   LOW INTENSITY CONFLICT & LAW ENFORCEMENT

competition between *vory* and state officials and the rise of young criminals who dismiss thieves' traditions.

Vory v zakone are but one set of actors in the extremely complicated and dangerous struggle for Russia. They are expanding their influence over vast territories and diversifying their activities, infiltrating legitimate commercial spheres particularly banking, import-export, real estate and the auto and entertainment industries while continuing to develop traditional criminal activities such as extortion, bribery, narcotics trafficking and bank fraud. If successful in their bid for continued influence, the consequences could be significant.

NOTES

1. This article is based on a number of most instructive sources, both written and oral. Written sources upon which the authors have relied most heavily include: Iu. M. Antonian, *Osobo opasnye lidery v ITU i vospitatel'noe vozdeistvie na nikh* [*Particularly Dangerous Leaders in Prison and How to Reform Them*], Moscow: Vsesoiuznyi nauchno-issledovatel'skii institut, MVD SSSR, 1989; *Bor'ba s organizovannoi prestupnost'iu: problemy teorii i praktiki* [*Combating Organized Crime: Problems of Theory and Practice*], Moscow, Akademiia Ministerstva Vnutrennikh Del SSSR, 1990; A. I. Dolgova (ed.), *Organizovannaia prestupnost'* [*Organized Crime*], Moscow: Iuridicheskaia Literatura, 1989; M. Dyomin, *The Day is Born of Darkness* New York, Alfred A. Knopf, 1976; A. I. Gurov, *Professional'naia prestupnost'* [*Professional Crime*], Moscow: Iuridicheskaia Literatura, 1990; S. Ia. Lebedev, *Antiobshchestvennye traditsii, obychai i ikh vliianie na prestupnost'* [*Antisocial Traditions, Customs and Their Influence on Crime*], Omsk, Vysshaia Shkola Militsii (Militia Higher School), MVD, SSSR, 1989; G. Podlesskikh and A. Tereshonok, *Vory v zakone: brosok k vlasti* [*Thieves Professing the Code: Striving for Power*], Moscow: Khudozhestvennaia Literatura, 1994; and J. Rossi, *The Gulag Handbook*, New York, Paragon House, 1989. Interviews include those conducted with G.F. Chebotarev, deputy head of the Sixth Department for Organized Crime Control of the Ministry of Internal Affairs, USSR; 'The Georgian', former athlete turned businessman who had many close ties to the Georgian underworld; A.I. Gurov, head of the Sixth Department for Organized Crime Control of the Ministry of Internal Affairs, USSR; 'Sasha', *vor v zakone* serving a sentence in a Russian prison; and A.N. Volobuev, pioneer in the research of organized crime in the Soviet Union.
2. The Russian title *vor v zakone* is frequently rendered in English as 'thief in law' which is the literal translation (see S. Handelman in 'The Russian Mafia' *Foreign Affairs*, vol. 73, No.2, p. 86, and K. Fireman in *Newsday*, 'Moscow's Latest Menace: Mob Hits', 16 May 1994, A15. S. Erlanger, 'A Slaying Puts Russian Underworld on Parade' *New York Times*, 14 April 1994). This, however, says little to the reader. I prefer 'thief professing the code', which is somewhat more indicative of his role.
3. Gurov confirms that the title *vor v zakone* is not to be found among pre-revolution studies, and believes its emergence to come at the beginning of the 1930s (Gurov, p. 108).
4. See Dyomin, *The Day is Born of Darkness*.
5. *Tsekhoviki* supplied the black market with goods of higher quality than those being produced for the state market. The Soviet Union could claim many millionaires long before official steps were taken toward the transition to a 'market economy'.
6. Most statistics in the former Soviet Union should be handled with care, particularly those regarding crime. The figure of 20,000 criminal leaders came from Volobuev who confirmed that he did not use a very scientific method in arriving at that figure. He said it could be 10,000, it could be 40,000. Chebotarev claims that the number of *vory* is fairly accurate since the MVD keeps close track of all of them.

APPENDIX A

Thieves' Song

I'm the son of a man from the underground,
A worker, a Party man.
My father loved me, I treasured him,
But consumption laid him down.
And so, without a father to support me,
I left home and went to the street,
And the street turned me into a thief,
And I soon was behind prison bars.
I began to wander, with a plan and without one,
And five times I landed in jail.
And in '33, with the canal completed,
I decided to leave the thieves' life behind
And cut all my criminal ties.
I arrived in town; I've forgotten its name,
I decided on factory work.
And they told me: oh, dear, a record. What's this?
Please be sure to forget our address!
I trampled that canal release underfoot
And went out into the street again.
And the criminal life took me back in its arms
And once again I was back behind bars,
And going the rounds of the camps.
Bars and bunks, year in, year out,
Year in, year out, the same.
Ah, how hard it is to turn a new leaf
When the State won't come to your aid!
Deportation, deportation, cattle cars,
Once again, we're bound God knows where,
And with each day, and with each stop,
The taiga grows drearier, and all my hopes drop.

APPENDIX B
PROFILE OF A *VOR*
OTARI VITALIEVICH ('OTARIK') KVANTRISHVILI

On 5 April, 1994, three bullets from a sniper's gun brought down Otari Kvantrishvili, said by Russian law enforcement officials to be Moscow's top criminal figure (author interview with Chebotarev, May 1994). Attending his funeral was a virtual who's who of Russian society: entertainers, law enforcement officers, government officials, athletes. Flowers from veterans of the Afghan War, major Moscow banks and social organizations smothered his graveside as foreign-made luxury automobiles tied up traffic around the cemetery for hours. His story is important not only because of the role he played in the criminal world, but as an illustration of the extnesive interweaving of the underworld with the 'legitimate' world.

The Georgian *vor* got his start in the late 1960s in the infamous criminal group led by 'Mongol', perhaps the best-known criminal organization of the day. ('Yaponchik' received his criminal credentials in this same group.) In the early days, Kvantrishvili was a petty criminal, starting his career with gambling and card playing and eventually engaging in relatively minor hard currency frauds in special state stores in which only foreign currency was accepted (author interview with Kvantrishvili acquaintance, 1994; see Odinokova, p.6–7). In 1966 he was charged with rape but was released immediately, diagnosed as a schizophrenic, a common method of avoiding prison. Unlike many Russian *vory v zakone* who worked their way up the ciminal ranks and usually spent more than half their lives in prison, Kvantrishvili gained influence in part thanks to the vast contacts he made as a wrestling coach for the police team, Dynamo. As a result, Kvantrishvili developed close contacts with many police officials and was suspected of having been an MVD informant and perhaps even a KGB informant (author interview with Kvantrishvili acquaintance, 1994).

This is only one of many speculations made about Kvantrishvili. He seems to have befriended at one time or other representatives from every corner of society. As chairman of the Lev Yashin Fund for the Support of Athletes, Kvantrishvili attracted all types of athletes, in particular boxers, wrestlers and martial arts specialists, some of whom would find themselves in such criminal groups as Baumansky, Liuberetsky, Domodedovsky and Balashikhinsky, over which Kvantrishvili was said to have had considerable influence.

As vice president of a high profile 'charitable organization', Kvantrishvili had many business and government associates. The organization's president had traveled with Gorbachev to Europe to conclude contracts with Italian companies. A Russian business daily published an interview with the president of the organization, during which journalists presented rumours that his organization 'controls the most powerful mafiosi structures in Moscow' (*Kommersant*, 'Assotsiatsiia XXI vek: "Mafiia – eto ne k nam!"' Oleg Utitsin, Mikhail Mikhailin, p.29, No.45, 7–13 December 1992).

Another of the organization's vice presidents, and one of Russia's most popular singers, headed Kvantrishvili's funeral, assisting the mourning widow. Such public figures, generating credibility and legitimacy, frequently help top criminals to make inroads in society as a whole. Coincidentally, the singer travels to New York on occasion where 'Yaponchik', the most notorious of all Russian *vory* and longtime associate of Kvantrishvili, resides. In addition to 'Yaponchik', Kvantrishvili was said to have had close relations with underworld boss Kuchuloria ('Piso'), who died in 1988, and Bagdasarian ('Svo'), who passed away last year.

As there was much speculation about his life, so was there about his death. In the months prior to his murder, the Georgian godfather appeard on television with increasing frequency, developing a high profile, mingling with society. Hardened criminals came to see him as a 'clown', no longer respecting his authority, though it is unlikely that they ordered the contract.

Some police officials believed that the Chechen community had organized the murder, stating that it was the only group able to raise the several million dollars needed for the job (author interview with MVD official, May 1994). The Chechen community had clashed with the Kvantrishvili family before when, in August 1993, they gunned down Otari's elder brother, Amiran, when he tried to collect 'protection' money from an unwilling client. It is doubtful, however, that the Chechens were the only group with access to the necessary financial resources, particularly considering the vast amounts of money that have been made in Russia in the past several years. Also, there is no evidence indicating that the Chechens specially targeted the Kvantrishvilis.

Kvantrishvili is said to have indirectly owned several Moscow casinos, controlled many hotels and restaurants and generally influenced hundreds of criminals, business and government officials. Some observers point to the government as the likely source of the contract because of Kvantrishvili's growing power in Moscow business and politics. One cannot rule out the MVD or the KGB as possible hitmen given the speculation that Otari was an informant for one or both of these agencies.

Another possibility is that the fatal bullets came from up-and-coming criminal groups who do not acknowledge the authority of *vory v zakone* and wanted to flex their new found muscle.

It will in all likelihood never be known who ordered Kvantrishvili's murder as the list of potential candidates is endless. In life and in death, Otari Kvantrishvili demonstrated the degree to which the upperworld and the underworld are deeply intertwined in the former Soviet Union.

[8]

The Russian 'Mafiya'

Stephen Handelman

POLITICS BY OTHER MEANS

ORGANIZED CRIME IS the most explosive force to emerge from the wreckage of Soviet communism. The so-called Russian mafiya has undermined reform, spawned extraordinary levels of violence in major cities, and helped fuel a growing ultranationalist backlash. Although it is considerably less organized than its Western counterparts, and for that reason often misunderstood or underestimated in the West, Russia's crime syndicate constitutes a serious threat to post-Soviet democracy.

The "mafiya," Russian-style, is a hydra-headed phenomenon that feeds on the emerging market economy. Between 3,000 and 4,000 gangs operate in Russia, including several hundred whose activities span the territory of the Commonwealth of Independent States and cross the old Soviet borders into Central Europe and the West.

The definition of Russian organized crime is sometimes stretched for domestic political purposes. Police and politicians still fall into the Soviet habit of ascribing mafiya connections to anyone who possesses what seems an unreasonable amount of money. Total active gang membership in Russia is estimated at less than 100,000 people. Nevertheless, the hazy boundary between criminal and legal business activity has allowed mafiya groups to penetrate most areas of the Russian economy, giving them disproportionate influence.

STEPHEN HANDELMAN, a Visiting Scholar at Columbia University's Harriman Institute, was Moscow Bureau Chief of *The Toronto Star* from 1987 to 1992. He is completing a book on Russian crime.

Stephen Handelman

According to the Russian Ministry of Internal Affairs (MVD), organized crime controlled as much as 40 percent of the turnover in goods and services by 1993. Few entrepreneurs can expect to remain in business for long without being asked to pay money or provide shares in their companies to gun-toting "protectors." In the absence of government regulation, criminal cartels have infiltrated banks, real estate markets, stock exchanges and even the rock music industry. Meanwhile, more traditional criminal pursuits have transformed the economy of regions like Central Asia, which is fast becoming the newest hub of the world narcotics trade. Most unsettling of all, perhaps, is the involvement of organized crime groups in the marketing of stolen Red Army weapons, which then turn up in the ethnic quarrels on Russia's southern borders.

What makes the Russian mafiya distinctively menacing is its connection to key sections of the government bureaucracy.[1] No criminal enterprise of this complexity could have succeeded without the support and encouragement of officials at every level. According to government investigators, more than half the country's criminal groups in 1992 had ties to government. A number of cartels are fronts for the former Soviet elites—the "nomenklatura capitalists," who have shed their party cards en route to becoming wealthy monopoly financiers. Mounting evidence indicates that nomenklatura capitalists use organized crime groups as instruments in the fierce struggle over the spoils of the former Soviet Union: the industries, banks, defense facilities, ports and factories once exclusively controlled by the Communist Party.

In one notorious 1992 case, Chechen mobsters were intercepted in an attempt to swindle about $350 million from private banks in Moscow and other cities by using promissory notes, a form of interbank transfer inherited from the Soviet era. Four employees of the Russian State Bank were later accused of supplying the false promissory notes to the Chechens in return for a cut of the profits.

---

[1] I have spelled "mafiya" using its Russian phonetic translation in order to distinguish it from its Western counterpart. All figures cited in this article, except where otherwise noted, come from the Russian Ministry of Internal Affairs. Since facts about organized crime are still largely unpublished, much of the material presented here is based on private interviews with leading police officials, politicians and gangsters themselves.

Is America's past Russia's future?

Profit may not have been their only motive. The president of the country's largest commercial banking association believes the inspiration for the swindle came from senior Finance Ministry officials determined to undercut private commercial banking activity. Crime in the post-Soviet era, in other words, is often a continuation of politics by other means.

THE GREENING OF RED GANGS

To UNDERSTAND THE Russian mafiya's role in the nation's political wars, a brief look back is useful. Russia's criminal underworld has an impressive history. Societies of smugglers, thieves and highwaymen existed on the margins of national life for centuries. In the late tsarist era, outlaw bands were glamorous symbols of struggle against

Stephen Handelman

landowners and the oppressive state. The traditional gang structure, fortified by a code of honor and rituals that discouraged outsiders, became a model for the early Bolshevik clandestine organizations.

The future founders of the Soviet state not only admired the gangs' antiestablishment ethos. They also secured employment for them in the revolution. Bandits were recruited for so-called expropriations— bank heists and kidnappings—carried out in order to raise funds. The young Josef Stalin counted gang leaders among his closest associates, eventually recruiting some of them into his secret police. After the establishment of Soviet power, members of the criminal underworld were used as enforcers and informers against political dissidents in the gulag prison system.

But the most profitable form of cooperation emerged in the 1960s with the rise of the black market. Soviet gangsters acted as unofficial middlemen in the "gray" and "black" economies, circulating privately produced goods or state materials with the tacit cooperation of factory managers and apparatchiks. At the same time, the archaic structure of the old Russian gang began to change. Large criminal organizations surfaced in many Russian cities, led by mob chieftains known as *vory v zakonye* (thieves in law), who ran the equivalent of territorial monopolies in trade. As traditional underworld proscriptions against involvement with authorities weakened, many mob leaders began to operate in tandem with government officials in their regions. By the close of the Soviet era, more than 600 *vory* populated the length and breadth of the Soviet Union.

Communist authorities themselves, however, took second place to no one in criminal behavior. During the 1970s and 1980s, scandals such as the Cotton Affair, in which party bosses in Uzbekistan raked in huge profits by falsifying production reports, revealed a previously unsuspected talent for larceny beneath the puritanical exterior of the Soviet leadership. Russians first began to use the word "mafiya" in those decades to describe the vast networks of corruption lurking inside regional and central ministries.

Perestroika did little to break the power of these networks. In fact, it brought various criminal strands of Soviet life together. "Perestroika was the real beginning of organized crime in our coun-

The Russian 'Mafiya'

try," said one senior MVD investigator, a comment others repeated dozens of times. The secret wealth accumulated by underground tycoons and party barons found a legitimate outlet when the government expanded the permissible area of private commerce. Black and gray money poured into the stock exchanges, joint ventures, cooperatives, banks and joint stock companies that were otherwise celebrated abroad as harbingers of economic reform. At the same time, party bodies (and the KGB) quietly siphoned funds to trading companies and export-import firms that were being positioned to take advantage of the widely anticipated new era of "market socialism." Russian entrepreneurs who tried to operate by the rules found it impossible to survive in the face of both official and criminal competition. By the late 1980s, according to Russian analysts, the majority of small cooperative businesses established during perestroika was either controlled by or heavily in debt to criminal elements.

> Unbridled capitalism, organized crime and official chicanery have produced a crisis of governance.

The stage was thus set for the shifting alliances and violent struggles that have come to characterize modern Russian organized crime. Russian mobsters have been as unwilling as their political counterparts to abide by the rules of compromise and consensus required of large organizations. This diffusion of mafiya power across the country has had a devastating effect. Gangland murders, bomb explosions, kidnappings and gun battles have become part of daily life in dozens of Russian cities. This increased violence has been the most visible sign of underworld competition for a stake in the new economy—and of a criminal sophistication beyond anything seen before in Russia.

The Russian gang is arguably the only Soviet institution that benefited from the collapse of the U.S.S.R. Once the powerful party machine that administered the old empire fell apart, the 15 new nations that emerged represented easy pickings for criminals who perceived the entire Eurasian continent as their natural domain. For instance, the smuggling trade flourished as enormous quantities of copper, zinc and other strategic metals were shipped

Stephen Handelman

from central Russia in unmarked trucks or military aircraft to
Baltic ports and then to Scandinavia or Western Europe. The
smugglers took brilliant advantage of the Commonwealth clash of
sovereignties: products stolen from a Russian factory were
regarded as legal goods the moment they left Russia's borders. So
much illicit metal from Russian defense factories passed through
Estonia on its way overseas—an estimated half a million dollars'
worth a day in 1992—that the tiny Baltic republic earned the distinction of being one of the world's largest exporters of finished
metal without operating a single metal plant.

Smuggling profits have formed the foundation of postcommu-
nist mafiya wealth and the basis for the working cooperation
between criminals and the nomenklatura. By the time Commonwealth governments awoke to the dangers created by their porous
borders, and hastily began signing (largely ineffective) customs
treaties, the income from the illicit trade in Soviet resources was
being plowed into real estate, privatization vouchers and financial
institutions. It soon became difficult to separate the gangs from
their government patrons.

Russian authorities readily acknowledge that the mixture of unbri-
dled capitalism, organized crime and official chicanery has produced
a crisis of governance. A frustrated Boris Yeltsin said last year that
mob activity had "acquired such scale and character" that it threatened the future of the Russian state. He complained it was destroying the economy, destabilizing the political climate and undermining
public morale. "Crime," he concluded, "has become problem number
one for us." It was impressive rhetoric. But it sounded, unfortunately,
like an admission of defeat.

CRIME AND PUNISHMENT

THERE HAS BEEN much bluster in the Russian parliament about
crime prevention but, since casting aside communist rule in 1991,
Russia's new leaders have failed to adopt any significant measures to
curb organized crime. What's more, the reformers' most substantial
achievements—demolishing the last vestiges of the police state and

The Russian 'Mafiya'

lifting most restrictions on private ownership—have had the perverse effect of creating the perfect environment for mafiya growth.

Russian policymakers committed a fundamental mistake: they tried to develop a free market before constructing a civil society in which such a market could safely operate. As a result, businessmen, politicians and law enforcement agencies suffer at the mercy of the lingering ideological prejudices of Soviet jurisprudence. Many activities that are required for a market economy to function remain illegal or unprotected by legislation; other activities that are considered unlawful according to Western norms, such as organized crime, are not specifically prohibited.

Under the existing system, police may arrest a group of felons caught in a criminal act, but the lack of Western-style conspiracy laws means police cannot prosecute the mastermind if he or she stays off the scene. Under Soviet law, "racketeering" was considered a capitalist concept and therefore inapplicable to Soviet reality. On the other hand, making a profit—"speculation," a serious offense under the old Soviet criminal code—remains an ambiguous area for post-Soviet law enforcement. Provisions for settling disputes between private companies have yet to be clarified, and no guidelines yet exist for establishing contracts or declaring bankruptcy. Russia has no independent judiciary and no way of tackling more sophisticated varieties of white-collar crime. Current laws offer no means of impounding the records of fraudulent companies or checking the criminal provenance of bank accounts. Even if such provisions existed, their enforcement would be doubtful. Russian policemen are so poorly equipped that some pursue criminals by bus and taxi. In such an environment, it is no wonder that crime flourishes.

Several ambitious plans to increase spending on police and security forces and replace the old Soviet criminal code languished in the last parliament. The new Russian constitution, approved by a narrow margin last December, establishes some important principles for reforming the justice system, such as an independent judiciary and the right to private property and business. But it remains to be seen whether those principles and plans will be translated into law.

The greatest obstacle to a coherent anti-mafiya policy remains per-

Stephen Handelman

ceptual. Many Russian policymakers (and some foreigners) believe that corruption and crime are the price that must be paid for Russia's experiment with free enterprise. They argue that other nations (including post-1917 Russia) also experienced high crime rates during periods of acute social and economic change. Today's smuggling tycoons and shady entrepreneurs are often compared to the robber barons of nineteenth-century America. Perhaps, too, it is only reasonable for those whose notions of order were shaped by Soviet authoritarianism to wonder whether the cure might not be worse than the disease. But arguments for accommodating the mafiya break down at a critical point. It is one thing to tolerate the excesses of future Russian Carnegies, Vanderbilts and Morgans; it is quite another to grant them free grazing rights in the political system.

> The mafiya's connection to government makes it a dagger pointed at the heart of Russian democracy.

The Russian mafiya's connection with government, born of its symbiotic relationship with the former communist establishment, makes organized crime a dagger pointed at the heart of Russian democracy. The danger is especially apparent outside the urban centers of Moscow and St. Petersburg, where local crime lords and their government allies have filled the vacuum created by the departure of communist authority. These alliances are joined for political as well as economic reasons. As regional leaders seek more power over resources, they share a common interest with black-marketeers and underworld figures in resisting central control.

Organized crime has infected the central nervous system of Russian politics. Throughout 1993, successive corruption scandals paralyzed the Yeltsin government. No institution was left untainted: senior commanders of the Red Army were caught in smuggling rings; cabinet ministers and police officials were discovered working for shady commercial firms. In the most celebrated case, members of the ill-fated Supreme Soviet, led by then Vice President Aleksandr Rutskoi, forced several reform ministers out of office over charges of corruption. Government officials, in retaliation, released

The Russian 'Mafiya'

documents attempting to prove that Rutskoi and his political allies were guilty of money laundering and weapons smuggling.[2]

The burlesque of charge and countercharge politicized even the slender efforts the state was making to halt corruption and further reduced the government's credibility. Russians could easily remember how corruption cases during the Soviet era coincidentally affected only the losers in political battles. While Yeltsin himself was not linked to any scandals, the president plainly found it awkward to deal with evidence of wrongdoing among his political allies. Several of his top anticorruption investigators quit in disgust. As the euphoria of August 1991 faded, most people concluded that hardly anything had changed except the faces in power. "To tell you the truth," one prominent Moscow journalist admitted to me, "if someone staged a new coup tomorrow, I would not know what or whom to defend."

To suggest to an increasingly disillusioned populace that crime is an unfortunate but unavoidable by-product of political and economic transition is an insult. The rising cost of living might be politically acceptable to ordinary Russians who, as they are the first to inform foreigners, have endured tough times before. But when economic discontent is joined to anger over official corruption and criminal violence, it becomes a potent political force. The sight of the country's newly rich emerging from luxury restaurants and gambling casinos, of Western cars jamming the roadways, of gunmen strutting down the streets, intensifies the nationwide sense of betrayal and, more significantly, the loss of personal security.

Rising crime rates have turned what was once an ordered, communal society into a land of fearful strangers. In a 1992 survey, three out of four Muscovites admitted they were afraid to walk the streets at night. And in 1993 another opinion poll found that 49 percent of Rus-

---

[2] In February 1993, Russian Defense Minister Pavel Grachev announced that 46 generals and top officers were to be court-martialed on corruption charges and that an additional 3,000 officers were to be disciplined for "illegal business deals" ranging from smuggling weapons to black-market sales of military equipment. A few months later, Grachev himself was hit with corruption charges related to the acquisition of official cars from Germany.

Stephen Handelman

sians rated crime higher on their list of concerns than unemployment.[3]

The strong support for the neofascist Vladimir Zhirinovsky in the December 12, 1993, parliamentary elections owed at least as much to the backlash against crime as to economic populism. The continuing appeal of both ultranationalist patriots and neocommunists is largely based on their invective against "mafiya" (read Western) values. Zhirinovsky, like many opposition candidates, campaigned on a harsh law-and-order platform. In his last television appearance before the election, he advocated a return to Russian civil war-era decrees ordering the shooting of criminals on sight.

Draconian solutions to the law-and-order crisis are now part of mainstream political thinking and will probably dominate the agenda of the new State Duma. Having failed to develop a society guided by the rule of law, the first post-Soviet government is reverting to the habits of its predecessors. Retrograde attitudes emerged in the aftermath of Yeltsin's battle with parliament during the crisis of October 1993. Shortly after the assault on the Russian White House, the government imposed a curfew on Moscow and sent squads of soldiers and police to patrol the streets. Not surprisingly, crime rates plummeted. The incidental success of these temporary measures strengthened the advocates among police and politicians for a Soviet-style war on crime. Yeltsin ordered police to drive "unregistered aliens" out of the capital in an effort to cripple the powerful crime syndicates who move easily between Moscow and other cities across the Commonwealth. The measure was targeted primarily at gangsters from the Caucasus. Chechens and Azeris in particular are responsible for a large percentage of drug trafficking. But the blunderbuss approach resulted in the expulsion or beating of thousands of otherwise innocent traders. Such violence indicated growing racial intolerance among Russians as much as any serious determination to root out crime. And, as some observers noted dryly, most

---

[3] In the first year after the fall of communism, the Russian public prosecutor reported 2.7 million crimes, an increase of 33 percent over 1991. The rates for murder, rape and aggravated assault continued to climb during the first six months of 1993, along with categories of crime that had been negligible during most of the Soviet era, such as drug trafficking, embezzlement and theft of government property.

The Russian 'Mafiya'

of the Russian crime lords welcomed the move as a way of eliminating their biggest competitors.

There are also signs that the government is preparing to take a harder line against entrepreneurs, conforming to right-wing prejudices that identify private business with crime. The Ministry of Internal Affairs dusted off a KGB tactic used in the last year of the Soviet era—the search of commercial enterprises and confiscation of property without a warrant—and proposed it as part of an anticrime package. Yeltsin rejected the proposal after it was leaked to newspapers. But it surprised no one that the idea received sympathetic attention from nomenklatura capitalists and the right wing.

A reversal or slowdown of reforms is the goal of the former Soviet establishment, which prefers a subsidized, corporate capitalism to the unlimited expansion of private property. It also happens to be the goal of the larger criminal syndicates, which are eager to transform their wealth into political influence. Gangsters ranked among the staunchest defenders of democracy during the August 1991 coup, partially because of their traditional antipathy toward communists. But several have since confided that they no longer support reforms because of the "disorder" in the Russian economy. "In this kind of environment, who can do any business?" said one gangster without a trace of irony.

During the December campaign, some opposition candidates in the regions were believed to have received campaign contributions from mafiya groups, and there are reliable reports that ultranationalist parties have used gangs to harass Caucasians and other ethnic minorities. Whether or not such reports can be believed, the maneuvering room of the Yeltsin government has already been narrowed.

GOOD COP, BAD COP

WESTERNERS UNDERESTIMATE the extent to which organized crime and corruption have hampered Russian political and economic reforms. Early assumptions that the introduction of free enterprise would smooth the way for democracy failed to take into account the lingering power of the former Soviet establishment. Organized crime has

Stephen Handelman

reinforceed the old structures in their battle to retain control over key sectors of the economy and strengthened popular hostility toward the free-market democratic policies pursued by pro-Western reformers.

The West should to take Russian organized crime far more seriously than it has up until now. The current situation poses a double dilemma to policymakers in Western capitals. While internal Russian developments have moved once again to the top of the international agenda, the West has increasingly less influence over Russia's domestic affairs. Western advice and financial assistance, albeit limited, have been discredited by Russia's bruising encounter with the chaos of the marketplace. Nationalist and authoritarian remedies are now ascendant. But important areas of influence remain unexplored.

> Nationalist and authoritarian remedies to chaos and crime are now ascendant.

The first area requires a conceptual change in economic aid policies and in strategies for developing the Russian market. Until recently, the West concentrated on helping Russia meet its international debt load while encouraging it to carry on with austerity policies. Since the December elections, opinion has shifted toward providing more overt support for social safety net programs as a way of easing economic discontent. But these policies still do not address the central problem: the legal vacuum at the heart of the Russian economy. Western advice and assistance in creating a commercial infrastructure, including a viable banking system and regulatory agencies, and in developing a legal framework for business activities would go far toward meeting the security concerns of Russian and foreign investors.

If the obstacles in the Russian marketplace hamper Russian entrepreneurs, they have a chilling effect on foreigners, for whom the nexus between organized crime and politics exacerbates the cultural barriers between the ex-socialist East and capitalist West. Bribery was always a hidden cost of doing business in the Soviet era. Today, the hapless foreign businessman can find himself the target of extortion demands or worse. And he finds little sympathy from already overworked police and courts.

International assistance in bringing Russia's justice and law

The Russian 'Mafiya'

enforcement system into the modern era is therefore crucial. This task involves more than familiarization courses in the principles of Western jurisprudence and police exchange programs. Russian police are deficient in just about every area, from police cars and computers to techniques of crime detection and prevention. Aid in reforming the hoary machinery of Soviet justice, with its bias toward prosecution and disregard for individual rights, would go a long way toward removing a principal factor behind the widespread Russian contempt for law.

The Western police establishment, for understandable reasons, has been gun-shy about working closely with its Russian counterpart. The recent decision by the FBI to open a liaison office in Moscow is a step forward, but several agents admit that widespread corruption inside Russian law enforcement has kept relations less than collegial. However, the West has more than an academic interest in forging a collaborative relationship with Russia's police agencies.

The old rhetoric of the "evil empire" has been replaced by fears of Russian mafiya penetration of Western economies. Those fears are well grounded. Russian gangs have been responsible for a wave of violent crime in Central Europe and Germany. The smuggling of Russian resources abroad has depressed world prices for commodities such as aluminum. Weapons-grade uranium and other by-products of the Soviet nuclear arsenal have turned up for sale in West European capitals.

Russia's criminal syndicates are also attracting unsavory partners in the West. Gang leaders from Moscow and the Baltics have held "summits" with members of the Italian mafia, and Russia's growing importance as a drug transit corridor has aroused interest from Colombian cartels. Post-Soviet gangsters have become active in the United States, as suggested by the growing number of murders, interceptions of smugglers and evidence of substantial capital transfers. The MVD estimates $25 billion was transferred from Commonwealth states to Western banks by organized crime structures in 1993. The sobering possibility that the former communist establishment, through its mob allies, could become a major investor in Western economies reinforces the need for closer attention to the West's own economic security.

Stephen Handelman

Russia's internal conflicts have dampened the triumphant mood of the post-Cold War era. The turmoil of the past two years has shaken several assumptions made by the West after the fall of the Soviet Union: that the communist establishment has lost its grip on politics, that Russians would eagerly grasp democracy with both hands, and that capitalism would provide the engine of Russia's transformation. The uncertainty surrounding the third assumption is the most troubling. As Russians increasingly identify free-market democracy with organized crime and corruption, they will turn toward much less congenial forms of governing. Unchecked economic chaos and gang violence could well foster the rise of a hostile, authoritarian power on the Eurasian continent, instead of the prosperous partner the West requires for a stable 21st century world.◈

[9]

Journal of Contemporary Criminal Justice
Vol. 11 • No. 4 • December 1995

Primitive Capitalist Accumulation:
Russia as a Racket

Robert J. Kelly
and
Rufus Schatzberg
and
Patrick J. Ryan

ABSTRACT

The function and structure of Sicilian institutions
provide an historical lesson in how and why the Mafia
flourished to the extent that attempts to imprison its
leadership havethreatened the stability of the very
government that is tolling its death knell.
Extrapolating from that experience, the workof Follain,
Jousten, Varese and others provide the authors with a
theoretical framework for understanding the
dependencybetween the liberal democratic system
being introduced in Russia today and the current mafia
activity in that country.Crime, be it "organized" or not,
is not new to Russia. Until ther breakup of the
Republics, Western researchers knew little of its nature
or its scope. Should the violence associated with
Russian crime continue it may overwhelm the entire
society or we may see an alliance of wealthy elites and
multi-layered criminal conspiracies justaposed but
miles apart from the non-criminal, "ordinary " citizens.

Primitive Capitalist Accumulation: Russia as a Racket

We have become a mafia state on a world scale. Everyone thinks that political
issues could lead to an explosion but crime could as easily blow us asunder. (Boris
Yeltsin cited in Handelman, 1995). Organized crime is destroying the economy,
interfering in politics, undermining public morals, threatening individual citizens
and the entire Russian nation . . . our country is already considered a great mafia

258   Primitive Capitalist Accumulation:
      Russia as a Racket

power. (Boris Yeltsin cited in Sterling, 1994).

Sterling and Handelman, the writers who quote Boris Yeltsin, warn continually and clearly that the Russian "mafia" (the Italian term has been appropriated into the Russian language tout court) has so deeply penetrated government, business and state security forces that it has virtually transformed and reconstituted the entire post-perestroika society into a criminal formation. Yeltsin, the political maestro who, astride a tank not long ago, defied a communist putsch, now admits unabashedly - not in cautionary tones but as matter-of-fact that the state has been hijacked by hit men, racketeers and extortionists, that its corrupted politicians have brazenly amassed huge fortunes in bribes, and that military men have shamelessly peddled weapons - from Kalashnikovs to nuclear missiles - for the right price.

As we argue below, there appear to be two major crime waves that now hold Russia and the independent republics making up the amorphous Confederation of states in a stranglehold. Actually, the former state structure in the Soviet Union could itself have been identified as a mafia. The Communist Party was never a political party in the Western sense, but rather a ruling elite that used terror and intimidation to appropriate the entire economic mechanism of a vast empire. Its rulers paid no more mind to the principle of political legitimacy than the dons of Castellammare and Palermo. While the analogy is imperfect, the Soviet communist party was more akin to La Cosa Nostra than Il Partito Communista Italiano, and its dispensations of power and wealth were unchallenged by either elections or law. Party chiefs ruled the Republics just as surely as John Gotti and crime family bosses ran their fiefdoms in New York. According to Vaksberg (1991), in Azerbaijan, a southern republic, the Caspian Sea caviar mafia, the Sumgait oil mafia, the fruits, vegetables, cotton, customs and transport mafias - all reported to the party chief and enriched him in return for his turning a blind eye to their rackets. To carry the analogy further, one might say that when Gorbachev achieved power in 1985, he became "boss of bosses," the leader of a Communist Party Politburo most of whose members were sultans of crime and corruption. The Central Committee too was filled with hacks whose principle purpose was the protection of the Party as a privileged caste by turning Leninist ideology to their own advantage. In a state in which property theoretically belonged to all - in other words, to no one - the Communist Party owned everything, from the docks of Odessa to the citrus groves of Georgia. Before Gorbachev and the semblance of reform, party chieftains in the Brezhnev era understood that the imperative of stability obliged them to pay homage to and grease the Moscow Don.

In Brezhnev's days, the political environment encouraged the growth of crime and thrived under the direct patronage of party leaders in Central Asia, the Transcaucasus and the Black Sea Coast. These were remote areas and provinces, distant from Moscow, where local wealth and clan loyalties, existed even before the hectic ascendancy of Communism and allowed the growth of a second economy and second power, albeit one restrained by the need to display a proletarian rather than a Czarist propriety. To be fair to the Soviet rulers, the system they inherited from

Leninism could only survive with a large black market that counterbalanced the effects of suffocating bureaucracies filled with greedy officials. Those engaged in trade as either entrepreneurs or managers had to know how to operate within that system: who to pay off, who to grant favors, and how to line their own pockets.

The collapse of the Party apparatus was the death knell of the greatest mafia the world has ever known. From dissidents within the "nomenklatura" and officials in satellite countries making up the Warsaw Pact, the wholesale corruption and, social brutalities of party apparatchiks was revealed after the breakup (Dijilas, 1992; Simis, 1982). In these portraits the Party functioned as the equivalent of a large criminal syndicate whose defining, essential aspects were the acquisition of personal wealth and the exploitation of power through extra-legal means.

Corruption in the Soviet system was not merely a matter of exceptions and lone deviants - the "rotten apple" theory used routinely by embarrassed police officials in the West to exonerate their departments - but of systemic, pervasive malfeasance and misfeasance which leads to the inescapable conclusion that the structural criminal character of the Party apparatus and the whole political system facilitated crime and protected criminals from exposure. And in other ways, Stalin's terror mirrored mafia tactics; he used intimidation and credible threats of violence as instruments of coercion and discipline that fostered an atmosphere of secrecy and widespread suspicion. As the Stalinist terror faded under Khrushchev and then Brezhnev the Communist Party's business became "business" in the sense of the word when describing organized criminality.

In the Khrushchev era a penitential mood took hold, temporarily, with the acknowledgment of Stalinist excesses. (We are tempted to see the period as one not dissimilar from the obsessional war preparations in the Coreleone Family where the veteran boss, Clemenza, tells Michael that a major gang war from time to time is a healthy purgative usually followed by an Arcadian period of cooperative relations and alliances that are profitable, stable and safe.) Still, in spite of the meltdown and loosening of the ideological rigidities of the Stalinist era, we believe that the failure of the Khrushchev experiment was not only disastrous for the Soviet Union, but somehow fundamentally crucial for the rest of global history, and not least, for the future of socialism itself. Indeed, it appears that the Khrushchev generation was the last to believe in the possibility of the renewal of Marxism, let alone socialism; or rather, the other way around, that it was the failure of egalitarianism generally, which now determines the utter indifference to Marxism and socialism seen in several generations of younger intellectuals. But we think this failure was also determinant of the most basic development in other countries as well,.

While we do not want the Russian comrades to bear all the responsibility for global history, there seems to be some similarity between what the Soviet revolution meant for the rest of the world positively, and the negative effects of the last, missed opportunity to restore that revolution. Both the anarchism of the 1960s in the West and the Cultural Revolution in China are to be attributed to that failure, whose agonizing prolongation, long after the end of both, explains the universal triumph

260   Primitive Capitalist Accumulation:
       Russia as a Racket

of cynicism in the omnipresent consumerism of the post modern contemporary era. It is therefore no wonder that such profound disillusionment with political praxis should result in the popularity of the rhetoric of market abnegation and the surrender of freedom to a now lavish invisible hand.[1]

It was only in the post-Stalin time after the violence of collectivization and industrialization was over that the Party's mafia structure took shape. In the 1960's a trade mafia developed which was a pyramid of payoffs originating in the top ministries and Central Committee and trickling down to shopkeepers where everyone "got a piece." The scams and bribes were tributes to the human imagination, matching the guile and adroit styles of the best con men and professional criminals anywhere in the world. And it was not that this swamp of corruption was a secret to the Soviet people any more than the existence of the Mafia is a mystery to Palermo's retail merchants forced to pay protection money. Like their Sicilian counterparts, the Soviet mafiosi made themselves known at every turn.

Perestroika and Glasnost: The Grand Machinery of Various Apocalypses

In 1992, one of the authors [of this article] traveled through two of the major urban centers of Russia and then south through the Ukraine, the Donets region and across the Black Sea to Istanbul. Short of a calamity, the politics of a foreign country are ordinarily of meager interest to a traveler and were it not for the locals cloying interest in organized crime and its reverberations, this trip would have been no different. Surprisingly, it was the foreign visitor whose imagination was exercised by Road Warrior visions of catastrophe and dystopia. Some of the simplest questions about Russian politics and organized crime remain almost beyond objective analysis, clouded as they are by the rather generalized acceptance by the populace of organized crime as an ordinary way of doing business, indeed of life. As the legitimizing myths of the former political system slip away, will the State fail and implode into anarchy and banditry? Has it already collapsed?

The organized crime problem may actually be more apparent than real if it is remembered that law enforcement agencies are busy coping with daily survival themselves so their capacity and initiative to enforce the law is somewhat blunted. Informal market related producers, or, in less euphemistic language, the black markets, are openly tolerated and in some instances explicitly authorized. In Moscow, St. Petersburg and throughout various Republics there is agreement between many ordinary citizens and government officials that competitive forces, processes and economic incentives were sorely needed to overcome the clogged state allocation systems. Also evident from the trip across the southern tier was little overt expression of political criticism of the government's handling of crime control; the voices of opposition, clearly disgusted with the organized crime problem, seemed muted more, we suspect, out of inertia and nostalgia than from a sense of fear and censorship. Of course, some members of Parliament who were aggressively anti-mafia paid with their lives so there was also a general sense of anxiety and intimidation in the air, but the tentative impression was that the law enforcement agencies were anxious about resorting to wholesale repression which would only awaken popular resistance. With the exceptions of the diehard communists, the young and the insane, the Russian people now seem to avoid politics altogether. Generally, one could say that Russians have, by and large, no sympathy left for Communism (though most feel a strong sense of nationalism) and that the democratization that has occurred in terms of a rapid transition from an administrative command system to a market economy constituted the genesis of a process resulting in the wholesale criminalization of the economy by new sets of actors. That the change over is yet underway only bolsters the criminals' efforts. The criminalization is no less real for the fact that the transition is ongoing; indeed, it enables it.

The outcomes of Perestroika and Glasnost enabled the private sector to achieve legal status during Gorbachev's regime. Unlike capitalism in China, where corruption is also massive, its major support comes from the "Nomenklatura," the upper echelons of the Communist Party, and even their approval is ambiguous; cadres in regional and local party committees were hostile, or demanded a large cut of private profits, or both. The first private businesses, known as a cooperatives, were obliged to bribe, lie to authorities and hire goon squads in order to stay in business, even if they wished to work honestly, which most did not (Kampfner, 1994). These cooperatives were regarded by most citizens as criminal enterprises. Today, according to Handelman (1995) and Sterling (1994) virtually every small business across Russia pays protection money to some gang; former Party commissars appropriate lucrative businesses for themselves; most fortunes in raw materials are smuggled out though the porous borders of former Soviet Republics; and ministers and government officials peddle property and favors (Shabalin, et al, 1995). Moscow has become a sort of frontier town reminiscent of Dodge City in nineteenth century America. Almost all the new commercial space is controlled by Russia's gangsters.

Thus it is possible to conceive of two "mafias" or two waves of organized crime with the latter, the post-perestroika version connected with and indelibly stamped by its predecessor. In the West, (United States) the mob historically moved in where no legal economy existed - in drugs, gambling and vice in general -creating an informal, shadow economy. Occasionally, where it could compromise or reach a politician, the Western Mafia meddled in government contracts and operated protection schemes. But in the Soviet Union, as we learn now, no economic transaction was untainted. It was as if the entire Soviet Union were ruled by a great crime family known as the Communist Party. The party's intricate bureaucratic layers offered countless opportunities for mischief, and no one could afford to avoid a certain amount of complicity. In short, it was impossible to be honest and as if to deepen the gloom Solzhenitsyn recently wrote,

262   Primitive Capitalist Accumulation:
       Russia as a Racket

> The corrupt ruling class - the many millions of men
> in the party/state nomenklatura - is not capable of
> voluntarily renouncing any of the privileges they have
> seized. They have lived shamelessly for decades at the
> people's expense - and would like to continue doing so
> (Solzhenitsyn, 1991: 75-76).

With Gorbachev's purges of Party mafiosi in the Politburo amounting to little, Solzhenitsyn's jeremiads seem retrospectively prophetic indeed. After aborted coups by party officials and conspirators from the army, state collectives, party security organs and military-industrial complex, ideology was hardly the point any longer.[2] With the Party in ruins, remnants of its structures actively collaborated with new illegal clans that emerged in the post-Gorbachev period.

As in Eastern Europe, party apparatuses often remain in power because so few outsiders are competent enough to run factories and administer huge bureaucracies. Consequently, former Party executives, collective enterprise chairpersons, factory bosses, and security chiefs remain in firm control. Party men cling to their properties with a death grip, perhaps in the vain hope of a resurgence of the old regime amid the anarchy of the current situation. At the same time, a sense of lawlessness prevails in many cities and towns out in the peripheries of the great conurbations of Moscow, St. Petersburg, Kiev, Odessa, Kharkov, Rostov and geographically proximate Siberian communities; where a second wave of mafia emerged with new sets of mobsters - independent of the communist party structures. They too are called mafia which they resemble but many are more like the unscrupulous figures of primitive capitalism; the "robber barons," the Vanderbilts and Rockefellers with their attendant thugs and stooges. Whereas these early capitalists were not labeled criminal because their activities were not yet entered in the penal law, the activities of their Russian cousins are legally criminal and the gang's structure clearly denotes organization.

The new Russian mafia gets rich in a number of ways, with drugs being among the most lucrative of illicit businesses. According to Sterling (1994), the former Soviet Union produces twenty-five times more hashish than the rest of the world — another example of the Almighty's enigmatic generosity in seeing that the country has so many valuable raw materials. Drug production and dealing were not unknown in Soviet times but they were limited. "When Soviet controls fell apart," Sterling writes,

> . . . things changed. By 1992, family-sized poppy
> fields yielding two crops a year materialized and put
> under heavy armed guard. New plantations in
> Uzbekistan increased by 1000%. Around 200,000 acres
> were planted with poppies in Kyrgyzstan. Plantations
> were springing up in Tajikistan. Others were spreading
> over a thousand square kilometers of empty radioactive

> terrain around Chernobyl ... underground laboratories
> started to produce synthetic drugs such as Crokodil and
> Chort, a thousand times stronger than heroin. Russia
> had the rare distinction of being at once a user country,
> a transit country and a producer country, all on its
> customary extravagant scale (1994: 106).

The newer, even more ominous trade (if that is conceivable), which is possibly unique to the former Soviet Union, is in fissionable nuclear materials. Little has been written about it, and what is available says nothing really definitive, probably because no one knows the extent of this "emerging" black market. It is known that Russia is the world's largest or second largest producer of such materials. Handelman (1995) speculates persuasively, in our opinion, that few of the more than 150 mining and manufacturing sites in Russia for nuclear raw materials, are secure and serve equally as centers of smuggling and thievery as they do as mining sites. It would be hard to believe that the administrators and security managers of these sites and stockpiles of uranium and weapons materiel are immune to the temptation of sudden wealth in a political climate of lawlessness.

With all of the turbulence since 1991, one can imagine a quasi-Italian scenario, with another "revolution" in a decade or so when a more enfranchised, civically conscious, generation of Russian middle class, law-abiding citizens - similar to that which rose in Sicily after the mafia murders of Falcone and Borsellino, and many others, who were appalled by decades of elite accommodation with organized crime -will forcefully demand an end to it. Perhaps Russians will have more luck than the Italians have had at interdiction of criminal groups.

We can extrapolate from Italy's experience with organized crime and tentatively formulate a theory of criminal development in Russia. Follain, for example, suggests on the basis of his analysis of Italian organized crime that the malevolent relation between the liberal democratic system Russia is attempting to introduce and the current mafia activities is inevitable (Follain, 1995). His argument is that when the mafia gains a political purchase, the appearance of free choice will serve only to consolidate organized crime's position in the society. The dilemma in Russia would then be that Parliamentary elections might do no more than place power in the hands of those forces with the determination and wealth to the pack the Duma with compliant stooges. Characteristically, such dependency is mutually parasitical, of tenuous loyalties and fleeting in the face of serious challenge. The opposite, of course, might occur in the form of counter institutional developments among those in religion, business and education that just may become powerful enough to resist the criminal forces and push the government into taking strong anti-crime measures. Significantly, the experience in Italy barred the "fair weather friend" nature of the criminal/politico associations as inter-gang violence intensified. This bespeaks the domination of both upper and underworlds by the Russian criminals and the elimination of the cozy partnerships evident today.

264   Primitive Capitalist Accumulation:
      Russia as a Racket

In Italy's case, when drug trafficking became the most profitable criminal activity by far, and when the struggle to centralize its operation in one Cosa Nostra group, the Corleonesi, precipitated viciously fierce infighting among mafiosi, the historic collusive symbiosis between organized criminal activists and members of the government began to dissolve. The Italian mafia and the government were on a collision course in the 1980s that led to violence and murder against the former silent partners and protectors of the underworld (Stille, 1995). Similarly, to the extent that Russia moves along like criminal pathways, the associated violence may eventually overwhelm the entire society.

In contrast to the power of a "Nomenklatura mafia" of pre-perestroika times, post-perestroika Russia exhibits an uncanny resemblance to Sicilian mafia dynamics in Italy before the great benchmark events of 1992 involving the murders of Falcone and Borsellino, the crusading anti-mafia magistrates. Until recently, many Sicilian politicians, out of a misguided sense of local patriotism or self-protection, pretended the Mafia was largely mythical, a scare created by northern politicians and economic interests to discredit southern Italy (Kelly, 1994). Subsequent events culminating in a rash of brutal murders exposed the dreadful results of the failure to face obvious facts. This is another explanation which is germane to theories of organized crime in Russia. In defiance of the traditional code of omerta (silence), many Sicilian journalists and law enforcement officials demonstrated the extent of the Mafia's deep penetration and collusion with successive governments in Rome that guaranteed the mafia's own immunity from prosecution (di Argentine, 1993; Tarormina, 1993). Mafiosi were employed by the Government as tax collectors and were recipients of government building contracts; hundreds of politicians in Rome as well as Palermo worked with Mafia leaders. In Italy the mafia flourished when it was linked to the political hegemony of the Christian Democrats.

Similarly, organized crime and its "first wave," flourished in the former Soviet Union under the predominant influence of the Communist Party.[3] Finckenauer sums up the political/economic conditions that resulted in the "second wave" of organized crime:

> The perestroika reforms of the late 1980s, out-lawing the Communist Party, and the demise of the USSR itself in 1991 - followed by the horrendous economic problems of the past several years - have all fed an enormous growth of new forms of organized crime. Under the conditions, some of the traditional staples of western organized crime (mostly unknown in the old Soviet Union) such as drug trafficking and prostitution, but especially extortion of new companies, businesses, and restaurants, have become among the more prevalent forms of current criminal enterprises in Moscow and other former Soviet cities (1995, 279).

The changes in the structure of crime have prompted some interesting efforts at theoretical explanation. In looking at this phenomenon from a perspective that is broader and more encompassing than in the former Soviet Union, Jousten (1995) sees the growth of the "second wave," of organized criminality as affected by at least three factors: the expansion of crime opportunities, a substantial increase in the numbers of actual and potential offenders, and the lack of available control and containment capacities within law enforcement agencies.

The later descriptive factor may not be as empirically accurate as we might wish when applied to Russia in its pre—and post—perestroika phases. The Soviet police function was not sensitive to entrepreneurial crime conducted on an individual basis as occurs in Western societies where corrupt ties do exist between law enforcement and professional criminals but where a significant amount of enterprise crime is initiated by non-governmental actors. That qualification aside, Jousten (1995) appropriates the theoretical perspective of Cohen and Felson (1979), very persuasively in attempting to understand the growth of organize crime occasioned by perestroika in Central and Eastern Europe. The first of the three master variables making up the model, increased criminal opportunities, reflects a structural change in the nature of the economy from a state-controlled system to one guided by market forces and this means that the amount of goods available increases considerably. In addition, as state controls slacken, the security crusts around borders break down thus expanding the opportunities for criminal smuggling to develop. Secondly, the existence of a "shadow economy" as a consequence of an unrelentingly poor standard of living, unemployment and inflation means that people often turn to the black market and crime as a way of supplementing income. The numbers of likely and motivated offenders increase as the Gulag (prison system) is dismantled. Compared to the West, prison populations in former Warsaw Pact and Soviet Republic countries have always been greater. Where little was done to rehabilitate inmates, prisons became a recruiting pool for organized criminal enterprises that include organized crime. Third, according to Jousten (1995), Russia lacks the criminal justice resources to cope with organized crime; there are shortages in adequate personnel, facilities, training of personnel, equipment and inadequate legal tools to help police and prosecutors. Lacking the experts, and tools — such as RICO laws, electronic surveillance equipment and witness security programs — organized crime will probably grow before serious efforts are introduced to control it. In the West, the fear is that organized criminals will migrate and cross borders (Finckenauer 1994).

In an approach that complements Jousten (1995), Varese (1994) adapts an analytical framework that attempts to understand the genesis of the Mafia in Sicily and applies it to the social structural conditions in post-perestroika Russia. Varese (1994) takes Gambetta's theory of the emergence of mafia in Sicily and examines the extent to which it can be applied in Russia. Gambetta (1993) sees the Sicilian experience as a response to a massive structural change in its political economy during the transitional phases from feudalism to capitalism when property was

266   Primitive Capitalist Accumulation:
       Russia as a Racket

privatized and made an exchangeable commodity in a system of market relations.
According to Gambetta, the state, during this extraordinary period, lacked the
resources and skills to protect private property rights that became salable through
market forces. Historically, the latifundia (large estates) were guarded by private
security forces known as gabellotti (proto-mafia) who functioned as agents and
landlords for the landed gentry and aristocracy that owned much of the arable
acreage in Sicily's agricultural economy (Blok, 1974). With economic changes and
the breakup of land monopolies, property was redefined as an exchangeable
commodity, and entrepreneurs and owners needed protection that the state could
not provide. Thus, the mafia emerged to satisfy the demands of the new land owners.
The mafiosi were prepared to employ violence in their roles as land agents and
regulators. Over time, mafiosi ventured into other activities where violence and
extortion were their defining behavior.

   A parallel set of conditions exists today in Russia, where the reappearance of
private property and its exchange value, according to Varese (1994), has meant the
emergence of extralegal groups prepared to provide protection services that state
agencies cannot offer. The privatization reforms brought to an end the Soviet
monopoly over property and created a market condition in property and enterprise
business in which the state law enforcement apparatus could not or would not serve.
Because criminal justice agencies were themselves implicated in extortion rackets
or were too incompetent to confront them, non-state groups and individuals (often
the very perpetrators of criminal acts against property and businesses) appeared,
ready and able to supply that protection. The conclusion is obvious: Until and
unless Russia realigns its criminal justice system to control extortionate predation
against the commercial sector of the emergent market economy, the past of Sicily
may be Russia's future.

   It is doubtful that anyone who has tried to do business or lived in Russia in
recent years, has not broken one of its laws. A legal system deliberately constructed
for a socialist police state has proven hopelessly inadequate for modern commerce.
In reality, Russia's market economy provides the milieu for mafia-type activities.
Simply put, Russia lacks a network of statutes in its enforcement apparatus to
capably facilitate lawful operations of private and state owned enterprises.

   It is noteworthy and somewhat amazing that the system has not collapsed into
utter anarchy given the levels of crime, chaos and dismay, and it being terribly
vulnerable to what Yeltsin ruefully and laconically describes as a "mafia State"
where major portions of the nation's economic activity are relegated to gray zones
of violence, corruption, black markets, shortages and inefficiencies. It is a
frightening image of Russia that shows. It is a starving giant of a nation in economic
chaos, threatened by civil war, lurching toward fascism, and hijacked by organized
crime. It seems that "bad" money is being pumped into the upper world's legitimate
economy so fast that a logical (and intriguing) question is whether Russia will
survive its dealings with the robber-baron climate of business, culturally and
socially intact and with sufficient resources and energy to mature into a real market

economy.

Despite the models having been developed in different contexts, the logical possibilities linking the two theoretical models of Jousten and Varese plausibly describe changes in the nature of Russian organized crime. Doubtlessly, the temptation is strong to see "family resemblances" inherent in the structures of otherwise culturally and politically heterogeneous societies. The structural debate goes back to Ianni/Albini who detected the genesis of organized crime in the dynamics of the social institutions and the ethos of society - not necessarily in the cultural artifacts of particular sub-cultural and ethnic minorities. What appears to be happening in Russia with the collapse of the Soviet Union and the repudiation of its institutional setup, is the emergence of new progressive forces springing to life, forming a new sense of "the political," "the economic," "privacy," "business," "life style," and that crucial psychological sensibility, "success". For the committed communists the historical lessons of 1991 must be especially bitter, for it has often been said that every age is dominated by a privileged form, or genre, which seems by its structure the fittest to express its secret truths and that function is now gone for the hard-liners.

The period of capitalism in Russia drove the ideologically sacred sense of partinost to extinction; the deep, underlying materiality of all things has finally risen, dripping and convulsively into the light of day; and it is clear that the political culture itself is one of those things whose fundamental materiality is now, not merely evident to Russians, but quite inescapable. "Politics" in Russia now means simply the care and feeding of the economic apparatus (in this case the market rather than the collectively owned and organized means of production); and "crime" - organized crime - is no longer limited to colorful rural bandits and comparatively small vice gangs in some cities. It is an appendage and expression of "primitive capitalist accumulation."[4] What is to be done?" - that famous question of Lenin's could not be more pertinent today as Russia reels from crisis to crisis. Organized crime in Russia much like it counterparts elsewhere is not part of one gigantic organization. There is a multitude of gangs in addition to criminal groups with origins in the former Communist Party, the state-owned industries, the military and the KGB.

It seems evident that the Russian government has been utterly incapable of containing the frenzied criminal conspiracies and behavior unleashed when the Party system was overthrown and the country moved toward capitalism. A reasonable conclusion from the available research, commentaries, writings and analyses of events would have to lay most of the blame for the anarchy and crime at the doorstep of the government when it hastily abandoned most economic controls before attempting to devise, develop and deploy institutions essential for a market economy. Instead of doing the latter, the government behaved in ways that stimulated criminal instincts and opportunities, for example, by installing confiscatory tax rates that invited tax evasion and implementing artificially low domestic energy prices that created incentives for vast corruption in the energy

268   Primitive Capitalist Accumulation:
       Russia as a Racket

export trade. Even more fundamentally, however, it seems that in large part the failure to control crime has occurred because many elements in the government became partners in criminal enterprises. Lacking any meaningful conflict-of-interest laws, and with many ministries managed by greedy bureaucrats more concerned with self-aggrandizement than performing their duties, it is no surprise that the Russian government itself appears to be a major source of the problem of organized criminality. Although President Yeltsin has repeatedly declared war on crime and made it one of his top priorities, law enforcement agencies have only meager results to show despite periodic anti-crime campaigns.[5] Gangsters are arrested from time to time, yet the arrests often seem as much the results of inter-gang warfare whose publicity demands a police response than of police efficiency.

Were it not for the widespread violence connected with criminal activity, many might consider the ugly scramble for the acquisition of commercial assets regrettable but no more than an essential prelude to a capitalist economy. After all, the "buccaneers" of American capitalism - Rockefeller, Carnegie, the Vanderbilts and Mellons - were not squeamish in hiring professional thugs to do their bidding in labor disputes or in destroying competition without regard for the personal devastation that ensued. Added to this clamber is the fact that there was no legitimate private capital in the Soviet Union, so aggressive and extra-legal attempts by officials and managers to secure a place in the new economic system are to be expected and should not be considered a uniquely Russian development.

Unfortunately, the surge of crime in Russia has not been just a matter of cunning bureaucrats cutting corners to cull as much personal benefit as possible from privatized state assets. It is additionally associated with more dangerous criminal activities in drug trafficking and abuse, gang wars and the illicit trade in everything imaginable including fissionable material. The Proudhonist formula "property is theft" has been modified and converted for bureaucrats and gangsters in the proto-capitalist world of Russia to "power becomes property." This is quite different from the American saying that "money is power". In Russia the power to do crime yields property (wealth). In America, at least on the surface and idealistically, one legitimately amasses the wealth, and then wields power.

In quantitative terms, it is impossible to measure the power of organized crime but there are some estimates: For instance, Handelman says that Russian law enforcement officials believe organized crime accounts for 30% to 40% of the national turnover in goods and services (1994). But even if we take such an estimate as approximately correct, it is difficult to determine just what it means. Here, problems of definition plague inquiry. Is a business person forced to pay 20% of his earnings to a gang for "security services" thereby a part of organized crime? His extortion fees help to sustain the criminal but he is obviously a victim who doubtless would be quite willing to save the money if local police could provide adequate protection. As in the Sicilian experience, absent government services, someone, usually a bad guy, will step in to provide "protection". How too, does one distinguish between victims and perpetrators; between those who hire assassins and traffic in drugs and those who occasionally bribe an official for a favor? All are involved in criminal activity that tends to increase the power of criminal syndicates and enterprises, but there are vast differences in the effects on society.

As the struggle for Russia intensifies it may begin to resemble the mafia infested island of Sicily and southern Italy in more ways than even Varese envisions. Should current trends continue, Russian society could be sharply polarized, with wealthy elites and multi-layered criminal conspiracies forming out of a deft use of the incoherent tax system, and a lack of controls on international capital market flows, on the one side and, on the other, everyone else. As they do, and have, in Italy, criminally assisted elites, living side by side with impoverished masses of people in the cities, towns and countryside, could further fracture the Russian society to a point where it devolves into a plutocracy with the powerful, the criminal and the wealthy arranging matters so that they live in a different country from their ostensibly fellow citizens. They, like their mafiosi counterparts in Italy, will have their own schools, banks, resorts and information networks; their own private police and security systems, and their own politicians and government officials. Communism is over but organized crime could become the perfect tool for reinstalling another Machiavellian power elite thriving on the formula of divide and rule.

Shelley does not think that the post-Soviet phase will necessarily lead to democracy and the installation of an effective anti-organized crime control apparatus. Indeed, she says:

[T]he existence and pervasiveness of organized crime may preclude the transition to democracy, limit personal freedom, and thwart legitimate foreign investment and open market economies. Since organized crime has already partially supplanted many of the governments of the successor states, the citizens may be trading one form of control for another; domination by the Communist Party may be replaced by the controls of organized crime (1995: 7).

A democratic capitalist economy may be no more than a pipe dream in the post-Soviet states where mafias are deeply entrenched; more like y, a parasitic politics, a type of political clientelism that cripples local markets in capital, commodities, industrial and consumer goods, seems like a natural consequence of a subculture of extortion and intimidation where criminal groups have deeply penetrated the institutional structure of the society.

CONCLUSIONS: EMPIRE AND CRIME.

In terms of criminal phenomena, the collapse of the Soviet Union should not be a celebration of hope for the renewal of history - that may be illusory; perestroika merely serves as host for the metastases of empire crime. Our hypothesis is that we are dealing here not with a disappearance, but with a dispersal of the Soviet empire and its attendant criminality from closeted centrality into all the local, provincial and territorial micro-empires. The dismantled systems (and the process is not over yet) finds the means to perpetrate themselves in other ways - not by dynastic filiation

270   Primitive Capitalist Accumulation:
       Russia as a Racket

with the Communist Party as in the past, but by something like fractal division, by
scission. We now find micro—autarkies, micro--criminal activities, bearing within
themselves, in miniature, all the vices of the past. Thus crime, like politics, is
perpetuated in other forms - fragmented, peripheral and new, infecting all phases of
social and economic life; and like politics, which becomes transpolitical, crime is
transnational and is governed by a single passion: recycling lucrative criminal
enterprises that worked in the past and inventing accommodations for new criminal
opportunities and actors.

It was observed above that Russia resembles Sicily as a structure of political
expediency that generates mafia. But Sicily has also recently given birth to a
strategy of mafia dissolution. Can the same kind of energy be harnessed by Russia?
In Italy and Sicily, anti-mafia policies emerged as forms of repentance and revenge
captured by the concept and figure of the "pentito" which appeared in the 1980s
among Red Brigade terrorists (Kelly, 1991). To achieve this, Italy utilized some
American law enforcement techniques - RICO, electronic surveillance, witness
security programs - that helped to bring about the conversions and cooperations that
were previously unthinkable. Involved in the moral housekeeping (prodded by
outrageous assassinations and acts of outlaw defiance that enraged the public) were
not only mafiosi, but politicians and government officials. As if to buttress the
purgation was the willingness of the Italian government to expose its own collusive
transgressions with the mafia - a spectacle, incidentally, not likely to occur in the
United States where the anti-organized crime policy has been one of "control and
containment" (Edelhertz, 1987).

Many of the Red Brigade terrorists experienced a self-abnegation, a
disenchantment, as they told it. In the confessional mode they engaged in a
psychology of self-dispossession, giving up their predilection to destroy, murder,
and create mayhem in the name of some structures of power for which the public
that had shown some sympathy began to increasingly and implacably oppose such
terrorist methods of implementation. Repentance passed first from the ultra-left
Brigades, to communism, to the whole revolutionary movement, then to the mafia.
It affected the avant-garde, then, like a contagion, washed back into collective
ideologies and practices of crime and corruption. The rather astonishing ease with
which it occurred in Italy was an obvious sign that the country was tumbling down
the slopes of history. Was this the energy of a corpse? The "pentiti" in seeking
redemption suddenly went back on all their previous beliefs and came to serve
Italian society as a vaccine against all radical temptation. The same with the
mafiosi: after several "confessions" and expurgations from contrite and remorseful
murderers there was a drop in the voltage of public interest and these individuals
became pathetic as persons but powerful as witnesses, an antidote to the societal
level plague of which they were a part.

Glasnost in Russia has meant an opening up of modernity, but not just the area
of human rights evinces change - economic catastrophes, political upheavals and
crime all increased with the liberalization of the regime in the former USSR. Before,

it is now obvious, all these things had been repressed and are now returning. The consequences of the destabilization and demolition of institutions has not only meant the dismantling of the "Evil Empire" (which at least was visible, however much opaque and localized in the eastern bloc countries) but also its insidious metamorphosis into something more fluid and elusive, more able to metabolically infect the West. Some law enforcement officials openly worry about the threat of the now recognized organized crime entities in Russia.

Russia's great weapon is not its arsenal of nuclear weapons (which it is selling off) but a reciprocal crime contamination between East and West — not so much through aggressive actions against criminals but by the disintegration of the walls separating and shielding the two former antagonists. As Russia comes out of its deep freeze and as economic and social structures become more and more porous, flexible, international and progressive, it will be interesting to see if in its defrosted form its organized criminality is imitative of the West, and thereby containable, or an emission of new, frightening energies that lay trapped for more than a half century by the great experiment called Communism.

END NOTES

1. Communism and Marxism were extinct dogmas in the Soviet Union and Eastern Europe long before the disillusionment occurred in the West. While not especially relevant to the themes of this essay, there is the oddity of influence where the message of Marxism and Communism exercises a spell on Western intellectuals long after their rejection among Soviet workers, citizens, and even party officials. One wonders how can this be: Why Marxism haunts the air, lingers and virtually mesmerizes a significant number of Western social scientists. Radical and mainstream criminologists in the United States have always been respectful of Marxism as a body of ideas and have resorted to Marxist-inspired explanations of crime with great conviction and enthusiasm. It is very likely that for many of the same reasons that individuals are attracted to the social sciences, they find Marxism interesting; its leading questions go to the core of the social science enterprise and at the same time that it offers an analysis of social organizations, it suggests a diagnosis for redressing social flaws and defects. Marxism's "historical inevitability" is, in a way, emotionally uplifting. The Marxist analysis offers a way out of the pessimism of inevitability through the notion of planned human intervention (Communism) into social processes to raise the welfare of people. Criminology has also been affected by the implications of the analysis of problems Marxism initiated. For example, organized crime analysis has moved from a Lombrosian focus on the criminal as a deviant and defective to institutional flaws in social structure as a precipitant and progenitor of criminal behavior.

272   Primitive Capitalist Accumulation:
       Russia as a Racket

2. Daniel Bell's premature announcement of the "end of Ideology" some four decades ago has a new and unexpected plausibility in Russia and eastern Europe. But ideology is now over, not because class struggle has ended and no one has anything to fight about, but rather because the fate of ideology can be understood to mean that conscious ideologies and political opinions have ceased to be functional in perpetuating and reproducing the system. In the great Communist Manifesto, Marx urges us to do the impossible, to think about economic development and its social expressions, positively and negatively, all at once; to achieve, in other words, a type of thinking (dialectical) that would be capable of grasping the demonstrably baleful features of capitalism along with its extraordinary and liberating dynamism simultaneously, within single thoughts, and without attenuating any of the force of either judgment. We are expected somehow to lift our minds to a point at which it is possible to understand that capitalism is at one and the same time the best thing that has ever happened to the human race, and the worst. Central to the nineteenth century debate and now in Russia and other former Communist societies is the rhetoric of the "market" which amounts to a fundamental struggle for the legitimation or de-legitimation of communist/socialist discourse on the nature and purpose of social institutions. The surrender to the various forms of market ideology - on the left, not to mention everybody else - has been perceptible and universal. Everyone is now willing to grant that no society can function efficiently without the market and that government planning is obviously impossible. More boldly, the proposition of anti-communism comes to this: The market is in human nature. In terms of the "end of ideology" thesis, "politics" now means simply the care and feeding of the economic apparatus - or, the market. Needless to say, the classical notion of the market (which conservative ideologies conveniently ignore) is meaningless in the realm of multinational corporations and giant oligopolies. As Galbraith suggested long ago, oligopolies are an imperfect substitute for planning of the socialist type.

3. This not to say that organized crime did not exist before the Communists came to power. On the contrary, in parts of Russia, the Ukraine, Georgia and elsewhere, traditions of organized crime preceded the Bolsheviks but were never more that parochial ventures by comparison with the Communist era. See Finckenauer (1994); Kenney (1995); Amir (1986).

4. It will be noticed that we are here projecting some conception and hypotheses about conditions and factors and their reproductions making up the milieu of organized criminality. This is perhaps the moment to say something about contemporary discussions on organized crime theory and of efforts to stigmatize various models as merely descriptive and ad hoc. Reuter complains that there is no significant organized crime theory (1994). His sketch of an acceptable theory amounts to little more than a formalization within the frameworks of industrial organization theory. Reuter's recommendations are an attempt to think about a

specific phenomenon, organized crime, within the large paradigmatic structures of economic theory and one is left with the impression that a complex, multifaceted phenomena like organized crime is reducible to axiomatic statements within the calculus of industrial organizational theory. We think such strictures are damaging and ultimately self-defeating when theory is construed as the elite language of privileged scientific discourses and idioms. Organized crime is simply too complex and too vulnerable to historical exigencies to be confined to any particular paradigm and when it is, its insularity becomes apparent. It is not as if an ethnographic account of organized criminal activity is short on theory, while an essay on the business-like parameters of a vice activity becomes the exemplary model of scientific work on the phenomenon. They are both forms of discourse and to that extent they produce rather than just reflect their objects of reference. The difference between them may lie in their operational qualities. The ethnographic account is more expository, temporally bound to events it describes; while econometric analyses of vice make their contribution by informing and edifying about "business-like" characteristics of some types of organized criminality. The latter does not invalidate the former; nor does it necessarily precede it. They exists side by side - the one as an enabling part of the other, ideally speaking - like the recto and verso of a sheet of paper., For an elegant piece of theorizing still in its formative stages see, Albanese (1995) "Where Organized and White Collar Crime Meet: Predicting the Infiltration of Legitimate Business."

5. Private communications among the authors and Russian law enforcement officials, June 1994. Russian law enforcement experts clearly recognize the threat of rampart crime and its impact on the possibilities of a democratic society. The seriousness of the problem is also acknowledged by the United States Congress. In a rare move, the Senate Select Committee on Intelligence invited James F. Collins, the State Department's senior coordinator for Russia and other former Soviet States, to testify on the subject of organized crime. Before outlining government policies designed to protect American citizens and to assist the Russian government in coping with the problem, Collins observed that: "... Crime now poses - some three-plus years after the end of the Soviet Union - a major challenge to the government and the citizens of the NIS (New Independent States) as they pursue the uncharted road from communist totalitarianism authority to democracy and market economies (1995,270).

BIBLIOGRAPHY

Albanese, J. (Ed.). (1995). *Contemporary Issues in Organized Crime*. Monsey, New York: Willow Tree Press, Inc.

Amir, M. (1986). Organized Crime and Organized Criminality Among Georgian Jews in Israel. In R. J. Kelly (Ed.), *Organized Crime: a Global Perspective* (pp. 172-191). Totowa, New Jersey: Rowman and Littlefield.

274   Primitive Capitalist Accumulation:
       Russia as a Racket

Blok, A. (1974). *The Mafia of a Sicilian Village, 1860-1960: A Study of Violent Peasant Entrepreneurs*. New York: Harper and Row.

Cohen, L. & Felson, M. (1979). Social Changes and Crime Rate Trends: A Routine Actively Approach. *Criminology*. 25 933-947.

Collins, J. F. (1995, April 3). Crime in the New Independent States: The United States Response. *U. S. Dept. of State Dispatch*. 269-273.

di Argentine, A. B. (1993, August). The Mafias in Italy. In E. U. Savona (Ed.),*Mafia Issues* (pp. 120-124). Milan: International Scientific and Professional Advisory Council of the United Nations Crime Prevention and Criminal Justice Program.

Dijilas, M. (1982). *The New Class*. New York: Harcort, Brace Jovanovich.

Edelhertz, H. (Ed.). (1987). *Major Issues in Organized Crime Control*. Washington, DC: US Government Printing Office.

Finckenauer, J. (1994). "Russian Organized Crime in America." In R. J. Kelly, R. Schatzberg, and K. Chin (Eds.), *Handbook of Organized Crime in the United States*. (pp. 245-268). Westport, CT: Greenwood Press.

Follain, J. (1995). *A Dishonored Society*. New York: Little Brown.

Gambetta, D. (1993). *The Sicilian Mafia: the Business of Private Protection*. Cambridge, MA: Harvard University Press.

Galbraith, K. *The New Industrial State*.

Handelman, S. (1995). *Comrade Criminal: Russia's New Mafiya*. New Haven: Yale University Press.

Jousten, M. (1995). "Organized Crime in Central and Eastern Europe." In Albanese, J. S. (Ed.). *Contemporary Issues in Organized Crime*. (pp. 201-211). Monsey, New York: Willow Tree Press, Inc.

Kampfner, J. (1994). *Inside Yeltsin's Russia*. London: Cassell.

Kelly, R. J. (1994, July). Breaking the Seals of Silence: Anti- Mafia Uprising in Sicily. *USA Today*. (pp. 72-76).

_____ (1991). "Terrorism and Intrigue." Italian Journal. 5, 148-158.

Kenney D. J., & Finckenauer J. (1995). *Organized Crime In America*. (chap. 10). New York: Wadsworth Publishing Co.

Reuter, P. (1994). "Research on American Organized Crime." In R. J. Kelly, R. Schatzberg and K. Chin (Eds.). *Handbook of Organized Crime in the United States*. (pp. 91-120).

Shabalin, V., Albine, J., & Rogers, R. E. (1995). "Organized Crime and Business: A Report on the International Seminar for Honest Business." *Criminal Organization*. 7, 23-25.

Shelly, Louise I. (1995). "Post-Soviet Organized Crime: Implications for Economic, Social and Political Development". Trends in Organized Crime 1.1 (Fall) reprinted from Demokratizatsiya 2.3 (Summer, 1994): 341-358.

Simis, K. (1982). *The Corrupt Society*. New York: Simon and Schuster.

Solzhenitsyn, A. (1991). *Rebuilding Russia*. (pp. 75-76). (A. Klimoff Trans.). New York: Farrar, Strauss, Giroux.

Sterling, C. (19934). *Crime Without Frontiers: The Worldwide Expansion of Organized Crime and the Pax Mafiosa*. Boston: Little Brown.

Stille, A. (1995). *Excellent Cadavers: The Mafia and the Death of the First Italian Republic*. New York: Pantheon Books.

Tarormina, G. (1993, August). Organization and Functions of the Direzione Investigativa Anti-Mafia - DIA (Anti-Mafia Investigative Board). In E. U. Savona (Ed.), *Mafia Issues* (pp. 18-21). Milan: International Scientific and Professional Advisory Council of the United Nations Crime Prevention and Criminal Justice Program.

Vaksberg, A. (1991). *The Soviet Mafia*. (J. & E. Roberts Trans.). New York: St. Martin's Press.

Varese, F. (1994). "Is Sicily the Future of Russia? Private Protection and the Rise of the Russian Mafia." *Archives of European Sociology*. XXXV: 224-258.

ABOUT THE AUTHORS

Robert J. Kelly is a Broeklundian Professor of Social Science at Brooklyn College, and Professor of Criminal Justice at the Graduate School, City University of New York. He has conducted research on organized criminal activities, terrorism, violence in maximum security correctional facilities, and minority students in higher educational institutions. His publications, include Deviance, Dominance and Denigration; Organized Crime: A Global Perspective; Handbook on Organized Crime in the United States (Co-Editor); and numerous essays and articles in various journals.

Rufus Schatzberg retired from the New York City Police Department as a detective first class. His publications include Black Organized Crime In Harlem: 1920-1930; Handbook on Organized Crime in the United States (Co-Editor); and a soon to be released book titled, African-American Organized Crime in the United States: A Social History, which he co-authored with Robert J Kelly. Schatzberg has published numerous articles on terrorism, organized crime, and crime in schools.

Patrick J. Ryan a retired sergeant from New York City Police Department currently is an Associate Professor in the Department of Criminal Justice, Long Island University. He is President of the International Association for the Study of Organized Crime, former Editor of Criminal Organizations, and director of the Center for Drug Studies, Long Island University, School of Public Service. He has published several articles on RICO and defining organized crime; Ryan's most recent work is Organized Crime: A Reference Handbook.

[10]

Journal of Contemporary Criminal Justice
Vol. 11 • No. 4 • December 1995

Russian Organized Crime:
Its History, Structure and Function

Joseph L. Albini, Ph.D.
R.E. Rogers, Ph.D.
Col. Professor Victor Shabalin, Ph.D.
Gen. Professor Valery Kutushev, Jur.D.
Lt. Col. Professor Vladimir Moiseev, Ph.D.
Julie Anderson, B.A.

Abstract

In analyzing Russian organized crime, the authors describe and classify the four major forms of organized crime: 1) political-social, 2) mercenary, 3) in-group, and 4) syndicated. Though the first three classifications of the aforementioned types of organized crime existed throughout Soviet history, it was the syndicated form that began to emerge in the late 1950's, expanding during the corrupt Breznev years (1964-82), exploding during perestroika, and reaching pandemic levels after the demise of the Soviet Union in 1991. The abrupt transformation of the Russian society from a centralized command economy to one driven by the forces of market capitalism created the socio-pathological conditions for the malignant spread of mercenary and especially syndicated organized crime. New criminals syndicates were created by an alliance of criminal gangs/groups and former members of the Soviet Union's communist nomenklatura (bureaucracy) and the consequence was the criminalization of much of the Russian economy. The social structure of these syndicates is based on a loose association of patron-client relationships rather than a centralized hierarchical system; their function is to provide illicit goods/services desired by the people. The authors conclude their study by emphasizing that what has taken place in Russia is not peculiar to the Russian people, but exemplifies what can happen to societies that experience rapid and intense social change.

214   Russian Organized Crime:
       Its History, Structure and Function

The study of Russian organized crime encompasses the challenge and the acknowledgement of all the facets of human behavior, of historical and social change, the many forms political and economic development can take, and the complexity of the psychology and creativity of the criminal mind that seeks the path to acquiring money and power. The Russian experience with organized crime is an experience with many lessons, - - economic, social and political - - from which the discipline of criminology and, indeed, nations and governments, can benefit and learn. For the Russian experience with organized crime is a lesson in reality. Absent here is the romance and mythology that has surrounded the image of organized crime in the United States as one originated by, controlled by and centrally organized by the "Mafia" or "Cosa Nostra." To expect that the American public will finally begin to read the scholarly works on the subject to show that a belief in "Mafia" and "Cosa Nostra" has only served to excite readers and visually stimulate movie audiences is too much to ask, for mythologies die with a great deal of difficulty. They die hard because they serve a purpose; they serve to excite, entertain and construct social reality. But, history has taught us that mythological constructs are mythology, not reality. And this is true of organized crime in America and the American public's conception of it. The study of Russian organized crime should serve as a laboratory within which the basic features of organized crime reveal themselves. These features and characteristics are basic to its nature and, although historical and cultural factors exert their influence and create some differences in the countries in which it exists, the essence or basic characteristics of organized crime are inherent to its nature.

As we read the literature on organized crime in Russia both scholars and journalists seem to agree that Russian organized crime is not like the "Mafia" in the United States. What this comparison means precisely is hard to discern, particularly when some of these authors refer to organized criminals in Russia as "the Russian Mafia." But this usage is at the core of our discussion; that is, the term "Mafia" has become a synonym for organized crime. This confusion emerged as a result of the indiscriminate use of the term "Mafia" among American scholars and journalists. In the senior author's pioneering work, The American Mafia (1971), the argument was made that there never was nor is a secret criminal society called "Mafia," either in Sicily (its supposed country of origin) or in the U.S. (the country of its supposed exportation). If we correctly understand its origin in Sicily, mafia was not and is not one organization, but rather, the term is better understood as a method or modus operandi of a criminal endeavor which has the following components (Albini, 1971: 88):

1. The use of force, intimidation or threats of such;
2. The structure of a group whose purpose is that of providing illicit services through the use of secrecy on the part of its associates;
3. The assurance of protection from the legal structure which is necessary for its continuous operation.

ALBINI, ROGERS, SHABALIN, 215
KUTUSHEV, MOISEEV & ANDERSON

As a method, then, mafia can exist anywhere. As for its being exported or imported, we should understand that it is organized criminals that migrate; the system and the criminal's ability to employ it in any given country, by contrast, depends upon the social conditions and social system of that country which may either foster its use or stifle its development. Thus, as has been noted, (Albini, 1992: 87) it is argued that the Sicilian "Mafia" migrated to the U.S. during the period of 1870 to 1920. During the same time there was an equally large migration of Italians to Brazil and Argentina; yet, Della Cava (1977: 197) notes that - - "not only are Italians and their descendants rarely associated with professional criminality, in either country, but also 'organized crime' itself exists on a greatly reduced scale." So, too, as Albini (1986) has noted in his study of organized crime in Great Britain, Italians are virtually non-existent as a major force in organized crime activity.

Contrary to popular "Mafia" lore, it is not specific ethnic groups that create or determine if mafia will exist; rather, it is the existence of social, economic and historical factors present in each society that set the stage for its emergence and success. Thus, in the history of United States, virtually every ethnic group has been found to have had members that participated in organized crime. Their method has always been the same. Yet, because of a need for mythological belief, the Sicilian "Mafia" has caused the word "Mafia" to become a synonym; it can be a synonym, but not one for referring to a secret criminal organization; rather for what is a method of organized criminal activity.

So, as we move toward understanding the nature of organized crime in Russia, the Russian experience allows us and forces us, if we truly wish to understand its reality and the reality of organized crime in any other country, to apply clear and useful distinctions to the term organized crime itself.

As one reads the scant literature (Kenny and Finchenauer, 1995: 276 and Abadinsky, 1990: 264-165) on Russian organized crime, particularly that concerning Russian organized crime in the United States, one immediately notes that there is confusion. There is confusion regarding whether or not Russian organized crime is, in fact, organized crime, whether it is a form of "Mafia", how it is structured and a variety of other elements. By contrast, Lydia Rosner (1986) presents a more useful portrait of the Russian immigrant and Russian organized crime in the United States by examining this immigrant's value system regarding how it relates to crime in Russia and then examining the adaptations these immigrants have made regarding criminal activity in the United States.

Once again, we stress that mafia as a method is dependent for its effective development upon the social setting in which it exists far more than it is upon the structure or organization of the groups that engage in it. We can stress the logic behind this observation by simply asking— "Is there any ethnic, racial or other type of group, irrespective of its organizational structure, that has not been successful in their involvement with organized criminal activity in the United States?" The Irish, Poles, Germans, Japanese, Chinese, motorcycle gangs, Jamaicans, prison gangs, Cubans, Colombians, Mexicans, the Black Guerilla Family, the Aryan Brotherhood

216   Russian Organized Crime:
        Its History, Structure and Function

are just a few we mention, but the list goes on. Why does it go on? Because America is the land of opportunity for success in organized crime. The American society with its historically changing but ever present needs and demands for illicit goods and a public that has continuously hidden under a guise of morality has set up a system where great financial wealth can be made. This wealth can be acquired providing that one wishes to take the risk of possibly death and/or imprisonment and has the ingenuity by which to provide some form of political protection for their criminal enterprise by providing favors for their protectors of by simply giving them direct "pay-offs."

This is the American way of crime. The mythology of the "Sicilian Mafia" has been just that — a mythology.

The Sicilians have been no different from any other group in their modus operandi or structure in terms of their having achieved success at organized criminal ventures in America. For the past three decades, they simply became the show that America watched in an effort to convince itself that the real threat of organized crime lies from outside its boundaries in the form of an invasion of foreigners and their mystical secret society. It is social and political systems that allow for the creation of organized crime. That is a fact. And so the Russian social system in the past and particularly since the collapse of the Berlin Wall has laid the breeding grounds for organized crime to breed and flourish in Russia. That, also, is a fact. As we shall demonstrate, the Russians are no more or less moral than Americans. In fact, indeed, as we will show, American and Russian patterns of organized crime are, in many respects, similar. Their differences emerge only as those influenced by such factors as historical development and the rapidity of the economic, political and social changes that occurred in Russia at the turn of this decade. Indeed, along with those found in America, there are similarities between the Russian patterns and structure of organized crime and those found in the history and development of organized crime in Sicily.

The basic problem with the literature that grapples with the question of whether or not Russian organized crime in America and Russia is really organized crime, we feel, comes from the mistaken need for writers to continue to emphasize the structure of criminal groups more than their function.

Noone makes this point more succinctly than Southerland and Potter (1993: 264). Speaking to the structure and function of criminal groups, they conclude:

> "The empirical evidence suggests that criminal enterprises are small, centralized organizations with short hierarchies, little specialization, and unwritten formalization based on socialization. The logic of the situation based on organization structure theory demonstrates how unlikely it is that a very large tightly controlled and organized criminal conspiracy could function in operational reality.

ALBINI, ROGERS, SHABALIN,   217
KUTUSHEV, MOISEEV & ANDERSON

A monopolistic syndicate by definition would have an extremely large number of employees and numerous functional specialties such as drugs, prostitution, gambling and loansharking. To achieve its goals, the syndicate would have to provide constant instruction and information to street-level purveyors. It would have to monitor employee performance, keep careful records, and engage in considerable discussion about specific plans. These behaviors would imperil the very existence of the organization. If such a conspiracy existed, removing its leadership would cripple the enterprise. Experience demonstrates that this has not happened despite extensive successful prosecutions of prominent organized crime figures."

We are in agreement with Southerland and Potter and feel that it would be more productive to study the functions of organized crime groups since the structure is assuredly based upon that function. Many writers it seems are so influenced by a belief in a conspiratorial model of criminal enterprises that they go searching for large complexly structured groups of participants. In doing so, they miss the trees for the forest. As we observe Russian organized crime, we find that, like American organized crime, the function—that is, what the criminals are trying to accomplish in terms of goals—definitely influences the structure. Therefore in our search and discussion we find it productive to employ Albini's (1971, chapter 2) classification of the four major forms of organized crime. These are:

1. Political-social organized crime - - where the goal is not direct financial profit, or the changing of or maintaining of the existing political-social structure. An example of this would be terrorism or the Ku Klux Klan.

2. Mercenary organized crime - - where the goal is the attainment of direct financial profit. Here would be included racketeering, extortion, organized theft of goods, confidence games and other forms of profit-oriented crimes.

3. In-group organized crime - - here financial gain is not the direct goal, but instead the purpose lies in the individual's psychological and social gratification of belonging to a group that engages in deviant and criminal activity. Here would be included the hedonistic or violent gangs that engage in thrills or violence but do so for the adventure itself - - examples of this are the adolescent and street-corner gangs found in most cities which frequently engage in street fights over territory or "rumbles."

4. Syndicated organized crime - - here the goal of the criminal group is to attain direct financial gain by providing illicit goods and/or services through the use of threat, the use of violence and by attaining forms of police or political "protection" which will safeguard the criminal from legal nterference. An example of this would be gambling, prostitution and drug syndicates.

The reader will note that each of these forms of criminal activity has a different goal and the structures and size of the group will vary based upon the structural and personnel differences required in the achievement of each goal. It is here that we

218   Russian Organized Crime:
        Its History, Structure and Function

find that the confusion that so often occurs in the literature arises from the fact that many authors employ the term "Mafia" to describe organized criminal activity which is mercenary or political-social in nature. The term mafia, if it is used properly to describe a method, is really correctly used only when it refers to syndicated crime. But, even here, because the term has become so indiscriminately, erroneously and randomly used, we are advocating that it not be employed (because of the misunderstanding its use creates. We, instead prefer and will employ the term - - syndicated crime.

As we move now to the analysis and description of Russian organized crime, we do so within a theoretical background that views its development from a historical and social perspective; for to argue that Russian organized crime is a current phenomenon is to miss its existence within Soviet society in the past.

To say, however, that it is not a current phenomenon is to fail to understand that the breakdown and breakup of the Soviet Union in 1991 has opened new roads and new opportunities for organized criminal ventures to develop within Russia itself and to reach out across international boundaries. This phenomenon has become so pronounced that recently the Russian government has appealed for international help from legal agencies in its fight against organized crime (Las Vegas Review Journal, Nov. 22, 1994: 9A). So, too, because Russian organized crime is now viewed both by the American public and by American law enforcement agencies as part of America's growing crime problem, we wish to present our discussion in the context of comparing the Russian and American experience. Also, as we noted earlier, because Russian organized crime manifests a profile of emerging from the rapidity and abruptness of swift historical and societal change, it serves as a laboratory of socio-scientific research. Also we feel that because of the confusion concerning the nature of "Mafia" in Sicily it will be of heuristic value to the international study of organized crime to compare the similarities and differences of syndicated criminal development in Russia and Sicily; for indeed, there are many similarities along with drastic differences.

Let us move on then to the investigation and understanding of this complex, multivariable, socio-cultural phenomenon known as organized crime.

As we stated before, to say that Russian organized crime is a new phenomenon is to miss a major lesson learned from the Russian experience; mainly, that although totalitarian political systems can control most aspects of social life, they cannot totally control all of these. So as V.L. Dedenkov (Report No. 9: 5-6) notes, following the Russian revolution, there appeared a variety of criminal groups or organizations that have been given the name "thieves within the code." These groups varied in size, had a leader, and had rules of behavior for their members, one of the major rules being that the members not become involved in politics. It is difficult to construct an accurate profile of these organizations because one of their major features was secrecy. Sterling (1994: 47), citing the work of the Russian poet and ex-thief Mikhail Dyomin, notes that such organizations date back to the 1600s. However Sterling seems to agree with Dyomin that these were organized on the model of the Sicilian mafia. At this point we should note that what both Sterling and Dyomin are using as their basis for this argument is based upon an erroneous confusion; mainly that of viewing "Mafia," the so-called Sicilian secret society with other Sicilian criminal groups known as "Frattellanze" or "brotherhoods." Mafia, as we define it as a method could not and did not emerge in Sicily until 1860 when the institution of universal suffrage provided the third ingredient of what constitutes syndicated crime or Mafia as method - - political protection (Albini, 1971: 127). These "brotherhoods" arose in the 1700s to fight the Bourbons whose rule began in 1738. The frequent mythological and erroneous belief that the Mafia in Sicily began as a benevolent organization to fight the French oppressive government is born here. These brotherhoods, as Antonino Cutrera (Albini, 1971: 114) states, although they stressed secrecy and each were indeed organized and had a leader, were organized not for noble purposes but instead, to make profits from theft and extortion. As such, they seem to have had the same structure and function as the "thieves within the code." We argue then, that the "thieves within the code" in Russia, from the little information we have regarding them were, at least during the early years of Soviet Security Police and later Stalinist repression from 1920 until 1950, at most, criminal organizations that engaged in mercenary, not syndicated crime. Later, particularly after the breakup of the Soviet Union, as we shall argue, some of these "thieves within the code" groups did begin engaging in forms of syndicated crime.

During the 1920s there was a struggle for power among different factions in the Communist Party; it was especially intense after the death of Lenin in 1924. By 1928, Stalin had eliminated the opposition and ruled with an iron fist until his death in March 1953. The Stalinist era was from 1928-1953.

We should note at this point and in reference to the organized criminality of the "thieves within the code" and of organized crime in general in Russia during the communist era that, officially, the Soviet government took the position that such activity was a product of a capitalistic system and therefore could not by nature exist in a socialist society (Report No. 9: 1). Hence, any information regarding evidence or allegations of its existence was flagrantly suppressed to the point that when KGB and military personnel themselves reported such activities, they were simply told - - "There is no organized crime in the Soviet Union." We should also add that, during this era, the majority of the crimes for which people were arrested such as those arrests resulting from the purges of the 1930s were those that were politically motivated and viewed as crimes against the state (Report No. 9: 6).

But, although there is nebulousness about the nature of organized crime groups in Russia before the revolution and in the post revolutionary 1920s and Stalinist era, this nebulousness begins to clear as we move into the 1950s.

There exists, currently, a mistaken but prevalent belief that, in Russia, organized crime in its contemporary forms did not exist until the tearing down of the Iron Curtain or, put another way, that Russian organized crime first appeared as a result of Glasnost and Perestroika.

Lydia Rosner (1993) is quick to counter this point of view and we agree with

220   Russian Organized Crime:
      Its History, Structure and Function

her that, indeed, various forms of Russian mercenary and syndicated crime were in existence even though they were being hidden by the Iron Curtain. In fact we would argue that the current forms of mercenary and some forms of syndicated crime began appearing and evolving in complexity by the end of the 1950s and flourished during the period of stagnation - - the label given to the period of rule of the Communist party leader L. Brezhnev (1964-1982) (Report No. 9: 7). This period is important to our later discussion of the development of various forms of organized crime. It is important because during this time, the breeding grounds for the development of organized crime emerged by the fact that capital investment was allocated to the military in an effort to gain missile parity with the United States, all at the expense and sacrifice to the Soviet people's standard of living (Report No. 9: 7).

Konstantin Simis, writing in 1982, had already labelled the U.S.S.R. as the "corrupt society" and stated then that both "...the Soviet state and society alike [were] rotten with corruption from top to bottom." (Simis, : 179, authors' italics).

To say that organized crime in Russia is a new phenomenon, then, is to miss the role of its historical development since the 1950s and the changes in the political, economic and social system of Russia and its republics during the era of stagnation.

Nonetheless, we must here make an important distinction between the era before and following the breakdown and breakup of the Soviet Union between 1989 and 1991; that is, that prior to this period, organized crime in the Soviet Union focused primarily on enterprises within its political and territorial boundaries; after the fall, we see it extend its enterprises and boundaries to international markets and territories.

When Eastern Europe broke away from Communist control in 1989, it had a profound effect on the Soviet Union. Many nationalists wanted independence for their republics. 1989 was also the year the Communist Party competed with other parties for seats in the new Duma (Parliament). When the military and KGB failed in the August 19-21, 1991 coup, Boris Yeltsin dissolved the Soviet Union and created Commonwealth of Independent States (C.I.S.). He also outlawed the Communist Party (It later became legal under a different name) and seized its assets of over 3 billion rubles.

In order to understand organized crime in Russia during both periods, we must examine the nature of its origins within the cultural and historical development of the Soviet Union itself. For it is within the values of this culture juxtaposed and in conjunction with the economic, political and other aspects of Soviet society that this form of criminality took roots. After its various types had developed and its various groups formed, its exportation into other countries and the nature of these exported forms of criminality became dependent upon the social, economic and political environment of those countries into which they were exported and upon the demand for illegal goods and services which existed within the global marketplace itself. We are here trying to emphasize the distinction between the phenomenon of a criminal system that develops within a society generated by individuals born and

ALBINI, ROGERS, SHABALIN,   221
KUTUSHEV, MOISEEV & ANDERSON

raised in that society and their individual participation in similar forms of that criminality outside that system. Thus, although mafia as a method developed and exists in Sicily, it is a composite of the Sicilian life and culture of Sicily. If Sicilians who participated in that system came to America, as some of them did, it is not the "Mafia" that is transported. A cultural system, as such, cannot be transported; instead, it is individuals who migrate and bring with them their criminal values and techniques. However, ultimately, whether or not such criminals are successful in effectively instituting these criminal enterprises in their country of destination depends upon the amenability of the social system of that country to foster such development.

By contrast, criminal groups or criminal secret societies with a particular modus operandi could migrate to a foreign country as a group. If their style of criminality is new to that country, then we can speak of these groups as having exported a new form of crime. If, however, that form of criminality already exists within the country they enter, we can hardly refer to these criminals as having exported it into that country. In either respect, as we noted, whether or not these groups are successful in implementing their criminal operation depends, ultimately, upon the social, economic, political and other conditions of the country into which they migrate.

We make the above distinctions because, in the literature concerning organized crime, particularly that of Russian organized crime, we so often note the use of the term "export" in the discussion of what are described as new forms of organized crime in America and other countries. A major illustration of this is witnessed in the argument that indeed has become a part of American folklore; mainly, that the Sicilians "exported" the mafia to the United States. History shows us that "mafia" as a method existed in America as early as the time of the Civil War, long before the conditions surrounding the prohibition era in the 1920s allowed the Sicilians and many other ethnic groups to take their turn at engaging in a pattern of crime - - syndicated crime - - that is as American in origin, as apple pie.

**Let us return now and concentrate on our discussion of the
basic topic of this paper - - Russian organized crime.**

It is true that many changes in the types of organized criminal enterprises and the organizations of the groups operating them took place after the fall of communism in 1989-91. But to argue that the fall in itself, created this surge in Russian criminality is to miss the realities of what was occurring in Russia before the coming of Glasnost and Perestroika. Lydia Rosner (1993) makes this point succinctly in the title of her recent article - - "Crime and Corruption in Russia are nothing new." And indeed we agree with her that the seeds of what has grown to become the formulation of criminal groups that now threaten international peace and safety through the terror of the potential sale of nuclear material (Time, August 29, 1994: 47-51) were sown in the very system of communism and its inherent and absolute policy of the

222   Russian Organized Crime:
       Its History, Structure and Function

state owning all goods and services. In the reports of recent conferences and seminars held in Russia, Professor V. Shabalin and A.I. Dolgova and various other social scientists, government representatives and lawyers have noted that the current practice of bribery and corruption certainly existed during the time of the Tzars and have been, historically, an embedded part of the very nature of Russian society itself. Indeed N.G. Chernyskevsky speaks of Russia as a land "...rich in bribetakers...since time immemorial" (Report No. 9: 18).

Our purpose here is not to degrade or pass judgment on Russian society or its people, for most Russians are indeed honest citizens; instead we wish to observe, analyze and discuss a way of life which Rosner (1986) refers to in the title of her book as - - "The Soviet Way of Crime." This system, indeed, incorporates a cultural "way" of social interaction brought about by political and economic restrictions that has come to constitute the arena of life in Russia for most of the twentieth century.

It is a way of life and crime that arises out of needs, values and social interaction patterns that can be understood only within the web of a historical development and social structure that is unique to Russia. This does not mean that there are not similarities here to other cultures. Indeed, one could argue that, in the way of crime, Russia has several historical-social patterns that are similar to those of Sicily. But history and social forces do not form societies so that they are identical; hence, the differences far exceed the similarities. Yet in the social potential for the development of syndicated crime, we find that both the people of Russia and Sicily definitely have one feature in common; that is, they both have a distrust of government and governmental power. Sicilians developed this distrust because of the many and rapid foreign invasions in which the conquerors took over the land, took what they needed and either left or were forced to leave by cultural revolutions or other foreign invaders. Under such conditions one learns to rely on family and communal ties as resources for sustaining life and human relationships as opposed to relying upon the typically unfulfilled promises of central governments. In Russia, governments both under the rule of the Tzars and that of the Communist state represented totalitarianism in one form or another where individual freedom was suppressed. As such, like the invading foreigners of Sicily, the internal governmental system of Russia has made the Russian, like the Sicilian, distrustful of government. This common historical inheritance in both Sicily and Russia has produced a method of social interaction in which patrons and clients become the basic social format for interaction. The terms "patron" and "client" describe power relationships that gain their meaning only within the context of social interaction. It is important to note that this power is not formalized in the legal system nor is it established by conventionally prescribed rules. Yet it lies at the basis of interaction, both legal and illegal, in both Russian and Sicilian society. To describe these terms, we turn to the work of Jeremy Boissevain (1966: 18) who defines a "patron" as any person in a position of power and influence and thereby can help or protect others who are not in that position. The "client", by contrast, is the person who seeks and receives the assistance and protection for which he in return offers services to the patron. Eric Wolf (1966: 16-17) further elaborates on the description by noting that no two functionaries in a "patron-client" relationship are equal. So, too, he notes that patrons and clients can engage in both legal and illegal actions where the patron provides assistance and protection with the client returning the favor by being loyal to the patron, giving him political support and by providing the patron with information that is vital to his personal and social welfare.

We should emphasize that patron-client relationships are not governed by legal norms but instead are based upon social norms in which there is an accepted faith between the two participants that each will carry out his or her end of the bargain. Most importantly, we should note that the power relations between patrons and clients are constantly in a state of change so that a "patron" at one time or in one situation may later become the "client" of his or her original "client." So, too, a "patron," while serving as such to a "client" may himself or herself simultaneously be serving as a "client" to another patron. Thus, the patron-client relationship must be understood as a system of interaction taking place at and between various levels of social strata and one that involves constantly changing power positions. The nature of patron-client relationships varies from society to society, but in Sicily and Russia the system operates to form networks of relationships in which the more clients a patron has, the more power the patron gains from favors he or she can request. This power is enhanced further by the vital information the patron obtains; in turn, the more patrons a client has, the more power he or she obtains from the protection and service the client can receive. As such, it is a mutually-reinforcing system in which, in terms of cost-benefit analysis, it serves both parties to cooperate and help one another. As such, both parties can gain and retain power.

Because of the distrust of government in both Sicily and Russia and the development of the patron-client system of interaction, the breeding grounds for syndicated organized crime were entrenched in both social systems. In Sicily, the catalyst for the development of mafia as a method resulted from ownership of land in the "gabellotto" or landlord system, a system that developed following the abolition and breakdown of the feudal system in 1812 (see Albini, 1971, chapter 4). These landlords slowly established themselves in the social structure by developing patron-client relationships in which they could offer services, legal and illegal to a variety of clients. In time, they hired men skilled in the use of violence and through time, the landlords threatened and employed violence against those who opposed them. Finally, when Italy obtained universal suffrage, the landlord could now provide votes for governmental officials who in turn, if elected, would be in a position to offer the landlord and all his clients protection from the law.

In Russia, the catalyst was not land as land and its tenure under the Tzars never had or took the format of Sicily's "gabellotto" or landlord system. Hence, the criminal activity that we find described during that era and following the early days of communist rule as "thieves within the code" or bands of thieves organized around the major element of secrecy, was primarily that constituting forms of mercenary crime. These groups stole for financial gain or profit but had no political protection.

224   Russian Organized Crime:
       Its History, Structure and Function

It remained to the days of the full development of the communist state, to the development of the political and economic system of the 1960s Soviet society, for syndicated crime to emerge as a pattern which took hold and continues to the present day. There is no doubt that Perestroika and Glasnost exerted their influence in the direction and volume of syndicated crime, but the system of the patron-client way of crime in the Soviet Union was already alive and doing well before these political programs were introduced.

What land was to the spawning of syndicated crime in Sicily in the 1860s, state owned goods and services were to become in the Russia of the 1960s, the bartering ingredient which generated the development of Russian syndicated crime. Here we should note that by contrast to Russia and Sicily, in America, where syndicated crime has existed as early as the 1860s, it was and continues to be the desire for illegal goods and services on the part of American citizens that has historically created a multitude of criminal syndicates that procure political protection and threaten and employ violence in order to make such goods available.

Organized crime, then, particularly syndicated crime is a complex phenomenon. The structure of the groups that engage in it reveals many variations; thus, ethnicity, kinship, business and other bases for organization and cooperation appear and vary in the societies in which syndicated crime exists. Indeed, in contrast to the belief in a large, centralized, bureaucratic format of syndicate structure, research reveals the opposite; that the existence of structures small in the number of functionaries, with continually changing involvement of personnel and power-relationships and constantly changing webs of networks and enterprises are the features that make this form of criminality the menace that it is. It is not the secrecy in which these groups conduct those enterprises for the practice of secrecy is a natural ingredient to all criminals enterprises. Nor is it the largeness of the group that sustains such enterprises for largeness would indeed hamper rather than aid their effective functioning; instead it is the existence of large numbers of small syndicates with their multitude of network patron-client relationships and the demand for their goods and services that gives syndicated criminals their strength and persistence in societies that allow them to function. For at the end of the argument concerning its existence lies the reality that it is societies, not individuals, that create the basis for syndicated organized crime.

Let us turn now to our discussion of the nature of organized
crime in the Soviet Union and Russia.

The basic source of the emergence of syndicated crime in Russia arises, as Rosner (1993) explains, in the fact that in the Soviet Union, all goods and services were owned by the state. As such, theoretically there could be no private enterprise. We say, theoretically, because, in reality, there was a way, the Soviet way of crime; that way was to steal goods from the state or illegally barter for the performance of services, in a manner which, like, theft, would have been considered a crime against the state.

The state, of course, was caught in a dilemma; it needed to provide goods and services to its populace, but it was also concerned about developing and keeping its military strength equal, if not superior to that of its then adversary - - the United States. In the 1960s, particularly under the rule of L. Brezhnev, most capital investment was diverted into the science and military establishment in an effort to counteract the new U.S. threat of missile development. In doing so, the state seriously reduced the production and supply of goods and services that constituted the basic necessities for life and comfort among the general population. As a result, a black market for all goods and services emerged.

This condition was further complicated by the political reality of what Simis (1982: 26-27) calls, "the dual system of government," that existed at that time; that is, the existence of bodies of government such as the Council of Ministers and other agencies empowered to govern by the constitution and, alongside this, the Communist Party, which is not even mentioned in the constitution, yet became the real ruling body of the Soviet Union. As Simis further explains, since the state, which owned all goods and services and was the sole employer of the population was subject to the Communist Party's decisions, this translated into the Party really being the sole controller of all aspects of Soviet life.

And so, it seems that when shortages in goods and services were created by the state's allocations of money for military purposes in the 1960s, the Soviet citizens at all levels began to create their own manner of obtaining the goods and services which often constituted the basic necessities of life, or those that make living easier and more pleasant.

Lev Timofeyev, (1990: 58) a Russian critic of the Soviet regime puts this reaction on the part of Soviet citizens very succinctly when he observes; "no violence or brainwashing, however intensive, could make man forego the basic relations of supply and demand. Apparently, nature has not provided any other mechanism for supporting the social life of homosapiens."

And so the shortage brought into action the use of patron-client relationship. As Rosner (1993: 1) describes it:

> "Thus a state employee could find work doing private repair jobs for those who could pay him with meat or clothing stolen from their jobs. The state employee had to obtain his supplies from a network of 'friends' whose favors he rewarded with favors of his own. A state cement truck driver would exchange some cement, delivered to a private job, for some coats for his children. A state clerk in an automobile licensing agency would exchange the right to drive a motor vehicle for gasoline for his own use or sale."

226   Russian Organized Crime:
      Its History, Structure and Function

As Lev Timofeyev (1990: 58) notes further - - "Everything is bought and sold in this country. Everything including the official positions in the Communist Party".

And indeed, Rosner (1993: 1) adds to Timofeyev's observation by noting that further alienations from the central government took place as the national organization in the republics themselves became totally corrupt, the people in charge staying in power and increasing their power by granting and exchanging political favors as well as employing private procurers in order to obtain all types of goods and services.

It is indeed difficult here to argue that syndicated crime, as a form, existed at this time since it is difficult to distinguish the criminals from the political protectors. Since many people, if they could, were stealing goods from the state and wheeling and dealing in the game of exchanging goods and services, it is ludicrous to argue that criminal syndicates were established to provide illicit goods to those who desired them. Why? Because this entire system of citizen's and governmental agents' obtaining goods and services was so widespread as to have become, itself, the social norm. So, too, violence, although it seems to have occurred in the form that Rosner (1986: 9) mentions as the use of violent force by "thugs" working for corrupt district party members, was not, during this time period, a pronounced feature of this system or the Soviet way of crime. Ironically, and further confusing the issue of the existence of syndicated crime, is the fact that during this era of communist rule, as Timofeyev (1990: 56-57) notes, any entrepreneurial activity, whether engaged in by criminal groups or honest business people was, by definition, considered illegal and punishable by law. But since so many of the governmental officials were themselves engaging in corrupt practices, it is difficult not to argue that the government itself consisted of a form of organized crime. For if the corruptor is simultaneously the corrupted, where are the boundaries for establishing the definition and essence of the legal system itself?

It seems then that the period prior to the fall of communism and the breakup of the Soviet Union became the training and breeding ground for the development of syndicated crime in contemporary Russia. For up to that time, the criminality, if one indeed can call it that considering the fact that stealing from the state and the rampant exchanging of goods and services among Soviet citizens had become the social norm, was, for the most part, confined and contained within the Soviet Union itself. But with the breakup of the Soviet Union and the movement toward the development of a market economy, and the privatization of business and industry, the former Soviet Union experienced one of the most rapid and tumultuous changes in the history of social change. The breeding and training grounds now having been established, Russia and its republics were a ripe market for the development of an international market of criminal ventures. And so, it is in the late 1980s and early 1990s that this Soviet way of crime extends its boundaries and develops its various forms of contemporary organized crime including the clear development of syndicated organized crime.

ALBINI, ROGERS, SHABALIN,   227
KUTUSHEV, MOISEEV & ANDERSON

The picture of the contemporary scene in Russia is best painted by the 1993 U.S. News and World Report publication most timely entitled - - Focus on Change (1993: 16). The report reads:

> "The former Soviet Union is a cauldron of contrasts. It is now 15 separate countries, the sum of the new parts much less than the old whole. Russia dominates, undeniably weakened; Its military is dispirited and underfunded, its economy in a steepening plunge, its political reform stalemated. But it is also strong. Its arsenal of 30,000 nuclear weapons is intact; it has vast reserves of natural resources, a solid labor base and a growing entrepreneurial class. In Russia and the other new states, many younger leaders haven't abandoned hopes of radically reforming political systems."

This report then describes the current process of converting the military and defense industry into civilian production by using the Russian term (p.17) "KONVULSIYA" - - convulsion; and, indeed, "convulsion" is probably the best word for describing the entire current social system of Russia and the Federation.

In a state of "convulsion," the human body loses equilibrium. Convulsing political units do the same.

We use the analogy of disequilibrium because, indeed, Russia and its former republics are caught in a web of contradictory and conflicting political and social forces often serving to frustrate and block the desperately needed move toward a unified and cooperative approach toward the resolution of economic and other problems. This situation is a perfect setting for the proliferation of crime, particularly organized crime. For as the movement and changes geared toward privatization began to emerge slowly in 1989 and 1990, the forces - - business, political, and criminal - - of the old and the new power groups began to clash. Young entrepreneurs who honestly believed that a private and free economy was the new mode of doing business, did, in fact, begin creating business enterprises. At first, it seems that the old time communist bureaucrats simply expected these young businessmen to fail since these bureaucrats believed that any capitalistic venture, by its very nature, could not succeed. When, however, these bureaucrats saw, that, indeed, these entrepreneurs could or were becoming successful, they either used their legal power and the law itself to arrest them, often as Timofeyev (1990: 58-59) notes, labelling them as "mafia-profiteers" or, recognizing that there was gold in those capitalistic hills, decided to join them and allow the capitalistic system to work for them.

And so privatization, definitely established as an economic program in 1992, became, as Rosner (1993: 2) puts it - - "...the ultimate shakeout of a bureaucratically corrupt system." But, with privatization, the world, not just Russia and its federation, became the stage upon which the current drama of Russian organized

228   Russian Organized Crime:
       Its History, Structure and Function

crime would be enacted.

Internally, the breakdown of the Soviet Union sounded the bell for various republics to demand and/or fight for independence. A look at the military operations of the Russian special forces reveals that since 1989, political-social organized crime became a major concern for the new Russia. In 1989, political unrest demanded military intervention in Uzbekistan. In the spring of 1990, ethnic unrest in the Trans-Caucasian republics demanded Russia's military action. Indeed, the months of May and June 1992 saw political upheavals in the form of riots, protests, civil war, terrorism and other forms of political-social criminality in Kazakhstan, Uzbekistan, Georgia and Dagestan. These and the continued conflict between Azerbaijan and Armenia over Nogorno- Karabakh created a continuing sequence of criminal acts of a political-social nature. Jim Shortt, (1993, Preface) who has trained KGB personnel and police and security forces in the Baltic states before, as well as after independence, cites numerous cases of terrorism and other forms of social-political organized crime. What is interesting about Shortt's description and analysis of these political-social actions is his mentioning of the involvement of Russian "mafia" functionaries. Quick to note that, in Russia, "mafia" is a generic term for racketeers, black marketeers, and gangsters (p.39), Shortt mentions that these criminal gangs were frequently employed to help the cause of interior ministers in various former republics. As such, Shortt notes, in Latvia, in March 1992 a criminal group went to the extent of disguising themselves as members of a military unit by wearing the Russian military red beret and camouflage. These groups, as Shortt observes, (p.27) disguised as official Russian special units, were actually paid criminals whose task was to protect and facilitate the escape of other criminals in the event of attack by authentic Russian forces.

Probably the most voluminous form of organized criminality ushered in by the breakup of the U.S.S.R. and the movement toward privatization lies in the category of mercenary crime. For, here, the goal is not the seeking or retaining of political power; rather - - outright profit itself.

Russian research (Report No. 9: 7) concludes that a direct relationship exists between the growth of contemporary organized crime and the improvement of the economic system. Russian students of the topic agree that "...the level of organized crime is closely associated with the state of the economy...." and that "....within the economy is hidden the nucleus of the criminal corporation."

We note once again that the breeding grounds for the growth of organized crime and the accompanying patron-client system of social interaction necessary for its development were already intact prior to the coming of privatization; one, then, can readily understand that when the economic gates were open, a flood of criminal ventures began to flow through Russia, its former republics, and the world.

This growth has brought to the foreground a term that has come to be widely used in the discussion of contemporary Russian organized crime - - "the shadow economy"; and rightly so, for it is within the context of this economic system that organized crime seems to have increased in both types and number of enterprises

ALBINI, ROGERS, SHABALIN, 229
KUTUSHEV, MOISEEV & ANDERSON

as well as its extension into international markets.

But we must be quick to note that the shadow economy and its frequently employed synonym - - "the black market" - - has its roots in the past social patterns of Soviet society. Its evolution into contemporary forms spawned by criminals must be viewed from the perspective of a system where, formally, all goods and services were owned by the state to one slowly trying to change to a system of individual entrepreneurs. We define the shadow economy as "...the entire complex of non-accounted, non-regulated and illegal types of economic activities (different from normative documents and rules of the economy)." (Report No. 9: 12)

But, in offering this definition, we heed the words of Lev Timofeyev (1990: 59) who reminds us that the entire Soviet economy has been nothing else but an "...enormous 'black market' of goods, services, official positions and privileges." Timofeyev also answers the question of why "the black market" nonetheless has helped create the current growth and expansion of organized criminality. He explains:

> "the chief drawback of the Soviet black market in
> comparison to the free market is that in the former the
> profit is not genuine capital, it cannot be used for
> investment, for expanding production and improving
> productivity. Untaxed cash acquired in this market is
> typically used for personal consumption or converted
> into gold and valuables which in the recent period are
> increasingly apt to be taken out of the country via illegal
> routes." (p.56).

It is this practice that casts the shadow of criminality across Russia. And the shadow it casts takes many forms.

Paul Klebnikov, writing in Forbes magazine (Nov. 21, 1994: 74-84) compares current Russia with that era of the robber barons in America where the robber barons dominated American capitalism. Men like Cornelius Vanderbilt, John D. Rockefeller and others gained control of a large number of assets, not through theft, but through their organizational skills and financial leverage. Klebnikov then describes several Russian businessmen who have become wealthy. It is here worthwhile, for the purpose of our discussion, to note briefly the description of how one of these men became successful since it illustrates our point that the old political-economic system in Russia has blended with the new. Klebnikov writes about Mikhail Khodorkovsky, chairman of Menatep Bank, a Russian bank with close to one billion dollars:

> "His first financial backing came from one of the
> communist-controlled district councils of Moscow.
> Later, Khodorkovsky apparently bought out the district
> council. Now this swarthy young man runs a vast
> conglomerate. It includes Menatep Bank, a dozen other

230   Russian Organized Crime:
      Its History, Structure and Function

banks, Moscow real estate, a steel mill, one of Russia's
largest producers of titanium as well as food processing
and chemical companies." (p. 71.)

This article goes on to tell how Khodorkovsky lives in luxury but is surrounded
by a host of private security guards.

The web of patron-client relationships, apart from allowing for the creation of
robber barons, has also allowed for the old and the new to come together in the
establishment of a variety of new mercenary organized criminal adventures.

The fear of nuclear war spawned by the threat of nuclear missiles falling into
the hands of terrorists, has caused concern over organized crime and its involvement
in the sale of plutonium as well as nuclear missiles themselves. It is difficult to
estimate the extent of such ventures, but the fact that two attempted illegal sales of
radioactive materials were thwarted by Russian police in 1994, and that, since
1991, close to 440 cases of the attempted smuggling of nuclear material into
Germany, most being rendered ineffective by sting operations (Time, Aug. 29,
1994: 46-51) make the possibility of such sales loom as real threats.

In his discussion of the problem regarding the sale of nuclear material, William
Burrows (1994: 54-55) states the reality surrounding this issue by reminding us that
Iraq, Iran, Libya and other countries would indeed be interested in purchasing
plutonium. With such a demand, the possibility always exists that both lone free-
lancers and/or criminal syndicates in Russia or one of its former republics may serve
as the avenue for establishing and facilitating these connections. Obviously, the
sale could come from some scientist or official who has access to such material or
organized criminals could bribe the source of access in order to obtain the nuclear
material and arrange for its sale.

A great danger is posed by the conversion of the Russian Army as an object of
the activities of criminal associations. These associations have the following aims:
obtaining valuable raw materials; acquisition of technology for next to nothing;
control over the sale of military technology abroad; utilization of army
transportation capabilities for illegal conveyance; the seizure of various types of
weapons; recruitment of discharged service-men into subunits for guarding
criminal structures. So, too, organized crime leaders are attempting to corrupt and
infiltrate special military detachments such as the Russian Cossacks and other elite
units entrusted with guarding military supply depots in an effort to attain weapons,
and nuclear and other valuable materials.

In contrast to the questionable sale of nuclear material itself, Dr. Louise Shelley
(1994), testifying before the Commission on Security and Cooperation in Europe,
alerts us to the fact that there is a large illicit trade in military equipment which, she
notes, is alarming because it is helping to support armed conflicts within the former
Soviet Union and in other parts of the world. This information which Dr. Shelley
cites is given credence by the recent scandal and accusations against Russian
Defense Minister, Paval Grachev (Time, Dec. 5, 1994: 80-81) who, in answering the
accusations from the Russian Parliament, accused the Parliament of being the real

ALBINI, ROGERS, SHABALIN, 231
KUTUSHEV, MOISEEV & ANDERSON

culprits, since it controls the purse-strings. In either respect, the scandal surrounds the illegal sale of military property in Germany.

According to another article by Seymour Hersh (June, 1994: 75), sixty kilos of highly enriched uranium were seized by the Russian Ministry of Security in April, 1994 at Izhevala, Russia. Twenty people were arrested and charged with smuggling. This article also argues the possibility (p.76) that Russian scientists, because of losing the basic necessities of life - - housing, health care and regular paychecks - - may be leaving the country and taking not only their scientific knowledge with them but high-tech weapons components as well. This article does note that the Department of Energy feels that there really is no evidence that nuclear weapons or materials have, in fact, been exported from the Soviet Union (p.75). However, there is always that possibility, as Claire Sterling (1994: 215) suggests, that nuclear sales outside Russia and its republics have been made, but the reason the world does not know anything about such sales lies in the fact that "a solid wall of secret agents...blocks the view." It does appear that there is a legitimate concern in Russia and one of its republics - - Kazakhstan - - over the control and exporting of nuclear weapons into the hands óf terrorists when we saw recently that 1300 pounds of uranium stored in the republic of Kazakhstan, which evidently Saddam Hussein was desperately trying to obtain, went instead to the United States and is now safely stored in Oak Ridge, Tennessee (Time, Dec. 5, 1994: 38-39).

We should note that, legitimately, Russia, at the tune of 2.2 billion dollars in 1992 alone, has been aggressively selling weapons to India, China, Syria, Iran and other countries in its effort to convert industrial defense production into civilian production. Unfortunately, the fact that the Russian government cannot offer long-term support and service for its technologically complex weapons has not made this the effective conversion finance-raising solution it was intended to be (U.S. News & World Report, Focus on Change, 1994: 17-20). No doubt, however, the demand for these weapons will allow for criminal groups to continue the illicit sale of such weapons to those countries or groups who, even though the continued servicing of such weapons cannot be guaranteed, will nonetheless purchase them out of dire need.

Along with these ventures, we have in Russia and its former republics other types of mercenary crime. There are the scams concerning credit and banking violations in which capital made from illicit activities is employed in establishing businesses that serve as fronts for illegitimate transactions. In a sophisticated version of the "long-firm fraud" scheme developed and practiced widely by British criminals (Albini, 1986: 103-104), a Russian criminal group stole 200 million dollars from the Russian state in 1992. This scheme, described by Claire Sterling (1994: 108-109) entailed the creation of a straw bank in the small republic of Chekenya which sent Russia's central bank fraudulent or phoney "credit advisories" for 200 million dollars which the directors of the straw bank indicated they had on deposit. The straw bank then asked Moscow for a credit line in order to import computers. The central bank sent the money to a dozen commercial banks

232   Russian Organized Crime:
       Its History, Structure and Function

in Moscow. When informed that the computer deal had not gone through, these twelve commercial banks simply allowed the cash to be withdrawn and sent back to the straw bank, no questions asked, and minus their cut. Sterling (Chapter 5) also cites numerous other cases of fraudulent business ventures, sometimes involving American and other foreigners working in conjunction with Russians, in which petroleum and other goods and materials resulted in the increasing of the wealth of these individuals and the depletion of the Russian economy. In Moscow, in January 1994, a seminar entitled, "For Honest Business" was sponsored by the Russian Criminological Association. Here, as V. Shabalin notes in his summary of the seminar, Organized Crime and Business, material and discussions showed that there is in Russia today a fast growing network of commercial banks and stock and currency exchanges which, through their illegal investment of funds, are literally running rampant simply because the state control over such activities has been seriously weakened. This weakness comes from the fact that these illegal deals are made possible because these criminal associations can and do, by lobbying practices, influence political decisions and the legislation process itself. According to the Analytical Center of the Academy of Sciences of Russia, 35% of capital and 80% of election shares today are transferred into the hands of criminal and foreign capital.

Along with enterprises involving the use of fraud, a number of other organized mercenary criminal enterprises exist in Russia. These typically function as they do in other countries. An example would be the enterprise of counterfeiting. With the increasing use of sophisticated photocopiers, counterfeiters in many countries are producing bills and transporting them across international boundaries. Some of these bills have already made their way from Iran to the former Soviet Union (U.S. News and World Reports, Dec. 5, 1994: 79). The widespread use and flow of counterfeit bills in Russia is demonstrated by the case involving the kidnapping, in 1993, of a teacher, busdriver and schoolchildren by criminals in Rostov, Russia. After demanding and receiving the ransom money paid in U.S. currency, the kidnappers made a final demand - - that they receive a machine that could distinguish between real and counterfeit bills (U.S. News and World Report, Dec. 5, 1994: 73). As we move now into our discussion of the organized "protection" and "extortion" forms of organized crime, those typically referred to as "rackets" we do so with the aim of using this topic to bridge and lead us over into our discussion of syndicated crime in Russia. We do this because these forms of "rackets", depending upon the format they take, can be of the mercenary or syndicated type.

There are those types where the organized perpetrators have no political or police protection. For the most part, the "Black Hand" in America, for example, because it typically did not have political protection, used fear and intimidation by sending letters to Italian immigrants in an effort to extort money from them (Pitkin and Cordasco, 1977). So, too, currently in New York and other cities, as Kelly, Chin and Fagan (1993) have found, Chinese street gangs in the Chinese communities of these cities extort money from Chinese business people. As Kelly, Chin and Fagan

ALBINI, ROGERS, SHABALIN,   233
KUTUSHEV, MOISEEV & ANDERSON

(p.226) note, these activities persist not because the criminals have political or police protection, but rather because, out of fear, the victims refuse to file charges or testify against these criminals. Hence, in Russia, we find that there are criminal gangs who, simply because they are adept at using intimidation and force, "work" the "protection" and "extortion" schemes without police or political protection. Like the Italian and Chinese criminals in America, these groups rely on the fact that their victims are too fearful to report the crime or serve as witnesses in any possible legal action taken by the authorities. Typically, when they sell "protection" to businesses, such "protection" is based upon an agreement. Thus, as Arthur Fisher (Popular Science, Aug. 1994: 24) reports, thugs who guard the multitude of street kiosks which sell everything from imported camcorders to video games in Moscow usually offer their services for twenty percent of the sales.

The "protection" operation, both in Russia and other countries where it is practiced, often originates out of a symbiotic need created by the social conditions themselves. Thus, often times, it is not the criminal that forces protection on the businessman, but, instead, the businessman who, recognizing the need for protection in an environment where theft is so rampant, will often seek and agree to be protected for a price.

In many of the contemporary "protection" and "extortion" schemes in Russia today, however, the reality is that many of these rackets have the backing and protection of political and/or police alliances. Recently, organized criminal associations have been subsidizing the education of young participants in criminal associations studying law with the goal of having them later assume positions of power within this legal system; thus further assuring protection to their criminal enterprises.

Political protection can and is obtained either by having a powerful patron in the legal system that grants it in return for money, favors, or because the political protector is part of the criminal enterprise itself. Thus, a minister or high government official can himself become the "protector" for a criminal venture or, in many cases, create the criminal venture itself and then offer protection to those who are operating it. In this respect, it would be like the case of John Morrissey (Albini, 1971: 186-189) in the United States, who because of his patronage to Tammany Hall and his support from fellow Irish voters, was elected to the position of New York Senator as well as becoming a representative in the U.S. Congress itself. As such, he was able to offer political protection for his own criminal syndicate operations.

At this point we must note the role played by the KGB, police and other governmental officials in the Russian saga of organized crime.

Typically referred to as "state rackets" (Report No. 9: 22) these subsume those types of criminal enterprises where official position and power is employed to "extort" and/or "protect" the victims. Lydia Rosner (1993: 3) tells us how party officials, with the backing of the law itself, have imprisoned over 200,000 entrepreneurs and then often took over their enterprises. The growth and proliferation of

234   Russian Organized Crime:
       Its History, Structure and Function

these criminal types organizations, as Timofeyev (1990: 60) observes, have come to control large regions, as was recently demonstrated in Uzbekistan and have come to serve the interests of the Communist Party, armed forces and the secret police. Rosner (1993: 1-2) notes that in the quest for wealth and power, KGB leaders and other officials of the state looted state-run industries and turned these positions into vehicles for increasing their own personal wealth. Indeed, some KGB officers added to their personal wealth through the practice of confiscating the personal property of those arrested for state crimes, often burglarizing the homes or apartments of those incarcerated and then either kept the goods for their own use or turned them over for sale in the black market.

The KGB was reorganized in May 1991 and became known as The Ministry of Security of the Russian Federation. As such, it became for the first time a "union-republic" agency. There is a belief that the new KGB has the intent of "repenting" itself of its past political misdeeds (Azrael and Rahr, 1993: 5); however, as R.E. Rogers observes, many believe that the organization changed only in the upper echelons in that the basic membership of the organization itself remains the same. For this reason, as Stephen Hendelman (1994: 15), testifying in June 1994 before The Commission of Security and Cooperation in Europe stated, American police are reluctant to get involved not only with the KGB but with most police forces in Russia because they suspect that they continue to be generally corrupt.

The severity of the current status of "state" rackets operating in Russia is revealed in Handelman's testimony when he notes (p.11) that in 1993 alone, no less than 1500 Russian governmental officials were charged with serious corruption and another 4500 cases of bribery went to trial. These statistics, as Handelman observes, hardly begin to match the real volume of corruption that continues to go on undetected.

Added to this level of corruption is that found among the police and the military. The chief of Moscow's police force estimates that on his force alone, 95 percent of his men are on the take (The Economist, July 9, 1994: 22). Those who are honest have to work under the most dire conditions with no equipment or using antiquated equipment. As Handelman states (1994: 11), detectives in some cities literally are forced to chase their suspects by using taxis or bus services.

Speaking to the issue of police problems in Russia, in 1992, V. Kutushev noted that in America, with the exception of inner city residents, there typically is respect for the police and friendly interaction between citizens and police. In Russia, this is not the case. Police, in Russia, when they attempt to arrest a citizen, are most likely to meet with resistance. The number of policeman killed in 1991 numbered 140, and each year the number continues to grow.

As for the military, in February 1993, Russian defense officials stated that they plan to discipline 3000 army officers for questionable business enterprises and 46 general officers were facing court martial proceedings regarding corruption charges (Hersh, 1994: 67-68). Such corruption and the delving into of criminal enterprises by military personnel no doubt has been spawned by the deplorable living and

ALBINI, ROGERS, SHABALIN,   235
KUTUSHEV, MOISEEV & ANDERSON

fighting conditions which military personnel have been subjected to in recent years. The extreme state of these conditions is revealed in the fact that Russian soldiers and their families have recently been forced to go without the basic necessities of water, heat and food to the point that four recruits died of malnutrition (Time, Dec. 5, 1994: 81).

And so the "protection" and "extortion" groups, those with political or police protection and those without, have established themselves on the streets of Russia and its independent states. And violence has become a common part of these ventures. In Nizhni Tagil, a city in the Ural Mountains, the extreme form that this violence can and does take was illustrated when a group of Russian criminals hijacked a T-90 tank, drove it to the local market and fired upon a criminal group of Muslims who were trying to wrestle protection money from the venders (U.S. News & World Report, Mar. 7, 1994: 42). The Russians, in doing so, let the Muslim criminals know that this was and would continue to be solely their enterprise.

The complete evolution of the growth of syndicated crime in Russia and the former republics is evidenced, however, in the development of those criminal ventures where the three elements of syndicated crime are fully established; that is, the rendering of illegal goods and services, the use of violence or the threat of it and the assurance of protection from legal interference.

Here we see the establishment and functioning of syndicates that involve and evolve from a variety of ethnic, social class and other social backgrounds. Their major enterprises are the smuggling of drugs and other goods, and prostitution. Since both of these enterprises necessitate that the public seeking the illicit service and the criminals who deliver them interact or make contact with one another, political protection is necessary for their continued operation. Thus, in prostitution, women, homosexual men and other types of individuals whose services can be sold for profit are made available in certain areas of the cities or are "on call" for the customer who seeks more privacy in the encounter. If necessary, these women or men are transported to various regions or even into other countries based upon trade demands and profits. Reminiscent of the prohibition era in the United States, these women and homosexual men often are subject to physical and other abuse if they disobey those who oversee their work.

It is in the realm of drug-trafficking, however, where much of the high profit is made. It is true that the smuggling into Russia of automobiles stolen in America and used Japanese cars from Japan, along with the smuggling of antique artworks out of the country constitutes a form of high profit for criminal syndicates, drug smuggling is the venture that reaps the largest profits. By its very nature, as Albini (1992, chapter 4) explains, drug syndicates typically involve functionaries from various countries interacting with one another. Since, as Claire Sterling (1994: 105) notes, the Russian former republics produce 25 times more hashish than the rest of the world and opium poppies flourish in abundance in Afghanistan, Uzbekestan and other territories of the former U.S.S.R., the drug trade in contemporary Russia is alive and well. Drug traffic flows both within and outside Russia and its federated

236   Russian Organized Crime:
       Its History, Structure and Function

states. As such, it has attracted smugglers from all parts of the world and the ties between Russian syndicates and those in other countries literally encircle the globe. This has created what Phil Williams (1995: 60-61) calls "strategic alliances", alliances where the functionaries of criminal syndicates in various countries, like the functionaries of businesses which engage in legitimate ventures, seek and form alliances which are mutually beneficial to their operations. Claire Sterling, in her book, (1994) speaks, repeatedly, of "The Pax Mafiosa", giving the impression that syndicates, particularly those in Sicily, have now established and made an everlasting peace with one another based upon their realization that cooperation rather than conflict will more effectively divide the spoils for all. This, we feel, is an uneasy conceptualization describing an uneasy form of peace-treaty. So, too, Sterling seems to give the impression that such peace treaties are new to the world of drug smuggling and exist primarily among and between large, well-established syndicates. Phil Williams shows us, however, that such alliances are existent among many small syndicates as well. But we feel that Sterling's "Pax Mafiosa" can be misleading because of the impression that it has now become a new, continuing and lasting form of interaction. As Julie Anderson, drawing from simulation or game theory notes, the n-person, non-zero-sum-game model, theoretically, would indeed explain why such cooperation takes place; mainly because both or all parties stand to gain in the venture. But, as Anderson observes, this assumes a rationality of action that may appear valid in theory; but, in the reality of life itself, all too often human behavior manifests a logic predicated upon emotion, culture and attributes other than those based upon cold logic. Thus, as Phil Williams (1995: 68-69) illustrates in regard to the interaction of the Medellin and Cali cartels in Columbia, although in the early 1980s they began in a state of alliance and cooperation, by the end of the 1980s, they were, in effect, at war with one another. Speaking to the point of the cooperation and conflict that typically occurs among functionaries of criminal syndicates, Stephan Handelman (1994: 22) makes our point succinctly when he states:

> "...criminals are just like governments...I mean... governments...can't get it together, criminals can't either."

The contemporary syndicates now operating in Russia and its federation, primarily those involved in drug smuggling and other organized syndicated crimes, have evolved from various socio-cultural origins. Thus, many of the "thieves within the code" gangs, having the "brotherhood" structure which they manifested during the era of the Soviet Union, have increasingly, over time, provided themselves with political and police protection; in so doing, they have moved into syndicated forms of organized crime such as drug smuggling and prostitution. Others continue to operate primarily in mercenary forms of organized crime. Thus, according to one source (The Economist, July 9, 1994: 20) when Russia moved toward privatization, these "thieves within the code" gangs, because they had amassed large sums of capital, proceeded "...to buy a state that was in the process of being rebuilt."

ALBINI, ROGERS, SHABALIN,   237
KUTUSHEV, MOISEEV & ANDERSON

According to Handelman (1994: 13) these "thieves within the code" generated further wealth after the fall of the Soviet Union through their participation in the black market. Many of these "thieves", Handelman notes, are functionaries on both upper and lower levels in both syndicated and mercenary types of organized criminal enterprises in contemporary Russia.

As is true of many organized crime groups in Russia and other countries, ethnicity is a factor in the origin and development of such groups. Ethnicity often serves as a basis from which organized criminals draw membership in gangs and serves as a basis for trust among gang members. Hence, the Chechen syndicate has an ethnic and historical base (Serio, 1992: 6-7). The Chechen are largely a Muslim group that was deported from their homeland in the Caucaus region of Russia by Stalin in 1944 on charges of collaborating with the Nazis. They returned in 1957. According to Serio, the Chechens are different from many other criminal syndicates operating in Russia today in that they draw their membership exclusively from their ethnic ranks and have a hierarchical arrangement based upon clan relationships. This group, according to Serio, is involved in a variety of mercenary and syndicated crime activities including smuggling automobiles and the sale of narcotics. A group known for its extreme use of violence, it operates not only in Russia but in Germany, Austria, Hungary and other European countries. The Chechens supposedly have recently sent members to New York to set up operations in the United States.

Although it is difficult at the moment to assess the full extent and ramifications of Russian organized crime in the United States, Rosner (1986, chapter 4) discusses its presence in Brighton Beach, New York, and Kenny and Finckenauer (1995: 275-280) mention its presence in New York City, Los Angeles, and Philadelphia. These groups, it seems, are involved in extortion, drug trafficking, medical fraud and a variety of other enterprises. As we said, it is still too early to determine the full extent of their criminality and what directions it will take. However, their patterns and enterprises suggest that they are engaging in organized criminal ventures similar to those of other American syndicates currently functioning in American society.

This then, is the nature of organized crime in Russia. We have here presented a portrait of its history, structure and function in order to lay a foundation for future study. We hope that our description and classifications will serve to become the basis for comparisons with organized crime in other countries and cultures as there are many lessons to learn from the Russian experience.

But, in ending our discussion we do so with an understanding that what has taken place in Russia exemplifies what can happen to societies that experience rapid and intense social change. The portrait we have painted here should not be viewed as one of Russian society or the Russian people as being totally morally corrupt. If such were the case then we would not have so many voices in Russia seeking solutions and turning to other countries for help. By comparison, America has not been a land without its own forms of corruption. Watergate, and the S & L loans scandal have indeed had their impact on American society and serve as reminders that America, when it comes to morality, is not a nation without its own moral

238   Russian Organized Crime:
       Its History, Structure and Function

weaknesses. Indeed, it is because of its moral hypocrisy concerning illicit drug use that syndicated crime in America is doing so well.

As we take a departing look at our portrait of Russian organized crime, let us depart with an understanding that what took place and is occurring in Russia and its federation at the present time has its basic roots in the social upheaval that results from rapid social change. The roots lie in the nature of the destructive forces that accompany a nation that has truly experienced "convulsion" resulting from a series of intense shockwaves that have politically, economically and socially battered Russia and the Soviet Union during this century. First came the Russian Revolution which appeared to be a movement geared toward freedom for the proletariat; but was it really freedom that resulted when, in fact, as Jim Shortt (1993: 3) reminds us "....Lenin maintained himself in power by force of arms"? Then, in 1941 came the Nazi invasion and the Soviet struggle for survival against this oppressor. Then, in the 1950s came the Cold War and the potential threat of conflict with the United States. Then, in 1989-91 came the breakdown and breakup of the Soviet Union and its republics.

When humans undergo such rapid changes and stress we refer to this situation as "trauma". Although we do not normally use the term to apply to societies, "trauma" is what Russian society has repeatedly experienced over the course of this century. As the wall of Communism came down, various sectors of Russian society and its republics began their own attempts at effecting or resisting further change. Indeed, as Shortt (p.39) points out, the Russian organized criminals at the time, themselves, opposed the breakup because they feared that the breakup would create, as it did, new national borders; thus, now making the payment of bribes a requirement for transporting their illegal goods across these borders. Political officials, serving as patrons to their sympathizing clients purposefully attempted to create political upheaval; these upheavals, indeed, produced many forms of political-social organized crime. During the same time-period, however, many of these political officials, while engaging in their efforts to create social disturbances, continued to receive money for services rendered, sold ranks and protected one another by participating in the criminal enterprises of a shadow economy (Report No. 9: 26).

This social "trauma" reached the point where President Yeltsin, on June 14, 1994 issued a decree - - "On the Urgent Measures to Defend the Population against Gangsterism and Other Kinds of Organized Crimes". As V. A. Shabalin (1994) notes, the decree introduced some strict legal measures that could be used against organized crime groups. Whether these measures can and will be applied successfully remains to be seen. Rosner (1993: 3), writing long before this decree was issued, had already addressed the issue and expressed the opinion that a crackdown on the newly formed criminal groups "...would be an arbitrary act in the battle for power, under the guise of a crime-control solution".

And so, as we end our discussion, we do so with the awareness that Russia and its former republics have arrived at and are currently at that stage of social change

ALBINI, ROGERS, SHABALIN,   239
KUTUSHEV, MOISEEV & ANDERSON

where it is difficult to predict, with accuracy, which direction they will go. Some critics fear a return to a complete state of communist rule, while others fear that Russia will become a dictatorship if Vladimir Zhirinovsky (Time, July 11, 1994: 39-45) were to come to power. Others, like Vladimir Kvint (Forbes, Dec. 5, 1994: 45-152) suggest that Yeltsin could restore the Russian monarchy and make himself a regent for life.

Although public opinion polls in Russia, as Pipes (1990, pp.ix-x) indicates, show that Russians are in favor of conversion to a free enterprise system, Pipes warns that this may be merely a reflection of a panacea and that "it will take a long time to reorient the psyche of the people in a direction conducive to genuine economic freedom". Paul Klebnikov (Forbes, Sept. 12, 1994: 228), on the other hand, believes there is a strong possibility that the Russians, by swapping foreign bank credit for shares in Russian oil and gas companies, will put their economy back together again. If what Klebnikov suggests does in fact happen, this would serve as a motivating factor that would strengthen what some see as a very strong desire on the part of the Russian people to move toward privatization and democracy.

Oddly enough, the social upheaval that has taken place in Russian society in the past century is reflected once again in the current plans to reconstruct the Cathedral of Christ the Savior in Moscow (U.S. News & World Report, Dec. 5, 1994: 67-68). This cathedral serves as a dynamic symbolic reminder of Russia's century of "trauma". In 1812, Tzar Alexander I ordered its construction in gratitude to God for Russia's victory over Napoleon. It took 70 years to build. In 1931, Stalin ordered it destroyed in order to obtain the copper and marble from its structure and make way for a monument to Communism, a building that was to be taller than the Empire State Building and an accompanying statue of Lenin bigger than the statue of liberty. However, this palace of Soviets never materialized. Today, there are plans to reconstruct the cathedral, making it identical to the one destroyed by Stalin.

We must remember in closing that, despite its major problems, Russia has produced, during this century of conflict, some of the world's most beautiful music and art, a large number of Nobel Prize winners, the awe-inspiring sculptures of Vadin Sidur (Daniloff, 1994: 516-521) and one of the world's most successful space programs. Indeed, it is to the Russians that American astronomers are turning for help in a menace to Earth currently more far-reaching than organized crime; mainly, the potential dangers to Earth from destructive, near-earth asteroid collisions (The Planetary Society, 1994). It is believed that between 1000 to 2000 objects - - asteroids and husks of old comets - - now orbit the sun in Earth's immediate neighborhood. Any of these, scientists hypothesize, if they were to collide with Earth could, potentially, put an end to human civilization. It is hoped that Russian and American scientists, working together and studying this phenomenon, can avert it. We hope that they do, because if one of these objects of sufficient size strikes our earth, there will no longer be any reason to worry about or study the phenomenon of organized crime.

240   Russian Organized Crime:
      Its History, Structure and Function

About the Authors

Dr. Joseph Albini is recognized as one of the foremost experts on American and international organized crime and has written numerous books, monographs, book chapters and papers on this subject. His book The American Mafia, (1971) is considered a classic in the study of organized crime. Professor Albini is Visiting Professor of Criminal Justice, University Of Nevada, Las Vegas and is currently Co-Director of The Joint Russian-American Academic Committee For the Promotion Of The Study of Comparative Criminal Justice. He is also Emeritus Professor, Wayne State University, Detroit, Michigan. Dr. Albini and Dr. R. E. Rogers co-presented a paper to the MVD Conference on organized crime, May, 1995, in Irkutsk, Russia. They and their Russian colleagues have co-authored several articles on the Russian Criminal Justice System and are involved in numerous collaborative research projects.

R.E. Rogers, Ph.D. has been studying Russia/The Soviet Union for thirty-five years as a student and professor. He has taught a variety of courses in history and the behavior sciences including Russian history, The history of world communism, criminology and abnormal psychology. Among others, he has taught at Eastern Michigan University and Khabarovsk Pedagogical University in Khabarovsk, Russia. Dr. Rogers was also a guest speaker at the Irkutsk Graduate Militia College and also addressed the staff of the Kharbarovsk Woman's Reformatory #12 and Men's Reformatory #13 (both labor prisons). He is the American Co-Director of the Joint Russian-American Academic Committee for the Promotion of The Study of Comparative Criminal Justice at Eastern Michigan University and is also a consultant on the Russian criminal justice system. Dr. Rogers is currently a professor of history and psychology at St. Clair Community College, Port Huron Michigan.

Colonel, Professor Victor A. Shabalin is a Professor of Political Science at the Khabarovsk Graduate Militia (national police) College in Khabarovsk, Russia. He completed post graduate courses at St. Petersburg University and doctorate courses at the Social Science Academy in Moscow. He is considered to be one of the foremost political and historical experts on the Russian Far East. In addition, Professor Shabalin is a member of the Criminological Association and has participated in the drafting of new laws to fight organized crime in Russia. He is also considered to be one of the foremost scholars on Russian organized crime.

General Professor Valery Kutushev, Jur.D. is Rector (president) of the Kharbarovsk Graduate Militia College in Kharbarovsk, Russia. He is the author of numerous papers and monographs on the Russian criminal justice system.

ALBINI, ROGERS, SHABALIN,   241
KUTUSHEV, MOISEEV & ANDERSON

Lt. Colonel, Professor Vladimir P. Moiseev, Ph.D. is Professor of Philosophy and Chairman of the Department of Philosophy at Irkutsk Graduate Militia College in Irkutsk, Russia. He is a graduate of the Irkutsk Teacher's Training College and has taken post-graduate courses at Moscow University. He is an expert on juvenile delinquency and the underclass in the Russian Far East. Professor Moiseev has written academic papers and monographs on these topics.

Julie Anderson recently completed her Bachelor of Arts degree at the University of Nevada, Las Vegas, with a major in Political Science. She is currently enrolled in the Master's Program in Political Science at the University of Nevada, Las Vegas. Her specialty interests are conspiracies, studies in nationalism, and foreign and domestic affairs.

REFERENCES

Albini, J. (1971). *The America Mafia*. New York: Appleton Century Crofts.

Albini, J. (1986). Organized Crime in Great Britain and the Caribbean. In R. Kelly (Ed.), *Organized Crime: A Global Perspective* (pp. 95-122). Totowa, NJ: Rowman and Littlefield.

Albini, J. (1992). The Distribution of Drugs: Models of Organized Criminal Organizations and Their Integration. In. T. Mieczkowski (Ed.), *Drugs, Crime and Social Policy* (pp. 79-108). Boston: Allyn and Bacon.

Avinsky, H. (1990). *Organized Crime*. Chicago: Nelson Hall.

Azreal, J. and Rahr, A. (1993). The Formation and Development of the Russian KGB, 1991-1994 Report prepared for the Under Secretary of Defense for Policy. National Defense Institute. Santa Monica, CA: Rand.

Boissevain, J. (1966). Patronage in Sicily. *Man. I* (Marek). pp. 16-27.

Burrows, W. (1994). Nuclear Chaos. *Popular Science* (August), pp. 54-76.

Daniloff, R. (1994). An Artist who faced down suffering with his eyes wide open. *Smithsonian*. (December), pp. 119-126.

Della Cava, R. (1977). The Italian immigrant experience. Views of a Latin-Americanist. In S.M. Tomasi (Ed.), *Perspectives in Italian Immigration and Ethnicity*. New York: Center for Immigration Studies.

Efimov, S. (1994). Scientific Investigation of Anomalous Phenomena in Kozakhstan. *Skeptical Inquirer*. 18 (Fall), pp. 516-521.

Fisher, A. (1994). Moscow Rules. *Popular Science*. (August), pp. 24-79.

Focus on Change (1993). *U.S. News and World Report*.

Handelman, S. (1994). *Crime and Corruption in Russia*. Briefing of the Commission on Security and Cooperation in Europe. Washington, D.C.: (June).

Hersh, S. (1994). The Wild East. *Atlantic Monthly*. (June). pp. 61-86.

242   Russian Organized Crime:
       Its History, Structure and Function

Kelly, R., Chin, K. and Fagan, J. (1993). The Structure, Activity, and Control of Chinese Gangs: Law Enforcement Perspective. *Journal of Contemporary Criminal Justice.* 9 (August), pp. 222-239.

Kenney, D.J. and Finchenauer, J.O. (1995). *Organized Crime in America.* New York: Wadsworth.

Klebnikov, P. (1994). Sovereign Junk. *Forbes.* September 12, pp. 228.

Klebnikov, P. (1994). Russia's robber barons. *Forbes.* Nov. 21, pp. 74-84.

Kvint, V. (1994). Restoring the Romanovs. *Forbes.* Dec. 5, pp. 145-152.

Las Vegas Review Journal. (1994). Nov. 22, p. 9A.

Pipes, R. (1990). *Forward.* The Anti-Communist Manifesto. L. Timofeyev (Ed.). Bellevue, WA: Free Enterprise.

Pitkin, T. and Cordasco, F. (1977). *The Black Hand.* Totowa, NJ: Littlefield, Adams.

Report No. 9. (1990). *Organized Crime.* Press Group Report. V. Shabalin, J.L. Albini, and R.E. Rogers (Eds.). Novosibirsk. Prepared by the Joint Russian-American Academic Committee To Promote the Study of Comparative Criminal Justice.

Rosner, L. (1986). *The Soviet Way of Crime.* MA: Bergin and Garvey.

Rosner, L. (1993). Crime and Corruption in Russia are nothing new. *Law Enforcement News.* (XIX), March 15, pp. 1-3.

Serio, J. (1992). Shunning Tradition: Ethnic Organized Crime in the Former Soviet Union. *CJ International*, 8 (November-December, pp. 5-6.

Shabalin, V., J. Albini, and R.E. Rogers, "Organized Crime and Business: A Report on the International Seminar for Honest Business." *Criminal Organization.* Vol. 7 (1995).

Shabalin, V., and R.E. Rogers, "The New Stage of The Fight With Organized Crime in Russia." *Criminal Organization.* In Press.

Shelley, L. (1994). *Crime and Corruption in Russia.* Briefing of the Commission on Security and Cooperation in Europe. Washington, D.C.

Shortt, J. (1993). Preface. In KGB: Alpha Team Training Manual Boulder, CO.: Paladin.

Simis, K. (1982). *U.S.S.R.: The Corrupt Society.* New York: Simon and Schuster.

Southerland and Potter (1993). Applying Organization Theory to Organized Crime. *Journal of Contemporary Criminal Justice.* 9 (August), pp. 251-267.

Sterling, C. (1994). *Thieves' World.* New York: Simon and Schuster.

The Economist. (1994). *Russia's Mafia.* July 9, pp. 19-22.

The Planetary Society (1994). Letter to the Senior Author from Louis Friedman, Executive Director. Pasadena, CA.

Time (1994). July 11, pp. 39-45.

Time (1994). August 29, pp. 47-51.

Time (1994). Dec. 5, pp. 38-39 and 80-81.

Timofeyev, L. (1990). Some notes on the black market economy. In L. Timofeyev (Ed.), *The Anti-Communist Manifesto.* Bellevue, WA: Free Enterprise.

ALBINI, ROGERS, SHABALIN,   243
KUTUSHEV, MOISEEV & ANDERSON

U.S. News and World Report (1994). March 7, pp. 36-47.

U.S. News and World Report (1994). Dec. 5, pp. 73-82 and 67-68.

Williams, P. (1995). Transnational Criminal Organizations: Strategic Alliances. *The Washington Quarterly* 18 (Winter), pp. 57-69.

Wolf, E.R. (1966). Kinship, Friendship and patron-client relations in complex societies. In M. Banton (Ed.), *The Social Anthropology of Simple Societies*. New York: Praeger.

[11]

F E D E R I C O   V A R E S E

Is Sicily the future of Russia?
Private protection and the rise
of the Russian Mafia

IT IS DIFFICULT to discuss a phenomenon when one does not know precisely what it is. This problem is particularly vexing in the case of the Mafia. It has been argued that 'the need for a definition [of the Mafia] is crucial; not just for any definition with some degree of contingent empirical plausibility, but for a definition with some analytical clout' (1). The word 'Mafia' itself has travelled far to distant lands, such as the former Soviet Union. For instance, according to Arkadii Vaksberg, Russian journalist and author of *The Russian Mafia*, the Mafia is 'the entire soviet power-system, all its ideological, political, economical and administrative manifestations' (2). In an article published in a magazine for British executives dealing with Russia, the label *Mafiosi* is used to lump together bureaucrats, smugglers from the Caucasus, the CPSU *nomenklatura* accused of embezzling state funds, the late British businessman Robert Maxwell and many others (3).

Russian police authorities and criminal specialists seem to have a better feel for the phenomenon, although their particular interest is more in the degree of organization displayed by criminal groups and in the extent of their connection to the state apparatus, rather than in what they actually do. According to Anatoli Volobuev, organized crime as experienced in Russia is:

a negative social phenomenon, characterized by the unification of a criminal group on a regional or national basis with a division on hierarchical levels and selections of leaders, having organizational, administrative and ideological functions; use of corruption, attracting into criminal activities state officials (including law enforcement officials) for maintaining security for the participants in the community; monopolization and widening of spheres of illegal activity with the goal of achieving maximum

---

(1) D. GAMBETTA, *The origins of the Mafias* (Cambridge: Mimeo, 1991), p. 2.

(2) A. VAKSBERG, *La Mafia sovietica* [*Sovietskaya Mafya*, 1991], trans. by S. GIORDANO

(Milano: Baldini e Castoldi, 1992), p. 247.

(3) *Russia Express-Executive Briefing*, issue no. 83, 27 July 1992, 26-7.

224

Arch. europ. sociol., XXXV (1994), 224-258 — 0003-9756/93/0000-641 $02.50 © 1994 A.E.S.

MAFIA IN RUSSIA

material income while maintaining maximum protection of the highest echelons from prosecution (4).

Despite the fact that this definition does not exhibit more than a 'contingent empirical plausibility', it goes at least some way to testify that Russian specialists recognize the existence of the phenomenon, vaguely defined though it may be.

Confusion over the definition is rife among scholars of the Italian Mafia as well. D. Gambetta remarks that proper definitions are either dismissed as unnecessary or extremely capricious in the literature on the Italian Mafia: 'in one essay the Mafia is identified with everything criminal which happens in or below Naples; in another essay bandits, landowners and Mafiosi form an inextricable tangle; in yet another, the Mafia is identified with violent handling of the political tensions which affected Sicily soon after unification' (5). Amid such confusion, Christopher Duggan has reached the conclusion that the Mafia does not exist (6).

Unfortunately, the Mafia does exist, as magistrates, ordinary people and Mafiosi themselves in Sicily know only too well. Gambetta has provided a working definition of Mafia as 'one particular instance of an industry which supplies private protection' (7). Armed with this definition, he offers a model that is intended to explain the origin of the phenomenon in Sicily.

How the Mafia emerged in Sicily: a property rights approach

Gambetta has argued that 'the Mafia can be understood as a response to the lack of trust affecting Southern Italy and that endemic distrust is the crucial difference which explains why the Mafia did not emerge elsewhere in the Mediterranean world' (8). The lack of trust in the new Italian state produced a high potential demand for protection, and the Mafia supplied such protection to whomever wanted to buy it. Gambetta's argument is thus organized around a crucial distinction between a *demand* for protection and a *supply* of the same.

---

(4) Anatoli VOLOBUEV in A.I. DOLGOVA, *Organisovannaya prestupnost'* [*Organized Crime*] (Moscow: Iuridicheskaya Literatura, 1989), p. 31, quoted in J. SERIO, Organized Crime in the Soviet Union and Beyond, *Low Intensity Conflict and Law Enforcement*, vol.1, no. 2 (Autumn 1992), p. 129.

(5) D. GAMBETTA, *The origins of the Mafias*, p. 1.

(6) According to Duggan, Mafia was a word of abuse that political factions of all sorts levelled at each other. C. DUGGAN, *Fascism and the Mafia* (New Haven: Yale University Press, 1989).

(7) D. GAMBETTA, *The origins of the Mafias*, p. 2.

(8) D. GAMBETTA, *The Sicilian Mafia* (London: Harvard University Press, 1993), 77-8.

FEDERICO VARESE

Building on Leopoldo Franchetti, a nineteenth century Italian social scientist largely neglected among contemporary students of the Mafia, Gambetta regards the Mafia as a by-product of the end of feudalism and the beginning of a democratic society. The main effect of the demise of feudalism in Sicily was the transformation of land into a market commodity subject to legally defined individual property rights. Trading in land became conceivable in the South of Italy in the early nineteenth century. At the same time, vast extensions of both common and Church land were auctioned for the benefit of private purchasers (9). From 1812 to 1860, the number of landowners of large estates in Sicily went from 2,000 to 20,000; from 1860 to 1900, the number of hectares in private hands increased from 250,000 to 650,000 (10).

Gambetta subscribes to what we might call the 'property rights theory'. There is no single universally acceptable statement of the theory, but its essence may be summarized as follows: the existence of well-defined private property rights and their enforcement by the state is viewed as the basic precondition to the proper functioning of a market economy and its development. Well-defined property rights typically include the following three basic elements:

1) to every property is assigned a well-defined owner or owners with exclusive rights of ownership;
2) the owner of the property is the recipient of the residual income accruing to the assets;
3) the owner has the right to control or determine the use of the existing assets, to restructure the property and to sell or lease it (11).

That Sicily did not experience a smooth transition to the market economy is considered by Gambetta as a significant factor in the rise of the Mafia. Property rights—'an unprecedented novelty' in Sicily—proved 'difficult to enforce and [...] a source of constant strife' (12). The abolition of feudalism and the widespread introduction of private property rights greatly enhanced the demand for protection. However, the endemic distrust in Southern Italy in the ability or commitment of the state to clearly define and protect property rights produced a peculiar solution to the problem of protecting property. Protection did not undergo the customary process of centralization to become the monopoly of the state, but was supplied by autonomous suppliers, who were the ancestors of today's Mafiosi (13).

(9) *Ibidem*, p. 84.
(10) *Ibidem*, p. 91.
(11) E.G. FURUBOTN, S. PEJOVICH, *The Economics of Property Rights* (Cambridge, Mass.: Ballinger Publishing Company, 1974).
(12) D. GAMBETTA, *The Sicilian Mafia*, p. 94.
(13) *Ibidem*, p. 80.

MAFIA IN RUSSIA

The absence of trust is only part of the explanation supplied by Gambetta for the growth of the Mafia. 'If trust is scarce, then it is reasonable to infer a high potential demand for protection. [...] Lack of trust implies simply that there will be more opportunities to meet that demand [for protection], and hence that meeting it will prove more profitable than elsewhere', but it does not necessarily follow that someone will do so (14). In fact, lack of trust remained uncompensated in various parts of Southern Italy and the Mediterranean world, such as in the village studied by Banfield (15). Elsewhere, a system of patronage developed, as in the town of Pisticci studied by Davies (16). Gambetta offers evidence of the emergence of the *supply* of protection. He locates the emergence of the supply of private protection among the *bravi* released from baronial control at the crucial historical juncture that saw the end of feudalism and the birth of a democratic society. In Sicily, noble landlords maintained private armies of field guards, known as *bravi*, to protect their estates, to enforce their rights and to keep peasants in submission (17). One nobleman, for instance, is reported in 1750 as employing a 'company of twenty-four dragoons [...]' (18). In addition to the *bravi*, Sicily witnessed a long period of 'semi-private protection of public order', endorsed by the Bourbons, and that came to an end only in 1892 (19).

Once the breakup of huge patrimonies occurred and the Italian state abolished these forms of semi-private policing and started by the end of the century to rely upon *carabinieri* and police officials, many professional protectors found themselves unemployed. *Bravi, compagni, militi*, disbanded soldiers of the Bourbon army and bandits 'began offering their services to classes other than the aristocracy. [...] Gradually those who succeeded as protectors became *autonomous* suppliers. Autonomy was the key element missing in other parts of the Mediterranean' (20). Franchetti, as early as 1876, wrote:

> The villains, still ready to serve the purpose of others, have become self-employed, and their industry represents a new course of crimes which are far more numerous than those committed by the *bravi* of the previous era. Thus becoming more

(14) *Ibidem*, p. 78.

(15) E.C. BANFIELD, *The Moral Basis of a Backward Society* (New York: The Free Press, 1958).

(16) J. DAVIS, *Law and Family in Pisticci* (London: London University Press, 1975).

(17) See H. HESS, *Mafia and mafiosi: The Structure of Power* [*Mafia: Zentrale Herrschaft und lokale Gegenmacht*, 1970], trans. by E. OSER (Lexington Mass.: Lexington Books, 1973), 17-18.

(18) A. BLOK, *The Mafia of a Sicilian Village* (Oxford: Basil Blackwell, 1974), p. 90. The campieri constituted a kind of private police force which, in the absence of an efficient formal control apparatus, claimed to preserve law and order in the countryside. *Ibidem*, p. 61.

(19) HESS, *Mafia and mafiosi*, p. 19.

(20) D. GAMBETTA, *The Sicilian Mafia*, p. 80.

FEDERICO VARESE

democratic, the organization of violence is now accessible to many and can support even small interests which formerly could count only on the muscle and energy of their bearers [...] (21).

Gambetta's argument may be summarized as follows:

o) Once a monopoly over property exists, there is no scope for the emergence of private suppliers of protection.

1) The end of monopoly over private property produces an increase in the number of people owning assets.

2) From *(1)* above it follows that the number of transactions in which individual agents with property rights engage will grow substantially.

3) From *(2)* above it follows that a demand for trust in whoever enforces property rights will emerge.

4) This demand will not necessarily be entirely met by the state, or at least not efficiently or not quickly enough.

5) From *(4)* above it follows that there will be scope for the private supply of protection as a substitute for trust.

6) A potential supply of private suppliers of protection is present (22).

It should be clear that some conditions are factual, while others are deductive. Namely, *(2)*, *(3)* and *(5)* are deduced from *(1)*, *(2)* and *(4)* respectively, rather than being a possible alternative between two courses. Other elements are not ineluctable and need to be established factually. It may well be, in fact, that the end of the monopoly over the means of production never takes place, as it would most probably have happened if the authors of the August 1991 coup in the Soviet Union had been successful. Alternatively, once the transition to a market economy has started, the state might succeed in efficiently protecting property rights, as happened in England during the transition from feudalism to capitalism, or that a supply of private entrepreneurs of violence does not emerge, as in the cases studied by Banfield and Davies. The following figure may help to visualize the above points.

Gambetta's account of the emergence of the Mafia in Sicily thus disposes of the 'cultural' argument advanced both in Sicily and abroad to explain the rise of this very peculiar institution. According to

---

(21) L. FRANCHETTI, *Condizioni politiche ed amministrative della Sicilia* [1876], vol. 1 in L. FRANCHETTI and S. SONNINO, *Inchiesta in Sicilia* (Florence: Vallecchi, 1974), 90-1,

quoted by D. GAMBETTA, *The Sicilian Mafia*, p. 79.

(22) See D. GAMBETTA, *The origins of the Mafias*, p. 14-15.

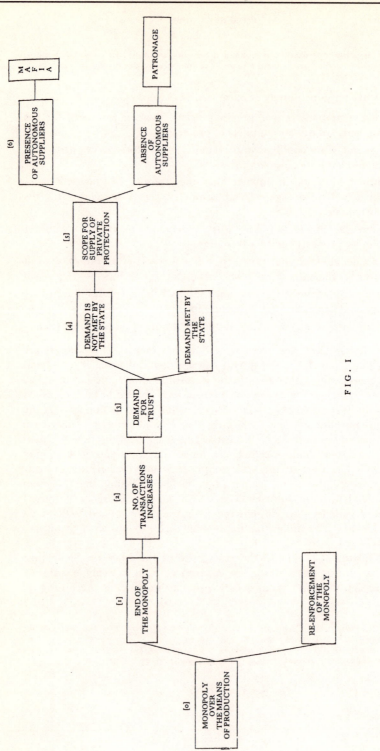

FIG. I

FEDERICO VARESE

this argument (23), individual agents are *pushed-from-behind* by an immaterial substance called 'Sicilian' culture. People's behaviour is considered as mechanically shaped by a set of beliefs, norms and cultural values, which determine the preferences and the set of feasible alternatives. Hess in particular provides an account of Mafia activities in terms of a sub-cultural system which would explain the resistance of Southern Italy to change (24). This argument exhibits various flaws, all of which are factual. Firstly, Sicilian resistance to change is highly disputable. A number of courageous Sicilian public persecutors (most notably, G. Falcone and P. Borsellino) started a massive anti-Mafia campaign that resulted in a number of trials known as *maxi-processi*. As a result of that campaign and of subsequent investigations, the *cupola* of the Sicilian Mafia resides in state prisons and, though the phenomenon is far from being on the verge of disappearing, there is no doubt that a considerable sector of Sicilian society did a great deal to bring Mafia bosses to justice. Moreover, the overwhelming political victory of Leoluca Orlando (an outspoken former member of the Christian Democratic Party and founder of the anti-Mafia political movement *La Rete*) in his bid to be mayor of Palermo in the December 1993 elections points to the conclusion that Sicilian sub-values are not so helpful at predicting what Sicilians will actually do (25).

The cultural argument may be refuted in another way. If another part of the world experiences the same conditions witnessed by Sicily in the nineteenth century and a Sicilian-like Mafia emerges, then Sicilian sub-cultural values will have been proved to be an unnecessary causal pre-requisite. This paper will explore the question of whether present-day Russia is such a place, thus pursuing a suggestion advanced by Gambetta himself (26). In the following sections we will explore to what extent the data so far available are consistent with Gambetta's model; whether, in other words, the future of Russia may be in some respect similar to the history of Sicily (27).

(23) For a critical review, see P. PEZZINO, *Una certa reciprocità di favori: Mafia e modernizzazione nella Sicilia post-unitaria* (Milano: Franco Angeli, 1990), and N. TRANFAGLIA, *La mafia come metodo* (Roma-Bari: Laterza, 1991).

(24) HESS, *Mafia and mafiosi*.

(25) Arguably, the electoral results in Corleone, a high-density Mafia town outside Palermo and Totò Riina's birthplace, are even more significant. The left-wing 31 year old candidate obtained 70 % of the votes, ousting the Christian Democratic Party rival, Michele

La Torre, mayor almost without interruption since 1968 (*Repubblica*, 7/XII/1993).

(26) D. GAMBETTA, *The Sicilian Mafia*, 252-4.

(27) The present paper's title, *Is Sicily the Future of Russia?*, refers to 'Is Mexico the future of Eastern Europe?', by M. CROAN, published in S.P. HUNTINGTON and C.H. MOORE (ed.), *Authoritarian Politics in Modern Society: The Dynamics of Established One-Party Systems* (New York: Basic Books, 1970), 451-483.

MAFIA IN RUSSIA

The data supplied in section I point to the conclusion that organized criminal organizations proliferated after perestrojka. The monopoly over the means of production during Soviet times meant that autonomous suppliers of private protection did not emerge. Only the end of such a monopoly has set in place the first condition envisaged in Gambetta's model, namely, the spread of ownership and the increase in the number of people engaged in economic transactions. What a great number of observers labelled as Mafia-like activities in the pre-Gorbachev era were, in fact, instances of 'organized' corruption involving mainly top state officials.

Economic reforms from 1986 onward have produced a dramatic increase in the number of property owners and transactions in which individuals with property were involved, as documented in section II. The spread of property ownership has not been matched by clear property rights legislation and administrative or financial codes of practice. Nor has it been matched by a corresponding ability on the part of the authorities to enforce such legislation as does exist. The new Russian state has proved to be as riddled with corruption as the Soviet Union of the Gorbachev era. In addition, it has proved to be as inefficient in producing clear legislation and in protecting property rights. The new owners found themselves powerless. As a consequence, fear of losing property and vulnerability to frauds increased and so correspondingly did the demand for protection. An independent supply of potential 'protectors' has also appeared on the scene: an increasing number of dismissed officers and soldiers from the Army, the KGB and the police are looking for jobs and the only skill they possess is physical force. They perfectly qualify as autonomous private suppliers of protection. It seems to be the case that all the factual conditions of Gambetta's model do in fact apply to Russia today.

Having established that both a demand for and a supply of private protection is rising in Russia, I will turn to two instances where demand and supply met and I will argue that, in an untrusting world like present day Russia, it is highly rational to buy private protection, despite all the collective evils it produces. In such a world, suppliers of private protection—including Mafia groups—can only thrive. A general conclusion to be drawn is that a hasty transition to the market, in particular a transition which is not accompanied by clear property rights legislation and enforcement, may lead to disastrous consequences.

FEDERICO VARESE

I

Russian organized crime

J. Serio has reported that officials in charge of combating organized crime estimate that four to five thousand criminal groups are active in the former Soviet Union.

The size of most groups ranges from 5 to 100 members. Some of the largest groups may have anywhere from 100 to 1,500 people and several specialized subunits within the organization. Until now, groups have existed for one-and-a-half to two years on average and committed 18-20 crimes per group. [...] According to official statistics, in 1987, 12,000 criminal groups displaying signs of organization were revealed and broken up, including 400 groups in Uzbekistan and Ukraine, 119 in Krasnodar territory, 29 in Moscow, and 21 in the Moscow region. As of January 1992, there were said to be some 80 organized groups in Moscow and St Petersburg alone. On average, every third group in the country had firearms, and three-quarters have motor vehicles at their disposal (28).

Soviet specialists claimed that organized criminal activity developed rapidly from 1986 onward. Criminal investigation teams exposed 2,600 groups and discovered around 50 'deeply conspiratorial' groups which had been operating for three or more years. During this time, they committed around 20,000 crimes including 218 murders, 785 armed assaults and 1,469 robberies (29).

The official data reported in table 1 indicate that the late eighties were the crucial years during which almost all groups started to operate.

Some groups are named after the territory they control (for instance, the group known as 'Solntsevo' hails from the Solntsevo region of Moscow); others after the ethnic background of the group's members (such as the 'Chechen', which consists of people originally from the Chechen-Ingush Autonomous Republic); other groups are known by the name or nickname of the group's leader (such as the 'Boris' Mafia) (30). According to *Kommersant*, there are ten major 'brigades' in Moscow, though some of these groups seem to be simply street gangs, while others appear to be ethnically homogeneous street beggars involved in petty crimes, such as the Gypsies (31).

(28) J. SERIO, *Organized Crime in the Soviet Union and Beyond*, 134-5.

(29) V.S. KOMMISSAROV, O nekotorykh problemakh bor'by s organizovannoj prestupnost'yu *in* G. MIN'KOVSKII, (ed.), *Bor'ba s organizovannoj prestupnost'yu: problemy teorii i praktiki* [Combating organized crime: theoretical and practical problems] (Moscow: Ministry of Internal affairs, USSR National Academy, 1990), p. 50, quoted in J. SERIO, *Organized Crime in the Soviet Union and Beyond*, p. 135.

(30) *Ibidem*, p. 135

(31) Moskovskii reket: Khotyat li gangstery voiny? [Moscow Racket: Do the gangsters want war?] *Kommersant*, no. 46, 26 November-3 December 1990, 24-5. The *Tsigane* (Gypsies) are most visible as beggars on the

MAFIA IN RUSSIA

Composition, time span and geographical extension of activities
of organised criminal groups as reported by Soviet police in 1990

Group's feature	Numbers of groups (Total 1,641)
Composition	
Up to 3 members	902
4-10 members	644
More than 10 members	81
Unknown	14
Time span	
Up to 1 year	1,172
From 1 to 5 years	392
More than 5 years	19
Unknown	58
Geographical extension	
Inter-provincial or inter-territorial within a Republic	379
Inter-republican	154
Unknown	1,108

Source : *USSR Criminal Statistics, 1992*, quoted in *Annual Report on World-wide Organised Crime*, Interior Minister, Republic of Italy, May 1993, p. 42.

TABLE I

Though they are partial and diverse, the sources available so far point to the fact that the constellation of groups known as the Mafia emerged after 1985, following the introductions of the Gorbachev reforms, which allowed a private sector to emerge and, in particular, after the law on Co-operatives became operative (32). These data strongly support the model advanced in this paper. They indicate that the end of the

streets and are known for being involved in minor robberies. 'Now in Moscow there are 20 major groups, involving approximately 8,000 members. It is typical to have from 25 to 300 soldiers in each group'. SERIO, *Organized Crime in the Soviet Union and Beyond*, p. 138.

(32) On the co-operative movement, see A. JONES, W. MOSKOFF, *Ko-ops. The Rebirth of Entreprenership in the Soviet Union* (Bloomington and Indianapolis: Indiana University Press, 1991).

233

FEDERICO VARESE

monopoly over private property is connected with the emergence of the Mafia and further evidence for this claim will be analyzed below. Nevertheless, this account would be incomplete without an exploration of the Russian scene prior to the end of the state monopoly over property. We need to first establish that a Mafia did not exist before the end of the Soviet Union; that is, before the end of the state monopoly over the means of production and economic transactions.

Private property in the Old Regime and the Soviet Union

In Russia the very concept of private property was unknown until it was introduced in the second half of the eighteenth century by the German-born Catherine II. Until then, the peculiar feature of Russian absolutism in its early form (which lasted from the fourteenth until the late eighteenth century) was marked by the virtual absence of the institution of private property. This type of regime has been known since the time of Hobbes as 'patrimonial' (33). Its distinguishing feature is the fusion of sovereignty and ownership; the monarch views himself, and is viewed by his subjects, as both the ruler of the realm and its proprietor. The patrimonial system rested on the assumption that there existed no separation between the properties of the ruler and those of the state. 'Russians failed to distinguish either in theory or in practice among three types of property: those belonging personally to the monarch; those belonging to the state; and those belonging to private citizens' (34).

The first attempt to separate royal from state lands in Russia was made by Paul I (1796-1801) who created a Department of Appanages in charge of the Romanov family properties. Under Nicholas I in 1826 this department was elevated to the status of a ministry (35). Until then, revenues flowing from the two types of property were pooled. Until then, too, Russian emperors felt perfectly at liberty to hand over or sell to private individuals vast tracts of state property (36). Richard Pipes has further argued that:

(33) R. PIPES, *The Russian Revolution 1899-1919* (London: Collins Harvill, 1990), 53-7.

(34) In France, such a distinction appeared as early as approximately 1290, when custom required the king to safeguard crown estate as inviolable trust. After 1364, French kings had to swear an oath that they would not alienate any part of the royal domain as constituted on their accession. In the sixteenth century, it was further specified that the King's conquests were at his disposal for only ten years, after which they merged with the crown domains. R. PIPES, *Russia Under the Old Regime* (London: Weidenfeld and Nicolson, 1974), 65-66 and 69.

(35) *Ibidem*, p. 70.

(36) *Idem*.

MAFIA IN RUSSIA

The institution [of private property] came late to Russia, but once introduced it soon made itself thoroughly at home. While harassing its subjects for the slightest political offences, the imperial regime was very careful not to violate their property rights (37).

He quotes two rather telling instances as examples. Alexander Herzen never failed to receive his rents while abroad, despite being 'a powerful irritant to the authorities'; Lenin's mother continued to draw the government pension due to her as a civil servant's widow, despite having a son executed for an attempt on the tsar's life and two of her other children being jailed for revolutionary activities (38).

Pipes argues that property rights were effectively enforced in Imperial Russia, and that no autonomous organization was more effective than the state in protecting property rights. The results of Pipes' research thus correspond with the argument advanced here, namely, that once a state is able to define and protect citizens' property rights, the chances of private protectors emerging to perform such a job are very dim. In fact, no Mafia is recorded as having emerged in Imperial Russia.

Private property was not abolished in the Soviet Union. One of the corner-stones of the Marxist programme was, of course, the abolition of private ownership of the means of production, but the abolition of ownership of individual property was never advocated. Marx and Engels stated in the *Communist Manifesto*:

The distinctive feature of Communism is, not the abolition of property in general, but the abolition of bourgeois property [...] We communists have been accused of wishing to abolish the property that has been acquired by personal exertion; the property that is supposed to be the foundation of individual liberty, activity and independence [...] We have no wish to abolish this personal appropriation of the product of labour, which is indispensable for the production of the immediate necessaries of life (39).

Soviet citizens were entitled to own items of personal property. According to Article 10 of the Constitution:

The right of personal ownership by citizens of their income and savings from work, dwelling-house and subsidiary household husbandry, articles of domestic and everyday use, articles of personal consumption and convenience, as well as the right to inherit the personal property of citizens, shall be protected by law (40).

At first, the Soviet regime made some gestures toward abolishing inheritance rights, but soon reverted to a rather liberal policy. In 1926, a progressive inheritance tax, up to 90 % of the value of the estate, was

(37) *Ibidem*, p. 313.

(38) *Ibidem*, p. 313-14.

(39) *The Communist Manifesto of Karl Marx and Friedrich Engels*, introduction and notes by D. RYAZANOFF (London: Martin Lawrence Limited, 1930), 43-5.

(40) *Constitution (Fundamental Law) of the Union of Soviet Socialist Republics* [1936 text] in A. UNGER, *Constitutional Development in the USSR* (London: Methuen, 1981), 140-58. Art. 10 became Art. 13 in the 1977 new Constitution. See *Ibidem*, 230-66.

FEDERICO VARESE

substituted for a 10,000 ruble limitation. Since 1943, the government appropriated only a small fee, not to exceed 10 % of the value of the estate, for issuing an inheritance certificate. Thus, there was no limit on the amount which could be inherited in the USSR, and since some people earned very high incomes, fairly large properties could be bequeathed to heirs. The Soviet citizen could own and inherit property and money, have a bank account, a dwelling place and household equipment. Possession of dachas was also rather common among professionals (41). There is no evidence that the Soviet state failed to protect the property of personal items.

Criminal activities were of course widespread in the former Soviet Union, though they qualify as corruption rather than as Mafia. The Soviet economic system fuelled various forms of corruption. K. Simis noted that the Soviet 'underworld' was not ruled by gangsters and drug peddlers so much as by 'store and restaurant managers, and directors of state enterprises, institutions, and collective and state farms' and politicians (42). They mainly busied themselves with large-scale embezzlement from the state and with the diversion of goods from trade enterprises into their pockets. The common link among them was membership of the Communist Party of the Soviet Union. Membership of the CPSU was mandatory for anyone aspiring to gain an important position not only in the Party itself but also in the government apparatus. A list of acceptable candidates (*nomenklatura*) to fill the most important jobs was the vehicle for upward mobility of loyal Party members. The organizational structure of the Party and the state apparatus took the form of a huge hierarchical pyramid. At the base were the thousands of district secretaries and executives of the local government, heads of branches of KGB, MVD [Interior Ministry] and other organs. Above them were their counterparts at the regional level, making up the middle-level of the party state apparatus. At the summit of the pyramid were top functionaries of the Central Committee, the chairmen of the Council of Ministries, the deputies, members of the government, secretaries of the Party, as well as their counterparts at the level of each republic. At the very top, of course, sat the Politburo and the Secretary of CPSU (43).

The district elite supplied a constant stream of illegal tributes and gifts to regional centres. Each level of the political system extorted tributes from subordinate levels. 'Regional leaders bought a degree of

---

(41) K. HULIKA and I. HULIKA, *Soviet Institutions and Society* (Boston: The Christopher Publishing House, 1967), p. 584.

(42). K. SIMIS, *USSR: The Corrupt Society*

(New York: Simon and Schuster, 1982), p. 94-5.

(43) I am drawing here upon J. SERIO, *Organized Crime in the Soviet Union and Beyond.*

MAFIA IN RUSSIA

autonomy from the centre and conducted local affairs in a way they saw fit as long as it did not encroach on the centre' (44). Under Khrushchev and to a greater extent Brezhnev, an era of unfettered corruption among the elite flourished. This era is

epitomized by the exploits of Krasnodar Party boss Sergei Medunov who had run his whole region like one great commercial concession, [...] and the Uzbek cotton scandal, where a series of fictitious cotton harvests were used to swindle the state of three billion rubles and involved Brezhnev's son-in-law, Yuri Churbanov (45).

Competition among groups within the state apparatus produced cracks in what Simis calls the 'corrupt society'. The Suslov-Andropov-Gorbachev axis was especially active in exposing corrupt officials and promoting inquiries, in open conflict with the group which rallied behind Brezhnev and Chernenko. Andropov, in particular, made use of a special KGB section which devoted itself to fighting against corruption. As is well known, this struggle went through various phases, and in the end Andropov managed to discredit Brezhnev's men and become General Secretary of the CPSU.

Corruption in the Soviet period is a different phenomenon from the Mafia as defined here. The coalitions of corrupt officials did not resort to structures outside the state apparatus in order to produce violent threats. They had to bargain with the army or police heads for their backing. Sometimes they used petty criminals to organize small traps for irritant figures: for instance, they set up compromising situations, photos were taken and then were used to blackmail antagonists (46). However, they did not create an alternative military structure. The Soviet Army and the various police branches of the state retained the monopoly over force and corrupt functionaries were able to use the state agencies for their purposes so long as their head had struck a deal with the police or army commander. The power of a Regional Party Secretary was almost absolute, and he could control the appointment and the careers of many cadres, including police officials, judges, Ministry of the Interior and KGB agents at the local level. Often, unwelcome investigations were hindered or never started. Some conventions to signal willingness to enter into the corruption scheme—such

(44) J. SERIO, *Organized Crime in the Soviet Union and Beyond*, 133-4. See also S. WHITFIELD, *Industrial Power and the Soviet State* (Oxford: Clarendon Press, 1993), especially p. 105-9.

(45) M. GALEOTTI, Organized Crime in Moscow and Russian National Security, *Low Intensity Conflict and Law Enforcement*, vol. 1, no. 3 (Winter 1992), p. 239. Further evidence on Medunov, and more generally on corruption, is provided by W.A. CLARK, *Crime and Punishment in Soviet Officialdom* (New York-London: M.E. Sharpe, 1993), 167-71.

(46) See A. VAKSBERG, *La Mafia sovietica* (1992) and V. COULLOUDON, *La Mafia en Union Soviétique* (Paris: JC Lattes, 1990), for various instances.

FEDERICO VARESE

as accepting small gifts—emerged among the corrupt elite, and such coalitions lasted as long as they were mutually advantageous for their members. A ritual that could resemble in some ways the Mafia initiation ceremony did not exist to enjoin the Soviet bureaucrats.

There is another phenomenon which allows us to draw a clear distinction between Mafia and corruption, namely, the fact that Mafiosi do not commit suicide. As we have already mentioned, competing coalitions in the Soviet Union often used branches of the judiciary and the police apparatus to expose corrupt bureaucrats. Once exposed, the latter sometimes committed suicide, for reasons not dissimilar from the ones that led those Italians involved in the recently exposed corruption scandals of *Tangentopoli* (Bribesville) to choose a similar solution: they committed suicide out of shame, of fear of more severe sanctions (always possible according to the criminal code), or as an attempt to save their good name. In these cases, suicide occurs because the person has been caught deviating from the function he was supposed to perform on behalf of the community. On the other hand, a Mafioso who is arrested by the police is caught while performing his job, namely, engaging in a criminal activity. He has no reason to be ashamed. In fact, no cases have been recorded of Mafiosi committing suicide *because* they were caught by the police (47).

The widespread corruption fostered a black market where a variety of goods was exchanged. Different regions of the USSR experienced this in different degrees, Georgia being a region in which black market activities were notably extensive. Perhaps the most striking illustration of this is the underground Georgian millionaire Babunashvili, who was able to procure for himself the post of Minister of Light Industry. Furthermore, every major enterprise had its *tolkach* (fixer) whose job was to navigate the channels of the shadow economy and pilot the complex series of deals and undertakings necessary to operate in the Brezhnev era. Deals were also made with other enterprises. Nevertheless, the black economy did not operate independently from the state apparatus: state officials retained control over enforcement agencies as well as production. In this respect, they closely resembled the Sicilian landlords of the eighteenth and early nineteenth centuries, rather than the little property owners of the late nineteenth century. In the pre-

(47) There are altogether very few cases of Italian Mafiosi who committed suicide. They usually do so in order to signal to their 'family' that they did not give away the secrets they knew or to protect relatives. Recently, A. Gioé, a Mafioso from Altofonte investigated for the murder of Giovanni Falcone, killed himself (*Repubblica*, 3/VIII/1993. I am grateful to V. Pizzini for bringing this article to my attention and for an enlightening discussion on this point). In a letter he left behind, he explicitly wrote he did not regret his various deeds.

MAFIA IN RUSSIA

Gorbachev Soviet Union, independent agencies powerful enough to supply protection more efficiently than the state did not exist.

II

Spread of ownership

A crucial distinction must be drawn between property ownership prior to the Gorbachev period and from 1986 onwards. By 1992, a Western journalist provided the following vivid account of this new situation.

Buying, selling, trading, haggling, lowering the price or raising it to adjust the customer, Russians have taken to the streets, not to protest but to indulge in a huge, nationwide rummage sale [...] A woman hawks a bottle of vodka, another a pair of shoes [...], a third is selling six months' worth of birth-control pills (48).

Boris Yeltsin's decree on free trade (23 January, 1992), which virtually liberalized any form of trade, brought people out by the thousands on the city pavements. Russian citizens are now permitted to open any sort of shop and sell any sort of goods (except certain ones explicitly prohibited) without licence (49).

The percentage of private firms involved in Russian industrial production rose to 14 % of the total in 1991, though the value of their fixed capital was only 4 % of the total. Small and medium private enterprises jumped from 20,000 to more than 50,000 in the first months of 1992, when the first wave of the privatisation programme hit Russia. In 1992, 33,000 small-scale state enterprises were privatized (50).

Partly influenced by the Polish and Czechoslovak examples, the Presidential decree on privatisation, promulgated on 29 December 1991 (decree no. 341), put most small enterprises into the category of 'obligatory privatisation'. Auctions of state assets took place in many parts of Russia (51). By February 1992, 50,000 agricultural firms, 9,000 companies, 1,300 commercial banks and 110 commodity exchanges had been officially registered (52). In 1993, the number of privatised enterprises has reached 82,000 units and between 700 and 800 medium and large enterprises are still being auctioned off every month (53). In all of Russia 30,000 small and large shops have been privatized, of which 9,399 were in Moscow. Between January and April

(48) *Independent*, 27/III/1992.
(49) *Repubblica*, 24/I/1992.
(50) In total, 1,547 of the 26,000 companies that employ more than 200 workers or have assets valued over 1 million rubles, were sold by the end of April 1993. *Financial Times*, 27/V/1993.
(51) *Sole 24 Ore*, 30/VI/92.
(52) *Byt*, II/1992.
(53) *The Economist*, 11/XII/1993.

FEDERICO VARESE

1993, 2.5 million apartments or houses were privatized, bringing the total to 5,300,000. By May 1, 1993, 16 % of all flats were privately owned, and the government forecasts that by the end of the year the figure will be 40 % of the total (54). The third wave of the privatisation programme is about to hit Russian industry. According to the Russian Government's plans, by the end of 1993 up to one third of the entire value of Russia's productive capital will be privatized and the projected figure for 1994 is to be about 50 % (55).

Land is slowly but steadily being freed from the bonds of state ownership. By January 1993, 49,770 private peasant farms were operating in the Russian Federation (56). The President's decree on the Regulation of Land Relations and the development of Agrarian Reform in Russia, which enhanced the ownership of land (57), was published in October 1993 and it is supposed to implement the right to own and sell land, which is enshrined in the newly adopted Constitution (58).

That the reforms generated by Gorbachev and Yeltsin constitute a radical change in approach from what had come before can be illustrated by the enactment of a Law on Inventions in the USSR, approved on 31 May, 1991, which came into force on 1 July, 1991 (59). The key provision in regard to registered inventions was that inventors would have exclusive right of use (as in most Western patent laws), and therefore could sell or license such rights of use over the invention to others. This was a major departure from the old 'inventors' certificate' regime, in which inventions were treated as public property and inventors had no right to restrict or monopolize their use. One could say that the traditional socialist system amounted to a giant company suggestion scheme, in which the *USSR, Inc.* exercised a monopolist's power to set the terms of any reward to inventors (60). The effect of this new law was to further undermine state monopoly and to spread ownership (61).

(54) *Repubblica*, 4/VI/1993.

(55) *Programma uglubleniya ekonomicheskikh reform* (Moscow: Government of Russian Federation, 1992), p. 90.

(56) S.K. WEGREN, *Trends in Russian Agrarian Reform*, RFE/RL, vol. 2, no. 13, 26 March 1993, p. 51. According to Alexander Kalinin, leader of the government agro-industrial complex department, there are now 48 million land plots—8 % of all agricultural areas—in the hands of private owners, and 180,000 private farms on which around 0.5 million Russian citizens are working (*Izvestia*, 28/I/1993).

(57) *Rossiyskaya Gazeta*, 29/X/1993.

(58) Art. 9, sub-paragraph 2. Text in *Rossiyskaya Gazeta*, 10/XII/1993, p. 3-6.

(59) Text in *Izvestia*, 14/VI/1991, p. 3-5.

(60) 'In a centralized economy, the supreme political and economic authorities coalesce, the Politburo is at one and the same time the supreme arbiter of politics and board of directors of USSR Ltd., the largest firm in the world'. A. NOVE, *The Soviet Economic System* (London: George Allen & Unwin, 1980), p. 25.

(61) Guidelines for a Law of Contracts have also been approved in the last months of the USSR's life. *Principles of civil legislation of the USSR and the Republics* were approved on 31 May, 1991 and came into effect on 1 January

MAFIA IN RUSSIA

The above discussion of the various data relating to property ownership has attempted to show that conditions in today's Russia are congruent with propositions *(1)* and *(2)* of Gambetta's model. These propositions can be captured in the statement that the end of the monopoly over the means of production and commerce increased the number of people owning assets and their involvement in economic transactions.

Demand of protection

Proposition *(3)* of Gambetta's model is inferred from *(2)*, namely, a demand for trust in whoever enforces property rights will emerge after the spread of property. In this section we will attempt to establish whether such a demand for trust and protection of one's property was met by the Soviet and Russian state (62).

Whether a state protects property rights efficiently depends to a great extent on whether such rights are clearly defined. In Russia the increase in property owners and economic transactions was not matched by clear property rights legislation. For a number of years property regulations were a mixture of procedures from the previous regime, which were heavily influenced by socialist doctrine in matters of property, and new regulations. In a paper on reform priorities, Rudiger Dornbusch observed that

Among the key elements [of a smooth transition to market economy] is a functioning legal system that protects the right to conduct economic transactions and provides the possibility of sanctions and redress (63).

He then goes on to argue that the most suitable way of handling this issue is to 'adopt wholesale and without question the entire civil code, including corporate law, of a well-functioning legal system, say the Netherlands or Finland' (64). This is hardly a viable suggestion, and in fact the Soviet Union and the newly independent republics did not take up this advice. Since late 1989, Soviet policy-makers have put forward a number of laws, statutes, decrees and presidential edicts that were intended to create the legal framework for a Western type mixed

---

1992 (replacing a law of 8 December, 1961). Text in *Izvestia*, 25/VI/1991, p. 3-7.

(62) This is no doubt an empirical question to be established. Nevertheless, it could be argued that under certain conditions—namely, pressure to develop markets—*invariably* the institutions of an old regime will change more slowly than private markets.

(63) R. DORNBUSCH, *Priorities of Economic Reform in Eastern Europe and the Soviet Union*, Centre for Economic Policy Research Occasional Paper no. 5 (London: February 1991), p. 7.

(64) *Idem.*

FEDERICO VARESE

economy. They dealt, among other things, with joint stock companies, small firms, security transactions and banks.

An important step toward the full-scale extension of property rights came in 19 November, 1986, with the adoption of the Law on Individual Labour Activity (that went into effect in May 1987). This Law laid the ground for the potential development of business organizations that were not simply individual enterprises or even small scale family businesses, but also businesses that could be made up of people not related to each other. These businesses, along with their assets, would be owned by the members of the cooperative. While the law permitted a wide range of activities, authorities were given the power to decide for themselves what should or should not be allowed and ultimate power to give or deny permission to operate an individual business (65).

Since 1986, the legal situation in Russia has developed in a chaotic fashion. A plethora of often overlapping and conflicting laws and decrees emanates from a variety of jurisdictions. 'The same subjects are often covered by many different and mutually contradictory normative pronouncements, and it is difficult to ascertain their ultimate validity' (66). Naishul' has shown that the weakening of vertical hierarchical links and the collapse of the party destroyed the former network of administrative coordination. State authority has been transformed into 'a system of autonomous administrative offices with overlapping jurisdictions, each pursuing its own rather than the general state interests' (67).

The privatized state industries are thus subject to a considerable degree of uncertainty, as pointed out by a commentator: 'at the heart of the debate [over the newly privatized enterprises] is the uncertainty about the nature of the property rights that have notionally been transferred from the state to shareholders' (68). The same verdict applies to the legal status of land and flats. 'If Russian law is a sea of uncertainty, nowhere the waters are murkier than around questions of ownership. And in practice, the most energetic battles are over who owns a particular building or piece of land' (69). Tax regulations are also

(65) JONES and MOSKOFF, *Ko-ops*, p. 5-6.

(66) R. FRYDMAN, A. RAPACZYNSKI, and J. EARLE, *The Privatization Process in Russia, Ukraine and the Baltics* (Budapest: Central European University Press, 1993), quoted in J. CHARAP and L. WEBSTER, Constrains on the development of private manufacturing in St Petersburg, *Economics of Transformation*, vol. 1, no. 3 (September 1993), p. 315.

(67) V. NAISHUL', Liberalism, Customary Rights and Economic Reforms, *Communist Economies and Economic Transformation*, vol. 5, no. 1 (1993), p. 55.

(68) *Financial Times*, 27/v/1993.

(69) *The Moscow Letter*, vol. 1, no. 3, 1 February 1992. This is a newsletter published by a pool of western legal firms operating in Russia. In the article I am quoting from, the author is narrating a story of legal uncertainty involving a western company, Capital Contracts.

MAFIA IN RUSSIA

unclear and ever-changing (the law regarding taxation for joint ventures has changed three times since early 1992) (70). The absence of any form of legislation has characterised the life of the 600 Commodity Exchanges (where traders exchange commodities instead of stocks), and produced great uncertainty on what is allowed and what is illegal (71). Banking transfer payments and mortgage loans still await a law to regulate them, and therefore a wide variety of transactions has been conducted in cash, such as the purchases of flats and houses (72).

The absence of a copyright law has either fostered piracy or withholding of investment, or both. A case in point is that of the Russian publisher of *Scarlet*, the sequel to *Gone With the Wind* by Alexandra Ripley. Despite having legally purchased the right to publish *Scarlet* in Russia, the Muscovite publisher abandoned the book's distribution, because Moscow was flooded by unauthorized versions of the book published by more than ten Russian publishers, and he could not find a legal way to stop others publishing the Ripley's sequel (73). Finally, the Russian Government approved a Law on Copyright and Related Rights on 25 January 1993 (74). The law itself provides for a 'transitional period' (which will end on 1 January 1994) during which users have the right to use, for example, computer software and data banks without the author's consent and without paying compensation. '[In Russia] piracy of all types of intellectual property, and indeed in the other countries of the cis, is the rule rather than the exception [...] and the actual enforcement of the law may prove very difficult' (75). Even the officials involved in the drafting of the law and its enforcement reckon that, at best, piracy would fall from more than 90 % to 60 % during the next four to five years (76). According to expert estimates, up to 95 % of the computer software distributed in the former Soviet Union is pirated (77).

As late as April 1992, the Siberian baseball player Rudolf Razhigaev's response to a travelling scout for the California Angels baseball team, who offered him a *contract* to play in the United States, was: 'A what?' (78). This anecdote shows that legal procedures, even when they

(70) *The Moscow Letter*, vol. 1, no. 22, 15 November 1992.

(71) See *The Times*, 18/IV/1992, *Repubblica*, 21/I/1992 and *Sunday Times Magazine*, 12/I/1992.

(72) *Repubblica*, 4/VI/1993.

(73) *Il manifesto*, 12/IX/92.

(74) *ITAR-TASS*, 27/I/1993.

(75) V. YASMANN, *New Russian Copyright Laws Protect Computer Software*, RFE/RL, vol. 2, no. 11, 12 March 1993, p. 48.

(76) This is the Rosapo (Russian Agency for the Legal Protection of Computer Software, Data banks and Topology of Integrated Circuits) Director General's opinion. *Poisk*, no. 10, 1992.

(77) V. YASMANN, *New Russian Copyright Laws Protect Computer Software*, p. 48.

(78) *Newsweek*, 20/IV/1992.

FEDERICO VARESE

exist, are far from being internalized by the citizens. And often such procedures are simply not yet in place.

The Russian state has not only proved itself unable to produce clear property rights legislation, but is increasingly lagging behind in the protection of its own citizens' lives, a feature that further debases trust in it. According to official statistics, the 'serious crime' rate has increased 32 % in one year alone (1989), while the average Soviet citizen was in 1989 four to five times more likely then a Briton, Frenchman or Japanese to die a violent death (79). Although the detention rate increased 7 % in the first quarter of 1990 compared with the same period in 1989 (and by 16.3 % in the case of serious crime), the overall crime rate rose 15.3 % during the first three months of 1990 (80). Demands on the police are increasingly burdensome and dangerous: in 1989, policemen used firearms 3,891 times (almost four times the figure for 1988) and more than 350 MVD officers were killed in the course of their duties (81).

Russian crime rates 1989-1992

Year	Total reported crimes [A]	% increase on the previous year [A]	Number of unresolved crimes [B]	% increase on the previous year [B]	Number of murders [C]	% increase on the previous year [C]
1989	1,619,181	=	619,375	=	13,543	=
1990	1,839,451	+ 13.6 %	782,128	+ 26.2 %	15,566	+ 14.9 %
1991	2,167,964	+ 33.8 %	1,041,107	+ 68.0 %	16,122	+ 19.0 %
1992	2,760,652	+ 70.5 %	1,380,526	+ 122.8 %	23,006	+ 69.8 %

Source : *Crime—The Threat to Russia*, Documents prepared for a Closed Conference on Organised Crime held in the Kremlin, Moscow, Russian Federation, 12-13/II/1993.

TABLE 2

The total number of reported crimes in 1992 rose 70.5 % on 1989, while the total number of unsolved cases has gone up 122.8 % on 1989 (82). Aleksei Kazannik, the current Russian Federation Prosecutor

(79) *Izvestia*, 26/II/1990 and *New Times*, no 35, 1989.

(80) *Pravda*, 31/VI/1990 and *TASS*, 27/VI/1990. Figures after the first half of 1991 were no longer comparable because of the independence of the Baltics. All the same, all the figures show a continued growth in crime.

See L. SHELLEY, *The militia and crime control* (Mimeo, 1993), 4-5.

(81) *Krasnaya Zvezda*, 4/VII/1990.

(82) These data are taken from *Crime—The Threat to Russia*, documents prepared for a closed Kremlin Conference on Organized Crime in Russia (12-13/II/1993). See *Nezavi-*

MAFIA IN RUSSIA

General, said that his office is in a position to complete no more than 50 % of the bills of indictments in the already investigated cases (83). It has become dangerous to walk even in the most central streets of Moscow (84). These data match growing concerns over personal safety related to the rising number of kidnappings reported in the Russian press (85). Collective panic spread in 1992, when bottles of paralysing gas against thieves could be bought everywhere in Moscow (86). L. Shelley, an expert on Soviet and post-Soviet crime, has concluded that 'the crime increase of the final years of the Soviet period [...] did not represent the continuation of a trend'. Instead, it was a 'new phenomenon' (87).

The absence of a credible state, which provides rights and enforces them, undermines not only trust in the state, but also among citizens. The business community has so far not developed a set of rules of the game which holds in the absence of an enforcing central agency. There is, in fact, a high rate of crimes committed by business people against other business people. A number of cases have been reported in which the arrested criminals were members of trade and purchasing cooperatives with ambitions to rid themselves of their competitors, employing guns and explosives. 'Competition here means that you grasp the throat of your competitor and beat money out of him', says Sergei Siderenko, chief of the St Petersburg's special anti-Mafia unit (88). Of more than 5,000 private retail outlets that were reported as operating in Moscow in 1991, 80 % do not have elementary security systems. Vladimir Novikov, of the Moscow Criminal Police Department, told the weekly *Golos* that the privatisation of retail trade that started in 1991 has led to a dramatic increase in theft, armed robbery and murder (89).

Both self-declared Mafiosi and law enforcers in Russia seem to agree on the fact that the state is not a credible protector of individual property and safety (90). According to an anonymous Mafioso interviewed

simaya Gazeta 12/II/93, and *Kommersant-Daily* 16/II/1993.

(83) *Nezavisimaya Gazeta*, 28/X/1993.

(84) See, for some instances, ITAR-TASS, 18/X/92.

(85) See *Trud*, 24/VIII/1990, *Rabochaya Tribuna*, 30/XI/1990, *Komsomolskaya Pravda*, 1/1993.

(86) A boy in Moscow exploited the security mania by selling spray cans of de-icers as if they were paralysing gas (such as CS gas) against thieves. It should be noticed that the rising demand for protection has given him the opportunity to perpetuate the fraud and sell

what people believed was an imperfect substitute for protection.

(87) L. SHELLEY, *The militia and crime control*, p. 5.

(88) *Newsweek*, 5/X/92. See also *Moscow News*, 21/V/1993.

(89) According to him, a 'commercial shop' thief can boast an average daily scoop of 100,000 rubles (*Golos*, 2/III/1992). Many of the new shop owners themselves invite crime. A day's earnings are very often left overnight in flimsy outdoor kiosks (*Ibidem*).

(90) Business people operating in Moscow and other major cities are reported as having

FEDERICO VARESE

by the magazine *Sovetskaya Torgovlya,* 'in the absence of clear moral values and beliefs, the Mafia has permeated the entire fabric of society [...] The laws of the state do not work, or work selectively. It is useless to fight the Mafia, and wise people have understood this and are collaborating with us' (15/XI/1991). This opinion was shared by A. Gurov, head of the USSR Interior Ministry department combating organized crime. In an interview with *Sovetskaya Rossiya* (10/XI/1990), he described the situation as one in which 'everyone lives by his own laws and instructions [...] A veritable war of sovereignties is on. Almost every neighbourhood or block has proclaimed its sovereignty'. All this contributes to the increasing 'legal nihilism and anarchy'.

A sort of do-it-yourself approach to protection has been endorsed by top magistrates and has made its way into the new Russian Criminal Code. Valentin Stepankov, until recently Russian Prosecutor General, proposed an amendment to the criminal code that would abrogate the legal concept of proportionate self-defence. In the Soviet Criminal Code, as in most criminal codes in the world, the notion authorised citizens to defend themselves in ways proportionate to the threat. According to Stepankov,

If an individual is trying to defend himself, his life or his properties, then he is entitled to use any means and we should not ask wether he is going beyond the limits set by the concept of proportionate self-defence (91).

Stepankov's proposal has been included in the new draft of the Criminal Code, which has already been signed by the President and awaits final approval from the newly elected Federal Assembly (92).

The demand for protection is quickly growing in Russia. Following the January 1992 price deregulation, private farmers in the Kemerovo region, Siberia, have seen many armed visitors to their farmsteads take away their cattle and poultry. The local racketeers have told the farmers they will leave them alone provided that they receive a monthly 'protection sum' of 5,000 rubles. 'Those guys carry grandfather's hunting rifles, they tote army submachine guns, and I would feel much better off if I had a machine gun in my house', one farmer told a *Kuranty* reporter. Siberian farmers have asked their local associations to buy

appealed to foreign police to assist them (L. SHELLEY, *Post-Soviet Organized Crime: Implications for the development of Soviet successor states and foreign countries,* Mimeo, 1993, 14-5). The FBI is to open an office in Moscow (Paddy Rawlinson, personal communication).

(91) Stepankov also notes that the Russian penal code does not take into account economic crimes. 'Russian justice cannot do any-

thing to persecute economic crimes, because it cannot apply old Soviet laws which referred to socialist property'. *Corriere della Sera,* 12/II/1993.

(92) A furtner relevant novelty of the new Criminal Code concerns the collective responsibility of members of organized criminal groups. See *Moscow News,* 3/XII/1993.

MAFIA IN RUSSIA

them firearms (93). Farmers have to protect not only their cattle, poultry and the expensive farm machinery from occasional thieves, but also the right to cultivate their own plot from collective state farmers who have not embraced the new framework of individual private property in land. In an interview with one of the first private farmers—Mr. Sergei Boyakov, owner of 228 hectares of land in Russia's rich southern Penza region—it was reported that he was plagued by the problem of persuading state farmers to keep their cows off his pastures and, despairing of a negotiated settlement, has decided to hire private police to guard his fields (94).

Fear has spread among farmers across the Federation. During the Russian Farmers' Congress held in Moscow in early February of 1992, a major concern voiced by the delegates regarded protection of property, and Deputy Prime Minister Gaidar promised that they would be allowed to carry firearms to protect crops (95). Private farmers in the Cheliabinsk Region, the Urals, have been allowed to carry shotguns for the protection of their lives and property after the Ural Farmer, an association of private farmers, pressed the police to give such permission in the aftermath of a spate of crimes against rural households. Under an agreement with the association, the police have also said that they are ready to provide farmers with patrols to protect them from attacks on their property (96). According to the Minister of the Interior, there are more than 1.5 million firearms possessed illegally by the population (97).

The data supplied above seem to indicate that present-day Russia is a potentially rich pasture for suppliers of private protection.

Supply of protection

So far we have explored the issue of whether there is a potential demand for protection. It cannot, however, be argued that demand is going to be met inevitably, otherwise we will yield to a functionalist reasoning. Lack of protection implies that there will be more opportunities

(93) *Kuranty*, 22/I/1992.
(94) *Times*, 13/V/92.
(95) TV Programme *Novosti* and *ITAR-TASS*, 4/II/1992.
(96) *Megalopolis-Continent*, 16/III/1992.
(97) Data taken from *Crime—The Threat to Russia*. See *Kommersant-Daily* 16/II/1993. An intriguing feature of the transition to the market and the spread of ownership is the increase in petty frauds where everyone entering transactions is liable to be a victim. Demand of protection from fraud should be taken into consideration, even if the threat is not posed by a machine gun. Details of the most common of them have been spelled out by a canny swindler interviewed by state TV, Andrei Ujutnov, currently in jail (TV Programme *Novosti* 27/VIII/1992).

FEDERICO VARESE

to meet that demand, and hence that meeting it will be more profitable than elsewhere. But it does not follow that a Mafia-like solution will arise inevitably. Together with the demand for protection, it is essential to provide some coherent idea of the origin of its supply (condition *(6)* in Gambetta's model). In what follows we will assess the independent evidence that points to the presence of a considerable number of potential private suppliers of protection.

The supply of private protection usually derives from few specific sources. Vigilantes, ex-soldiers, private guards, bandits, prison inmates, as well as some individuals with spontaneous aptitude, provide a pool of potential suppliers already trained in the use of violence (98). It has been estimated that in the span of three years—from 1987 to 1989—economic reform was responsible for 3 million people losing their jobs in industry, only 20 % of whom were offered suitable alternative employment (99). Prime Minister V. Chernomyrdin stated that unemployment in Russia currently stands at 4.5 million (100). Among the newly unemployed, it is not uncommon to find people trained in or accustomed to the use of violence.

A number of servicemen have now been made 'redundant', due either to economic structures of the Russian state or to dismissal for offences ranging from corruption to abuse of authority. At the end of January 1992, Viktor Barannikov, chief of Russia's security service, announced a cut of staff from 36,000 to 2,800, a reduction unprecedented in KGB history. Those retired include chauffeurs, medical personnel, highly skilled specialists (in particular 'code crackers' and experts in computer security), who, according to *Kommersant*, are already being courted by Western security agents (101). 25,000 officers of the former Soviet Army have been fired on political grounds. The Russian Defence Ministry's press services stated on 2 February 1993 that the programme for the gradual reduction of Russian armed forces' numerical strength will result in an annual discharge of between 40,000 to 50,000 officers (102).

A series of dismissals has affected the police as well. This is due not so much to an effort to cut down the number of officers (the police are in fact trying to expand their ranks), but to reduce corruption and slop-

---

(98) D. GAMBETTA, *The Sicilian Mafia*, p. 78-9.

(99) In one survey of Muscovites, 26 % thought they themselves would become unemployed after marketization of the economy. JONES and MOSKOFF, *Ko-ops*, p. 127. See also D. J. PETERSON, New data published on Employment and Unemployment in the USSR, *Report on the USSR*, vol. 2, no. 1, 5 January, 1990, p. 4.

(100) *Rossiya*, no. 9, 24/11/1993.

(101) *Kommersant*, 3/11/1992.

(102) *Repubblica*, 13/1/1993 and *Interfax*, 2/11/1993.

MAFIA IN RUSSIA

piness (103). In 1988 alone, for example, 1,500 policemen were convicted for offences ranging from negligence to abuse of authority. Following a major investigation conducted in 1987-88, 25,000 policemen were discharged on various grounds, and a further 32,000 were dismissed in 1989 (in 1990 it was estimated that there was a total of 475,000 personnel in the police as a whole) (104). The police are finding it difficult to attract quality personnel, 'particularly given the new opportunities to earn considerably more as bodyguards and private investigators' (105). Moscow's Main Administration for Internal Affairs was about 4,000 under strength in 1989. The best trained and equipped forces of the MVD were offered a three year contract and 200 rubles a month in 1989. (The MVD forces are largely made up of conscripts) (106). In the first six months of 1990, over 100 skilled law enforcement experts in the Khabarovsk Territory quit their jobs because of low salaries (107). An Interior Ministry spokesman voiced the concern that the Ministry lacked 60 % of skilled experts considered necessary to fight effectively organized crime, and that the equipment the officers use 'is just nothing to talk about' (108). According to figures revealed at a closed conference on Organized Crime by Russian Internal Minister Viktor Yerin, 63,000 professionals left the militia in 1992, and one in every five of them 'went over to the enemy' (109).

Sometimes private protection may also be supplied by gangs of young people who—out of pure pleasure—enjoy patrolling a certain area and exercising their physical strength on some scapegoats. A gang of such young people, who make a cult of physical fitness, has appeared in Moscow in 1990. The *Lyubery*, named after a working class suburb of Moscow, are a party of hard-hat, clean-cut, karate-trained lads who have raided the capital in order to 'cleanse' it of hippies, heavy-metal rock fans and other representatives of 'Western decadence', apparently with the tacit support of police (110).

---

(103) See M. GALEOTTI, Police and Para-militaries: Public Order Forces and Resources, *Report on the USSR*, vol. 2, no. 23, 8 June, 1990, p. 6-9.

(104) *TASS*, 27/vi/1989 and *Radio Moscow*, 13/iii/1990.

(105) M. GALEOTTI, Police and Paramilitaries: Public Order Forces and Resources, p. 7. Dr. C.A. Thomas, of the Socio-Legal Studies Centre of Wolfson College, Oxford, has informed me that the Russian judiciary is experiencing a similar out-flow of quality personnel. Increasingly, judges prefer to work for private law firms.

(106) M. TSYPKIN, Workers' Militia: Order Instead of Law?, *Report on the USSR*, Vol. 1, no. 46, 17 November, 1989, p. 16.

(107) *Trud*, 24/viii/1990.

(108) *Izvestia*, 9/vii/1991.

(109) *Crime—The Threat to Russia* and *Kommersant-Daily* 16/11/1993.

(110) M. TSYPKIN, Workers' Militia: Order Instead of Law?, p. 16. According to *Kommersant* (26/xii/1990), the gang controls some prostitution and most of its income is derived from shell games and other confidence games.

FEDERICO VARESE

To organize an efficient firm providing a private supply of protection, it is necessary to have not only a labour supply, but also a minimal level of equipment, most importantly weapons. Lack of morale and pressing economic problems have pushed many members of security services and the army to sell a considerable amount of weapons on the black market. According to Gennadi Deinega, of the St Petersburg police investigation department, the local firearms black market offers for the most part weapons stolen from the army, KGB and police units. Since 1989 in St Petersburg alone 45 pieces of firearms have been registered as 'unaccounted for' by police and KGB officers. Another significant source is the so-called 'conversion business'. Warrant officers at military warehouses often sell stolen weapons on the black market that are later listed as 'written off and destroyed' (111).

Economically pressed army soldiers and officers are not the only suppliers. A steady flow of weapons also comes from 'amateur manufactures' ('Any turner who has the basic skills can make hand-guns', says Deinega) as well as the so-called 'diggers', those who looked for and collected WWII weapons. Prices are not extremely high given the current situation: at the St Petersburg Sennoy market, hand-guns are priced between 3,000 and 10,000 rubles, while a sub-machine gun goes for 100,000 rubles. According to Deinega, the same amount of governmental effort which goes into combating the illicit flow of drugs should be devoted to combating the vast firearms black market (112).

When supply and demand meet

So far, we have been trying to establish whether the conditions of Gambetta's model, outlined at the beginning, obtain in Russia. In the following sections, we are going to look at some solutions to the problem of private protection, i.e. at some instances where the demand for protection met its supply. We envisage two different solutions to the problem of protection:

1) the 'internalizing' solution: an entrepreneur produces protection only for himself. (Protection is private and each supplier has himself as the only customer).

2) the 'Sicilian' solution: autonomous suppliers sell protection to selected customers.

(111) *Megalopolis-Express*, 11/III/1991.   (112) *Idem.*

MAFIA IN RUSSIA

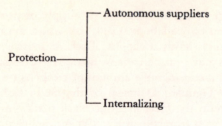

FIG. II

Internalizing protection

Internalizing protection is a solution to the problem we have been dealing with so far. It amounts to being a thug or hiring a number of thugs on a permanent basis, who will perform a variety of tasks, such as making sure partners comply with the terms of an agreement, obtaining credits and punishing non-payers. The absence of a clear legal framework and of a credible state able to enforce laws and contracts has led a number of business people in Russia to resort to firepower. According to a police officer, 'now every respectable man from the business world deems it necessary to hire several armed bodyguards or at least to buy a weapon on the black market' (113). A recent investigative newspaper article reported that 'the accumulated firepower available in Russia is being employed more and more often by seemingly respectable businessmen as a last argument in settling property and financial disputes' (114). For instance, a guard of the *Most* company shot a member of another commercial set-up, *Bayazet*, during an argument over office space (115).

One company that seems to have internalized protection is *Top*, a commercial enterprise based in Moscow, which has been defined as a 'criminal-commercial organization' by a MVD officer (116). In addition to the legitimate sphere of operation, which was the 'nerve centre of the entire organization', it developed two detachments of 'fighters', one of them headed by a known criminal and the other by the commercial director of a small business venture named *Spetsstroi*. Strong-arm tactics were used to win advantageous deals, punish non-payers, obtain credits and settle scores with rivals (117).

(113) *Idem.*
(114) *Moscow News* (21/v/93).
(115) *Idem.*

(116) Lt-Col. Nikolai Tsiplenkov, in *Idem.*
(117) *Idem.*

FEDERICO VARESE

Letting an army of thugs sit idle for most of the day, however, amounts to a waste of resources. In fact, the *Top* thugs, in addition to protecting *Top*, developed their own network of extortionist and protective activities which brought them to the attention of the police. They began to demand protection money from newly-opened shops in a peripheral district of Moscow. The 'protection department' of *Top* slowly emerged as a new business in itself, not just as a subsidiary. In fact, a two-stage pattern may emerge in a business that has internalized protection: first, if disputes arise between the legal business people and the 'fighters', the latter are more likely to win the argument, since they can be extremely intimidating; secondly, the legal side of the firm may tend to rely more on threats of violence and less on quality and price to keep its customers and partners. This implies that the production of efficient threats may eventually become the core business activity of the company and the 'fighters' will expand their role in the company. A possible transformation may then occur: a firm that has internalized protection may either split into two or evolve into one that specializes in selling protection only (118).

Autonomous suppliers

We now turn to instances of the solution to the demand for protection which bear crucial similarities to the solution which emerged last century in Sicily. In such instances, protection is a commodity sold on the market by autonomous suppliers. The first of such suppliers we encounter is the state itself, the agency that by definition should precisely do the opposite. The Interior Ministry issued an order allowing local Soviet policemen to enter into contracts with the cooperatives to provide security services for commercial establishments. In 1989 contracts totalling 600,000 rubles for such services were signed by the Moscow militia. The head of the MVD even suggested that policemen might form private cooperatives which would be supervised by their own department (119). The Ministry itself thus encourages private—not universal—protection.

It may be the case that the Ministry has not considered a perverse by-product of providing protection only to some commercial outlets.

(118) This is not, however, the only possible pattern and further qualifications need to be adduced to explain the peculiar equilibrium reached in the case of *Top*.

(119) JONES and MOSKOFF, *Ko-ops*, p. 92.

The idea for this was put forward earlier in 1989 by MVD Chief Bakatin. See A. TREHUB, Hard Time for Soviet Policemen, *Report on the USSR*, vol. 1, no. 23, 9 June, 1989, p. 21.

MAFIA IN RUSSIA

Assuming that selective police protection is effective, thieves will be deterred from stealing from the places which enjoy the extra police protection, if such outlets are clearly signposted. This means however that unprotected agents can be easily identified by default and crime will tend to be more concentrated there. Since protection is selective, it will be easier to spot the unprotected enterprises and target them (120). The choice for the entrepreneurs was between paying for the extra police protection or being exposed to *greater* danger. Not only is the basic right to security effectively abandoned as a universal right, but also the effect of such a policy is to shift the burden of crime onto the segment of the public which does not pay the extra fee to the police officers.

Privately distributed police supervision need not be the most efficient or welcomed form of protection. In Moscow, many owners of commercial outlets were offered extra police protection at a price. They were in no hurry to take up this opportunity, despite the dramatic rise in thefts, armed robbery and murder targeting the thousands of retail outlets that have sprung up in Moscow in the recent past (121). Lack of confidence in the efficiency of the service could be a good reason not to buy protection from the police. Vladimir Novikov, of the Moscow Criminal Police department, has suggested another possible explanation, which would not stain the reputation of the militia: the reason why business people do not accept the extra services offered by the police is that many are themselves involved in the widespread activity of selling stolen goods (122). Cooperatives which obtained their supplies illegally would not turn to the state to secure their property rights, but to private suppliers. Indeed, only a private protector would do.

The streets of Moscow offer various insights into the reasons that may push sellers to buy private protection from autonomous suppliers. A sophisticated street code has emerged by which valued selling spots are rented out by what we call a 'traffic agent'. Sellers of homogeneous goods tend to cluster together and/or prefer certain spots to others. 'Those selling hardware have begun to gather outside the government hardware stores. Children's goods sell best outside children stores' (123). The former Gorky street (renamed Tverskaya) is the site of most of the selling, though the open space in front of McDonald's fast-food restaurant is a more valued selling position because of the large number of foreign customers going into the American restaurant. The number of sellers with their merchandise displayed on little tables or stalls nearby

(120) See D. GAMBETTA, *The Sicilian Mafia*, 15-34.

(121) *Golos*, 2/III/1992.

(122) *Idem.*

(123) *Independent*, 27/III/1992.

FEDERICO VARESE

McDonald's is surprisingly small: not more than five or six. The area is far from being chaotic and customers can easily buy the merchandise. This is strikingly different from the street nearby, where it is almost impossible to walk on the sidewalk, due to the large number of sellers of petty commodities. Near McDonald's, an invisible traffic agent 'rents out' public space (124). The agent assures the seller that no one will trespass on his pitch and that the business environment will not be a chaotic one.

It would seem rational for the traffic agent to rent out as many places as possible. At the end of the day, he would make more money. Nevertheless, if he is to provide effective protection, the more people he is protecting, the more difficult it will be to collect the fees and to assure general safety for all. In fact, it is in the traffic agent's best interest to protect the street sellers as efficiently as possible, because his daily income and reputation as a supplier of protection depends on the seller earning a sum and not being robbed. In order to do so, it makes sense for him to have a limited amount of customers as opposed to an unmanageable number. Moreover, the more people he protects, the higher the risk of attracting free-riders, who do not pay the fee but enjoy his protection (125).

The rights that people have over assets—or places—are not constant in the streets of Moscow; they are a function of their own direct effort at protection, of the competition posed by other people's attempts to capture those assets, and of police or other agents' protection (126). In the instance we just described of places outside McDonald's, agents other than the police protect the rights of street sellers. In addition to the protection of assets and earnings, those who pay protection money are assured that a high barrier to newcomers is put up by the protection agents. The sale is far from being a mad scrimmage (127).

Commerce has been closely followed by the emergence of protection agents. In the following, we will take a closer look at an instance of private protection supplied by an autonomous supplier. Zhenya Belova, 12, and Nadya Nekrasova, 13, are two young entrepreneurs involved in washing car windscreens at the crossing outside Kropotkinskaya subway station. The idea to take up such a trade came from reading about 'fantastic money' car washers make in the children's paper *Pionerskaya*

---

(124) The cost of a place outside the big hotels in Moscow—Cosmos, Rossiya and Intourist—was a thousand rubles a month in January 1992: 'Rich folks stay there [in the hotels], so you have to pay a thousand for a pitch there', *Moscow News*, 12/I/1992.

(125) D. GAMBETTA, *The Sicilian Mafia*, *passim*.

(126) Y. BARZEL, *Economic Analysis of Property Rights* (Cambridge: Cambridge University Press, 1989), p. 2.

(127) See *Independent*, 27/III/1992.

MAFIA IN RUSSIA

Pravda. They bought spray cans for washing car windscreens, procured some rags, pressed into service Nadya's little sister Varya and started working.

> The traffic lights there change slowly and you can wash more cars. Only we have to pay protection money to bigger boys. One is called Dude. We pay him a tenner first thing and then pocket all we can earn during the day. He makes sure adults don't take our money away and chases off competition. Further down the road two boys work at the crossing next to the embankment. They pay the traffic police there 25 rubles for each hundred they earn. They do not bother us because Dude makes a deal with them (128).

The story told by Nadya shows that protection agents do provide a service to sellers in post-communist Russia. Dude performs a number of tasks for which the two girls compensate him. Dude fends off competitors and thieves. He does not offer a *public good* in the same way as a light-house keeper does. He does not make the world more secure for everybody. He chooses two customers of the commodity *protection* at the expense of others and he has found a way to make them pay for it. This instance helps to dispose of the commonly held view that the protection agents offer protection only from the dangers they create. Dude imposes on Nadya and Zhenya an extra cost, though he makes sure that no one else will start competing with them in the same area (129). The two girls pay him to avoid competing with other sellers that may prove to be more efficient than they are (130).

It is in Dude's interest to protect only a few at the expense of others. The greater the number of agents Dude protects, the higher the chance of disputes arising among them. The Mafioso would then be constantly called to settle disputes, some of which might prove hard to resolve. Some of his customers could end up feeling insufficiently protected and further conflict would arise, including the possibility of new Mafioso offering a better deal to the dissatisfied.

Dude performs an additional task. In the absence of Dude, Nadya, Zhenya and Varya would be truly at risk; for instance, they might come under the investigation of the police (if for nothing else, for not paying any sort of taxes). Alternatively, they are in danger of being robbed, or of being forced by some customers to provide services they are not willing to supply.

> We meet different people, of course. One day a green car pulled up and the driver said: 'You want to make some money, girls?' 'Shall we wash your car?' 'No—he

---

(128) *Moscow News*, 12/1/1992.

(129) D. GAMBETTA, *The Sicilian Mafia*, 22-24.

(130) Nonetheless, a form of competition arises in a market protected by the Mafia, and it is a harmful one: sellers compete not by improving quality or reducing prices but by buying or developing internally more efficient violent skills.

FEDERICO VARESE

said—just spend a minute on the back seat.' We moved away but he didn't drive off. Then we went up close to the car and said: 'You gonna pay 30 if we stand round your car? Only we want the money first.' We looked inside, and the guy had already taken his pants off. We ran away.
One cabbie drove up and we cleaned his windows. He paid a fiver and then asked Nadya: 'What are you doing in the evening? We could take a ten minute ride and I'd pay you more.' Nadya said no. 'Too bad' he said and drove away (131).

Dude did not directly intervene in the two instances Zhenya recalls. However, it should be clear that the world where Nadya and Zhenya spend their working days is far from being secure. It does not take much to imagine that one of the customers might react rather differently from the cabbie who quietly drove away. This driver might have been deterred by Dude's presence, even though we cannot be certain of this. What we may expect, though, is that Zhenya and Nadya could have resorted to Dude's protection in case the taxi driver had been more persistent.

The optimal situation for a seller is to work without having to pay any money to thugs like Dude; nonetheless, the two girls still prefer to pay some protection money rather than give up the opportunity of earning a living washing windscreens. The costs of operation are higher than in a world based on a shared business ethics and the rule of the law, but returns for the girls are still higher than being idle in the courtyard of their periphery building. Despite obvious drawbacks, the price paid for the services of the Mafia has a rational justification in a untrustworthy world (132).

Not all young street entrepreneurs enjoy effective protection. Alexander Brovkin, 14, stations himself in front of the Novodevichy Nunnery wall, next to a Beriozka hard currency shop, where he sells rabbit fur caps, caviar, picture cards and pins. Unfortunately, he has hit an unlucky path: the police take him to the precinct nearly every day and seize his unsold goods and Western money. He claims to be a 'Japanese' dealer, namely, a dealer knowledgeable about customer preferences and the best sites for business. There is something wrong in his trading strategies, if he has to visit the police station so often. He himself furnished the reason for his misfortunes: 'Some guys came here

(131) *Moscow News*, 12/1/1992.
(132) D. GAMBETTA, *The Sicilian Mafia*, 28-33. Managers of the 'Red Zone' disco in Moscow are said to have directly asked for protection, agreeing on 1,200 US dollar per month. It has been reported from St Petersburg that, when a Russian businessman complained to his high level gangster friends that someone had stolen a million rubles from

his safe, his friends went hunting. Within three days, according to a source close to the gangsters, the million was returned safe (*Newsweek*, 5/X/92). For another instance of a successful businessman actively searching for mafia protection see CHARAP and WEBSTER, *Private Manufacturing in St Petersburg*, p. 310, 316.

MAFIA IN RUSSIA

once and asked me to pay them 500 a month. I paid up. Now they have disappeared for some reason'. This is the reason why the police were after him so much: nobody protected him. Alexander paid a gang which proved to be a fly-by-night protection agency. They proved to be an unreliable source of protection. They were phony Mafiosi. This illustrates that a seller needs to do more than just pay money to the first gang that happens to pass by, in order to enjoy sound protection (133).

The payment of protection money was already a widespread phenomenon in the last years of the Soviet regime, after private cooperatives were legalized. Estimates suggest that 75 % of Moscow's cooperatives and 90 % of Leningrad's cooperatives made such payments. Racketeers could often determine the size of their demands from exact figures about the cooperative incomes based on information they obtained from the local soviets for a fee. In 1988, there were more than 6,000 reported cases of racketeering; of these, in almost half the cases (2,800), the demand was for 500 rubles. In 535 cases it was for about 1,000 rubles, and in 928 instances, protectors tried to extort more than 1,000 rubles. Sometimes racketeers expected their extortion money to be a fixed percentage (usually 30 %) of the cooperative income (134). These data support the analytical distinction between 'predatory' and 'sensible' protection. The majority of racketeers' demands were clustered around the 500 rubles' level, an amount of money which we take to be the 'sensible' one, while others asked for exorbitant sums. Mafiosi who take a long term view and expect to remain in business for a lengthy amount of time are less likely to charge predatory prices for fear of risking future income. Otherwise, if the temporal horizon of the protection agent is uncertain and short, he will be more likely, *ceteris paribus*, to charge extortionate prices (135).

Conclusions

Russia is undergoing a transition to the market which is in some crucial respects similar to the one experienced by Sicily last century. The spread of property has not been matched by clear property rights legislation, administrative or financial codes of practice and, further, authorities seem ill-equipped to enforce them where they exist. Such a situation reduces trust in the state and fosters a *demand* for alternative

(133) *Moscow News*, 12/I/1992. On phony Mafiosi, see GAMBETTA, *The Sicilian Mafia*, 28-33.

(134) JONES and MOSKOFF, *Ko-ops*, 85-6.
(135) D. GAMBETTA, *The Sicilian Mafia*, 28-33.

FEDERICO VARESE

sources of protection. We have analyzed cases where entrepreneurs either internalize protection or buy it from a private supplier, and the price paid has a rational justification in their world. Internalizing protection may not be a stable solution, though definite empirical evidence to this effect is not yet available. A business that internalises protection may—under certain conditions—specialize in the production of protection only.

Demand need not always find its supply, otherwise we will yield to a functionalist reasoning. As a matter of fact, in parts of Southern Italy private protectors were not always there to take up the opportunities opened up by the demand for protection at the time of feudalism's demise, as shown by Banfield and Davies. Most probably, not all parts of Russia will find the same solution to protection. Demand for protection, by itself, is not sufficient to give rise to autonomous suppliers of protection. Other factors play a role.

The other central factor is the presence of a *supply* of individuals trained in the use of violence who suddenly find themselves unemployed, such as the disbanded army soldiers, the *bravi* and the bandits in Sicily, or the growing 'violent' proletariat in Russia, made up of former KGB, army and police officers and criminals taking up new opportunities. Though such a supply may not be the only factor that explains the emergence of a Mafia, it does have an important role. These findings produce rather disquieting thoughts on the nature of the transition that Russia is experiencing. It appears that the Russian state is not able to produce the basic goods and services which are associated with the definition, enforcement and protection of property rights. These are not minor failings. If such failings are not given the utmost attention and eventually overcome, Sicily is a reminder to Russians of the path they are likely to go down.

Part III
Assessments

[12]

Organized Crime in the West and in the Former USSR: An Attempted Comparison

Alexander S. Nikiforov

There are criminal structures in many countries similar, but not identical, to the Italian-American La Cosa Nostra, Yakuza in Japan, and Medellin Cartel in Colombia. There are white-collar conspiracies of licit big business tycoons, such as the multibillion-dollar financial schemes of the supergiant transnational corporations like Lockheed Aircraft, Northrop, Gulf Oil, Exxon, Mobil Oil, United Brands, Esso Italiana, and Montedisson, which inflict enormous monetary damage well above that caused by the criminal activities of mobs, or gangs, associated with syndicates. Sometimes, organized white-collar collusions pursue immediate political aims or result in political scandals (endless American "gates," e.g., Watergate, Koreagate, Billygate [Billy Carter], and Irangate; or the Uzbek cases and the Churbanov case in the former USSR). These are to be included with organized terrorism—rightist, leftist, fascist, fundamentalist, chauvinist, separatist, and so on. In other words, organized crime flourishes in the context of social systems distinct from each other in their sociocultural characteristics. As different as the versions of its background and forms could be, organized crime is closely related to the political and economic infrastructure of any society in which it emerges. Why? The emergence of organized criminal societies, criminal organizations of gangsters, and white-collar or terrorist-type crime syndicates comes to be a peculiar and proper response to the political and economic conditions in the nation. The biggest among them act on the international level; they are in fact international criminal organizations.

The term "organized crime," coined by the Americans, is rather broad if not empty. This legal concept of "organized" applies not only to gangsterism, that is, to what is traditionally perceived as organized crime in the West, but also to large-scale white-collar conspiracies, group terrorism, and, in general, practically any offense committed with previous collusion, using a mode of operation like those schemes previously elaborated by a criminal ring, hold-up band, or the like. It is not by chance that some Western scholars (e.g., Mack, 1973) believe that to deem an offense to be

---

This article was originally published in Russia in the April 1991 issue of the *Journal of State and Law* (Moscow) under the title "On the Organized Crime in the West and the USSR."

"organized" it would be sufficient to state a fact of complicity, a mere rudimentary division of roles therein, and the absence of what we Russians call the "situationality" (*situativnostb*). Meanwhile, in these days of ours, the term "mafia" has become a synonym to any properly organized underworld criminal group having impact in many spheres of social and political life (Reshetnikov, 1988). That is, today, not only gangster societies of any ethnic background but also organized criminal societies with non-gangster patterns are being termed "mafia."[1]

For the purposes of penal policy, the concepts of organized crime and the organized criminal should get purely or predominantly legal definitions. For example:

1. *Organized crime*: the activities of the members of a highly organized, disciplined association engaged in supplying illegal goods and services including, but not limited to, gambling, prostitution, loan-sharking,[2] narcotics, labor racketeering, and other unlawful activities of members of organizations (U.S. Omnibus Crime Control and Safe Streets Act, 1968).

2. *Organized criminal*: a person who, as U.S. Senator John McClellan (1968) put it in his organized crime control bill of March 1969, "with intent to perpetrate conduct" involving a number of offenses, plans, finances, organizes, directs, or carries out conspiracy under structual sharing of functions and purporting to participate in the said conduct or to perpetrate it as a part of the continuous activities.

3. *Corpus delicti*: membership of a criminal society of mafia type. At law, the term "mafia" is used synonymously with the combination of words "mafiosi band" or "criminal organization" (Section 416i of the Penal Code of Italy; in the version of Rosario Minna (1988), a judge in Forence).[3]

4. *Criminal group*: group involved in organized criminal activities, that is, according to the 1986 U.S. President's Commission on Organized Crime, acting on a regular basis; a structured society of persons committing crimes, using violence and willing to corrupt for gaining and retaining power and profit (U.S. Department of Justice, 1988).

5. *Complicity*: complicity in a crime or in criminal activities is being carried out as follows:

- complicity under no collusion previously made;
- complicity under previously made collusion;
- firm criminal group;
- steady combination of two or more firm criminal groups retaining within this combination their independence;
- criminal society.

Anatoly S. Emelyanov (in Dolgova & Dyakov, 1989), the drafter of this provision (Section I7 of the Fundamentals of Penal Legislation of the USSR and the Union Republics) has argued that the first two of these forms of complicity pertain to a crime; the other three, to organized criminal activities.

The following language might complete this list of formulae, which in itself is far from complete: organized crime — a firm combination of persons having been organized to jointly commit crimes of greed for gaining control (power) in a particular sphere of society or over a particular territory (Luneev; Emelyanov; both in Dolgova & Dyakov, 1989).

We believe it is not worth arguing in favor or against advantages or disadvantages of the available legal definitions. It is more important that these definitions, responding adequately to the needs of penal policy — namely of organized crime control by law enforcement in its broad sense, beginning with searches, seizures, and arrests by police through long-term or life incarceration or the death penalty — help to realize the essence of this complex, dangerous, and heinous social phenomenon.

Even within the available language, perhaps having it widened a little by some additional characteristics (Dolgova & Dyakov, 1989, pp. 260–309) we can make one more step on the way to a more essential and more realistic idea of the organized crime phenomenon. Among its basic elements, there are: (1) supply with goods and/or services prohibited by law or in shortage by (2) a well-organized and disciplined criminal society with (3) organizational succession, structural division, and a hierarchy of criminal functions and groups, (4) using violence and corruption (5) to gain power and profit.

This model can or shall involve too: (1) money resources necessary to solve "common" tasks (i.e., *obshak* in Russian slang); (2) the use for criminal purposes of dependence on the criminal society and omerta (law of silence) in respect thereof; (3) collection and communication of "intelligence" and "counterintelligence" data; (4) neutralization of law enforcement activities; (5) the use of basic social and economic services; (6) some "outer" legality of activity, in particular infiltration into licit business, unions, and politics; (7) restricted membership (by shown loyalty to the criminal society, willingness to commit crimes, race, common origin); and (8) the contractual use of outside professionals such as accountants, lawyers, pilots, and chemists (Dolgova & Dyakov, 1989; Edelhertz, 1988).

The above-mentioned traits are mostly characteristic of Western Europe, the United States, and long ago "westernized" nations in the Near, Middle, and Far East, that is to say, the traditional Italian-American, gangster-style version of organized crime in the context of a free market. But it means that mafia, gang, or mob, in its traditional "mafiosi" sense, does not, as Italian judge and criminologist Rosario Minna (1988) has written, mean only a band or group of persons jointly committing crimes.

A "mafiosi band," or "criminal organization," is usually a diversified business criminal enterprise, multi-crime syndicate (i.e., criminal conglomerate) providing its clients with, or forcing upon them, goods and services prohibited by law. So, gangsterism is not simple banditism in its conventional perception (e.g., under s. 306 of the Italian Penal Code or s. 77 of the Penal Code of the Russian Federation), but rather it results in "organized" armed hold-ups, robberies, murders, and violence. Gangsters, or mobsters, are not mere "organized" bandits, murderers, extortionists, blackmailers, or swindlers, but employees or bosses of the criminal conglomerate. Corruption, intimidation, and violence organized and carried out in a mob style are typical of the whole business of organized criminals. Gangsterism is an inherent, constituent element of practically any form or kind of organized crime in the context of free market nations, where it would be proper to equate the concepts of gangsterism and organized crime or to consider gangsterism to be an initial form of the phenomenon of "organized crime". Currently, some symptoms of the "Italian-American" version have emerged in the former USSR (or possibly have always been present).

At this point, we have come to the question of similarities and distinctions between Western, "Italian-American", and "Soviet" versions of organized crime. First, some considerations about the essence of this phenomenon. In any country, people (or some rather numerous groups thereof) need goods and services prohibited by law or in short supply. Continuous demand is the outward cause for continuous supply. The government and legal business do not provide people with prohibited or in-shortage goods and services, or if they do, provide them in insufficient assortments or quantities, or relate their provision with some specified conditions (e.g., the age of the purchaser). Therefore, the groups of people who are in urgent need of such goods or services get them from organized criminals. The positions (offices, ranks) held by the arrested bosses of the criminal underworld are taken on by the other even more sophisticated bosses. The system remains untouched and goes on working.

The point is not only that consumers are supplied in an organized way with drugs and prostitutes (in the West, in the former USSR) or with pantyhose (*colgotki*), color televisions, and cars (in the former USSR)). In the same "organized" way and upon demand, businessmen are being intimidated (not only in the West nowadays); trade unions, officials, and politicians are being corrupted and intimidated or served in gangster style (in the West as well as in the former USSR). In other words, organized crime—this "bastard," this "illegitimate child" of the conservative–liberal democracy in the West and natural product or alter ego of the communist partocracy in the former USSR—makes its dirty work for its clients anywhere licit business, unions, and politics despise it or dare not do it right now. As Kelly (1986) writes, "legitimate power has historically surrounded itself with criminal instruments" (p. 16).

There is more — organized crime does not only "make money." Though the "mafia does nothing greedlessly" (Reshetnikov, 1988, p. 21), it needs power not only for profit but also as an essential part of its existence. Hence, its role is not only as a "shadow economy" but likewise as a "shadow government." In his message to the Congress on April 23, 1969, President Nixon named "La Cosa Nostra" to be a totalitarian and closed society within a democratic and open society and said that the criminal syndicate corrupts American government institutions and undermines the democratic process in the United States. At the Second Congress of the USSR Peoples' Deputies in December 1989, it was said that "organized crime has really launched a challenge against the Soviet society" (Vtoroy syezd Narodnyh Deputatov, 1990, p. 687). There is a distinction between "organized crime" and "politically oriented" organized crime (e.g., Lasswell and MacKenna, 1972, p. 24). The first one, from this standpoint, is "non-ideological" in its outlook. There have also been statements of organized crime politicization, for example, in the former USSR: contacts with informal extremist organizations and, hence, opportunities for acts of terrorism; support, particularly financial, by organized crime of anti-Soviet nationalist processes in several former Union Republics; consolidation of all the "anti-perestroika" forces interested in retaining and widening the shadow segments in economics, ideology, law and order (Luneev in Dolgova & Dyakov, 1989). Stalinism has been held to be an organized crime system, "the very totalitarian regime — mafia," supported with all the gigantic power of government, which "sooner or later acquires a scent of greed" (Dolgova & Dyakov, 1989, pp. 126–129). There were, evidently, well-founded reasons to differentiate, in the context of the former USSR, three basic species ("branches") of organized crime: "general" (predominantly, of mob style), economic (greed-motivated), and politicized (Pobegaylo, 1990).

Finally, to gain profit and control, the criminal underworld not only preys upon and parasitizes its victims but also to some extent serves them (doctrine and practice of the "godfather"). Many avenues exist: to arrange employment, to secure labor agreements, to solicit law enforcement on behalf of young offenders, to provide with legal, but in shortage, or illegal (and therefore, to some extent, in shortage) goods and services (the latter being the main method).

These are the basic outlines of the organized crime phenomenon, granting the assumption tht this model fits both the West and the former USSR. Yet more can be said, for even 40 years ago, Russian criminologist Boris S. Nikiforov (1951) wrote: " 'White collars' differ from the other organized criminals only in that they don't use, as a common rule, either intimidation or violence. They have got their own field of activity—commercialized fraud" (p. 209). In the West, the symbiosis of gangster and white-collar patterns in organized crime—with traditional gangsterism continuing to get more "respectability" and white-collar crime continuing to go on in its furthering of "demoralization"—acquires more and more signs of this most dangerous syndrome. This trend is distinctly traceable to rather new definitions of white-collar crime, which can apply to some aspects of modern gangsterism: embezzlement, bribery, fraud, theft of services, theft of trade secrets, tax evasion, obstruction of justice, computer crime. The non-violent nature of white-collar crimes is accentuated (Edelhertz, 1988). Sometimes, the trend is expressed in titles of published works (e.g, Yeager & Matthew, 1973; Clarke & Thornsten, 1975). So now, we find (Reshetnikov, 1988, pp. 17–18), for example, the links between the Sicilian ("we can term it presently—Italian") mafia and international currency schemes (with reference to the cases of Roberto Calvi and Michele Sindona).

Similarity in methods of criminal activity used by "organized" white collars and gangsters may be explained by the fact that socially they have rather much in common. Surely, white-collar criminals differ from gangsters in that they are persons of respectability and of high social status, committing their crimes in the course of their occupation (Sutherland, 1961). As we have just seen, they commit their crimes with no violence (Edelhertz, 1988; U.S. Department of Justice, 1988). But whenever a white-collar crime purports to get an illegal gain or advantage for business (Edelhertz, 1988), moreover, for organized business, they rather often strive after predatory monopolization. In the United States, for example, predatory monopolization is deemed to be attempts to monopolize by "persistent below-cost pricing, to destroy a competitor, coercion of suppliers of customers of a competitor, or systematic boycotts in order to exclude a competitor.[4] The trend to set a monopoly, which is inherent to "organized" white collars, is no less typical of gangsterism. Moreover, irresistible, crazy, and omnipresent "passion" for monopoly is the dominant characteristic of the gangster version of organized crime.

Neither "organized" white collars nor gangsters are able to compete with licit businesses and licit politics by practices of fair competition. This is so because through such practices they cannot achieve the desired degree of profit or power. They lack professionalism and knowledge. Thse people are, basically, small fry: socially disorganized dropouts, lumpens, rootless immigrants, romantics of acute feelings of a rather dubious kind, or merely greedy and power-mad persons who did not find or did not wish to find a different path for self-fulfillment. Being aware of their economic (despite huge profits) and, particularly, their mental, vocational, and ethical weakness in comparison with the status of chieftains of big business and big politics, they for this very reason follow the way of organized commission of such crimes because it fills them with a vision of their own puissance, power, and even of being of societal use.

To examine it more closely, we can see that everything we have written is more characteristic of the Italian-American than of the Latin-American version of the Western-type of organized crime. The Sicilian version in the narrow sense of the word is similar to that of Latin-American nations.

Indeed, in the United States, Canada, and France, gangsters make and launder illicit money while infiltrating into licit businesses, unions, and politics, usually, at the local levels. But in Latin America and in Sicily they practice political (for their own purposes or on hire) terrorism, threaten with coups d'etat, and paralyze the life of the society. In Colombia, the narcomafia is waging, during the last several years, a virtual civil war against the government.

While the failure of the brilliant Bolshevist experiment of building Communism was becomining more and more evident, apostles and advocates of the "bright futurity" rushed into taking life in both hands and enjoying it with childish zeal. Formerly—in the famous epoch of Lenin, Trotsky, and Stalin—they, changing one another but *in corpore* being unchangeable in power, have practiced looting mainly by direct means of political banditism, taking lands, mills, factories, apartments, and jewelry (sold as "confiscates" at dumping prices only to State Security officers) by "organized means" away from "contras," "kulaks," "enemies of the people," "nationalists," "cosmopolites." The various "contras" have been shot by firing squads or sent to the concentration camps, doomed to almost inevitable death.[5] After the idolatry had ceased, during the *zastoy* (stagnation) under Brezhnev, the former builders of Communism began to earnestly steal and swindle while beating up, though with weaker hands, "dissidents," still by "organized means" and in huge masses. Formerly they held monopoly power in economics and in politics, but now they are chained together with and embracing "thieves at law" and other criminal rascals. That is being proved with the ventures of former Communist officials involved in crime and corruption: Shelockov, Churbanov, Galina Brezhneva, Medunov, Rashidov, Karimov, Adylov—their names are legion!

Crucially, organized crime in the former USSR has differed from that in the West as follows. In the former USSR, its figures have occupied key positions within the state bureaucracy. Identification with bureaucracy gave to criminal entrepreneurs a chance to successfully conceal large-scale larcenies they had committed by bribes and tampering with documents at their disposal. Therefore, they or their counterparts in the countries of Eastern Europe have been sometimes called, rather accurately, "white-collar gangsters" (in Kelly, 1986, pp. 21–22; see also Manin, 1992).

In the West, organized criminals do not, save some exceptions (Sicily,

Bolivia, Colombia), hold positions within the framework of government. So, if in the West, organized criminals and gangsters strive for monopoly in the field of their business, in the former USSR, organized "white collars" have already had this monopoly since October 1917—with fictitious interruption during the New Economic Policy in the 1920s and some decrease in the perestroika period.

An exception to the general rule in the West is the Sicilian version where a mafia boss may be at the same time a mayor, a police chief, and so on. As it was noted above, the Sicilian version resembles that of such Latin-American nations as Bolivia and Colombia. And one must not forget the major role the Sicilian stronghold of gangsterism plays in the deeds of the international mob confederation, primarily in its narcotics business.

Hence, the main result is that if in the West, organized crime appears to be first of all gangsterism in its traditional, Italian-American version, in the former USSR it consists of white-collar schemes. With no unnecessary details, let us state the basic traits of organized crime in the former USSR: greed-motivated economic crimes (larcenies by means of official abuse, bribes, consumer fraud) in close cooperation with leaders of the world of crime: thieves, murderers, swindlers, smugglers (Dolgova & Dyakov, 1989). The combination of efforts of "businessmen" and "criminals" ensures coordination of their criminal activities, mutual support while confronting society, retention of traditions and rules of the criminal milieu, and so forth. In this context, accumulation of large amounts of property at the disposal of criminals inevitably produces the need for political protection of their particular economic interests. Hence, there exists strife to control power in the state, resulting in corruption of high-standing officials or in promoting those corrupted to the higher positions. Though, as the Russian writer Hochryakov (1988; 1989) has argued, "our people" within the framework of government and law enforcement do not and cannot play the key role in organized crime of our domestic kind, they are nonetheless its inherent, constituent ingredient. High-standing functionaries of the "security group" provide conditions necessary for organized crime to function. The point to be made is that in the context of the still recently omnipotent state, our domestic mafia could not effectively work or even exist with no "security group" of high-standing government functionaries as an inherent element.

In the USSR we have had racketeering gangs. In the twenties, "wild," rudimentary bandit practices or extorting money from "nepmen," in our time, from "unorganized" drug peddlers; gambling and car rackets; exploitation of hard-currency dealers and in-shortage goods profiteers; attempts to control newly born cooperative enterprises. In the latter instance, racketeering is of genuinely American style: consent to collaborate results in protection of cooperative property, dealing in deliveries of goods, and destruction of other firms. Refusal to collaborate may, for example, get a cooperative café set on fire or "suddenly" make a shop selling sporting caps a subject of concern for criminal police (Lyhanov, 1988).

Newly born cooperative enterprises in the former USSR became at once a "sweety," a piece of "apple pie" for racketeering gangs. But these enterprises have been victimized even more (70–80%) by official racketeering of the bureaucratic departments. When a notorious American gangster and racketeer Al Capone said, "white-collar crime—it's a licit racket," nobody could imagine the new reality of those words in 60 years and under quite different socioeconomic conditions.

Let us imagine how a preliminary prediction of how organized crime in the former USSR would evolve, suggested by an American criminologist, James Finckenauer (1988):

1. As the Soviet economy shifts from public to private, the nature of organized crime should shift from a white-collar type to a more Western form of organized crime, à la the US model.
2. An increase in the supply of legitimate goods and services should result in a decrease in the black market and in the amount of white-collar crime in the state bureaucracy.
3. A decrease in the size and scope of the state-run economy should result in a decrease in white-collar crime by state employees.
4. An increase in the size of the private economy should result in more infiltration and victimization by organized criminal elements.
5. An increase in economic growth and prosperity should result in an increase in the demand for illicit goods and services.
6. Prosperity (and particularly an introduction of convertible currency) should especially result in an increase in drug supplies and consumption.
7. An increase in demand for illicit goods and services should result in an increase in organized crime of the American type.

Finckenauer's predictions appear reasonable. Free markets would dramatically decrease the scope of state bureaucracy and the shortage of commodities, and accordingly the criminogenic impact thereof. An increase in economic prosperity in the context of a rather poor mass culture would result in an increase in retreatism, that is, enhanced demand for alcohol, drugs, gambling, pornography, and prostitution.

As Finckenauer has noted, an increase in the demand for illicit goods and services would result in an increase in organized crime of the American type. In the meantime, an increase in the scope of the private economy would be an incentive to the infiltration of laundered mob money, and to racketeering.

So, summing up, we can make an overall definition of organized crime, fit for both its Western and "Soviet" models: the mafia — in the West as well as in the former USSR — is a multipurpose, multidimensional criminal business enterprise of mob or white-collar (nonviolent) type, providing its clients with goods and services prohibited by law or in short supply. If so, mafiosi are not mere organized bandits, killers, extortionists, blackmailers, and swindlers, but employees and chieftains of the criminal enterprise.

NOTES

[1]As far back as in 1953, Boris S. Nikiforov wrote: "Organized crime with no respect to its species in question — white-collar crimes, bootlegging, bookmaking, racket, gangsterism" and so on (Nikiforov, 1953, p. viii).

[2]Loan-sharking, the mob species of usury, synonymous to "juice loan."

[3]See Minna (1988, pp. 260, 306, 308–309). Section 416i was enacted by Law No. 646, September 13, 1982, "On pecuniary measures of prevention, on amendments to laws no. 1423 (1956), No. 57 (1962), No. 575 (1965), on making the Parliamentary Commission dealing with the mafia problem." See also: A.G. Pipya v knige: Organizovannaya prestupnost. Problemy. Discussii. Predlozheniya. Kruglyi stolizdatelstva "Yuridicheskaya literatura." Pod red. A. I. Dolgova i S. V. Dyakov. Moscow, "Yurid. lit-ra" (1989) (heretofore, Organizovannaya prestupnost); with reference to G. Lattanzi, Codici penali., Milano: A. Dott Giuffre (1984, p. 650); G. Spagnolo, L'Associazione di tipo mafioso (Padova, 1987. p. 14); Gazzetta Ufficiale (1956, 31 December, p. 327); Gazzetta Ufficiale (1965, 5 June, p. 138); Gazzetta Ufficiale (1982, 14 September, p. 253).

[4]The Antitrust Division of the U.S. Department of Justice has referred to the U.S. v. Minnesota Mining and Mfg Co., 249 F.Supp. 594/ED 111, 1966, which included price-fixing counts as well as attempts to monopolize. See President's Commission on Law Enforcement and Administration of Justice. (1967, p. 111).

[5]How many victims of Bolshevist repressions in the 1920s through the 1950s have perished, 15–60 millions of people? More? Less? See on the subject, in particular Dugin (1990).

REFERENCES

Clarke, T. & Tique, J., Jr. (1975). *Dirty money: Swiss banks, the Mafia, money laundering, and white-collar crime*. New York: Simon & Schuster.

Dolgova, A., & Dyakov, S. (Eds.). (1989). *Organizovannaya prestupnost*. Moscow: Uridicheskaya Literatura.

Dugin, A. N. (1990). Stalinism: legendy i facty, *Slovo*, 7, 23–26.

Edelhertz, H. (Ed.). (1988). Symposium proceedings, Washington, DC, September 25–26, 1986. Washington, DC: National Institute of Justice.

Finckenauer, J. (1988). Unpublished research proposal for a study of organized and white-collar crime in the USSR.

Hochraykov, G. F. (1988, February 13). Korni i derevo-takovy otnosheniya mezdu administrativno — komandnoy systemaoy i organizovannoi prestupnostyu; *Moskovskie Novosti*, 46, 12.

Hochraykov, G. F. (1989). Mafia v SSSR: domysly, vymysly, facty. *Unost, 3*, 85–91.

Kelly, R. J. (Ed.). (1986). *Organized crime: A global perspective*. New York: Rowman & Littlefield.

Lasswell H. D., & MacKenna, J. M. (1972). *The impact of organized crime on an inner-city community*. New York: Policy Sciences Center.

Lyhanov, D. (1988, May). No zdravstvuyet Korol. *Ogonyok. 7–14*, 18–30.

Mack, J. A. (1973). The "organized" and "professional" labels criticized. *International Journal of Criminology and Penology, 1*(2), 103–104.

Manin, E. (1992, January 10). Russkie prishli. *Novoye Russkoye Slovo*.

McClellan, J. L. (1968). 114 Congressional Record at 14697.

Minna, R. (1988). *Mafia protiv zakona*. Moscow: Progress.

Nikiforov, B. S. (1951). Sovremennye teorii opravdaniya bezzakonya i proizvola. *Voprosy Filosofii, 4*, 209.

Nikiforov, B. S. (Ed.). (1953). *Organizovannaya prestupnost v Soedinennyh Shtatah Ameriki* (sbornik materialov, opublikovannyh v S.S.h. A.) IL, M.

Pobegaylo, E. G. (1990). *Organizovannaya prestupnost* i sovershenstvovaniye ugolovno-pravovoy borby s nei. In *Ukrepleniye zakonnosti i borba s prestupnostyu v usloviyah formirovaniya pravovogo gosudarstvav*. Moscow: Instutut gosudarstva i prava AN SSSR. (p. 41)

President's Commission on Law Enforcement and Administration of Justice. (1967). Task force report: Crime and its impact—An assessment.

Reshetnikov, F. M. (1988). Vstupitelnaya statya. In R. Minna, *Mafia protiv zakona* Moscow: Progress.

Sutherland, E. H. (1961). *White collar crime*. New York: Dryden Press.

U.S. Department of Justice. (1988). *Report to the nation on crime and justice* (2nd ed.). Washington, DC: Author.

U.S. Omnibus Crime Control & Safe Streets Act. (1968). Public Law 90–351. 90th Congress, House of Representatives 5037.

Vtoroy syezd Narodnyh Deputatov. (1990). SSSR 12–14 dekabrya 1989g. Stenograficheskiy otchyot, Moscow, t.2.

Yeager, M. G. (1973). The gangster as white-collar criminal: Organized crime and stolen securities. *Issues in Criminology. 8*(Spring).

Alexander S. Nikiforov
Candidate of Law
Senior Researcher, Institute of State and Law
Russian Academy of Sciences, Moscow
Apartment 53
Yaroslavskoye Chaussee, 125
Moscow 129347
RUSSIA

[13]

Post-Soviet Organized Crime

*Implications for Economic, Social and
Political Development*

LOUISE I. SHELLEY

Introduction

Organized crime has penetrated most of the newly independent states of the
former Soviet Union at all levels of government. With such extensive
infiltration into the society it ceases to be merely a crime problem, and
should more aptly be described as a phenomenon that will play a significant
role in determining the future course of development in the Soviet successor
states. Moreover, as an international as well as a domestic phenomenon, the
impact and consequences of organized crime are already being felt in its
former East European sphere of influence as well as in Western Europe, the
United States and parts of Asia.

The existence and pervasiveness of organized crime may preclude the
transition to democracy, limit personal freedom, and thwart legitimate
foreign investment and open market economies. Since organized crime has
already partially supplanted many of the weak governments of the successor
states, the citizens may be trading one form of control for another;
domination by the Communist Party may be replaced by the controls of
organized crime. As in other societies, organized crime will limit free
elections, the development of civil society and freedom of the press and
media.[1] Labor markets once controlled by state planning and submissive
trade unions will instead be subject to the intimidation of organized crime
which is already a major employer. State ownership of the economy will be
exchanged for control of the economy by organized crime groups which
have a monopoly on existing capital.

The collapse of communism may not lead to democratization and the
transition to a competitive capitalist economy. Instead, the pervasiveness of
organized crime may lead to an alternative form of development—political
clientelism and controlled markets. The control will come from the alliance
of former Communist Party officials with the emergent organized crime
groups, groups that currently enjoy the preponderance of capital of the post-
Soviet states. Rapid economic differentiation in income and wealth is
already occurring, a process that will accelerate as privatization proceeds.

Louise I. Shelley is professor of justice, law and society at The American
University, Washington, D.C., and editor of *Demokratizatsiya*. The author wishes to
thank Ernesto U. Savona for his insights into the Italian experience with organized
crime and its possible applicability to the post-Soviet situation; and the National
Council for Soviet and East European Research for their support in the preparation
of this article.

The Distinctiveness of Post-Soviet Organized Crime
Organized crime is crime perpetuated with financial objectives. Violence is rarely indiscriminate but is used to promote the economic objectives of the organized criminal group. Most organized crime groups make the most significant share of their profits from the exploitation of the market for illicit goods and services (i.e. prostitution, gambling, drugs, contract killing, supply of cheap illegal labor, stolen automobiles).[2] These activities combined with the extortion of legitimate businesses provide the primary income sources of organized crime groups in most societies.

Post-Soviet organized crime encompasses all of these activities. It also includes such diverse activities as illegal export of oil, valuable raw materials, smuggling of weapons and nuclear materials, and manipulation of the privatization process. These commodities now dominate the CIS nations' participation in international markets.

The most lucrative element of its criminality both within the former Soviet territory and abroad lies in the area of large-scale fraud. In the United States, organized criminals from the former Soviet Union have perpetrated massive medicare frauds and gasoline tax evasion.[3] In Germany they have exploited the subsidies the German state provides Soviet military troops to promote multi-million dollar frauds.[4] This large-scale fraud has deprived the German state of capital needed to rebuild its infrastructure. In Israel, organized crime groups counterfeit American dollars for export to the United States.

In the former Soviet states where there are almost no control mechanisms in place and a law enforcement apparatus which collapsed along with the state, fraud can assume even larger proportions, especially at a time when there is a redistribution of the state's resources.[5] The criminalization of the privatization process[6] threatens the future financial security of CIS citizens and their perceptions of market reforms.

Financial fraud assumes such a significant role in organized criminality because there is a strong influence of the crime patterns of the Soviet period on the successor states. Embezzlement (theft from the state) was the most pervasive crime in the Soviet period and was not perceived as criminal by most citizens.[7] A culture of financial manipulation was endemic among managers of state businesses who constantly engaged in illicit activity to achieve unattainable state production targets. Citizens failed to distinguish between state and personal property.[8]

In contrast, the activities that form the basis of organized crime in most societies were tightly controlled in the Soviet period. Until perestroika, Soviet law enforcers closely supervised daily life and limited such deviant activity as gambling, prostitution or trafficking in narcotics.[9] Therefore, international prostitution and drug trafficking are only now beginning to develop as key activities of post-Soviet organized crime.[10] Western law enforcement, prepared to fight traditional forms of organized crime, has just begun to restructure its investigative organs to deal with the large-scale and sophisticated frauds and financial manipulations committed by post-Soviet groups.

POST-SOVIET ORGANIZED CRIME 343

Post-Soviet organized crime groups apply traditional means of intimidation—extortion and violence—differently. Unlike the extortion of organized crime groups in the United States, Italy and Germany, which usually extract a fixed but tolerable amount from the businesses within their territory,[11] post-Soviet organized crime groups often seek short-term profits rather than long-term relationships that allow both organized crime groups and businesses to prosper. They extract such significant sums that businesses shut down or, as in Sicily, they acquire a significant stake in the enterprise.

The level of violence used by Soviet organized crime groups is also often unknown in the countries in which they are operating. During the Soviet period, there was much violence by the state against its citizens but relatively low rates of interpersonal violence.[12] Many who perpetrated violence on behalf of the Soviet state now perform

> *"Some current members of the Russian Parliament have close ties to organized crime groups."*

this service for organized crime. Recorded rates for violent crime in Russia and other successor states have escalated rapidly. The displays of violence are much more dramatic than in the Soviet period. In Germany, the recently arrived crime groups from the former USSR are more violent than domestic criminals. Belgium and the Netherlands report that the violence used against prostitutes smuggled into these countries by post-Soviet and central European organized crime groups exceeds that known previously against prostitutes.[13]

The Implication of Organized Crime Penetration Into the State

The penetration of organized crime into post-Soviet governmental structures undermines citizens' perceptions of democracy. Opinion polls indicate declining confidence in the transition to democracy. The strong popular vote for ultranationalist Vladimir Zhirinovsky represents, in part, a citizen backlash against the current political order, the rise of organized crime and the decline of order.[14] The premium placed on order by former Soviet citizens may result in the future election of more authoritarian governments.

A symbiotic relationship exists between organized crime and national, local and municipal governments. As the Italian experience has shown, once organized crime becomes so intertwined with all levels of government, the relationship cannot easily or rapidly be reversed.[15]

Organized crime has undermined the electoral process, the emergence of a viable multi-party system and the establishment of laws needed to move towards a legally regulated market economy. Organized crime has financed the election of candidates and members of the newly elected Russian Parliament, as well as those of other CIS states. Some current members of the Russian Parliament have close ties to organized crime groups. As the chair of the Duma Committee on State Security, Viktor Ilyukhin has said, the mob, "Using loopholes in the present laws, influences the adoption of political decisions up to the level of member republics of the Russian Federation."[16] The alternative political power of organized crime is poised for future growth because it has the resources to fund candidates in forthcoming elections at the local and national levels.[17]

Corrupt officials and legislators with ties to organized crime impede the introduction of legislation that might circumscribe organized crime activity.

"As the Italian experience has shown, once organized crime becomes so intertwined with all levels of government, the relationship cannot easily or rapidly be reversed."

For example, members of the Russian Duma complained in July 1994 that their proposed law on corruption had its provisions concerning corruption in banking deleted at the presidential level.[18] The legislative framework needed to combat organized crime including banking laws, regulation of securities markets, insurance laws and such specific measures as a RICO statute, laws against money laundering and a witness protection program have been impeded by corrupt legislators and individuals at the executive level. Many of these legal measures have already been adopted in several central and eastern European countries.

As a consequence of the corruption of the law enforcement apparatus, the passivity of the procuracy, the close ties between mafia groups and the security apparatus[19] and the lack of a specific organized crime statute in the criminal code[20] there has been no major organized crime trial in the past three years in the former Soviet Union. The lesson of this is that large-scale organized crime enjoys impunity in the successor states.

Organized crime has supplanted many of the functions of the state. A coalition of organized crime and former Party elites provides the ruling elites of many regions of Russia and many other CIS states. Organized crime provides many of the services that citizens expect from the state—protection of commercial businesses, employment for citizens, mediation in disputes. Private security, often run by organized crime, is replacing state law enforcement. Ilyukhin estimates that 100,000 unregulated private law enforcers presently operate without any regulation.[21] While this number is far fewer than are thought to exist in Poland, it is still a large autonomous force that is increasingly visible in Russian society.[22]

Organized crime is assisting the rise of regional powers in Russia. This is not the decentralization and federalism sought by American promoters of democracy. Instead it represents the rise of local fiefdoms, protected by armed bands loyal to local leaders who seek political and economic controls over their regions. These local leaders may enjoy more power than in the Soviet period because they own rather than control property and the "law enforcers" are employed by them rather than the state. In the absence of a legal framework, citizens outside major urban centers may have great trouble protecting themselves from the abuses of organized crime.

Economic Consequences
The transition from a centrally planned Communist economy to a free market capitalist economy requires a fundamental reorganization of the

POST-SOVIET ORGANIZED CRIME   345

structure of society. If organized crime groups can infiltrate the economy at this crucial phase of transition, then, as in Sicily, it may be impossible to disassociate the economic development of the successor states from the development of organized crime. The Sicilian mafia was able to infiltrate the economy and the political development of the island because its flowering coincided with the rise of private property, the collapse of feudalism and with the industrialization of this region.[23] While industrialization has already occurred in many regions of the former USSR,

> *"The legislative framework needed to combat organized crime . . . [has] been impeded by corrupt legislators and individuals at the executive level."*

the emergence of large-scale private property in Russia and the other successor states recalls the need for protection which gave rise to the mafia in Sicily a century ago.[24] Recent Russian sociological research indicates that some businessmen willingly pay protection because of the state's failure to provide protection; they view their protection payments as a cost of doing business.

Organized Crime and Economic Development

Pervasive organized crime does not necessarily preclude economic development. Rather, it limits the development of certain legitimate forms of investment and of open markets that benefit a cross-section of the population. The economy becomes dependent on illegitimate rather than legitimate economic activity. These commodities become central ones in the state's participation in international markets. This is probably the greatest risk that threatens the post-Soviet economies. Precedent exists in the economies of southern Italy and Colombia which are heavily dependent on their illicit commerce in drugs.[25] While the post-Soviet economies are trading in a greater variety of illicit goods than these two societies, the dependence on this illegal commerce is already clear for many in the labor force. Furthermore, many of the successor states are dependent on the foreign currency acquired through this illicit trade.[26]

Unlike in central Europe, "Economic liberalization in Russia is not leading to the old-style black market evolving into legitimate business, but to the new, legitimate businesses being sucked into the old black market."[27] Concentration of an economy in a limited range of goods and services, either legitimate or illegitimate, places an economy at risk for long term development. Sudden decline in demand or in production may have a catastrophic effect on the economy. The decline of the Soviet economy and its replacement in the successor states by organized-crime-based activity is having a deleterious effect on the future development of these economies. Industrial production in the state planned economy is collapsing but organized crime activity is rarely leading to new forms of production. Instead their activity is focused on large short-term profits rather than sustainable growth. Moreover, much of their profits are being exported, thereby denying Russia and other CIS states the capital they need to rebuild their infrastructures.

The economic activity of organized crime is undermining economic growth in several ways. Foreign businesses do not enter the market not only because of extortion threats, but also because they cannot make profits legitimately. Much of the commerce of organized crime is in the export of strategic raw materials and military equipment. The theft of these strategic items deprives the post-Soviet states of important sources of revenue. Not all the items presently sold abroad could be legitimately marketed by the successor states, but many of the metals could be legitimately sold in Europe and the military equipment to Third World countries. Mineral shipments out of the Baltic port of Tallinn are so significant that the freighting charges are a major source of currency for the Estonian government.[28] Many of the weapons that have been stolen or bought from soldiers at military bases are bought by nationalist groups engaged in ethnic conflict in the successor states, particularly in the Caucasus and Central Asia.[29] Larger scale military equipment is being sold to Arab countries and other nations in the Third World. The profits that are obtained from the illegal sale of these items are often not repatriated to the country but are instead deposited in foreign bank accounts. Therefore, the state is suffering from a dual loss—the loss of materials as well as the problem of capital flight.

Commercial real estate is booming in Moscow and to a lesser extent in St. Petersburg. According to some estimates, organized crime controls half the commercial real estate in central Moscow.[30] The owners of many of the buildings now being renovated in Moscow acquired their properties through the highly criminalized process of privatization. As one popular news account reported, "The old bureaucrats dominate much of the privatization process, for example, often deciding who gets what at what price."[31] In Moscow city officials sold the rights to auction off a building to five criminal organizations for about $1500. "At the secondary auction, accessible to well-connected outsiders, if they paid heavy bribes, the property sold for 250 million rubles ($250,000). Finally the building went on the market selling for 1.5 billion rubles (about $1.5 million). The 1,000-fold appreciation in value took all of two months."[32]

> *"According to some estimates, organized crime controls half the commercial real estate in central Moscow."*

Recently created wealth, much of it of illicit origin, is also fueling extensive construction of homes in the capital as well as other urban areas. Yaroslavl, a secondary city, has also seen much investment of criminal capital in real estate. The explanation for this is its proximity to Moscow, a mere several hours by train.[33] The vibrant but highly criminalized real estate market indicates that organized crime can contribute to domestic economic growth.

Organized Crime and Capital Flight

The problem of capital flight is one of the most serious economic problems facing the post-Soviet states. The amount of money being exported is estimated at between four and 15 billion in 1992.[34] The extent of capital that is leaving the country is of such great proportion that it recalls the experience of Latin America during the so-called "lost decade" of the 1980s. Latin America in these years was deprived of the revenues that it needed for its economic development. The post-Soviet states are now experiencing the same problem: they are losing the capital needed to rebuild their depleted infrastructures.

All capital flight is not the result of criminal activity, rather, it is also a consequence of the instability and corruption of the banking system,[35] irrational tax policies, the constant depreciation of the currency and the failure of the legal system to protect economic interests.

Money exported abroad comes from several important sources. These are: the massive financial frauds committed on the territory of the former USSR and on post-Soviet military bases, the expropriation of state resources and raw materials, massive payoffs to post-Soviet officials in order to receive contracts, foreign aid assistance and the illegal privatization to members of the nomenklatura and organized crime figures.

The capital is exported and laundered by a coalition of former nomenklatura personnel, organized crime figures and former KGB personnel who have the foreign contacts and language skills[36] to successfully launder funds and invest them abroad. Many have developed ties with earlier emigrant groups of the 1970s and 1980s who have financial and legal expertise as well as bases of operations in Germany, the United States and Israel.[37]

Many of the successor states prefer to close their eyes to illegal financial activities because their economies benefit from these transactions. Until Russian Central Bank officials raised capital requirements in 1994 it was easier to establish a bank than to buy a luxury auto.[38] Banking is dominated by organized crime and banks are regularly forced to pay protection money. Former security personnel figure prominently in the emergent banking sector.

"Banking is dominated by organized crime and banks are regularly forced to pay protection money. Former security personnel figure prominently in the emergent banking sector."

Officials in Latvia have not inquired into the large-scale foreign currency exchange market in Riga (much of it the consequence of organized crime activity) because the proceeds from this exchange are necessary to keep the Latvian currency afloat. In the past year, the free-standing Latvian currency has been one of the few to rise significantly against the ruble. Riga's sophisticated financial services could be compared to the off-shore banking provided in the Bahamas.

Organized Crime and Regional Development

Organized crime often develops in areas that are relatively underdeveloped economically in relation to others in the region. For example, in Italy, the regions with the greatest concentrations of organized crime are Sicily, Campania, Calabria, and Puglia, areas which are underdeveloped in relation to the economies in the north. Yet those engaged in organized crime activity require proximity of individuals with superior skills in technology, communications and developed international business skills. Therefore, links have developed between the organized crime groups of the south and the more economically advanced economy of the north of Italy. A similar relationship exists in both Latin America and Asia. The Chinese in Hong Kong and Macao control the organized crime that exists in the less developed economies of Asia. The Colombians market and process the drugs which are produced in the less developed Latin American countries of Bolivia, Peru and Ecuador.[39]

A similar economic relationship seems to be developing between the less economically developed parts of the former Soviet Union and the more industrialized regions closer to Western Europe. The basis for this relationship already existed in the Soviet period when massive fraud was perpetrated in the cotton industry by the so-called Central Asian "mafia." By falsifying production figures, Party leaders in cahoots with collective farm chairmen and key justice officials received large payments from the central government for cotton that was not grown. Payoffs to key figures in Moscow, such as Brezhnev's son-in-law, the deputy minister of Interior, secured their immunity from prosecution.[40]

The illegal economic ties between the Central Asian republics and Russia have resurfaced with the collapse of the former Soviet Union. Members of the Central Asian mafias, prosecuted by justice officials from Moscow in the final years of the Soviet period, were released from prison almost immediately after the dissolution of the USSR. Their release showed the autonomy of the newly independent countries from Moscow's policies. Yet they also revealed the continuity in the links between Party officials and the legal apparatus. These reemerged organized crime groups are responsible for new forms of criminality not linked to state production. "Smuggling profits has formed the foundation of post-Communist wealth and the basis for the working cooperation between criminals and the nomenklatura."[41] Drug trafficking, already rising in the final Soviet period, an active arms trade to areas with ethnic disturbances[42] and increasingly visible smuggling of nuclear materials[43] have made post-Soviet organized crime very threatening to the world order.

Illicit drug trade has risen because Moscow's subsidies to the Central Asian republics declined along with the Soviet state. Furthermore, as now independent countries, they need foreign currency to act as sovereign countries. But Russia's appropriation of the resources of the former Soviet state left these countries in a much more disadvantaged position that they had known in the Soviet period. In the early post-Soviet period both Kyrgyzstan and Kazakhstan contemplated legalizing the cultivation of drugs.

POST-SOVIET ORGANIZED CRIME   349

But bowing to international pressure and the threat of curtailment of foreign assistance, these countries subsequently outlawed drug production.[44] Yet a significant drug market is developing between the drug producers of Central Asia and the more sophisticated organized crime groups in Moscow. Drug trafficking is also developing in the Far East with proximity to Asian delivery routes.[45]

The lowest-paying work of production is done in the areas of least development with great rates of unemployment and underemployment. For this reason, ethnic minorities are associated with drug production.[46] Little attention is given to the technicians who process the drugs in Russia or serve as couriers to the West. Russia is also serving as an important transhipment point for drugs. Those who launder the money from Russia and the Baltic states are dependent on the labor supply of the lesser developed regions of Central Asia.

The emergent drug trafficking from the former Soviet Union resembles the Latin American situation in several important ways. Drug production occurs in highly undeveloped areas with no alternative sources of income by populations with a tradition of drug cultivation and consumption. Processing of drugs is done in neighboring regions where there is a higher level of education and technology. The goods are then marketed in the most advanced countries. The profits made by these sales are then laundered in the countries where the drugs are sold or in others with advanced banking systems. The chain that runs from the poorest parts of Latin America through Colombia into Mexico and then the United States to the off-shore banking in the Bahamas is being replicated in the former USSR. The primary target of this illicit trade is the marginalized and unemployed youth of central and Western Europe rather than the United States.

The problems of severe underdevelopment in many newly independent Central Asian countries suggest that illicit commerce from these countries will develop further as organized crime groups become more entrenched and the states cannot offer alternative employment or sources of foreign currency. The weakly developed law enforcement systems in these societies and the lack of cross-border protection suggest that there will be great growth in organized crime activities in these less developed regions.

Organized crime groups may inflict significant ecological damage in these less developed regions. Like other investors concerned exclusively with rapid economic growth, they show no concern for the renewal of natural resources. Economic crime's domination of the economies of the successor states may prove as devastating for the environment as their domination by their Communist predecessors.[47] Already organized crime groups are responsible for over-fishing of sturgeon for caviar in the Caspian Sea and wholesale harvesting of lumber without concern for reforestation.[48]

Organized Crime and Foreign Investment
Organized crime has undermined foreign investment and trade by increasing the risks of capital investment. Foreign businesses have been subject to extortion and their personnel threatened. Capital is not protected because

of an absence of: clear and permanent legal norms to govern investment and trade, reliable and honest parties with whom businesses can negotiate, trustworthy law enforcement, courts which are impartial arbiters of economic disputes, and the absence of insurance and banking laws.

The alliance of corrupt officials and organized crime groups prevents the emergence of long term trade agreements because they are not in their financial interests. The new mafiosi prefer to sell a certain amount of the state resources for their own profits rather than open trade with multinational companies which might abide by established regulations and limit their short-term gains. Many businesses, therefore, choose not to trade in the former USSR because they cannot compete with the illegal practices of organized crime.

Foreign businesses interested in international trade in oil and raw materials cannot avoid the profound corruption in this sector. International businesses often have to bribe officials who have the right to grant licenses to export oil and other valuable materials. The numerous and recently established export firms are dominated by organized crime groups.[49]

Therefore, United States firms are forced to violate U.S. legal norms if they seek to enter the Russian market. *The East European,* an investment magazine, reported estimates in Fall 1993 that 80 percent of all American businesses in Russia have violated the Foreign Corrupt Practices Act at least once.[50] Investors have to pay bribes to acquire access to lists of commercial property to rent, violate norms on the export of capital and have to submit to extortion threats.

The ill-equipped, corrupt and demoralized police make it necessary for foreign investors to turn to private guard services.[51] But many of these guard services are run by organized crime groups. Their staff include former KGB and militia personnel who may also engage in industrial espionage against businesses, sometimes at the behest of their employers. Businesses operating in Moscow and other major cities have purportedly appealed to the German criminal police, the FBI as well as other international police organizations to protect their personnel from personal threats.

Capital in most of the successor states is at greater risk than in other countries. The former Soviet Union, therefore, cannot compete with many other countries for legitimate capital investment. Foreign investment, like in the former East Germany and other parts of central Europe, does come from foreign organized crime groups. They have the protection mechanisms and the willingness to take the risks in the hostile environment. While mafia investment may be more a phenomenon in central Europe than in the former Soviet Union, émigré Soviet organized crime figures are repatriating capital to establish businesses. Even for them the investment climate may not be secure because corrupt officials in conjunction with law enforcement personnel may connive to acquire their newly established businesses.

Daily Life
The threats posed to daily life are among the most serious consequences of organized crime because they affect so many citizens of all social levels and

POST-SOVIET ORGANIZED CRIME   351

in almost all regions of the former USSR. The impact of organized crime on daily life affects citizens' perception of the social, political and economic transition. Organized crime affects citizens through: the privatization process, increased violence in daily life, higher rates of personal and property crime, more deviance, higher prices, and reduced personal security.

Organized Crime and the Privatization Process

A voucher system was initiated to provide all Russian citizens the opportunity to acquire the assets of the Soviet state. Based on the Czech model, all citizens received supposedly untransferable vouchers to prevent their acquisition by organized crime members and other wealthy citizens. Organized crime has managed to sabotage the process in several ways. First, more vouchers were printed than were authorized. Second, organized crime members illegally acquired vouchers

> *". . . because of organized crime control of consumer goods . . . Moscow [is] the third most expensive city in the world after Tokyo and Osaka. But the average wage in Russia is a mere $100 a month."*

from economically desperate Russian citizens. Third, vouchers have been illegally re-used by organized crime figures.[52] Having access to more than their share of vouchers, organized crime has been able to acquire a disproportionate share of the businesses and the shares of larger private enterprises.

Corruption also results in the failure to cancel vouchers and their reuse. For example, a St. Petersburg official in the State Property Committee was arrested on charges of criminal negligence after discovering that city officials had canceled only 10 percent of the eight million privatization vouchers used at auctions. These already used vouchers could then be recycled and used again. Citizens have had their access to property auctions blocked[53] by violence.[54]

Individuals in charge of many of the large Soviet companies have managed to privatize the resources of these enterprises or the properties associated with them at ridiculously low prices. This has been done without allowing any citizens a chance to compete. For example, the apartments and dachas owned by large companies have been bought at prices that are a mere fraction of their value on the open market. Individuals residing in choice locations have been threatened or even killed by organized personnel in order to acquire their apartments.[55] The thugs of organized crime threaten the employees and retirees of enterprises eligible to acquire shares in their businesses. In this way, citizens are deprived of their property rights through violence.

The failure to regulate the emergent securities sector also places citizens' property at risk. Citizens have lost all their assets as the owners of unregulated voucher funds have disappeared with all the vouchers in their possession. Moreover, citizens' savings and their pension funds in the hundreds of unregulated banks dominated by organized crime are at risk. The emergent stock funds are not adequately regulated. In a July interview with the head of the Anti-Mafia Fund, the author was informed that there are criminal cases against 20 different stock funds of the approximately 50 which are registered. Illustrative of the problems is the Neftalmazinvest fund (the oil diamond fund). Its name is misleading because its investments include chemical plants and hotels but none in oil and diamonds. The authorities caught up with this fund and suspended it in March of this year on charges of embezzlement.[56] Yet this was only one of its misdeeds. Its advertised first annual return of 750 percent was paid to only 12 of its many shareholders.[57] Yet the state did not address the problem of advertising fraudulent returns until July 1994 when a presidential decree was issued.[58] Sufficient safeguards do not exist to address other stock irregularities. In August 1994, the much-publicized MMM pyramid investment fund collapsed, depriving thousands of citizens of their savings.[59]

Organized Crime and Consumer Goods
Organized crime members possessing large amounts of rubles have legally acquired, without much competition, a significant share of the service sector—food stores, restaurants and other businesses serving consumers. Their control of this market has meant that citizens pay higher prices in the marketplace than if a fair and competitive market operated in the consumer sector. For example, prices in Palermo markets, dominated by organized crime, are as high as in other parts of the country even though the products sold are raised in nearby Sicilian farms.[60]

In Russia, it is estimated that prices are 20 to 30 percent higher because of organized crime control of consumer goods.[61] Moreover, food prices and services are now so high in Moscow that a recent survey made Moscow the third most expensive city in the world after Tokyo and Osaka. But the average wage in Russia is a mere $100 a month. At one time, the central planners in Moscow fixed prices. Now they are fixed by organized crime. Central planning once made goods unavailable—now their costs make them equally inaccessible to the average citizen.

Organized Crime and Foreign Aid
Much foreign aid is diverted within the country. Some estimates placed as little as 6-7 percent of assistance reaching intended beneficiaries.[62] The appropriated assistance has been sold on black markets at prices that are inaccessible to the citizenry. Assistance has rotted rather than reached citizens. In other cases, it built dachas for the elite.

Foreign organizations have responded by alternative delivery strategies. Armed guards have escorted shipments to old age homes and orphanages. But the security of the distribution of these goods cannot be protected once the deliveries are made.

Organized Crime and Community Service
When organized crime controls much of the economy of a particular area,

POST-SOVIET ORGANIZED CRIME 353

it may contribute to the infrastructure of the community. There is also evidence that Russian crime groups are repeating the patterns of Sicily and parts of Colombia. In these two countries organized crime groups pay for the construction of hospitals and schools as a form of insurance against the collaboration of community members with the law enforcement community. In Russia, certain organized crime figures sponsor sports events and are associated with visible philanthropic groups.[63] Corrupt banks contribute to educational and other community projects on a regular basis.

Organized Crime and Street Crime

Organized crime results in increased violence, street crime, property crime and more visible and pervasive deviance.[64] The rivalries of organized crime groups have led to armed battles in such major cities as Moscow and in secondary cities like Yaroslavl. The homicide rate in Russia has increased dramatically and now exceeds the level in Western Europe and is equal or surpasses that in the United States. The explanation for this growth are the turf wars of organized crime and the increase in contract killings.[65]

Robberies against CIS citizens and foreigners have increased as a result of the growth of organized crime. A significant growth in apartment burglaries and car thefts also results from the increasingly organized and professional crime. The vast majority of Russian citizens have changed their daily life as a result of the crime threat.

Organized Crime and Deviance

Organized crime has contributed to significant increases in drug trafficking and use, prostitution and gambling. Drug use has spread as a result of greater access to drugs, the commercialization of markets by organized crime and the greater demand for drugs by a demoralized population.[66] Gambling casinos are sponsored by organized crime in hotels and tourist sites.

The feminization of poverty in the post-Soviet period has made many women either voluntary or unwilling entrants into prostitution. Some women are recruited because prostitution pays more than any available legitimate employment either in the former USSR or abroad. Others are tricked into this work by offers of foreign hotel jobs. The women are threatened with violence and also threats are made against family members in the former USSR if they do not comply. Russian prostitutes, under the control of organized crime, work in Belgium, the Netherlands, Israel, Poland, Hungary and the Middle East.

Organized Crime and the Labor Force

The work force, once controlled by the Communist Party and centralized trade unions, may face increasing controls from organized crime. Organized crime was estimated by the Ministry of Internal Affairs to control 40,000 enterprises in 1993.[67] As privatization proceeds, ever more enterprises fall under the domination of organized crime which has no concern for the labor rights of individuals.

Organized crime, one of the few growth sectors in the economy, can attract employees because it can offer jobs and pay salaries that are often multiples of what individuals earn in the state sector. Evidence of this is the numerous departures from the police apparatus for employment in the private security sector. The limited employment prospects of many individuals make them easy targets for the false employment schemes offered by organized crime members. Organized crime exploits labor by smuggling men to low paying jobs abroad and using child labor in unregulated conditions at subminimal wages.[68]

Crime groups may impede the development of trade unions independent of state control because this would restrict or at least diminish their control over the labor force. At present some crime groups exercise influence over established trade unions—the benefits of this are the same as in the United States and other countries—to gain influence over the labor force, and access to pension funds. In Russia, there is one additional incentive, to obtain the resources of privatizing enterprises. The successor states must take precautions to ensure that the collapse of the USSR does not mean the substitution of one form of labor market control for another.

> *"Organized crime figures are acquiring newspapers and attempting to buy television stations."*

Organized Crime and Ethnic Groups

Minority groups long assumed an active role in the second economy or black market. As the underground economy has evolved into the present organized crime phenomenon, ethnic minorities continue to assume an active role. Often they act in conjunction with Russians, the dominant ethnic group in Russia.

The active participation of ethnic groups in organized crime is leading to increased ethnic conflict and hostility. The Chechens are blamed for leading organized crime in Moscow and in many other foreign countries. After the storming of the Parliament in October 1993, non-Russians, particularly individuals from the Caucasus, were expelled from Moscow because of their alleged involvement in organized crime.

Access to Moscow residence permits is still restricted, although organized crime figures can always bribe local law enforcement to permit them to stay in Moscow. Yet the legal restrictions on their residence means that they are always vulnerable to extortion and expulsion by the police.[69]

Organized Crime and Civil Society

Organized crime is impeding the development of civil society. The establishment of institutions independent of the state is a fundamental prerequisite to the creation of civil society. Organized crime figures are acquiring newspapers and attempting to buy television stations. Courageous journalists are routinely intimidated and investigative journalists are offered significant bribes to cease their investigations. Articles on organized crime

POST-SOVIET ORGANIZED CRIME   355

may be purposely deceiving as organized crime figures plant stories against their rivals or purposely mislead the public. Commercialism and the influence of organized crime are contributing to a less probing press and are hindering the development of a legitimate free press.[70]

The involvement of organized crime in numerous philanthropic organizations is also evidence that the emergent civil society is being corrupted from within. Citizen volunteerism was once dominated by Communist Party institutions, now it responds to the needs of organized crime. This infiltration occurs because of the contributions often made by foreigners to these charities. Furthermore, these organizations lend themselves to money laundering operations.

While organized crime impedes the development of certain aspects of civil society, it cannot be denied that organized crime groups may be a manifestation of civil society. They are groups that exist outside of state control; they are helping to fill the vacuum in society. But they are not a positive force that check state authority, rather they exist as a parallel and illegitimate force within the society.

Conclusion

The most critical question concerns the future evolution of these illicit economic entrepreneurs. Will they remain like the mafia and Camorra and persist in their illegal activities at the expense of their home communities and international markets? Or will they develop like the robber barons of the United States in the past century who evolved into the major philanthropists of American society? The answer may be premature, however it is certain some unique post-Soviet variant will develop. Post-Soviet organized crime bears certain resemblances to the organized crime phenomena in other societies but it is unique because it is strongly affected by the socialist state which preceded it.

Comparing post-Soviet organized crime with Colombia or Italy rather than the United States reveals the political, economic and social costs which have touched all sectors of the society.[71] The penetration of organized crime into the state has limited democracy. Economic growth has occurred but it has been very unequally distributed within regions and commercial sectors of the societies. Homicides have increased in areas with concentrations of organized crime. Both Colombia and Italy have discovered that once organized crime penetrates the state, the latter will not be able to disassociate itself from the former—even with the investment of significant manpower, economic resources, the application of intense repression and the sacrifice of many well-meaning individuals.

The former states of the USSR which lack the resources and the will to combat the organized crime phenomenon may be in worse shape than Italy or Colombia. The consequences of their impotence will be apparent in the future political, economic, social and cultural development of their societies. As in Italy and Colombia, the consequences of such organized crime will be not only a domestic concern but one with broad international implications. Post-Soviet organized crime poses an even greater threat to the world order

356   DEMOKRATIZATSIYA

because of its access to nuclear materials.

Organized crime's domination of the economies of many of the successor states will determine many aspects of the post-socialist transition in the coming decades. It will not necessarily impede economic growth because as the Italian experience has shown, high rates of growth are possible even with organized crime penetration into the central state. But it will preclude certain forms of development. Illegitimate commerce may predominate at the cost of legitimate business funded by foreign investment. Environmental damage, such as was perpetrated in the Soviet period, may continue because organized crime entrepreneurs are more concerned with short-term profits than long term consequences.

A very unequal pattern of economic development may occur because organized crime thrives when there are greater variations in economic development. Residents in areas with high rates of unemployment, little prospect of development or investment may accept the employment offered by organized crime or may cultivate illicit crops like drugs because they have limited economic alternatives. Free labor markets may not emerge because the coercion of organized crime groups may supplant that of the Communist Party.

"The penetration of organized crime into the state has limited democracy."

The major economic threats from the present organized crime structures are the exportation of much needed capital and the depletion of the resources of the former Soviet Union. If too much capital is sent abroad there will not be the funds needed to develop the economy. Furthermore, the organized crime groups are depriving successor states of natural resources that they will need for the subsequent development of their economies.

The scenario appears depressing but a political consensus is now emerging that a legislative framework must be established. Non-governmental groups concerned with combatting organized crime are also developing. If the political will is mustered, Russia may be on the verge of beginning the long, sustained attack on organized crime that must be launched if it is to diminish the influence of organized crime on the future development of the state.

Notes

[1]   Ernesto U. Savona ed., *Mafia Issues Analyses and Proposals for Combatting the Mafia Today* (Milano: ISPAC, 1993); Donatella Della Porta, *Lo Scumbio Occulto Casi di Corruzione Politica in Italia* (Bologna: Mulino, 1992), pp.29-31.
[2]   Howard Abadinsky, *Organized Crime*, 3rd. edition (Chicago: Nelson Hall, 1990), pp. 267-395.
[3]   "The Russian Con Men who Took California" *Newsweek*, 13 December 1993, p. 28 and State of New Jersey Commission of Investigation, *Motor Fuel Tax Evasion* (Trenton, New Jersey: State of New Jersey Commission of Investigation, 1992).
[4]   »Alarm, jetzt kommen die Russen,« *Der Spiegel* No.25, 1993, pp. 100-111.
[5]   Sergei Khmelev, "Bank Fraud: New White-Collar Organized Crime," *CJ International*,

POST-SOVIET ORGANIZED CRIME 357

Vol. 9, No. 5, (September-October 1993), p.18.

[6] Leonid L. Fituni, "CIS: Organized Crime and Its International Activities," Center for Strategic and Global Studies, Russian Academy of Sciences, Wilbad Kreuth, 1993, p.12.

[7] Lydia S. Rosner, *The Soviet Way of Crime: Beating the System in the Soviet Union and the U.S.A.* (South Hadley, Massachusetts: Bergin and Garvey, 1986).

[8] Maria Los, *Communist Ideology, Law and Crime: A Comparative View of the USSR and Poland* (London: Macmillan Press, 1988).

[9] Anthony Jones, Walter D. Connor and David E. Powell eds., *Soviet Social Problems* (Boulder: Westview Press, 1991).

[10] Giovanni Falcone, »PM: Una Carriera da Cambiare,« *Micromega* No.3, 1993, p. 56; Rensselaer Lee and Scott MacDonald, "Drugs in East," *Foreign Policy* (Spring 1993), p.96.

[11] Diego Gambetta, *The Sicilian Mafia The Business of Private Protection* (Cambridge: Harvard University Press, 1993).

[12] Louise Shelley, "Interpersonal Violence in the Soviet Union," *Violence, Aggression and Terrorism*, Vol. I No. 2, 1987, pp. 41-67.

[13] Interview with Cyril Fijnaut in Budapest, Hungary, August 1993 who had prepared a parliamentary report on prostitution in these two countries.

[14] Citizen concern over organized crime is reflected in «Vzrosloe naselenie Rossii: Ezhemesiachnyii monitoring obshchestvennogo meneniia» (March-August), *Informatsionnyi biulleten monitoringa*, October 1993, p.26.

[15] Raimondo Catanzaro, *Men of Respect: A Social History of the Sicilian Mafia* (New York: Free Press, 1992); Pino Arlacchi, "La Grande Criminalita in Italia," *La Revista del Libri* (April 1993), p.38.

[16] "Duma Adopts Anticorruption Bills," *FBIS Daily Report*, 16 May 1994, p.32.

[17] A. Uglanov, «Prestupnost i vlast,» *Argumenty i Fakty* No. 27, (July 1994), pp.1-2.

[18] Interviews with members of the Committee on Defense and Security of the Council of the Federation, July 1994 in Moscow.

[19] Vladimir Ovchinsky, *Mafiya: Neobiavlennyi vizit* (Moscow: INFRA-M, 1993), pp. 114-115.

[20] For a discussion of the crisis in fighting post-Soviet organized crime see A.I. Dolgova and S.V. Diakova, *Organizovannaia Prestupnost*, Vol.2 (Moscow: Kriminologicheskaya Assotsiatsiya, 1993), pp.175-208.

[21] Interview by author in Moscow in July 1994.

[22] Michael Specter, "Guns for Hire: Policing Goes Private in Russia," *New York Times*, 9 August 1994, p. A4.

[23] Paolo Pezzino, *Una Certa Reciprocita di Favori Mafia e modernizzazione violenta nella Sicilia postunitaria* (Milano: Frano Angeli, 1990) and Gambetta.

[24] Gambetta.

[25] Lee and MacDonald; Pino Arlacchi, *Mafia Business: The Mafia Ethic and the Spirit of Capitalism* (London: Verso, 1986), pp.187-210.

[26] Seija Lainela and Pekka Sutela, "Escaping from the Ruble: Estonia and Latvia Compared," Paper presented at the Third EACES workshop on "Integration and Disintegration in European Economies: Divergent or Convergent Processes?", Trento, March 4-5, 1993.

[27] "The Rise of the Gangster-Industrial Complex," *East European Investment Magazine* (Fall 1993), p.106.

[28] "Global Mafia," *Newsweek*, 13 December 1993, p. 28.

[29] Joseph Serio, "Organized Crime in the Former Soviet Union: New Directions, New Locations," *CJ International*, Vol.9, No.5 (Sept.-Oct. 1993), p.15.

[30] Paul Klebnikov, "Joe Stalin's Heirs," *Forbes*, 27 September 1993, p.131.

[31] Ibid., p.124.

[32] "The Rise of the Gangster-Industrial Complex," p. 109.

[33] "Yaroslavl's Fight Against Organized Crime," *FBIS Daily Report*, 20 April 1994, pp. 12-13.

[34] Rensselaer Lee III, "Soviet Organized Crime," paper presented at the Wilson Center, Smithsonian Institution, 2 November 1993; Khlebnikov, p. 130.

[35] Ovchinskii, pp. 115-117.

[36] "Deputy Minister of Security Arrested for Corruption," *RFE/RL Daily Report*, No.125, 5 July 1993.

[37] Together these groups commit financial frauds. Some of these frauds have costs not only for the post-Soviet states but also for foreign governments. For example in Germany, complex financial schemes are developed to exploit the subsidies that the German government is to provide the post-Soviet military troops on their territory.

[38] Ernesto U. Savona and Michael A. DeFeo, "Money Trails: International Money Laundering Trends and Prevention/Control Policies," paper presented at the International Conference on Preventing and Controlling Money Laundering and the Use of the Proceeds

of Crime: A Global Approach, Courmayeur, Italy, 19-20 June, 1994, p.17.

[39] Louise Shelley, "The Internationalization of Crime: The Changing Relationship Between Crime and Development," in *Essays on Crime and Development* ed. Ugljesa Zvekic (Rome: United Nations Interregional Crime and Justice Research Institute, 1990), pp. 119-134.

[40] Arkady Vaksberg, *The Soviet Mafia* (New York: St. Martin's Press, 1991) and Virginie Coulloudon, *La Mafia en Union Sovietique* (Paris: JCLattes, 1990).

[41] Stephen Handelman, "The Russian 'Mafiya'," *Foreign Affairs*, Vol.73, No.2, p. 88.

[42] V.S. Ovchinsky, *Strategiya borby s mafiei* (Moscow: SIMS, 1993), pp. 96-100.

[43] Michael R. Gordon and Matthew L. Wald, "Russian Controls on Bomb Material Are Leaky," *New York Times*, 18 August 1994, p.A1 and A10.

[44] Rensselaer Lee III, "The Illicit Drug Market in the CIS: Scope, Dynamics and Policy Implications," Paper presented at the Conference on Narcotics in the CIS Region, Meridian House, Washington, D.C., 11 September 1992.

[45] Yelena Matveyeva, "Narcobusiness getting a foothold in the Far East," *Moscow News* No.26, 25 June 1993, p.13.

[46] Ibid.

[47] In an interview in Moscow with former Procurator General Alexander Sukharev in July 1994, he suggested that there were Party sanctions for those who caused environmental destruction. Now there are no controls on environmentally harmful activity.

[48] Richard Reed, "Plan to Log Planet's Largest Forests in Russia Run Into Opposition," *Mexico City News*, 17 October 1993, p.16.

[49] "The Rise of the Gangster Industrial Complex," p.108.

[50] Ibid., p.111.

[51] Georgy Ovcharenko, «Pokupaiu Pistolet,» *Pravda*, 23 March 1989, p.6.

[52] "St. Petersburg Gangsters Push for Economic Power," *Current Digest of the Soviet Press*, Vol.XLV, No. 51, 19 January 1994, p.14.

[53] Ibid., p.14.

[54] Jonas Bernstein, "Organized Crime Said to be Stifling Russia's Economy," *The Washington Times*, 28 January 1994, p. A16.

[55] Anya Vakhrusheva, "Flat-Swapping in Moscow: A Risky Business," *The Moscow Times*, 4 June 1994, p.1; "Yerin Calls for 'United Front' Against Crime," *FBIS Daily Report*, 16 May 1994, p.22.

[56] Elif Kaban, "No Regulation, No Security in Russian Securities," *The Moscow Times*, 6 July 1994, p.12.

[57] William Barclay, "Privatization Chief Vows Fraud Crackdown," UPI wire service, 23 March 1994.

[58] Mikhail Dubik, "Enforcers Vow to Target Fraudulent Ads," *The Moscow Times*, 6 July 1994, p.13.

[59] "MMM Shareholders Declare Hunger Strike," *RFE/RL Daily Report*, 8 August 1994, p.1.

[60] Gambetta, pp. 201-211.

[61] "Crime, Corruption Poses Political, Economic Threat," *Current Digest of the Soviet Press*, Volume XLVI, No.4, 23 February 1994, p.14.

[62] "Humanitarian Aid Said Diverted to Mafia, Trade," *FBIS Daily Report*, 27 January 1992, p.26.

[63] Khlebnikov, p.128; Igor Baranovsky, "To Jail in American from Russia—With Love," *Moscow News*, No.26, 25 June 1993, p.13.

[64] "Crime in Russia: The High Price of Freeing Markets," *The Economist*, 19 February 1994, p.58.

[65] Igor Baranovsky, "Professional Killers," *Moscow News* No. 52, 31 December 1993, p.12. and "Yerin Calls for 'United Front' against Crime," p.22.

[66] "Russia Seen Vulnerable to Widespread Drug Abuse," *FBIS Daily Report*, 6 June 1992, pp. 1-2.

[67] Brian Duffy, Jeff Trimble and Yuri Shchekochikhin, "The Wise Guys of Russia," *U.S. News and World Report*, 7 March 1994, p. 45.

[68] Louise I. Shelley, "Entrepreneurship: Some Legal and Social Problems," in *Privatization and Entrepreneurship in Post-Socialist Countries*, Bruno Dallago, Gianmaria Ajani and Bruno Grancelli eds. (New York: St. Martin's Press, 1992), p. 316.

[69] "Moscow City Official on Visitor Registration," *FBIS Daily Report*, 9 December 1993, pp. 47-48.

[70] Interviews with journalists in Moscow in July 1994.

[71] Rensselaer Lee III, *The White Labyrinth: Cocaine and Political Power* (New Brunswick, N.J.: Transaction, 1990).

[14]

ORGANIZED CRIME IN RUSSIA TODAY
By Alena V. Ledeneva

Aside from the criminals themselves, only two kinds of people know much about organized crime: journalists and those charged with combating organized crime. In Russia and elsewhere, journalists are fond of writing headlines about the "Mafia." Such labeling tells us little more than what some resentful "Mafiosi" want to tell the world or what the security services are prepared to allow to leak out. Journalistic investigations have been few in number and are fraught with danger. [1]

Those charged with combating organized crime in Russia say: "We wouldn't call it the Mafia. We prefer to speak of criminal groups and associations. In Russia, they are not grounded in tradition and family as they are in, say, Italy. Organized — yes, but the control exercised by these organizations is not total, and they could easily be eliminated. We have all the information and it would be elementary in technical terms, were it not for their 'roofs.'"

It is seen as axiomatic by these professionals that no organized crime could survive without a protective "roof" (krysha) or "umbrella." That is, without penetration of state institutions, without corruption and without the active involvement of officials (including law enforcement officers) in criminal activities. It is probably too late to search for an antidote to phenomena on this scale and to apply a radical remedy to them. It is crucial, however, to get to know the "disease" we have to live with, to understand its origins and to pinpoint those aspects that could be treated.

There are two dominant explanations for organized crime: one explanation stresses the violence; the other, the corruption. The first, a rational choice theory elaborated by Diego Gambetta and Federico Varese, offers a "supply and demand" model of protection services. [2] The rise of organized crime is viewed as compensating for the loss of the state's power to protect the citizenry. In circumstances where a weak state becomes incapable of wielding a monopoly of legitimate violence while the demand for protection is increasing (usually in connection with a change in property rights), private protection services appear on the market alongside other business activities. The emphasis in this line of argument is often put on violence, the private nature of the protection business, its criminal roots and its opposition to the state. For example, Varese argues that the Mafia can be seen as an alternative military structure — with its own initiation rituals — operating independently of the state and deriving from criminal roots.

The second interpretation accounts for the rise of organized crime by emphasizing the corrupt nature of state institutions and the interpenetration of state and criminal structures. Its main finding — that the state cannot combat organized crime because the latter has penetrated the state itself — may be illustrated by the many inconsistencies in the work of Russian state institutions: for example, the State Duma's continuing failure to adopt an anti-corruption law, the inability to sort out nonpayments, the use of dirty money for election campaigns, corruption in local privatization committees in the period 1992-94, the rigged privatization auctions of 1995, and so on. According to this interpretation, there is often no legal way to deal with organized crime, since the criminals are well connected or even hold public office. Holding public office might not be a problem if it were clear "who controls whom." Unfortunately, there is no clarity as to the interrelationship between the "fifth power," as organized crime is sometimes called, and more traditional types of power: the legislature, the executive, the judiciary and the mass media (the "fourth estate"). [3]

These two interpretations are not mutually exclusive. Gangs derived from the criminal underworld coexist in Russia with ex-Afghan or ethnic gangs as well as ex-KGB and militia-based protection and security businesses. All belong to a territory covered by a "roof" normally connected to corrupt authorities. The "supply and demand" argument is, perhaps, more useful in explaining the inception of organized crime while, to proceed with the analysis of its development and evolution, one must take account of other important considerations.

Let us outline some of the dimensions indispensable to the analysis of organized crime in Russia. Organized crime should be considered in relation to the socioeconomic processes of transition. Economic liberalization and marketization, privatization and restructuring of property rights must all be seen as factors fostering criminalization since they created a demand for protection services. The supply-side was based on the criminal legacy of the past but received additional impetus from the breakdown of Soviet value systems (loss of confidence in the future, undermining of notions of honesty, duty, respectability), social polarization (decline of mutual help, lack of trust and loss of social control) and the rise of nouveaux riches who think the law does not apply to them. As a result of these and other factors, the state's monopoly of legitimate violence was broken.

With the stabilization of the economy and the formation of a new financial and political elite, however, conditions changed. From a situation in which everyone lived by his or her own laws, while the laws of the

Continued on page 7...

PRISM   **April 17 , 1998**   7

Organized crime... from page 3

state either did not work or worked selectively, Russia had by 1997 moved to an order more or less consistently dominated by the so-called "empires" — big financial-industrial groups. As these grew larger, they became increasingly interested in a strong central government, economic and political stability, and a police force capable of combating crime. Already in 1996, data on crime and detection rates suggested that the police were becoming better able to control the situation. This is already true in Moscow and the pattern may be expected to be repeated elsewhere. Increasing efficiency on the part of the tax police has also contributed towards strengthening the state (according to businessmen, it is much better to pay the police than bandits).

Continued on page 14...

Organized crime... from page 7

Russian organized crime has also evolved. Some of the most conspicuous changes include:

a) *"economization"* (entrepreneurial approach, inter-penetration with business and state enterprises, investment of criminal money into legal businesses);

b) *"detraditionalization"* (breakup of criminal "authorities," wealth being seen as a substitute for status accrued through time in prison);

c) *"professionalization"* (new types of crime such as electronic crime, manipulation of banking and other financial institutions, divisions of territories and principal spheres of activity);

d) *"globalization"* (emphasis on import/export business, expansion of geographical arena to take on an international character;

e) *"legalization"* (search for legal status in the public domain; spread of at least partly criminal capital to the mass media, charitable donations).

All these tendencies have weakened the outlaw community. The criminal world has lost many of its "thieves-in-law" (*vory v zakone),* a loss which has damaged the criminal community and made the order of things much more contingent. The appeal of life in the underworld has lost its specific "ideology." Together with wealth comes the need for legitimacy, respect and security for those who will inherit that wealth. Partly, too, this is a generational phenomenon: those who started young have reached an age at which they want to secure their position. The logic is similar to the rise of any elite: at some point they repudiate their own values and become interested in maintaining the status quo. This general principle is consonant with the claim of former interior minister Anatoly Kulikov, that organized crime is "entering a new stage of development — that of liberalization and coming to power." It is therefore important to speak about Russian organized crime in relation to its present stage of development.

Geography is an important, but extremely complex, aspect of Russian organized crime. The uneven level of development of organized crime in different regions (for example, the new tendencies described above would most likely be noticeable in Moscow, whereas in other regions organized crime may still retain the features of earlier stages), access to transport and possession of specially motorized vehicles, and the availability of advanced mobile-phone and radio communication systems, introduced a new element to criminal operations and contributed to the rise of regional crime. The analysis of organized crime should therefore be carefully related to its regional aspects. These include: ethnicity and territoriality as bonding mechanisms that often provide a basis for gangs and organizations, division of territories (borders and customs offices, for example), cooperation and conflict between regional criminal groups, and their representation in local government.

Another serious dimension of analysis is the extent of interpenetration of criminal authorities and political institutions. The official status of the organized crime leaders or "roofs" is often a matter of considerable concern to the professionals chasing them. Even if criminals are not in the posts themselves, they may belong to a network of control and back up (*krugovaya poruka*). This is the least eradicable legacy of the past, providing protection for people within a certain circle (the institution of "*svoi lyudi*").

For example, certain deputies to the parliament will be backed up by the administrative authorities even if compromising information on them becomes available. Similarly, the administrative authorities will be backed up by the security and police forces. In practice, whenever allegations against high-up officials or criminals are raised, the cases are suspended or closed. Everyone within the "circle" backs up everyone else: one supports others in anticipation of potential protection for oneself when the day comes. Support and protection may also be viewed as an investment in the creation of new obligations. This practice has deep roots and is logical enough in a situation where legal rights and adequate law enforcement are lacking.

In general, one could say that old informal rules have outlived the formal ones and helped to shape post-Soviet realities. But they have not escaped a certain degree of detraditionalization under pressure from new market forces and social arrangements. Informal rules have not simply stretched over current contexts. Following economic necessity and market demands, they have undergone a certain "marketization" and even acquired some features in common with formal rules — an external enforcement (sanctions, violence, racket) by the structures opposed to the state. For example, pervasive and habitual practices of "*blat*" (the use of personal networks for obtaining goods and services in short supply) became "monetarized" and slipped into the domain of corruption. According to Kulikov, nearly half of all illegal profits are spent on bribing officials. Accounts are opened in foreign banks in the name of public servants, who are offered free trips to the best foreign resorts. What used to be a matter of morals and ethics based on the modest norms of Soviet society and notions of kinship, friendship and other social ties, came, in the transitional stage of "wild capitalism," to involve material and financial capital.

The pervasiveness of blat and informal codes in the Soviet era helps to explain the scale of present-day corruption and organized crime. The informal legacy of the Soviet order provides an answer to the question: "When our society is so chaotic, how is it that our crime

Continued on page 15...

PRISM   **April 17 , 1998**   **15**

Organized crime... from page 14

is so organized?" The idea of a society held together by its informal networks also provides a clue how to answer the question: "Why is the situation not more violent than it is?"■

NOTES:

[1] Dmitri Kholodov, a journalist working for *Moskovsky komsomolets*, was killed in 1994 by a bomb hidden in a briefcase while he was investigating high-level military corruption. Another journalist, Andrei Konstantinov, frankly acknowledges in his writings his debts to "experts both dead and alive."

[2] Diego Gambetta, The Sicilian Mafia, Cambridge, MA: Harvard University Press, 1993; and Federico Varese, "The Emergence of the Russian Mafia," D.Phil. thesis, Oxford University, (forthcoming from Oxford University Press)

[3] The catchy phrase "fifth power" is becoming an everyday idiomatic expression. In this sense, post-Soviet neologisms such as "*diskaunt*" (bribe), "*razborka*" (negotiations with potential violent sanctions), "*bratva*" (fraternity), "racket," "roof," a "bought judge" (*zakuplenny sud'ya*), are reliable indicators of the processes spread in Russian society.

Alena V. Ledeneva is a Research Fellow at New Hall, University of Cambridge, England. Previously, she lectured in sociology and social theory at the University of Novosibirsk. She is the author of Russia's Economy of Favors: Blat, Networking and Informal Exchange (Cambridge University Press, 1998). She is now coediting a second book with S. Lovell and A. Rogatchevsky: Bribery and Blat in Russia (Macmillan, forthcoming).

CJ INTERNATIONAL

November-December, 1992

Volume 8, Number 6

Page 5

COMMONWEALTH OF INDEPENDENT STATES

Shunning Tradition: Ethnic Organized Crime in the Former Soviet Union

by Joseph Serio

While the traditions of the Soviet underworld seem to be undergoing a period of rejuvenation, there is a simultaneous rise in the number of groups that are based on ethnicity, and that are shunning the customs and habits that grew up during the Soviet era. The ethnic groups are generally homogeneous bodies governed by interpersonal feudal-like clan and tribal relations rather than the simple protector-protected relationship.

Because the very existence of these groups is predicated on a notion of "family," the Russian understanding of "boss" as a single, powerful decisionmaker attempting to maintain relationships among unrelated individuals for mostly economic reasons becomes superfluous. This type of group is found frequently in Central Asia and the Caucasus region of the former Soviet Union. One prime example of such a group with a rapidly expanding power base is the Chechen organization.

The homeland of the Chechen nationality is found on the western shores of the

The Chechen group is a closed organization, making it difficult for law enforcement agencies lacking personnel that speak Chechen to infiltrate the group.

Caspian Sea and due north of the Georgian republic, and is called Chechen-Ingush Autonomous Republic. A largely Muslim people from the Northern Caucasus region of Russia, the Chechens were deported from their homeland by Stalin in 1944 on charges of collaborating with Nazi troops in World War II. They returned in 1957 and now number around 700,000.

The importance of the Chechens is that they represent an emerging type of organized crime in the former Soviet Union. The group is more structured than most. Most important for them is the strict hierarchical arrangement of their clan relationships. It is a closed organization, recruiting only from among their own people. Chechens actively recruit juveniles from the Chechen regions where unemployment is high. This also ensures a degree of "purity" in the membership, making it difficult for law enforcement agencies lacking personnel that speak Chechen to infiltrate the group.

The group has also become adept at using extreme violence in the commission of crime. With the downfall of the Communist Party as an organ of control, a burst of violent energy seems to have been released from organized crime groups. In January 1990, then-member of the central ruling body of the USSR Ministry of Interior (MVD) Aslakhanov wrote, "Recently organized criminal groups of racketeers have been actively operating in Moscow. The most dangerous of them is the so-called 'Chechens,' who commit crimes that are daring and particularly vicious."

While MVD officials have counted as many as a dozen Chechen groups working in Moscow, there are three main

groups operating in the capital. Each group has a clear structure: leader, senior advisors, soldiers, and associated members. Among the groups there is a strict division of spheres of influence— they each have their own interests.

The most powerful of these groups is the "central." Its base was the restaurant Uzbekistan, but it was forced to relocate to the Hotel Belgrade, The Golden Ring and the Rossiia Hotel after several attacks by other Moscow groups. One of the leaders of this group, who goes by the name of "Baldie," controls a collection of operations in the resale of goods in short supply, as well as the Moscow markets, prostitutes, homosexuals, restaurants and cooperatives, located in the center of Moscow.

The second of the three groups—"ostankinsky"—controls all inter-city shipping from Moscow to Chechen. They are based at the Ostankinsky, Voskhod and Baikal Hotels. The members of this group for the most part are engaged in the resale of large consignments of furniture, foodstuffs, clothing, building materials, and audio and video machines. For example, in one day members of the "ostankinsky" group shipped from Moscow to Chechen 58 cases of butter, 37 of milk, 65 of noodles, 40 of macaroni and 68 of baby food. The leader of this group goes by the nickname "The Big One" ("Bol'shoi").

Continued on page 6

CJ INTERNATIONAL

November-December, 1992

Volume 8, Number 6

COMMONWEALTH OF INDEPENDENT STATES

Continued from page 5

The last of the three is known as "automobile." Its domain includes seven service centers, a center on Khoroshovsky Highway and a major store in Southern Port. They also strive to control numerous joint ventures, and are actively involved in smuggling automobiles from the West. The leader of the group goes by the nickname "Little Bird" ("Ptichka"). As of April 1992, he was in prison.

All three groups are involved in the sale of narcotics. Their network expands even into the army. It is estimated that in 1989 there were approximately 150 Chechens serving in the army in Moscow and Moscow region. By 1991, this figure reached 1700. Many of these contacts were used not only in the narcotics business but also for gaining access to weapons.

The groups frequently work together and maintain a source of funding (*obshchak*) which is used for paying lawyers and informants in the MVD and KGB, and for supporting the families of arrested group members. Bribery of prison officials for upwards of a million rubles to release comrades in prison is an ordinary occurrence. According to sources, this has been undertaken on more than one occasion in the past. It is impossible to determine the holdings in the *obshchak* but apparently it reaches the hundreds of millions of rubles. A main supply for the *obshchak* comes from Chechen control over street vendors. Every Azerbaijani flower peddler and fruit merchant in Moscow—there are 5,000 to 7,000 in the capital—must pay up to 500 rubles a day to the Chechen group. In addition, the group operates through about 140 small enterprises, most often as middlemen.

According to sources, the Chechen groups in Moscow have their own systems of counter-intelligence and security. They are directed by Akhmet M. based in the Hotel Belgrade and by Musa "The Younger," brother of Musa "The Elder" who controls the *obshchak*.

There are about 1,500 active members of the Chechen organization in Moscow. In-cluding transient members from other parts of the country, the figure reaches 3,000. The group has some 500 apartments around the capital, some of which are used exclusively for receiving communiques and telecommunications. At one hotel it is possible for Chechens to obtain a directory of any other Chechen located in the capital.

One example of the group's power is the incident at the cafe Voskhod in October 1990. After an attack on the cafe in which three Caucasians died, more than 500 Chechens gathered. A death sentence was pronounced on the lives of five leaders of Russian groups. Several Chechen members volunteered to carry out the murders, and 5 million rubles was raised for their legal defense and support of their families while they served their prison sentences. On November 27, 1991, on the seventh floor of the Ukraine hotel in downtown Moscow, there was an "All-Union" meeting of the Chechen leaders. One hundred fifty members from Stavropol, Chimkent, Tver, Tashkent and Moscow participated.

According to sources, the meeting topics included new ways to launder money, creation of a separate fund for legal assistance, and expanded cooperation among Chechens in every possible type of commercial enterprise.

Chechen activity is by no means limited to the corridor between Moscow and the Chechen-Ingush republic. In a recent interview with *CJI*, the Minister of Justice of Uzbekistan confirmed that the Chechens are active in Central Asia. MVD officials in Moscow are struck by the fact that the Chechens have been appearing in virtually all parts of the country and have access to high-ranking government officials. Moreover, the organization has been found in Germany, Austria, Hungary and other European countries. According to officials in Moscow, the Chechens recently sent members to New York to set up operations in the United States.

Joseph Serio is a Research Associate in the Office of International Criminal Justice.

Part IV
Russian Organized Crime and the Russian Economy

[16]

Privatizatsiya and Kriminalizatsiya

How Organized Crime Is Hijacking Privatization

Svetlana P. Glinkina

Privatization in Russia has been carried out with great ruthlessness and with remarkable speed. At the beginning of July 1994 about 70 percent of enterprises were already in private hands. Is this good or bad? Does it represent a success or a failure for reforms in Russia? Of course, it depends on the quality of the privatization process and on other factors. Two worrisome features of privatization should be distinguished: its formal character and its high level of criminalization.

There are many reasons for the widespread criminal activity in the reform process in Russia. The first group of factors is connected to the general societal situation and its alarming degree of criminalization. New types of economic crime are evolving. Economic criminal conduct of businesses is becoming a necessary precondition for their very existence. The present-day situation is the result of several factors, including (1) the breakup of statehood; (2) the current economic policy; (3) an intentional weakening of the state's fight against economic crimes, backed by the government's hope to use the "shadow capital" as a resource base for economic reforms; and (4) a drastic stratification of the population's standard of living with a simultaneous loss, in a considerable part (especially among the youth), of socially important goals—replacing them with consumption ideals that have also contributed to the criminalization of the economy.

An essential factor in the criminalization of economic affairs is that monopolization of power has resulted in the formation of a state administration that seeks to derive benefits from businesses. As a result, economic bodies within the state and government structures are attempting to preserve their privileged positions in this age of capitalist reforms. According to estimates by the Research Institute of the Ministry of Internal Affairs, 25 to 30 percent of money obtained from criminal economic activity during 1990-1993 was used to nourish corrupt relations with government and state officials. Instead of fighting against corruption, modern political leaders announced the elimination of the state's role as an active agent in economic life. The resulting vacuum has substantially cleared the field for criminal economic behavior.

The result of this criminalization of the economic system is the trend to

Svetlana P. Glinkina is director of the Institute of International Economic and Political Studies at the Center for East European Studies, Russian Academy of Sciences, Moscow.

386   DEMOKRATIZATSIYA

match the economic policy (and, in addition, the entire state policy) to the specific economic interests of criminal structures which, in turn, prevents much-needed reforms in the material and technological bases of production. Failing to create a modern technological structure leads to corresponding adverse consequences for the whole society.

There is another group of factors that influence the criminal character of privatization. They are closely connected with the very method of privatization that was chosen when the process was launched. The vast sell-off that was to return Russia to capitalism had to be carried out at a breakneck pace. It is not difficult to understand why. The first stage of the government's reforms—near universal price liberalization—had already released a storm of inflation and caused industrial output to plummet. Unless private ownership of industry and commerce could be set in place with extraordinary speed, economic collapse might well provoke broad popular resistance before privatization was complete. Now it is clear that the key consideration was not whether privatization was an economic success in the sense of promoting growth and providing jobs; much more central in the government's strategy was that the process should be "irreversible," creating a new class of large property owners ready to fight to retain their wealth. As a result, many of the investors who are participating in privatization were created from shadow economic activity—speculation, racketeering, extortion, looting and so on. Thus, Russia's privatization process is turning many of the country's prime assets over to swindlers and thieves. Analyzing the process of primary accumulation of capital in the country shows that the average Russian citizen has neither the desire nor the possibility to become an active owner in this vast new market.

". . . the average Russian citizen has neither the desire nor the possibility to become an active owner in this vast new market."

Where, on what levels, can the criminal character of Russian privatization be faced? The following scheme, which shows that Russian privatization went through four stages, can help answer this question.

Stages of Privatization in Russia
Stage One of the Russian privatization process, in 1988-1991, created the majority of the healthiest economic entities (see table). The start-up and infusion capital for some of the largest and most respectable private banks, stock companies, and joint ventures is closely connected with this process. President Boris Yeltsin launched an effort after the August 1991 coup to find the Communist Party's hoard, estimated to be tens of billions of dollars. But the investigation was suddenly dropped around the time that former Party officials connected with the money died mysteriously.

The easiest and most popular method of privatization in Stage Two was the so-called "milking the credit cow." It works as follows. The Russian Central Bank gives a special loan to a factory at a low (for Russia) interest

PRIVATIZATION AND CRIME 387

rate of 25 percent per annum to pay overdue bills to other enterprises or back wages. The money, however, goes straight to the commercial bank associated with the factory, which re-lends it at something closer to the country's real interest rate of 250 percent per year. The difference then gets pocketed or deposited in an overseas bank account. The volume of such loans in the last nine months alone was 6.5 billion rubles. This may help explain why, although the Central Bank keeps pumping out more money, the country's enterprises never seem to get any healthier. Some managers and commercial bankers have made enormous profits, but Russia's factories are producing less, not more.

The process of Stage Three of privatization began not in July 1992 as some claim, but earlier, with the spread of so-called small cooperatives. At that time, pre-privatization of partial assets began through cooperatives created on the base of or near state enterprises.

Table: Subjects, methods and owners of the privatization process

Stage	Subject of Privatization	Methods of Privatization	New Owner
1	ownership of political and social orgs.	creation of commercial entities (joint cos.)	the people in or around these orgs., nomenklatura
2	state budget, social funds	wide system of special loans & tax benefits; commercial entities based on social funds	corrupt officials, receivers of benefits
3	assets of state enterprises	1987-1991: new coopera-tives since 1992: sale of enterprises a) by auction, b) via commercial investing c) leasing assets d) changing the co. into a joint-stock co. (sale of stock)	depends on the quality of property: a) workers & staff b) bosses, racketeers, speculators, corrupt officials c) émigrés from USSR
4	citizens' savings	a) voucher funds b) banking orgs. c) new orgs of social security	a) fund officials b) swindlers c) investors?

388   DEMOKRATIZATSIYA

Since cooperatives, unlike state enterprises, were for a long time entitled to cash accounting without restriction on the amounts involved, "unclean" relationships between cooperatives and state enterprises became increasingly common. Cooperatives frequently performed no work at all, although money was transferred to their accounts from state enterprises; money was then withdrawn from these accounts and dispersed. Trade-intermediary cooperatives offered cash in exchange for cleaning assets at a ratio of 1:3 (the cooperatives received three rubles worth of assets for every ruble in cash transferred to the account of a state enterprise). This device became a very convenient method for laundering money.

The activity of criminal groups in Stage Three of privatization depends on the quality of the privatized property. Where enterprises are making substantial profits, or own valuable property, workers have often failed to win control against the combined onslaught of bosses, racketeers, speculators and crooked officials. According to estimates made by the Ministry of Internal Affairs in mid-1993, there were 40,000 enterprises controlled or established by organized criminal organizations in Russia. Seventy to 80 percent of private and privatized firms and commercial banks were forced to pay criminal groups, corrupt officials and racketeers.

> *"The main portion of those swindled have been pensioners."*

In privatization, an economic nomenklatura still exists and enterprise directors often misappropriate shareholdings. In January 1993, workers at a cement plant in Vologda, north of Moscow, reportedly found that two-thirds of the shares in the plant were unaccounted for. The workers eventually discovered that the director and his mother-in-law had signed up for those shares. At the Orel Electronic Instruments Plant in central Russia, 2,000 workers early last year signed a petition demanding the help of trade union leaders in defending their rights during privatization. Plant bosses had sent most of the workers on forced leave before setting up a flagrantly illegal joint-stock company.

Criminal groups are very active in Stage Four of privatization as well. Hundreds of voucher funds—investment agencies resembling Western mutual funds—have sprung up to invest the vouchers of Russians who lack confidence in their ability to choose wisely in the share market. But investors who take this route still have to pick their voucher fund, and in a number of sensational cases, the funds have proven to be bogus. According to estimates for the last year-and-a-half alone, the different financial organizations in Moscow (banks, voucher funds and financial institutions) have cheated more than one million depositors, including approximately half a million citizens. The main portion of those swindled have been pensioners. Among the fraudulent companies are the Independent Oil Company, the Lenin Trade and Financial Corporation and the security company Aldzher. In mid-November 1993, 1,500 angry investors

PRIVATIZATION AND CRIME   389

blocked traffic for two hours in central Moscow demanding that the government compensate them for their losses when the Technical Progress voucher fund shut its doors in July. As many as 30,000 investors may have been defrauded when the fund's directors vanished. Two similar cases occurred in St. Petersburg early last year. There is no reason to believe that this outcome was not foreseen, in considerable detail, by Yeltsin and his associates. But, as discussed above, openness to crime is an obvious feature of the path of Russian privatization.

Even where the methods used to acquire property are legal, and frequently they are not, the money used may be tainted. The role of criminal circles is especially important both for creating the seed money for privatization and for the laundering of money in all stages of privatization. Smuggling and illegal trade are main sources of primary accumulation of capital in Russia. The Soviet collapse left Russia with 8,400 miles of new international borders. The opportunities have opened widest for Russia's natural resources.

During the past four years, the smuggling of oil, gasoline, radioactive materials, timber and metals has sharply increased. The most popular metals to be smuggled out are nickel, copper and cobalt—which can still be purchased at subsidized prices for internal use and sold for much higher ones abroad. As much as 20 percent of Russia's oil and one-third of the metals mined were smuggled out of the country in 1992. Ten percent of the materials smuggled were destined for the Baltic states. In the first nine months of 1993, $35 million in nonferrous metals passed over the border from Russia to Estonia—most of it illegally—and then to the West. Tiny Estonia is now one of the world's largest exporters of nonferrous metals, even though it produces none. Similarly, about 70 percent of the raw materials crossing through Lithuania never reach Kaliningrad. According to information from the Ministry of Internal Affairs in Lithuania, four powerful mafia structures exist which specialize in such operations. As a result, virtually every day in 1993 a trainload of as many as fifty oil-tank cars (each of which can carry 147 barrels of oil) vanished. A train is taken to a siding at a train station that has oil storage facilities, where the oil is drained off for sale on the black market or for shipment out of the country. Eventually the empty train returns to Russia. Criminal structures have their own people working at railway stations in the Baltic states and have close connections with many corrupt officials, customers, etc. Also in Lithuania, mafia structures specialize in creating bogus commercial firms in Kaliningrad because, like other Russians, Kaliningrad residents can still purchase oil and other resources at subsidized prices. Smugglers have exploited this by setting up phony companies in Kaliningrad to buy oil and other materials. To avoid export duties, the smugglers would show customs officials a contract between a mainland Russian and a Kaliningrad firm. When customs officials checked to see if such a company existed, they usually found that it not only was properly registered, but also had a bank account. However, it was usually a 24-hour company set up for this single operation.

Another very important channel for primary accumulation of capital is exporting. There are many methods for and benefits from exporting in Russia. Fifteen billion dollars is siphoned out of the country every year, much of it by exporters tucking their earnings away in offshore bank accounts, safe from Russia's high inflation, high taxes and political instability. One scheme that has become popular is for a Russian businessman to negotiate a contract with a Chinese firm and ship the goods abroad. After a few weeks, the Russian claims he was never paid. Since there is little he can do about it, he writes off the deal. In the meantime, however, his Chinese partner has paid for the goods by making a deposit in the Russian's overseas bank account. Another method is for a Russian businessman to buy "services" abroad. For example, a Russian businessman may pay a foreign company $10,000 for consulting services. In fact, the Russian sends the money to a phony company abroad, which in turn transfers it to the Russian's bank account. No one will be able to prove that no services were received. There are dozens of firms that will perform this job for Russian businessmen, for a fee of five to seven percent of the transaction.

> *"Russia . . . has become the world's newest money-laundering center."*

Although Russia has a commercial banking system less than six years old, it has become the world's newest money-laundering center. Billions of dollars are finding their way in and out of Russian banks and other enterprises. Likewise, Russian gangsters are finding ways to launder their new-found wealth, investing in legal enterprises and eventually transferring tens of billions of dollars out of the country.

The favorable climate for laundering dirty money in Russia is related to the special rules of depositing in Russia. If a person comes to a commercial bank in Russia and deposits one million dollars, he can only be asked for his passport. The bank cannot find the source of the money. Confidentiality laws forbid bankers from disclosing information about accounts except to the tax police. To get the information on a suspected criminal's account, the tax police must know at which particular branch among the country's 2,000 to look. As a result, it is almost impossible to trace the money, whether it is legal or not. Nor is it required that deposits be reported to the authorities, as it is in the United States where laws aimed at stopping money laundering necessitate that cash sums larger than $10,000 be reported to the federal government.

The cash nature of Russia's economy also creates unlimited opportunities for money laundering. For example, more than one-half of the Mercedeses sold in Europe are purchased in Russia. The luxury autos are purchased with illegal gains and thus constitute a form of money laundering. Since such car sales are not registered, there is no way to trace how they were bought or even who owns them. Numerous business

PRIVATIZATION AND CRIME 391

deals also look suspiciously like money laundering. Owners of luxury hotels built in strife-torn regions of the former Soviet Union report large profits that observers believe to be phony, or at least hugely inflated. There is also the practice of setting up a bogus investment company offering 100 percent interest for one month's worth of investments, with the sole purpose of laundering money. The bogus investment company can afford to pay such high rates because of the vast sums involved.

Russia is certainly not the world's biggest money-laundering center, but it is already offering one of the most advanced forms of money laundering: control of the financial institutions. Moscow police have estimated that more than 25 percent of local banks are controlled by organized crime. Bank control is particularly easy in Russia, where no regulatory controls over ownership of banks exist. Even convicted criminals are not forbidden to buy or open banks.

High-level corruption, however, still remains one of the biggest roadblocks in getting a regulatory handle on money laundering and other financial crimes arising from the process of Russian privatization. But that is a subject for another article.

[17]

Practices of Exchange and Networking in Russia

Alena V. Ledeneva

Western researchers studying the former Soviet Union first paid attention to the phenomenon of *blat* — to do with the use of informal contacts and networks to obtain goods and services or to influence decision making — in the 1950s. Yet although the importance of *blat* has been pointed to, there have been no attempts — and in fact no possibility — to study it. This article is based on original data gathered in 56 in-depth interviews conducted during fieldwork in Russia in August 1994–April 1995. The window of opportunity for such research occurred after people ceased being inhibited talking about *blat*, while still having a fresh memory of the Soviet period. These materials are unique. They enabled the author, first, to develop an ethnography of *blat* — that is to present it as a distinctive form of social relationship or social exchange articulating private interests and human needs against rigid control of the state; second, to record the daily problems which represent the ex-Soviet system in a light not readily seen by an outsider; and third, to conceptualise the phenomenon of *blat* thus relating to other informal practices. In this article focus will mostly be on the third angle of the research.

In Soviet society the phenomenon of 'blat' — how goods and services were obtained in an economy where money played little role — was pervasive. In the socialist system of distribution, with its omnipresent shortages and hierarchical privileges, the circumventing of formal procedures became the 'reverse side' of an overcontrolling centre — the reaction of ordinary people to the social constraints they faced. Despite its pervasiveness *blat* was never studied directly. Although familiar to every Russian and reported by scholars as early as the 1950s,[1] *blat* has never been adequately described or analysed. At least three conceptual issues have to be resolved before *blat* can be subject to focused study and feasible fieldwork. First, the vernacular term has to be translated into academic discourse and conceptualised; second, *blat* should be distinguished from other informal ways of getting around formal procedures with which it is sometimes associated; and third, it must be con-

sidered why such a pervasive phenomenon was left for so long undefined and unexplored.

ON THE DEFINITION OF *'BLAT'*

'Blat' is virtually impossible to translate directly into other languages. As Berliner has remarked, 'the term *blat* is one of those many flavoured words which are so intimate a part of a particular culture that they can be only awkwardly rendered in the language of another'.[2] Most dictionaries of the Russian language contain the pre-revolutionary meaning of *blat*, which refers to criminal activity[3] — although it was generally used to mean less serious kinds of crime, such as minor theft. The criminal underworld spoke a jargon of its own which was referred to as *blatnoi* jargon, or thieves' jargon. In early Soviet times the word acquired a 'new common vulgar' usage; in the expression *po blatu* (by blat) it means 'in an illegal manner'. Another Soviet dictionary defines *po blatu* as 'illicitly, by protection, by patronage'.[4] In vernacular, 'by blat' means 'by acquaintance' (*po znakomstvu*) and would be used to mean ways of obtaining (*dostat'*) or arranging (*ustroit'*) something using connections. *Blat* does not appear, however, in any of three editions of the Great Soviet Encyclopedia published in 1927, 1950 and 1970, although it is available in dictionaries of the Russian language at least since the 1930s.[5] For while the term was in wide currency in an informal way, it was banned from official discourse and the practices involved in *blat* were condemned by the Soviet authorities.

According to respondents, *blat* is easy to identify but difficult to define. 'Blat seems an obvious word, it does not need definition', remarked one of them. Interestingly, everybody knows what *blat* is about but cannot grasp its essence. One reason for it is that the term means different things in different contexts irreducible to some common ground: *blat* is an acquaintance or friend through whom some goods or services in short supply can be obtained, cheaper or better quality. Also, *blat* is a reciprocal relationship which people call *'Ty mne, ya tebe'* (I help you, you help me). *Blat* is about using informal contacts, based on mutual sympathy and trust, that is, using friends, acquaintances, occasional contacts. *Blat* also takes place where one arranges a good job for another, or where, on otherwise equal conditions, the one who is known or recommended gets chosen. Sometimes *blat* means influence and protection, all kinds of 'umbrella' (*kryshi*), using big names, so-called 'I am from Ivan Ivanovich' recommendations. Facing this multiplicity of contexts to which *blat* or '*po blatu*' is considered a relevant term, we have to consider the question what are the shared characteristics of situations that are referred to be solved 'by *blat*'. The question cannot, however, be answered satisfactorily because it is often the case that some characteristics present in one case are lacking in another: for instance, getting access to goods and services in short supply in any case is different from getting access to positions providing income (jobs or educational courses). The variety in regularity of favours, a kind of relationship between the parties, type of need, character of reciprocity, participation of an intermediary makes *blat* situations almost irreducible to any clear-cut classification. Rather, these situations are tied together in the way which is best grasped in the notion of 'family likeness' or 'family resemblance' enunciated by Wittgenstein in his *Philosophische Grammatik*[6] and developed in the *Blue Book*.[7] Entities which we commonly subsume under a general term, Wittgenstein wrote, need not have anything in common;

'they form a family the members of which have family likenesses. Some of them have the same nose, others the same eyebrows and others again the same way of walking; and these likenesses overlap. The idea of a general concept being a common property of its particular instances connects up with other primitive, too simple, ideas of the structure of language.'[8]

In what follows a range of such family features will be explicated which may not be available in every particular *blat* situation but which altogether should be associated with *blat* practices.

First, *blat* is a distinctive form of non-monetary exchange, a kind of a barter based on personal relationship. It worked where money did not. In the planned economy money did not function as equivalent in economic transactions, things were sorted out by mutual help, by barter. In his auto-

biographical story, an émigré Soviet writer described his temporary position on the editorial board of a journal as a source for such exchanges:

'I finally realised what kept these capable people on the editorial board. One would think why they need all this? Superfluous efforts, troubles, administrative cares. Only for 250 humble rubles? Why not just write books? It is not as simple as that. The journal is a kind of property, currency, an exchange fund. We publish N from another journal. N publishes us ... Or pays compliments to our work in the party regional committee ... Or does not criticise ... We give a possibility of earning to B. B in his turn ... And so on. ... C was responsible for the business trips abroad. D brought me batteries for my transistor radio. E arranged a swimming pool for my daughter ... Things went on and on.'[9]

Thus, apart from official rations and privileges allocated by the state distribution system to different occupational strata, every employee had a particular kind of access (*dostup*) which could be traded in *blat* relations. The relative unimportance of money in the command economy brought into being this specific form of exchange, intermediary between commodity exchange and gift giving.[10]

The objects obtained in *blat* relationships were rarely exchanged in a straightforward manner. It should be emphasised that *blat* involved relationships and not merely goods. What was exchanged are neither things for things, nor the relative values people quantified in things, but mutual estimations and regards. *Blat* was thus not a relationship for the sake of exchange but an exchange for the sake of a relationship. In gift exchange, inalienable objects of the same kind pass between people already bound together by social ties, while in commodity exchange alienable objects of different kinds pass between people acting as free agents. Gift exchange underwrites social relations and is concerned with social reproduction; commodity exchange establishes relations between things and ensures reproduction of the latter.[11] Although *blat* certainly does transfer alienable objects (favours), it does so on the condition that social relationships had already existed. 'The other' is not only functional but is regarded personally and in this sense becomes irreplaceable. The favours therefore bear, as it were, a non-alienable character. They are marked by the personal stamp of the donor. This can be best imagined as the occasional lending or borrowing of one's access (*dostup*) but the access itself is never alienable. Just as in gift exchange, where debt cannot be returned by a different kind of gift, a received favour is never equivalent to that which the recipient can provide in return. The original favour leaves a 'memory' even if an unlike return has been made. Thus, access could be 'lent', 'borrowed' or 'exchanged'. In this sense *blat* is a 'favour of access' (*usluga dostupa*) which someone chose to provide.

Favours of access became possible because they demanded no one's own resources and were perceived as 'sharing', 'helping-out', 'friendly support', 'mutual care' etc. Such help derived not from one's own pocket, but rather was given at the expense of state property or someone formally entitled to this resource. Sharing access with friends and acquaintances became so routine that the difference between *blat* and friendly relations became blurred: one almost became consequent upon the other. The use of public resources for private (even if not selfish) purposes reflected another paradoxical feature of the Soviet regime, the character of state property. State property was declared to be public and supposed to be guarded by everyone: the slogan 'Everyone — to guard the public property!' (*Vse — na okhranu obshchestvennoi sobstvennosti!*) was one of the most common. But 'public' could also be interpreted as quasi-private, which was grasped in the everyday sayings: 'public' means 'that part of it is mine', 'one has what one guards' ('*kto okhranyaet — tot imeet*'). The trickle-down of public property, through the access provided by those who 'guard' it, to a wider circle of people was a common practice, either denied or sincerely 'misrecognised' by the rhetoric of mutual help used to speak of personal relationships. Being not just mutual help or friendly support but help given at the expense of the state or others, *blat* therefore referred to a wider system of possibilities and to one's influence within it.

The functioning of informal contacts and connections was predicated upon the structural characteristics of the Soviet-type system. Soviet *blat* was similar to *guanxi* in China[12] or *zalatwic sprawy* in Poland[13] but had no direct analogy in the West. One reason for this was that the use of informal channels in Soviet-type society was not a matter of choice, it was an enforced practice necessitated by

perpetual conditions of shortage. One could argue that not every society characterised by scarcity and shortage generated *blat* and this may be so. *Blat*-like phenomena resulted from the particular combination of shortages and, even if repressed, consumerism; from a paradox between an ideology of equality and the practice of differentiation through the closed distribution systems. In so far as those who had no privileges in the state distribution system could by-pass rationing and queuing it had an equalising as well as a stratifying effect. It therefore had a bearing on the society's egalitarian claim and its actual inequalities.

'*Blat* was oriented to different needs in different historical periods (flourishing already in the 1930s) but it always — directly through obtaining goods and services or indirectly through obtaining jobs and status — related to the personal consumption and thus the distribution of material welfare.

> '*Blat* was simply a necessity for a decent life. You couldn't eat or wear what you bought in the shops, everything was in short supply, queuing and bad quality of services were appalling. To live normally, one *had* to have acquaintances and informal access to every sphere where needs arise',

remembered many respondents. *Blat* therefore became an everyday pattern of behaviour and mentality, penetrating personal relationships, such as friendship etc, and shaping specific attitudes towards legality.

Another characteristic feature of *blat* was that it remained 'mis-recognised' personally, but could easily be recognised in the case of the other. While practising *blat*, which was, in a sense, a necessity for everyone, people refrained from declaring it. They knowingly or unknowingly withdrew the term from describing their own contacts and personal relations while the informal contacts of other individuals or groups were described in such a way. Personal contacts through which a formal procedure was circumvented, or access to public resources was received, could not be seen by participants themselves as *blat* relations, because they were either personal and already perceived as kin, intimate or friendly relations, or mediated by those. These were the relations in which *blat* was embedded and which made it 'misrecognisable' for those involved.

In contrast to personal relations and simple barter, *blat* relations were not necessarily dyadic. *Blat* transactions could be circular: A provided a favour to B, B to C, C to D, and D to A, and the last chain might not have taken place. What was important is that there had to be no immediate repayment — reciprocity was to be masked by the delayed return. Mediated favours were even more efficient for avoiding practical and social constraints against immediate repayment. Psychologically, mediation was very important because 'it was terribly difficult to ask on behalf of oneself. It was much easier to ask for a friend, or for an institution, just to put in a word for somebody'. It did look respectable when an intermediary asked to help somebody 'unselfishly', or when a donor helped an unknown person just for the sake of the relationship with the intermediary. Everyone helped 'unselfishly' but this constructed an efficient system called '*blat*' by outsiders.

To summarise all these features, the following working definition of *blat* is offered:

— *blat* was an exchange of 'favours of access' in conditions of shortages and a state system of privileges;
— a 'favour of access' was provided at the public expense;
— it served the needs of personal consumption and reorganised the official distribution of material welfare;
— *blat* exchanges were often mediated and covered by the rhetoric of friendship or acquaintance: 'sharing', 'helping-out', 'friendly support', 'mutual care' etc. Intertwined with personal networks *blat* provided access to public resources through personal channels.

The resemblance of *blat* and some other ways of circumscribing formal procedures — manipulating access to resources through direct purchase as in bribery or diverting of state property for personal profit — makes *blat* a member of a wider family of informal practices and complicates the matter of drawing the boundaries between them. The problem can be exemplified with reference to another metaphor about 'family resemblance' discussed by Wittgenstein in his 'Philosophische Grammatik'.[14]

'Think of ball games alone: some, like tennis, have a complicated system of rule; but there is a game consisting just in throwing the ball as high as one can, or the game which children play of throwing the ball and running after it. Some games are competitive, others not.'

This thought was developed in a famous passage of the 'Philosophical Investigations' in which Wittgenstein denies that there was any feature — such as entertainment, competitiveness, rule-guidedness, skill — which formed a common element in all games: board-games, card-games, ball-games, Olympic games, and so on. Instead there is found a complicated network of similarities and relationships overlapping and criss-crossing.[15] There is a family of informal practices among which *blat* is but one subfamily (say ball games), itself consisting of the whole variety of balls and rules about them presented above.

BLAT AND ITS EXTENDED FAMILY

Let us now consider the connections and contrasts between *blat* and other phenomena in Russia, such as bribery, corruption, and informal economic practices with which it is sometimes confused. The main difference derives from the fact that although *blat* was often associated with shady aspects of the state command system it had positive features which led to its acceptance and toleration. Embedded in 'human' relationships (friendships, kin relations, acquaintance) *blat* differed from more negative forms of exchange and power. On the other hand, it had those negative overtones which distinguished it from mutual help or support in personal relations and made it closer to morally reprehensible practices. These negative connotations are rooted in the use of access to public resources for private benefit. The distinctions of *blat* are considered below in more detail.

Bribery

Certain criteria for a distinction between *blat* and bribery were already suggested by Berliner.[16] One element of difference appeared to be 'the nature of the entree into the arrangement'. In *blat* there is some personal basis for expecting a proposal to be listened to sympathetically, either because of past friendship, or because of the trust developed after a long business association (a subject-subject relation). In bribery it is only the offer of a bribe which links the two persons involved (an object-

object relation). Hence bribery has a more cynical quality than *blat* and is a more dangerous practice. Bribe-giving should never be witnessed and does not imply trust or continuity in relations. Bribery is illegal according to a statute in the Criminal Code, while *blat* is not in the latter at all. According to respondents who were asked how a person could accomplish a given end, *blat* was usually acknowledged to have high potential whereas bribery was considered unsafe.

In contrast to bribery, *blat* is a matter of belonging to a circle. *Blat* favours are normally provided to *svoim* (people of the circle, one of us). In such long-term relations, all kinds of favours are possible and not normally paid for directly (*za mnoi ne propadet*). It is thus another difference between the two that a direct and immediate payment is usually implied in bribery, whereas in *blat* the reciprocation may or may not take place some time in future and may take any form. In contrast to bribes, 'money etc. offered to procure action or decision in favour of the giver',[17] *blat* does not imply a straightforward offer and normally excludes money or any other immediate and equivalent repayment.

It should not be thought, as Crankshaw observes, that

'*blat* has anything in common with simple bribery. It is essentially the product of an under-the-counter mentality which causes friends and acquaintances to combine together to defeat the shortages, and the unlimited, obstructive, entangling red tape of the bureaucratic machine. The motive is self-defense; and the most incorruptible individuals deal in it freely. There is no other way to come through in a land where there is still far from sufficient goods to satisfy all needs, even for a price. Straight bribery is quite another matter. *Blat* stands for the exchange of personal favours and is human and warm. Bribery stands for impersonal corruption'.[18]

Bribery implies a conflict of interests where one is to be 'compensated' for doing something one would not do otherwise, while *blat* is a form of cooperation and mutual support with a long-term perspective implying trust rather than compensation for risk. In daily life, 'by *blat*' implies ordinary people using their contacts, which may be justified by the situation of urgent need and by their aims if they do not exceed modest norms of personal consumption, while 'bribery' implies a bribe-taker using a public office and his power for his own material gain which is reprehensible.

It follows that *blat* and bribery have different implications for a person's self-image. In case of bribery, a profit is drawn (not necessarily pecuniary) from a person's position. In cases of *blat*, even if the position is used, it is done not for immediate profit, but to help a friend, a relative or a good person, and the self-image is altruistic.

'It could be considered as bad by outsiders, but my conscience is clear. It is not like bribery, it is help. You help this person because you know well that she or he deserves it. I know this person won't get it without my help and I give him or her an opportunity',

said a high-status, experienced university boss. A younger academic adds:

'In *blat*, one's self-image is positive also because no money is involved. People often provide favours in anticipation of some return favours in order to create a certain image: "no need to pay, it is a sign of friendship, no calculations between friends, I could be in the same situation myself, one day you'll prove useful".'

Blat is more pervasive than bribery, for it penetrates spheres where money is not applicable (either because of an ethic of personal relationships, or because the favour is so petty or so large that it cannot be repaid). Within the same circle everything can be solved by *blat*, although to enter another circle one may need money, paid directly or through *blat* contacts. *Blat* is widespread both among the poor who have no money to pay premiums and among those who would not dare to receive a bribe, but would protect or promote someone or something by *blat*. For those who prefer to pay, *blat* is therefore restrictive. New businessmen seem annoyed:

'If it were possible to bribe, *blat* would not be necessary. You pay and get what you want. But there are spheres closed to bribery, and at a certain level *blat* is the only available means for getting what you want. Also, to give a bribe, one

Table 1: *Differences and similarities between* blat *and bribery*

Differences	Similarities
1. No personal basis for a request, no continuity in relationship after transaction, no network.	1. Bribery sometimes makes use of *blat* channels.
2. Explicit exchange, usually immediate payment, money is normally involved.	2. Goods and services obtained by *blat* may involve extra payment.
3. More limited areas of application.	3. Areas of application may overlap, eg allocation of scarce resources (apartments, cars etc).

has to know whom to bribe and how much is to be given. Such information can only be obtained informally: to give a bribe one has to be recommended as a reliable person to guarantee the safety of a bribe-taker, that is, *blat* relations mediate bribery.'

One needs a chain of *blat* contacts to work out how and who has to be approached in every particular case. With good contacts bribery may not be necessary at all, everything can be decided by *blat*. If there are people in the chain who are not tied by close personal relations, a bribe may quite often be paid in some form. Thus, some links in the chain are *blat* ones, some must be paid off. The cases where *blat* approaches or mediates bribery create juridical problems as well as everyday confusion. This is but one reason why struggle against bribery and corruption cannot be fully effective — only one link (bribe-giver/bribe-taker) in the chain gets involved in the case while most of it — to do with *blat* and personal networks — is not considered.

To summarise (see Table 1), *blat* is not based on immediate payment. Rather, it implies a personal basis for and continuity in relationships. *Blat* is embedded in personal networks and disguised by altruistic motives of friendly help. It is thus capable of pervading a wider range of areas of social life — people resisting bribery for ethical reasons would use their connections or 'help' people close to them. The use of *blat* is less morally reprehensible and defended by the mechanisms of 'misrecognition'.

Corruption

Both in literature and conversation *blat* is often referred to as corrupt practice. This may be accept-

able in everyday usage, but it is also misleading, for neither '*blat*' nor 'corruption' have an agreed meaning, nor are these terms independent of moral judgments. According to one of the basic approaches,[19] corruption is defined as the use of public office for private advantage (the latter term being understood not only in a pecuniary sense but also in terms of status and influence). However, as Friedrich,[20] following Weber, has pointed out, the use of public office for private advantage is not always widely perceived in a given society as corrupt. Particularly if an individual making personal gain is simultaneously making a positive contribution to the society, many will see such actions as at least acceptable and sometimes even a 'just reward'. Thus although corruption usually implies a form of betrayal of public confidence, the significance of that betrayal cannot be universally assessed. Because of the clash that can arise between an abstract definition of corruption and its application to a complex real world, some authors have distinguished between what can crudely be called 'good', 'bad', and 'ambiguous' — or white, black and grey — corruption.

According to Lampert, cases of corruption have a ranking specific to the society. The Soviets clearly felt that bribery and embezzlement on whatever scale were worse forms of corruption than small-scale use of public resources for private ends (such as using workers to do private jobs in enterprise time).[21] This is in tune with the distinction drawn between various forms of corruption in the Criminal Code and the different penalties applied for engaging in them. *Blat* is not on the criminal scale at all and can be characterised as legitimate (by reason of their small scale or recognised necessity) thus falling into the category of 'good' or 'ambiguous' corruption.

Scott suggests defining corruption in Communist societies as 'behaviour which deviates from the *formal* duties of a public role because of private-regarding (personal, close family, private clique) wealth or status gains; or violates rules against the exercise of certain types of private-regarding influence'.[22] What is designated as 'private-regarding' here conceals a whole dimension of horizontal relations, such as kin and friendship or relations of mutual understanding (*voiti v polozhenie*), which are not necessarily self-oriented. These horizontal, non-hierarchical chains of relations also embrace *blat* relations, in which favours are done not for a material reward but for the sake of relationships: 'she is my friend' or 'he is a good man', 'he is one of us' or just because one cannot reject a request of an acquaintance. These relations imply non-bureaucratic, human codes of behaviour at any level of social hierarchy. These codes occur in a hierarchical, repressive or totalitarian system or under similar constraining conditions as compensatory codes or codes of hidden opposition. It is this horizontal dimension of personal relations with their internal codes that is overlooked in the analysis of corruption as a systematic phenomenon. Most corruption studies are focused on bureaucracies, while *blat* is rather about common people. To concentrate on the phenomena of corruption, that is the advantages bureaucracy enjoys at the public expense, is to omit those informal practices which contribute to it, without being identified as corrupt, as well as the advantages over the system gained by common people.

Western definitions of corruption can be very misleading when applied to Soviet conditions. Definitions focusing on public and private interests or purposes have to confront differences in the economic system and the system of property rights. As Lampert concluded of the USSR: 'It is appropriate to interpret some typical abuses as "organisational" rather than "individual"; the purpose of illegal practices is to further the overall aims of the organisation, not the personal interests of individuals within it'.[23] The distinction between the organisation and the individual, however, becomes blurred, both because organisational success will often lead to status and/or material rewards to the individual, and because individual offences may be rationalised in terms of 'the good of the organisation'. It is this confusion of organisational and personal (which resulted from the

ideological norm of self-identification with the purposes of the organisation, the Party, the Soviet state) that created an appropriate environment for *blat*.

Another distinctive characteristic of corruption is what Palmier[24] calls 'moral condemnation'. A given act may not be clearly illegal, but if there is evidence that many people see it as improper (illegitimate), then such evidence is included in the analysis of corruption. As opposed to corruption, *blat* is related to mundane (and legitimate) favours. People were forced to engage in *blat* practices to obtain things which were legal to have. Enterprises had to obtain the resources to fulfil plan tasks, thus meeting the demands of the command economy through informal channels of *tolkachi* (pushers responsible for obtaining supplies so that the enterprise could meet the plan tasks). In this sense the acceptance of *blat* or any form of economic informal practices was a forced necessity for both people and the system. The morality of these practices is only an issue when one is not involved in them. A moral position which seems relevant for the case was expressed by Zinoviev:

'You, of course, will think that... the behaviour of [the] *Homososes*[25] in such a situation is amoral. But we look at it differently. It is easy to be moral if you live in conditions which do not force you into morally reprehensible actions. You are well fed and clothed; you have a nice house with books and other ways of enjoying yourselves. And it seems to you that to be moral is natural and not in the least bit difficult... Everything is simple and clear-cut. But if a man finds himself below the bread-line, beneath the minimum that is indispensable if moral norms are to be considered applicable in real life, then it is senseless to apply moral criteria to his behaviour. A man in such a position is not only freed *ipso facto* from moral norms, he is freed from them by these moral concepts themselves. It is immoral to expect a man to be moral if he lacks the minimum living conditions that permit society to demand morality from him. ... *Homososes* are born, are educated and live in such conditions that it is just ridiculous to accuse them of immorality ... '.[26]

In his study of 'corrupt consciousness' of Soviet people Simis put forward the same idea of forced corruption for both those who give bribes and those who take them — the very system of services, such as, for example, free medical care, forces both a patient to look for either personal contacts or possibilities of bribery and a doctor to accept 'candy, perfume, caviar, sausages, meat and anything else the patients can think of'. Structural (both economic and cultural) forces or constraints of the Soviet overcontrolling centre have resulted in the flourishing *blat*: life became impossible *unless* the rules were broken. Despite its extent and frequency, however, *blat* received little formal acknowledgement. When publicised it was treated as deviant acts of atypical people. In practice the reverse seemed nearer to truth — in many jobs indeed it was often abnormal *not* to be involved in *blat*. Simis tried to identify the structural conditions of the socialist system that brought these practices into being.

In Soviet conditions *blat* and other informal activities can also be considered as compensatory mechanisms against the planned economy and ideological pressure on the legitimacy of private gain. *Blat* articulates private interests and 'human' needs against the rigid constraints of the state order, allows people to meet harsh conditions, to maintain their social comfort and to enjoy a sense of 'beating the system'. *Blat* also implies a transgression of social boundaries predetermined by the system, not least by redistributing goods and services to which middle-ranking or senior officials of the regime have nearly or totally exclusive access, such as foreign consumer goods, special shops, exclusive hospitals etc to the less privileged.

Despite the similarities between *blat* and corruption, *blat* is restricted by its domain of everyday life, unlike corruption, to do with politics and bureaucratic organisations. Although it implies access to public resources and so-called 'working-place crime', as does corruption, *blat* is more legitimate, since it is aimed at satisfying everyday needs and basic necessities. Recourse to *blat* is normally enforced by hard conditions, inefficiency of formal procedures, and the inability of state institutions to cope with day-to-day demands. In contrast to corruption, *blat* derives from personal networks which govern, control and regulate *blat* on an ethical, rather than a legal basis (see Table 2).

Informal economic practices

Apart from being seen as corrupt, *blat* is also sometimes described in the literature as economic practice. Most approaches to informal economies are oriented towards calculating the share of informal practices in national economies, as a drain of resources from the working place, fiddling of all kinds. If mentioned in economic studies at all, *blat* is regarded as a part of a broader phenomenon of the 'second economy' complementary to the Soviet central planning system. It is then considered in economic terms, that is, as a channel for the flow of resources from formal into informal economy or as a way of gaining extra income. This section will illustrate what the differences between *blat* and informal economic practices are and what they have in common. A discussion of research on the informal economy is also relevant for understanding the conditions under which *blat* developed and acquired its semi-legal status, and which necessitated its correlation with illegal economic practices.

The study of informal practices goes under a variety of names: 'submerged', 'parallel', 'hidden', 'informal', 'unofficial', 'underground', 'black',

---

Table 2: *Differences and similarities between* blat *and corruption*

Differences	Similarities
1. Mainly involves misuse of high official positions.	1. Use of the working place and influence over accessible resources.
2. Implies private wealth on a fairly substantial scale.	2. *Blat* falls into the category of 'good' or 'white' corruption.
3. Transactions concerned with elevating one's economic status above that of others.	3. Misrecognition is also characteristic of corruption.

'shadow', 'illegal' economy etc. The most wide-spread term for Soviet-type economies is the 'second economy'. This was mainly the result of the work of Grossman, who used it to refer to economic phenomena 'ideologically alien to the Soviet system'. In particular, he suggested that the second economy comprised production and exchange activities that fulfilled at least one of the two following tests: (a) being directed for private gain, (b) being in some significant respect in knowing contravention of existing laws.[26] Although the definition has proved useful, there is something inherently unsatisfactory in its combination of two quite disparate elements: private gain and illegality. Apart from this, the term 'second economy' seems strictly divided from the 'first economy' — a distinction which in fact does not exist — on the one hand; and from non-economic aspects of analysis, necessary for the analysis of *blat*, on the other.

Gabor defines the second economy as 'activity aimed at earning and redistributing income outside socially organised production and distribution'.[27] In this sense, the second economy comprises all those activities for the production of income that escape the direction and control of the state and are performed by families or individuals independently from the organisations of the socialist sector. Although *blat* is not 'an activity for the production of income', it is an activity aimed at redistributing socially organised access to resources, rewards and privileges through individual or family channels, and thus indirectly connected with 'the non-regulated aspects of activity within state- and cooperative operated organisations and all forms of private, semi-legal and illegal activity'. This definition of the second economy includes, apart from the regular private sector, 'not officially recorded' activities in the private sector itself, earnings deriving from tips and other types of undeclared remuneration, the clandestine use — including theft — of state property (raw materials, semi-finished articles, machinery, spare parts, finished products, labour, services) for personal advantage and, finally, illegal financial and commercial transactions.

In a legal perspective, *blat* could be most adequately viewed as 'anti-systematic' behaviour.[28] which is not to be branded as unlawful (against the law), but as unjust towards the others or, perhaps, simply contrary to the prevailing system. Or it could be referred to as 'semi-legal' activity. Generally speaking, this term may be applied to activities and transactions that contain an element of illegality but for one reason or another do not attract serious governmental repression. Although those in informal activities are frequently harassed, informal practices as a whole tend to develop under the auspices of government tolerance. Governments tolerate and even stimulate informal practices as a way to resolve potential social conflicts or to promote political patronage. The informal activity may be undertaken on behalf and in the interest of a state enterprise; it may be private and legal but unrecorded and thereby in avoidance of taxation; or it may have been officially encouraged but lacking a firm basis in law. A well-known example of the first category is the already mentioned practice of *tolkachi*. The second category embraces the letting apartments and holiday houses, private tuition, paid services by doctors, dentists, nurses, lawyers (although such services are in principle available free of charge), and numerous other privately produced services. *Blat* practices do not appear in such a categorisation, rather these practices are about networks, channels and ways through which all these activities are accomplished. It is thus not in the list, but in fact shapes most of transactions which can be placed in the second economy.

The availability of resources and goods to some economic agents and consumers and not to the others fosters the growth of an 'irregular market' for their exchange. This market is irregular, either because it entails corruption or because it discriminates among purchasers in terms of availability, quantity or price of the goods traded; or else because it is not open to all on an equal footing but restricted to a more or less extended group of people with special charcteristics (acquaintances, relatives, those willing to pay a 'bonus' on top of a price, provide other scarce articles or to grant favours). These aspects are not readily grasped by quantitative methods, but rather lend themselves to analysis in terms of social and cultural context. The latter are predicated upon the role of *blat* as a way of life and an economic necessity, the importance of contacts in certain areas and for certain activities, and the population's distrust of the state and the government; a distrust which, in their eyes, legitimates *blat*. In this sense the lines of analysis of *blat* and other informal practices correspond; these phenomena are not exceptional but endemic; not marginal but integral to organisation and the rewards of work.

It should also be emphasised that contrary to informal economic practices *blat* practices relied on unwritten laws according to which '*by blat*' ways were normal and unproblematic. The analysis of such unwritten codes is not available. The fact that the informal economy makes use of non-contractual but binding relationships, for which kinship is often the base, is difficult to represent in quantitative economic analysis. Families often find in the informal economy the flexibility and accessibility that the formal economy does not have. By pooling resources, by engaging in informal practices, by the self-construction of shelter, by self-provisioning, and by the skilful use of social networks and families, it can be argued, people avoided entrapment in the Soviet regime. They became actors who engage in relations with others to get what they can out of the existing system.

To conclude, *blat* cannot be adequately grasped in terms of informal economic practices (see Table 3). It implies ties of reciprocity within personal networks, rather than profit-oriented activities and market-type exchanges, on which informal economic practices are often based. The study of *blat* therefore requires a socio-cultural analysis of personal relationships and their impact on *blat* exchanges.

To summarise the relation between *blat* and other related practices presented in Tables 1–3, *blat* should be viewed as:

(1) less morally reprehensible and therefore more pervasive than any of these other practices;
(2) a specific form of social relationship embedded in personal (horizontal, non-hierarchical, humane and warm) networks;

(3) a culturally grounded pattern of mentality and behaviour, a form of exchange based upon certain ethical and cultural codes;
(4) an attribute of the Soviet system and it therefore cannot be understood apart from such characteristics of the latter, as shortages and the state system of distribution.

Lacking space here to consider an even more extended family of *blat*, that is, its 'relatives in the West', such informal practices as 'patronage' in Italy, 'pilfering', 'fiddling' and 'old-boy' networks in England, 'skimming' or 'gypping' in the USA, '*le travail noire*' and '*le piston*' in France, let us move on to examine the third aspect of the conceptualising of *blat*: why was such a pervasive phenomenon left unanalysed?

MISRECOGNITION OF *BLAT*

In this section it will be argued that it is the misrecognised character of *blat* that accounts for the pervasiveness of *blat*, on the one hand, and the lack of attention to it, on the other. A conceptual idea of 'misrecognition' first formulated by Pierre Bourdieu in his critique of economic or objectivist explanations of gift exchange, helps to clarify this point. According to his account, though objectivist explanations uncover the underlying structure of strictly enforced equivalent exchange present in every act of voluntary gift-giving, they miss the fact that:

'gift exchange is one of the social games that cannot be played unless the players refuse to acknowledge the objective truth of the game, the very truth that objective analysis brings to light, and unless they are predisposed to contribute,

Table 3: *Differences and similarities between* blat *and informal economic practices*

Differences	Similarities
1. Runs counter to the law.	1. Both are non-regulated activities.
2. A regular activity for the production of income.	2. Use of access to state property and public resources.
3. Based on economic exchange (rather than ties of reciprocity) and implies a 'market' for such exchanges (rather than networks).	3. Both practices are functional in some ways and subversive in others.

with their efforts, their marks of care and attention, and their time, to the production of collective *misrecognition*.[29]

In other words, gift-giving should be seen as such, not only by gift-givers, but by the rest of the community as well. Otherwise, it is not gift-giving any more. In case of *blat*, misrecognition is not collective in the same sense. As in gift exchange, misrecognition of *blat* is normal for the participants, who can practise *blat* only if they recognise it as 'helping-out'. From the perspective of an observer, the deal is recognised as *blat*. Perpetual switching of perspectives enables one to engage in *blat* practices and at the same time to distance oneself from them.

The complexity of the *blat* 'misrecognition game' cannot be fully grasped by Bourdieu's concept of misrecognition, where even being outside of the gift exchange transaction, a member of community would admit that it is a gift that has been given. As not all individuals accept the internal rhetoric of *blat* relations, the misrecognition game is incomplete. The fact that people could question *blat* and recognise it indicates that this does not endanger the foundation of community, that is there was no universally shared sense of 'honour' involved in *blat*.

Attitudes to *blat* varied a lot. The practical implications and strategies of misrecognition were dependent upon the situation (type of need, social context and outcome), personal dispositions, social background and occupation of the actor, as well as broader social and political contexts. To analyse these multiple possibilities the notion of misrecognition has to be further elaborated. Misrecognition of *blat* should be understood as a phenomenon (with reference to different strategies of misrecognition) bound with a system of denial, a system of ambivalence and a system of power.

Misrecognition as a system of denial

The system of denial is based on a contradiction between what one sees in other people as an observer and in oneself as a participant. Some respondents were quite straightforward, saying basically 'if *I* do it, it is not *blat*'. The negative character of the term '*blat*' facilitated its denial even if the fact of providing or receiving a favour was accepted: 'In my environment this word is a bit critical. If we do a favour, we do not call it *blat*'; 'I can't do

anything by *blat*. If I do something, it is not by *blat*.' In this sense, *blat* is like 'gift-giving' where a 'gift' is recognised to be reciprocal, with a difference that in recognition of the reciprocal nature, 'gift' is deprived of its positive charge while '*blat*' retains its negative meaning. The negative character of the term introduces a new element in the misrecognition game: it can be recognised in the case of the other, and misrecognised in one's own case. *Blat* communities suppress the use of '*blat*' and prefer the 'we are friends' terminology. They cannot stop outsiders, however, from noticing '*blat* ties'. Involvement in *blat* relations thus determines whether the case is presented in participant's, personal and subtle, terms or labelled bluntly as *blat*. In general, it can be put like that — when one speaks of others — *blat* is a kind of bad, whereas in one's own case — it's never like *blat*.

Many people were inhibited from identifying things they did or were forced to do by *blat*, for it could have disturbed their self-perception as honest and respectable people, damaged their self-esteem or presented their personal relations in the wrong light. They claimed that there is something negative in *blat* that is incompatible with personal relations. Implying that *blat* is an equivalent exchange, motivated by expectation of return favour, people counterpoised *blat* relations to relations of friendship or kinship in which a return favour was considered unacceptable. In so doing they again distanced themselves from *blat*. Favour exchanges, however, are never equivalent and their performance demands the same kind of misrecognition game, that is, denial of the motives of reciprocity, as in gift exchange. Given that under Soviet conditions the routine use of friends for extracting services was justified by the necessity 'to help' or 'to be helped', the difference between friendly and *blat* relations became blurred.

The interviews showed that retrospectively some people were able to consider their relations in terms of reciprocity and return favours, or recognised the underlying cynicism of their 'help discourse' when relationships broke down and the other party refused to give a reciprocal favour or signs of indebtedness, gratitude, loyalty, etc. While actually practising *blat*, however, people cannot discursively admit that they seek a special good or service in exchange for something else, but rather grant or appeal for help and support. Otherwise, the one who controls a good or service in demand would be embarrassed to provide it. The discursive forms such as *'sochtyomsya'* (deriving from *schitat'sya* (to count), meaning both financial counting, of mutual favours and claims and also recognising significance with regard and appreciation) or *'Ya v dolgu ne ostanus''* (I won't stay in debt) still imply the continuity of the relationship rather than an immediate pay-off terminating it. The tactics and etiquette, the practical skills of making an offer without saying it, of promising a return without mentioning it, concealing the expectations if they are available, were shaped by the rules of this 'misrecognition game'.

Misrecognition as a system of ambivalence

The reverse side of denial of one's own participation in *blat* was blaming others. Negative attitudes in relation to *blat* expressed in the interviews were always focused either on some particular groups (mainly 'cadres' and tradespeople), unworthy people or unjust cases. 'There is no *blat* in our circle. It is a prerogative of powerful people, directos, chief accountants, those who can turn decisions for their own benefits. At our level, it is not *blat*, it is minor', said a housewife, now a 'shuttle-trader'. Talking about 'cadres' and administrators caused a great deal of resentment.

'*Blat* is not simply a protection or recommendation in general, but a recommendation for a complete idiot, that is, a fully incompetent person. It is a promotion of someone incapable, with no faculties at all or inferior in comparison to the other candidate whose only problem is lack of *blat*',

said a former waiter, now in business. 'It is disgusting when one supports somebody unworthy. It is not help, it is pushing him through. Pushing despite all rules', commented a worker. His wife went on blaming the high-ups: 'When we got robbed, everybody in the block began to install security metal doors. Our neighbour, the head of some personnel department, brought some soldiers and they made him a door in one day, clearly at public expense.' In all these cases, the fact of using public positions or resources for private goals was recognised and related to those in power.

Pushing one's own interests over those of others — as 'recognised' *blat* was often defined — gave

the term *'blat'* its negative meaning. This was not only because of a zeal for justice or because of personal resentment by the deprived, but also because in Russian tradition, as well as in Soviet official ideology, a preoccupation with everyday life for its own sake was considered unpatriotic and subversive. Such negative attitudes were often a reaction of resentful people, unwilling to make, or incapable of making, contacts.

'We do not use *blat*, but can watch others regularly. There is a superstore downstairs with its back door right in front of our windows. We can see cars and people approaching and leaving with huge bags. It was especially bitter in 1991, the hardest time, when we had nothing to feed our children while they went off with full bags. It is clear who they were: either *blat*-people, or tradespeople, or swindlers. For us, it's all the same though,'

remarked the same worker. The ambivalence of the attitudes towards *blat* was embedded in the ambivalence of the Soviet distribution system, in which the official ideology of equality came into contradiction with reality. This was acutely grasped by one respondent,

'I would not say people are negative. To be honest, *blat* causes bitterness only in those who do not use *blat*. But there is always a level, at which they do use it [misrecognising this]. The problem is caused by the dissociation of levels in obtaining particular material goods. It is not the negative attitude towards the phenomenon itself. It is not, however, clear whether *blat* is good or bad.'

Another respondent stressed the same point in speaking of relative deprivation as the main reason for blaming others:

'some people occupy better apartments, drive better cars, everything because of their acquaintances, while we work, work all our life and have nothing. What kind of attitude, then, do you expect us to have towards *blat*?'

The strategies of misrecognition of those who felt less deprived often stemmed from considerations about the efficiency or rationality of acts which allegedly improved the formal procedure. Even though *blat* results in a breach of some formal procedure, it does not necessarily subvert the formal targets, able people can be supported and promoted. Moral approval of what was received or given through informal channels derived from the discourse of justice and merit. The latter did not exclude the former, but an emphasis on the one side and repression of the other is a typical strategy of misrecognition:

'It depends on how you look at it. How did I change my job? First I became friendly with the boss (we are neighbours in a garage cooperative) and then he invited me. He invited me because he knew I was a qualified worker and worked hard. This was important, because it strengthened the situation morally both for him and for me. But for others it could have of course looked like *blat*.'

Another worker commented on a similar situation,

'I don't consider as *blat* the fact that my aunt helped my wife to get a job of book-keeper. Accountancy was not her profession, but she was educated, had a diploma, she could count. She was in her place, worked well. Those who come in by *blat* do not work, they just receive money.'

Ambiguity in recognition of *blat* overlaps with mechanisms of social control exercised over a person who has got what he was not worthy of getting. A recommendation for an appropriate person was not included in the everyday meaning of *blat*. To get a job by *blat* meant that one was not suitable, did not deserve it and got it for a return favour. 'If a good-for-nothing man got promoted, the case qualified as *blat*', an academic remarked. Two stages are thus to be distinguished here. In the first, speaking objectively, a job is arranged by *blat*, but people decide whether it was *blat* or a support for a good specialist retrospectively, on the basis of their subsequent experiences. It also happened repeatedly that despite the generally negative first reaction to the term '*blat*' and all forms of misrecognition strategies, by the end of the interview people provided examples, jokes and autobiographical details showing a great deal of practical competence.

Misrecognition as a system of power

In the case of *blat* there is no universally-shared code of 'honour' as in gift-giving. Rather *blat* became a counter-ideology of the Soviet system which nobody was supposed to follow, but could practice according to the rules of the 'misrecognition game'. Millar suggests that 'the Brezhnev regime contracted a deal with the Soviet population, especially with the urban population, tacitly agreeing to overlook an expansion throughout Soviet society of the quest for the individual's, but especially for the individual's household's, gain — as opposed to collectivist and traditional socialist aims', a so-called 'Little Deal'.[30] The metaphor of 'deal', however, is inappropriate, for the alliance of group (household, family, friends, acquaintances) and collective interests did not necessarily imply a compromise of beliefs. Nor can the question, 'how is it possible to be a good Communist and engage in *blat* practices?' be solved by the concept of 'double morality'. The Soviet system is often characterised as engendering a morality of its own, endowed with two ethical scales in everyday life: one of official ideology and one of human sets of values which governed relations between people. It is not the case, however, that one was generally adhered to and the other not, rather it was a complicated mixture which was intrinsic to being a Soviet citizen. In other words, the distinction is an analytical one; in practice people do not 'compromise', they follow the logic implied in concrete situations with reference to both scales of values. It would not be correct to say that personal relations were generally valued more than loyalty to the state, but somehow being a decent citizen and a Communist was not incompatible with rule-breaking.[31]

The metaphor of a 'deal' suggests that there was a 'tacit agreement' between the authorities and the population about the combination of formal and informal criteria which legitimised *blat* within certain determined limits: *infrequent transactions conducted in modest volume, with discretion, normally in situations of urgent need and within a closed personal circle*. *Blat* was deemed illegitimate by both the system and the people. It annoyed the authorities because it violated the state system of distribution, and it irked the people because of the inequality behind the façade of equality. In effect, *blat* practices were not accepted, but connived at in this double denial. They received a 'negative' legitimacy from the combination of the strategies of misrecognition, in other words, the 'overt disagreement' and denial of *blat* on both societal and individual level.

On the societal level, for ideological reasons, *blat* could not have been recognised by the state as an attribute of the Soviet system. Rather, *blat* was either left unnoticed (unspoken in official discourse) or subject to a limited, usually satirical, critique. It was criticised as an anti-Soviet phenomenon deriving from the moral perversion of some individuals (*'koe-kto u nas eshchyo poroi'*). Its origins were never related to the system itself; the shortcomings were always reported as *'otdel'nye'* (literally translated as 'separate' — meaning individual, unattached, non-systematic). Such incompatible-with-socialism phenomena were attacked in a sequence of critical campaigns in the press.[32] The critique of these phenomena was however doomed to fail in Soviet conditions, for it was limited and censored. Power institutions could not eliminate what in effect supported them and what they were coupled with; yet, in terms of the rules of the 'misrecognition game', the critique was sincere. The inability to recognise that *blat* was rooted in the institutions of power led to a situation where the success of a campaign was judged by the detection and punishment of scapegoats while the phenomenon as such remained untouched. The words *'blat'* or 'connections' were excluded from official discourse thereby automatically withdrawing them from research and analysis; they were left to satirical periodicals, such as *Krokodil*.

Individuals sheltered themselves from 'noticing' their own involvement in *blat* as indeed did the system. People used similar strategies: negating, criticising, laughing at *blat*. These strategies were sincere, for unless these criticisms were considered important, taken seriously and followed, it would not be possible to manipulate them for personal advantage. On the other hand, the logic of life took over, despite verbal disapproval and estrangement, people were forced to use connections. Personal excuses for the involvement with *blat* normally referred to the structural conditions, such as shortages, inefficiency of institutions and bureaucratic procedures etc whereas at the societal level shortcomings of the system were explained by inefficiency of some 'immoral' individuals.

These practices were not based on any conscious compromise or discursive agreement. Rather, they

implied a niche of practices exercised in misrecognised form. The objective necessity of redistribution and rule-breaking for the system to function and for the people to survive thus resulted in a specific form of 'negative' legitimacy. Such legitimacy resulted from both criticism and, in misrecognised form, performance of *blat* and other ambiguous practices of the Soviet system. Some of these are grasped in six paradoxes of socialism noted in the well-known Soviet anecdote:

'No unemployment but nobody works.
Nobody works but productivity increases.
Productivity increases but shops are empty.
Shops are empty but fridges are full.
Fridges are full but nobody is satisfied.
Nobody is satisfied but all vote unanimously.'

Therefore, roots of *blat* can be found in the nature of its legitimacy, negative legitimacy, ensuing from the 'misrecognition game' on the societal level. The latter also explains why the role of *blat* in the Soviet system was understated and unexplored.

CONCLUSION

Although it has not been directly discussed until now, *blat* was quite fundamental to the day-to-day working of Soviet society. *Blat* stood in a paradoxical relation to the Soviet social and economic order. Quite literally, the system could not have functioned without it: *blat* was the prime way of getting things done in a non-market society in which money counted for rather little. At the same time as it was the condition for continuation of the Soviet order, *blat* also subverted it. It ran counter to official ideology and meant that centralised control of economic life was routinely undermined and placed in question.

Blat was, and continues to be, the 'normal' way of getting things done when reliance on people was much more important than reliance on money and formalities. The Soviet interpretation of the proverb, 'Have a hundred friends, not a hundred roubles', indicating the importance of bartering favours and access which friends provide, gives an illustration of this outlook. The data provided in the article largely relate to the Soviet past, but their analysis shows that we cannot understand the nature of the ongoing economic and political changes in Russia unless we see how distinctive *blat* was, as a feature specifically of a socialist non-monetary 'economy of favours', and how definitive its influence remains in the post-socialist monetary economy.

Blat stands now as one among other available possibilities for influencing decision making and obtaining access to all kinds of resources, but in many contexts retains its importance. Of course, many goods and services which could formerly have only been obtained through *blat* are now acquired by the use of money. Market mechanisms have to some extent replaced *blat* transactions to do with everyday consumption. But *blat* is proving to be both durable and, surprisingly, to some extent functional for the emergence of market mechanisms. Just as *blat* had an ambivalent relation to the old Soviet economy, perhaps it has also to the new market system. In some ways the continued existence of *blat* is a barrier to the generalising of a money economy, because *blat* was and still is a non-monetary way of doing things. Recent discussions of Western economies have stressed that, in a fluid, electronic, globalised age, 'networking' starts to replace more hierarchical structures in business and elsewhere. Networks are precisely at the core of *blat* transactions. It is thus possible that what from one point of view looks like a wholly archaic set of practices might actually be directly relevant to a market-oriented post-socialist economy.

REFERENCES

(1) Berliner, J. S. (1957) 'Factory and Manager in the USSR', Harvard University Press, Cambridge; Crankshaw, E. (1956) 'Russia Without Stalin', Michael Joseph, London; Dallin, D. J. (1951) 'The New Soviet Empire', Hollis and Carter, London.

(2) Berliner, *ibid*. p. 187.

(3) According to dictionaries of etymology (Shansky, N. M. (1965) 'Etymologicheskii slovar' russkogo yazyka', 2 vols, Moscow; Vasmer, M. (1964) 'Etymologichesky slovar' russkogo yazyka'. Pod red. Larina, 4 vols, Moscow) the term '*blat*' came into Russian from Polish '*blat*', meaning 'someone who provides an umbrella, a cover' (*ukryvatel*), which in turn is taken from Jewish '*blat*' which means 'close, familiar' (*svoi*). In its original meaning, in phrasing '*Svoi? Stuchish' po blatu?*' meaning 'Are you one of us? Do you speak our *blat* jargon?', it was already used in the beginning of the century. *Svoi* is a pronoun but in such contexts it became used like an adjective and noun. It was used as a label to signify the belonging to *blatnoi mir* (*blat* world), and was also adopted by modern Russian language as synonymous to *blastnoi* in its second meaning. Like much other jargon, the term '*blat*' probably was coined in

Odessa — Russia's southern port, known as the leading conduit for linguistic imports. See Polivanov A. (1931) 'O slavyanskom slovoobrazovanii', Moscow, p. 154.

(4) 'Slovar' russkogo literaturnogo yazyka' (Dictionary of Russian Literary Language) (1950) Vol. 2, Moscow.

(5) Ushakov, D. N. (ed.) (1935) 'Tolkovyi slovar' russkogo yazyka' (Interpretative Dictionary of the Russian Language) OGIZ.

(6) Wittgenstein, L. (1969) 'Philosophische Grammatik', Basil Blackwell, London, pp. 75, 118.

(7) Wittgenstein, L. (1958) 'The Blue and Brown Books', Basil Blackwell, London.

(8) *Ibid*. 'Blue Book', pp. 87, 124; Pt 2, p. 67.

(9) Dovlatov, S. (1993) 'Sobranie prozy', Vol. 2, Limbus Press, Saint Petersburg, p. 79.

(10) Whereas Gregory counterpoises gift and commodity as a binary pair, Sahlins places them at the opposite ends of a scale: from the positive altruism of what he confusingly calls 'generated reciprocity' to the 'unsociable extreme' of 'negative reciprocity'. According to Sahlins, reciprocity is 'not a single relation between incomings and outgoings, but a "continuum", a "spectrum", ranging from the pure gift ... to barter and theft which are each an attempt to get something for nothing with impunity. In between are those balanced reciprocities in which social conventions stipulate returns of commensurate worth or utility within a finite and a narrow period.' Sahlins (1972) 'Stone Age Economics', NY & Chicago, IL., pp. 185–196. See also Davis, J. (1992) 'Exchange', Open University Press, Buckingham.

(11) Gregory, C. A. (1982) 'Gifts and Commodities', Academic Press, London.

(12) Yang, M. M. (1994) 'Gifts, Favours and Banquets: The Art of Social Relationships in China', Cornell University Press, Ithaca and London.

(13) Wedel, J. (1986) 'The Private Poland', Facts on File Publications, New York, Oxford.

(14) Wittgenstein, ref. 6, pp. 75, 118.

(15) Wittgenstein, L. (1953) 'Philosophical Investigations', Basil Blackwell, London, ss. 66, 67.

(16) Berliner, ref. 1, p. 191.

(17) 'The Concise Oxford Dictionary' (1982) 7th edn, Clarendon Press, Oxford.

(18) Crankshaw, ref. 1, p. 74.

(19) Palmier, L. (1983) 'Bureaucratic Corruption and its Remedies' in M. Clarke (ed) 'Corruption: Causes, Consequences and Control', Frances Pinter, London.

(20) Friedrich, C. J. (1966) 'Political Pathology', *The Political Quarterly*, Vol. 37, No. 1, pp. 74–75.

(21) Lampert, N. (1984) 'Law and Order in the USSR: The Case of Economic and Official Crime', *Soviet Studies*, Vol. 36, No. 3, p. 371.

(22) Scott, J. C. (1972) 'Comparative Political Corruption', Prentice Hall, Englewood Cliffs, NJ.

(23) Lampert, ref. 21, p. 370.

(24) Palmier, ref. 19, p. 208.

(25) *Homosos* is an abbreviation for Homo Sovieticus, a stereotypical Soviet person, outlined in the novel 'Homo Sovieticus'.

(26) Grossman, G. (1977) 'The Second Economy of the USSR', *The Problems of Communism*, Vol. 26, No. 5, p. 25.

(27) Gabor, I. R. (1979) 'The Second (Secondary) Economy', *Acta Oeconomica*, Vol. 22, No. 3–4, pp. 292–293.

(28) Feldbrugge, F. J. M. (1989) 'The Second Economy in a Political and Legal Perspective' in E. L. Feige (ed) 'The Underground Economies: Tax Evasion and Information Distortion', Cambridge University Press, Cambridge, p. 305, quoting Wiles.

(29) Bourdieu, P. (1990) 'The Logic of Practice', translated by Richard Nice, Polity Press, Cambridge, p. 105.

(30) Millar, J. R. (1988) 'The Little Deal: Brezhnev's Contribution to Acquisitive Socialism' in T. L. Thompson and R. Sheldon (eds) 'Soviet Society and Culture: Essays in Honour of Vera S. Dunham', Westview Press, CT, p. 15. The metaphor refers to Vera Dunham's analysis of the 'Big Deal' in the period from the end of the war to Stalin's death (Dunham, V. (1976) 'In Stalin's Time', Cambridge University Press, Cambridge, pp. 3–5). The Big Deal represented a dilution of the idealistic, egalitarian goals of Marxist socialism by means of a tacit accommodation in practice to the materialistic, self-regarding behaviour of the New Soviet middle class.

(31) Zinoviev remarked in *Homo Sovieticus* that all his efforts to explain the essence of the Party and its position in Soviet society, what it meant to be a member, and the relationship between ideology and morality in Soviet society were a total failure in the West. 'Everything would have been clear to them if I had said that I joined the CPSU for career reasons. But I never made a career and never tried to. Party membership did not hinder me in any way. On the contrary, it made life a bit more interesting. And there was no "double-think" about it. In general, "double-think" is an invention of Westerners who don't understand anything about the Soviet way of life or Soviet people. I'm a Communist not in the sense that I believe in Marxist fairy-tales (very few people in the Soviet Union believe in them), but in the sense that I was born, reared and educated in a Communist society and have all the essential characteristics of Soviet man. I mentioned casually that business people come in wearing ties and jackets, although it is hot outside. Why did they do this? For career reasons?' (Zinoviev, ref. 26, p. 63.)

(32) Campaigns against *semeistvennost'* (nepotism), *kumovstvo* (relationship of godparents), *zemlyachestvo* (association of people of the same origins, places, background, experience) etc are pervasive in the periodical *Krokodil* starting in the 1920s and throughout the 1930s in particular.

FURTHER READING

Giddens, A. (1984) 'The Constitution of Society: Outline of the Theory of Structuration', Polity Press, Cambridge.

'Istoriya SSSR v Anekdotakh: 1917–1991' (1991) Everest, Riga.

Ledeneva, A. (1998) 'Russia's Economy of Favours: *Blat*, Networking and Informal Exchange', Cambridge University Press, Cambridge.

Simis, K. M. (1982) 'USSR: Secrets of a Corrupt Society', Dent, London.

Alena V. Ledeneva, University of Cambridge.

This paper was originally published in Soziale Welt, *1997*

[18]

EUROPE-ASIA STUDIES, Vol. 51, No. 5, 1999, 741–754

Violent Entrepreneurship in Post-Communist Russia

VADIM VOLKOV

THIS ARTICLE IS ABOUT THE ROLE of organised violence in the process of market building and state building in Russia. But instead of offering yet another review of the notorious Russian organised crime I will analyse institutions and practices of violent entrepreneurship, criminal as well as legal. Violent entrepreneurship can be defined as a set of organisational decisions and action strategies enabling the conversion of organised force (or organised violence) into money or other market resources on a permanent basis. If consumer goods, for example, constitute the major resource for trade entrepreneurship, money for financial entrepreneurship, information and knowledge for informational entrepreneurship, and so forth, violent entrepreneurship is constituted by socially organised violence, real or potential. Violent entrepreneurship, however, is different in one important respect: throughout modern history, organised violence, unlike other resources, has been managed and controlled by the state alone, that is by public rather than private authority and used for public rather than private ends. That is why with the rise of modern centralised states this key resource has been largely excluded from the sphere of private entrepreneurship. In today's Russia it is back again: I intend to demonstrate that what from the macro perspective appears as the crisis of the state takes in everyday practice the form of violent entrepreneurship.

The main unit of violent entrepreneurship we shall call the 'violent entrepreneurial agency'. In post-communist Russia such agencies can be initially classified into three types: state and illegal (units of state police and security forces acting as private entrepreneurs); non-state (private) and legal (private protection companies); and private and illegal (organised criminal or bandit groups). These should be seen as ideal types, the boundaries between which in real life are blurred. Despite the differences in their legal status, violent entrepreneurial agencies perform similar functions and display similar patterns of action on the economic market. This derives from the specificity of their major resource—organised force. Their main function we shall define as 'enforcement partnership' (*silovoe partnerstvo*), the term which was used by one of my respondents to describe the practice of his criminal group and which conveniently lends itself as an analytical category. Enforcement partnership is a business function of an organised group or enterprise deriving from the skilful use of actual or potential force on a commercial basis, employed to maintain certain institutional conditions of business activities, such as security, contract enforcement, dispute settlement and transaction insurance.[1]

0966-8136/99/050741-14 © 1999 University of Glasgow

VADIM VOLKOV

The institution of enforcement partnership

The institution of enforcement partnership of the 1990s grew out of the regularised protection racket of the late 1980s which, in turn, goes back to the practice of extortion in the Soviet shadow economy. Nonetheless, protection racket should be analytically distinguished from mere extortion: the latter lacks regularity, reference to a broader organisation in the name of which the money is collected, and the claim to offer real or imaginary services in return. The surfacing of extortion and its conversion into a regular observable pattern of protection racket occurred in 1987–88 as the co-operative movement, the first effect of the economic liberalisation, gained momentum. Initially, co-operators and petty traders became victims of those extortionists who were formerly engaged in cards debts recovery and shadow business protection. Very soon new groups composed of former sportsmen emerged on the scene and began to earn money by selling protection to small entrepreneurs and traders at city markets.[2] Official statistics registered a 30% increase in racketeering offences between 1987 and 1988. The scale of the phenomenon in question was no doubt much wider than its reflection in statistical accounts: according to expert estimates only every fourth victim appealed to the police organs; the police reacted only in 80% of cases; only every sixth racketeer faced criminal charges; and only every eleventh served a sentence in prison, while the prison term for this kind of offence was rather soft, with a maximum of three years.[3]

What stimulated the spread of protection racket? Because a substantial part of the assets of the first private entrepreneurs originated from illegal shadow dealings in the Soviet era, they were naturally unwilling to have any relations with the state police. The state police, in turn, generally did not regard *kooperatory* as legitimate objects of protection—not least because of the negative Soviet moral attitudes towards private entrepreneurs—thus leaving an empty niche for alternative informal groups forcefully offering protection services.

Apart from insufficient protection of private business by the state police, another major factor that produced demand for enforcement partnership was high entrepreneurial risk caused by frequent non-repayment of debts and failure to observe contracts, not to mention the spread of swindling and theft.[4] The state organs were incapable of reducing these risks because of the poor definition of property rights, the inefficiency of the state courts of justice (*gosarbitrazh*) in resolving disputes and their incapacity to enforce decisions.[5] The combination of high risks and the shortage of protection and justice created institutional demand for enforcement partners, a kind of business mediators who could ensure the smooth functioning of private business.

In contemporary Russian business vocabulary the functions of enforcement partnership are referred to by the modest phrase 'to solve questions' (*reshat' voprosy*). What does it involve? The first racketeer groups were mainly engaged in physical protection from other such groups and debt recovery (*smotreli chtoby ne naezzhali i ne kidali*). As private entrepreneurship developed and the intensity of transactions increased, the functions of enforcement partners diversified. They actively participated in business talks, giving informal guarantees of transactions and demanding such from other enforcement partners involved in the deal. These tasks were performed either by organised criminal groups or state police and security employees acting on an

VIOLENT ENTREPRENEURSHIP IN RUSSIA 743

informal basis. Expert and interview sources indicate that even today the majority of high-value business agreements can only be concluded given the participation and mutual guarantees of enforcement partners. Apart from security, risk control, debt recovery, and dispute settlement, enforcement partners also came to mediate relations between private business and the state bureaucracy, helping to obtain permissions and licences, registration, tax exemptions, as well as using the state organs (police, fire inspection, sanitary control services, and the like) to impose damage on the companies of their competitors.

The evolution of patterns of enforcement partnership is described by the partici-pants by three terms: 'to get' (*poluchat'*), 'to control' (*kontrolirovat'*) and 'to hold a share' (*byt' v dole*). A brigade of racketeers 'gets' (the tribute in cash) from a business in return for protection from other such brigades. A criminal group 'controls' a business enterprise when in addition to physical protection it introduces its own book-keeper or regular auditor to this enterprise, who supplies information about business transactions and their value, while the group supervises and secures major contacts and transactions for a fixed share of profits. At this stage the group can be said to turn from racket to enforcement partnership. When a group of violent entrepreneurs that 'solves questions' for a business enterprise invests its money in this enterprise and introduces its representative on to the board of directors, it becomes a shareholder and increases its share of income. If at the earlier stage enforcement partners preferred one-time big gains achieved by active intimidation and violence, the increasing competition between them and their aspiration to control the business produced incentives for creating a more favourable environment for and sustained relations with the clients to achieve longer-term gains.

The institution of enforcement partnership rests on the power of deterrence—the capacity to use force and cause physical damage to those who cause financial or other losses to the businessman the criminal group claims to protect. Thus the value of force is determined in proportion to the value of the potential damage—financial, material or otherwise—that may be caused in the absence of protection. But later, if and when enforcement partners get involved in business transactions on a permanent basis and, consequently, turn from episodic damage and risk control to a broader set of tasks of securing and expanding the field of business activity of a given firm, it is the business skills of, as it were, non-violent use of force that become the source of value rather than force as such. No fixed price list for enforcement partners' services ever existed—the price varied depending upon the evaluation of risks, the income of the particular firm, the duration and nature of its relations with the enforcement partner and the latter's reputation. But the average price of 'question solving' by a criminal group has become established at the level of 20–30% of the profit of the client enterprise. When the group holds a share, it claims up to 50% of the profit. The price of debt recovery stabilised at the level of 50% of the sum recovered.[6]

For the client enterprise these payments constitute transaction costs. Transaction costs are the costs required to transfer and secure property rights, gain access to resources, and maintain business relations.[7] They refer to institutional conditions of business activity in the market economy and include costs of making an exchange, such as discovering exchange opportunities, negotiating, monitoring and enforcing exchange relations, and costs of maintaining a judiciary and police apparatus that

744   VADIM VOLKOV

protects institutional structures of economic exchange. A large number of small and medium-size firms ended up under the control of criminal groups either because of the shadow nature of their own economic activities or because they yielded to the intimidation tactics of criminal groups. In most cases, however, criminal groups were simply more efficient than the state organs in solving day-to-day problems of the new Russian entrepreneurs. Because of a predatory tax system and inefficient state protection and arbitrage, the transaction costs incurred by using private rule-enforcers were lower that the costs of legal economic activity.[8]

Thieves and bandits

The legendary Soviet criminal underworld, the world of thieves (*vorovskoi mir*), has received a fair amount of scholarly attention.[9] Formed in labour camps and prisons in early Soviet times, the world of thieves became a powerful informal organisation that survived until the end of the Soviet system. Thieves observe a complex set of mores and prohibitions that regulate their relations with one another, with authorities and with outsiders. Prohibitions are particularly strong with reference to having a legitimate job and a family, co-operation with prison or any state authorities, the use of violence towards other thieves unless a collective decision is taken, and personal luxury. The central element of the world of thieves is the so-called *obshchak*, the communal fund which accumulates the money acquired by theft and other illegal methods. Having donated the money to the *obshchak*, the thief then receives from it his share, which makes his living. But the bulk of the *obshchak* is used to support those who are serving prison terms. The élite of this underworld consists of the so-called 'thieves-in-law' (*vory v zakone*), whose main function is *obshchak* management and exercise of criminal justice. Recent journalistic publications claim that the world of thieves has been challenged by a new type of criminal structure—the world of so-called 'bandits'.[10] Because of restricted space we shall not reproduce the journalistic descriptions but will turn straight to the interpretation of the differences between thieves and bandits from the standpoint of the socio-economic conception elaborated in this article.

Unlike bandits, thieves are not engaged in violent entrepreneurship. The thief's major task is to steal (in a broad sense) and avoid being caught. They do not produce anything and tend to keep a low profile unless in their own milieu. The bandit, on the contrary, considers himself a supplier of certain services—or at least makes such claims to his clients. His claim to being productive and his ability to affect business transactions derives from his capacity to apply and manage organised force. This capacity should be conspicuous, since it represents the group's major market resource and the source of income. Hence the elaborate system of external symbolic attributes (gold decorations, sport haircuts, leather jackets, etc.) and easily recognisable assertive style of behaviour. One would find it hard to identify thieves in urban public places, while bandits are easily recognisable. The thief's income comes from illegal secondary redistribution of property and consists of the private property of other citizens or state property appropriated by illegal means. The bandit aspires to receive a share of income of other entrepreneurs, which, as he claims, has been produced under his patronage or participation of the organised group that he represents. His income, therefore, derives from the redistribution of profit and takes the form of either profit share or tax. Being a type of entrepreneur, bandits seek regular income on the basis of a long-term business relationship and often claim to establish and enforce order, which is why they can sometimes come into direct conflict with thieves, for instance, when forcing them out of city markets and night clubs.

The ethic of thieves is a projection of values and rules of prison life into civic ('free') life. Prison and labour camp terms are the major source of thieves' authority, respect and career advancement to the highest title of thief-in-law. The bandits' mores were formed in the domain of civic life, they are more rational and practical, containing less prohibitions and constraints. The bandit's reputation and his rise to the élite position of *avtoritet* (authority) is built on precedents of vigorous and successful use or management of violence; of central importance is the combination of skilful use of force and organisational skills. Unlike thieves, many bandit groups ban alcohol and drugs. Instead they cultivate a healthy life-style, strict discipline, and physical fitness maintained in specially rented gyms which serve as one of the permanent meeting grounds of the group. If the system of thieves' values and mores ensured their capacity for group survival in the severe repressive conditions of the Soviet labour camps, the value system of the bandits is functionally subjected to the reproduction of the group's capacity to participate in the economic life of society as violent entrepreneurs. Thus, if the world of thieves is a product of the strong repressive state, the world of bandits emerges out of illegal use of violence in conditions of the weak state.

The above characteristics are more like ideal types that in real life can display deviations and intermixing. In practice, the traditional values and rules of thieves have been undergoing change, adapting to the new post-socialist realities and adopting some features of economic rationality instead of the somewhat parochial values of the criminal sub-culture. The traditional thieves' sub-culture seems to have been evolving together with the Soviet system that once shaped it. No doubt the actual practice of both thieves and bandits is too varied to reduce to a finite set of rules and principles, but we need to accentuate the differences in order to articulate the main structural principle of the so-called 'bandits', their being violent entrepreneurs. This brief interpretative exercise also helps us to define analytically the genetic principle of this new type of criminal business specifically connected with Russia's transition to the market and to distinguish it from more traditional types of criminality, such as theft and illegal (drugs, arms, etc.) trade.

Criminal groups

So what is usually referred to by the Russian police organs as an 'organised criminal group' (*organizovannaya prestupnaya gruppirovka*) can also be seen as an illegal violent entrepreneurial agency.[11] How did they initially form in Russia? Commonplace assertions about either territorial or ethnic formation principles should be treated with caution.[12] One should not infer from that that the criminal group is tied to the name-giving territory (e.g. Solntsevskaya gruppirovka, from Solntsevo, a Moscow suburb) or that it recruits its members on a strictly ethnic basis (e.g. the Chechens), although it is generally true that the name of the group originally refers to the type of ties that enabled initial trust between members and established their common identity. In Petersburg the first bandit-like groups called 'brigades' (*brigady*) grew from two types of primary ties: non-resident students' communes (*zemlyachestva*) and sport schools. The most influential Tambovskaya group was formed in the late 1980s by several students who came to receive higher education in then Leningrad institutes (including the Institute of Physical Culture) from the town of Tambov. Many of such non-resident communes from other cities (Murmansk, Vorkuta, Perm', Kazan') became centres of gravity for other sport-like violent young people willing to earn a living by the use of force. Thus emerged Murmanskie, Vorkutinskie, Permskie, Kazanskie and the like. Groups formed by Leningrad residents recruited local sportsmen (mainly boxers, weightlifters, wrestlers and the like) whose primary cohesion and trust had formed throughout their joint sport careers. Unlike the migrant brigades that used topographical labels, the names of the local ones derived either from the kind of sport (e.g. Bortsovskaya brigada, the wrestlers' brigade) or from the name of the leader—thus emerged Malyshevskie (from A. Malyshev) or Kudryashevskie (from P. Kudryashev).

Many groups have gradually lost their original direct connection with some obscure suburb, sport club, ethnicity or founding leader. Actually, the meaning of the criminal group's name is its practical usage. In the practice of violent entrepreneurship such names are used as trade marks.[13] The licence to use the trade mark practically means the right to introduce oneself as 'working with' such-and-such criminal group or with *avtoritet* X. Such a licence is supplied to a brigade or an individual member by the *avtoritet*, the leader of the group, normally after the candidates have been tested in action. For example, for the killing of the managing director of Petersburg northern airport, Rzhevka, one Andrei F. received $500 cash and the right to introduce himself as Murmanskii (i.e. belonging to the Murmanskaya organised criminal group).[14] The amount of cash may seem surprisingly low, but what really mattered in this particular case was the acquisition by the young bandit of the right to exploit the trade mark.

The name of the group has a specific function in the practice of violent entrepreneurship: it guarantees the 'quality' of protection and enforcement services and refers to the particular kind of reputation that is built from the known precedents of successful application of violence and 'question solving'. Because the functional necessity of the institution of enforcement partners derives from high entrepreneurial risks, the media stories about 'horrible' and 'omnipowerful' bandit groups only help to sustain the functional necessity of this institution and support the reputation of such groups. Before signing formal business contracts, companies acquire information about each other's enforcement partners ('whom do you work with?') and arrange a meeting between enforcement partners (*strelka*). Besides that, each of the participating sides would check whether the others really work with the group they claim to, and would seek additional information about the real power (reputation as well as actual firepower) of that group. The deal with all its formal juridical and business attributes will only be signed after the enforcement partners have recognised each other and given mutual guarantees. Likewise, a *strelka* will be immediately set up if one of the sides fails or refuses to fulfil its obligations. The outcome may be either a peaceful solution as to how the damage will be repaired or a violent

VIOLENT ENTREPRENEURSHIP IN RUSSIA 747

showdown (*razborka*). But in the long term *razborka* may be a more costly and less efficient solution, especially if it leads to protracted warfare that causes severe damage—primarily to the business firms controlled by the opponents.

The reputation of the enforcement partner, embodied in the name of the group or its leader, is crucial for avoiding possible cheats in business and acts of violence, since it carries a message of unavoidable retaliation. The licence to use the name to conduct violent entrepreneurship, i.e. to act as commercial enforcement partner, presupposes an informal contract between the leader and the unit (the brigade) that acts in his name. The contract includes the obligation to pay into the common fund and to follow certain rules. The group that has no licence from one of the established *avtoritety* will have little success in its business and will either be exterminated or sent to prison with the help of the police. The latter will be glad to use the occasion to its own advantage to report a successful operation against organised crime.

The reputation of the group enables entrepreneurship based on virtual rather than actual violence and thus a more efficient and stable practice of conversion of force into money value. It also allows the leader to collect a kind of rent from franchising his name to brigades for their day-to-day business. A reference to the name is a crucial part of the business and presupposes an introduction ritual: 'we are such-and-such' or 'we work with X'. The biggest name rental *avtoritet* in Petersburg was A. Malyshev, who managed to unite many smaller groups and brigades in 1991 into a powerful Malyshevskaya 'empire' whose members used his name in exchange for a share of their profits. At this stage, physical presence of the *avtoritet* becomes unnecessary. He can be abroad or in prison: the sign of force can function in the absence of its physical bearer.

The older the group and the higher its reputation embodied in its name, the more stable is the mechanism of rent and the less is the amount of actual violence required to perform the functions of enforcement partnership. The use value of the sign of force consists in its capacity to substitute for actual violence and thereby to increase the efficiency of violent entrepreneurship by reducing its costs and potential combat losses. This, in turn, can free investment resources and enable the transition from external control to shareholding and thus to more legal and 'civilised' entrepreneurship. The earlier mentioned Tambovskaya group, it seems, displays this pattern of transformation into a business enterprise: it now owns the major share of the Petersburg Fuel Company (Peterburgskaya toplivnaya kompaniya), which dominates the Petersburg and north-western Russian oil and petrol market.[15]

There is a good deal of confusion (or bias) in the statistics reflecting the degree of criminal control of the new Russian market economy. The most widely cited data are those provided by the Ministry of Internal Affairs (MVD) in January 1994 with reference to the estimates of the Russian Government Analytical Centre for Social and Economic Policies. It established that criminal gangs controlled or owned (the terms were not specified) 40 000 businesses including 2000 in the state sector. The majority of businesses (up to three-quarters) paid illegal protection money.[16] The Analytical Centre of the Academy of Sciences provided even more alarming data, stating that 55% of the capital and 80% of the voting shares of private enterprises had been transferred into the hands of criminal capital.[17] These and similar estimates inspired the authors of the US Center for Strategic Studies report on Russian organised crime to claim that 'roughly two-thirds of Russia's economy is under the sway of the crime syndicates'.[18]

Later and more sober analyses, such as the study of privatisation in Russia conducted by a group of scholars from the USA, established that these figures were inaccurate and unspecified: they were either exaggerations or in fact related to small business only. Thus, the 40 000 businesses referred to in 1994 were four times the number of medium-size and large enterprises that were privatised at that time and twice the number of large enterprises in existence.[19] 'Many big privatised firms are unprofitable, and even organised crime wants a risk-adjusted return', wrote the authors of the study. 'It is hard to imagine why organised crime would want to control weak firms that are cutting employees, reducing capacity, confronting serious cash flow problems, and struggling to supply the kindergartens, housing and hospitals their employees need'.[20] Surprisingly, at the end of 1997 the MVD provided data that almost replicated those for 1994: 40 000 economic subjects, including 1500 state enterprises, over 500 joint enterprises, and over 500 banks were said to be controlled by criminal groups.[21]

Understandably, any quantitative account of the criminal control of the economy is bound to be rather rough because of the lack of adequate accounting methods and reliable information. Sociological surveys of entrepreneurs seem to draw a more accurate picture. Thus, according to a study conducted in 1996–97, 11% of the entrepreneurs sampled admitted that they were inclined to use force as a method of problem solving; 42% had experienced the use of such methods; 53% admitted regular payments for protection services, of whom more that a third described the level of such payments as substantial.[22] Importantly, this does not imply that all protection money goes to criminal structures. Rather, it indicates the existence of alternative structures that provide the same services.

The legalisation of private protection

With the adoption of the Federal law 'On private detective and protection activity' on 11 March 1992 and of the 'Regulation on the extra-departmental protection (*vneve-domstvennaya okhrana*) of the Interior Ministry organs' on 14 August 1992 the former state security officers legally entered the private market for protection and enforcement services. Before that former KGB and MVD cadres, professionals in the use of violence, had been participating in providing such services illegally, on a par with criminal groups. It is with their involvement in the business of illegal private protection and dispute settlement that the term 'roof' (*krysha*) gained currency. Such terms as *komitetovskaya krysha* (KGB-provided roof), *mentovskaya krysha* (MVD-provided roof) and *banditskaya krysha* (roof provided by criminal bandit groups) entered the business vocabulary in 1991 to refer to a standard package of enforcement partnership services, depending upon the origin of the supplier. Even today expert sources estimate that up to 20% of FSB (former KGB) cadres are engaged in informal 'roof' business.[23]

The legalisation of protection business introduced a new agent to the Russian market—the private protection company. The policy of setting up private protection companies was a complex and perhaps well-calculated response to the difficulties of

VIOLENT ENTREPRENEURSHIP IN RUSSIA 749

the market transition. On the one hand, the criminal market for protection and enforcement services had by then taken shape, and the demand for such services was increasing owing to the rapid privatisation campaign and the development of financial institutions. On the other hand, there were a number of factors inside the state coercive institutions that produced such a response. First, the functional crisis of these structures and the moral pressure put on them by democratic public opinion, accusing them of being the foundation of the 'totalitarian' state, stimulated the dismissal of security professionals and their search for alternative employment. Second, the decline in central financial support for the state security and police forces created incentives to search for alternative, extra-budget sources of support. Third, the involvement of the state security forces in the structures of private protection was initially part of the effort to infiltrate the criminal business, the tactic known as 'control from within'. But later, operative goals conveniently coincided with financial interests, as the legal business of private protection started to grow. Thus, the privatisation of the state security forces through their involvement in violent entrepreneurship reflected the state crisis, but it may have also helped to discover new forms of state control of the private economy, more appropriate to the new market conditions.

By the end of 1997 Russia had 10200 registered private protection and detective agencies with 140 600 employees. In the city of Moscow and Moscow region over 30 000 people work in more than 1500 private security structures.[24] The city of Petersburg and Leningrad region have 765 private protection and detective companies with over 15 000 employed.[25] These figures give us the average of 14 employees per protection company for Russia overall and 19.6 and 20 for Petersburg and Moscow respectively. In fact large companies are few, less than 20, most of which are Moscow or Petersburg-based. Private protection companies are grouped according to the personnel numbers, annual turnover, and the number of protected 'objects'. The large ones are those having over 100 licensed armed guards, over $1 million turnover, and over 15 objects; the medium have 50 to 100 guards, $500 000 to 1 million turnover and five to 15 objects; and the small ones have under 50 guards, less than $500 000 turnover and less than five objects.[26] No unified statistical survey reflecting the structure and geographical distribution of private protection companies has been published so far. From the scanty data available one may assume that the number of such companies and their size are generally proportionate to the scale of business activity in the region. Thus, the city of Chelyabinsk has 150 private protection companies, the city of Novgorod between 50 and 60.[27] According to expert estimates, the highest growth rates of this type of business were achieved in 1993–94; by the end of 1996 the market had stabilised and further possibilities of extensive growth were exhausted.[28]

The legalisation of the business of private protection also gave additional opportunities to criminal groups. Many of them either created their own protection companies or hired personnel of the companies established by the police to do part of the job—the latter phenomenon is known as 'combined roofs'. In Petersburg, for example, one of the oldest and most prominent protection companies, Scorpion, was set up and headed by A. Efimov (nickname Fima), one of the *avtoritety* of the Tambovskaya criminal group, and actively used to draw police officers to perform the 'roof' functions. Scorpion was closed down by the authorities at the end of 1996; its director managed to escape but was tracked down in Ukraine and arrested a year later.[29] In Moscow, the guards of the special police unit Saturn protected one of the *avtoritety* of the Koptevskaya criminal group, V. Naumov (Naum), and his company Merando on the basis of a formal contract—until the successful assassination of Naumov by a rival group in January 1997.[30]

Private protection companies

The majority of senior staff of large private protection companies are former officers of the state coercive organs—KGB (FSB), MVD and the Army Intelligence Department (GRU) in the rough proportion of 50%, 25% and 25% respectively.[31] The first private protection company set up in 1991 in Moscow to help to draft new regulations for protection business was the detective bureau Alex. The former army intelligence colonel A. Markarov became its director. Alex strengthened its position after its guards joined the defence force of the White House, Boris El'tsin's residence during the August 1991 coup. But its first serious 'object' was the Moscow night club Night Flight, defending which (unlike the White House) Alex guards several times used their firearms. The following year the bureau extended its services to Petersburg, where it signed contacts with the five-star hotels Europe and Nevsky Palace and a number of joint companies.[32]

Large protection companies are in fact privatised segments of the state security and intelligence organs. In Petersburg, for instance, the firm Zashchita was created by the North-Western Anti-Organised Crime Unit and is considered to belong to the MVD, while the protection companies Tornado, Komkon and Northern Palmira are headed by former KGB-FSB officers and are, accordingly, the domain of this ministry. Though the companies are financially and organisationally separated from the state organs they have access to information and operative resources of the latter through personal connections and informal relations. Many directors of private protection companies openly admit the fact of 'mutually beneficial co-operation' and 'friendly ties' as well as financial aid to the public security sector by the private one.[33] The activity of private protection companies is formally supervised by the Department of Licences and Permissions of the MVD.

What do private protection companies do? Being a type of violent entrepreneurial agency, the private protection company provides the standard set of 'roof' services to other business agents and 'solves' their 'questions'—the phrase also frequently used by heads of MVD and KGB-backed companies even in published interviews. These are protection, contract enforcement, dispute settlement, debt recovery, information gathering, and sometimes organisational consultancy. For instance, in 1992 the protection enterprise Komkon successfully solved the question of a large debt recovery for the Petersburg branch of Sberbank Rossii, the biggest state commercial bank, and subsequently became its permanent enforcement partner.[34] The work in this field implies competition as well as co-operation with illegal enforcement partners, i.e. criminal structures. According to its director, Alex had a dispute with a Petersburg criminal group over a 'well-known company'. 'On the second day after we settled there they tried to intimidate us by phone. Then [we] set up a meeting (*strelka*). In the end [they] threw a grenade into our office. But things worked out well in the end, we did not abandon the object'.[35]

Since criminal groups were first to discover this entrepreneurial niche, they also laid down the basic rules and terms of the game, which every newcomer in the field had to take into account. As the head of the Department of Licences and Permissions of the Interior Ministry, Yu. Buryak, noted, 'the business of private protection is impossible without relations with criminal structures. I do not mind *strelki*, they were and they will be. But I am strongly against what is called *razborki*' (violent showdowns).[36] Because of the similarity of functions private protection companies in many ways resemble their criminal rivals. At the same time, the ex-KGB and MVD structures assert their difference in that their service is more reliable, predictable, and has a more competitive price. The charge for debt recovery varies between 15% and 40% of the debt.[37] The claim of a better quality of service rests on the professional experience of the personnel of large private protection companies who are able to use not only violence but also informational and analytical methods acquired during their career in state service. The major emphasis is said to lie not on direct physical protection or intimidation but on the preventive neutralisation of potential conflicts and threats. The vice-chairman of the security service of the Association of Russian Banks, A. Krylov, described the methods of legal enforcement partners thus: 'To recover the debt one does not need to resort to violent means—it is sufficient just to demonstrate that you have information that compromises the debtor and the channels for its dissemination'.[38]

The commercial success of the major protection companies derives from the conversion of the *reputation* of the KGB into a market resource, not only of its technical and information resources. These companies assertively advertise their links with the state security structures, increase the value of their trade marks by siding with the state organs and pay them formal as well as informal fees. In search of new opportunities for marketing the professional analytical skills of the intelligence service, private protection companies set up investment and organisational consultancy divisions. Since both criminal structures and legal protection companies are not only force-managing agencies but also in the long run are subject to the logic of economic action, both undergo a transformation into more civilised business enterprises with complex structures. The staff of both is divided into rank-and-file fighters (either former sportsmen or special task force combatants) and upper-layer managers who style themselves as business elite.

Violent entrepreneurship and the state

Economic historians and sociologists have studied the use of violence and the role of states in the development of capitalism.[39] Against the background of this knowledge Russia's present experience becomes much less exceptional. Historically, before markets started to grow, territorial monopolies of force had been established as a result of continuous warfare. Max Weber's classic definition regards the state as the territorial monopoly of legitimate violence.[40] Norbert Elias used this conception in his study of state formation in western Europe, demonstrating the centrality of internal pacification, i.e. the removal of violence from everyday life, for the development of

VADIM VOLKOV

peaceful economic activity of civil society.[41] The monopoly of force together with the fiscal monopoly made possible the central function of the state: the enforcement of universal law and order and the exercise of justice. Exploring the economic side of the use of organised violence, the economic historian Frederick Lane identified early-modern governments with violence-using and violence-controlling enterprises which produced and sold a specific service—protection. He described the political economy of force which assisted the accumulation of capital during the pre-industrial phase. If the governments that commanded organised force received tribute for the protection they sold to the subjects of economy and trade, the latter could also gain from what appeared a mere protection racket: they received protection rent. The customers, for example, Venetian merchants, earned protection rent because of the higher efficiency of their protector compared with that of their competitors: all merchants had to pay tribute to avoid damage, but those who paid less for firm protection in a dangerous business environment earned protection rent as a result of more competitive prices reflecting lower costs. Thus the institutionalised protection rackets that offered lower prices to clients grew at the expense of their rivals. Lane's major point is that 'during the Middle Ages and early modern times protection rents were a major source of fortunes made in trade. They were a more important source of profits than superiority in industrial techniques or industrial organisation'.[42]

The monopoly management of organised force and the economy of protection racket, so central to the formation of European states, are of course much more relevant to the distant past than to the immediate present. Theories of state formation hardly envisaged a reverse process, so powerful and stable appeared the modern states, the Soviet Union included. But today, when the Russian state is in deep functional crisis, historical sociology of state formation can inform our vision of the processes that are unfolding in the present. Thus, the booming of violent entrepreneurship in Russia means in fact that the state has lost the monopoly of legitimate violence. The present condition can be defined as the covert fragmentation of the state: the emergence, on the territory under the formal jurisdiction of the state, of competing and uncontrolled sources of organised violence and alternative taxation networks. The Russian state does not have unconditional priority in those very areas that constitute it: protection, taxation, and law enforcement. But organised criminal groups are not the sole and most powerful agents in the sphere of violent entrepreneurship: there are also various semi-autonomous armed formations, such as the president's personal guard, special police forces of all sorts kept by several state ministries, and numerous private protection companies.

In these circumstances the struggle against organised crime cannot radically change the situation. Would it not be more appropriate to talk about the reconstruction of the state, a process that is much more broad and complex than police measures against organised crime? All measures—political, economic, cultural, juridical and so on— that work towards the restoration of the monopoly of violence and the establishment of firm public control over it contribute to the reconstruction of the state. Legal protection companies that force purely criminal groups out of the market are also part of the process. The development of the business of private protection, however, is ambivalent. On the one hand, the privatised segments of the state coercive apparatus display a dangerous tendency towards autonomisation; they have an intrinsic interest

VIOLENT ENTREPRENEURSHIP IN RUSSIA 753

in becoming autonomous market actors. Moreover, since the demand for their services depends upon the general level of business risks, the agents of private protection would harbour a hidden interest in preserving the criminal sector as the source of risk rather than eliminating it. On the other hand, the state origin of many of the cadres of the private protection companies, and their close relations with the state organs, carry a possibility of a new centralisation and establishment of close control over the agencies of organised violence, with a parallel transition to their centralised budgetary financing. The logic of the economic market has its positive aspect as well, expressed in a specific political economy of force: intensive violence is economically inefficient. Legal as well as criminal entrepreneurs of violence are compelled to take into account economic limitations of their action as well as the developing business culture. Thus, in theory, the reconstruction of the state and the pacification of society should work itself out independently of any conscious intentional project of those in power. Or, alternatively, incentives for the strengthening of the state will be reflected in the consciousness of businessmen and politicians— contrary to the earlier widespread beliefs that the strong state and the economic market are mutually exclusive.

The European University at St Petersburg

[1] In this study I rely on data obtained from different sources: recent journalistic publications and books, interviews with experts, businessmen, representatives of criminal groups and the state police organs as well as from personal observations. I am thankful to Andrei Konstantinov for generous help.
[2] On the genesis of regular racket in Moscow see V. Karyshev, *Zapiski 'banditskogo advokata': zakulisnaya zhizn' bratvy glazami 'zashchitnika mafii'* (Moscow, Tsentrpoligraf, 1988), pp. 30–40; also M. Kleimenov & O. Dmitriev, 'Reket v Sibiri', *Sotsiologicheskie issledovaniya*, 1995, 3, pp. 115–121.
[3] S. Dyakov & A. Dolgova (eds), *Organizovannaya prestupnost'* (Moscow, Yuridicheskaya literatura, 1989), p. 98
[4] The perception of entrepreneurial risks and ways of dealing with them are well reflected in a recent study of the emerging markets in Russia. See V. Radaev, *Formirovanie novykh rossiiskikh rynkov: transaktsionnye izderzhki, formy kontrolya i delovaya etika* (Moscow, Tsentr politicheskikh tekhnologii, 1998), pp. 116–127.
[5] Evidence of this is provided in the dissertation by Federico Varese, *The Emergence of the Russian Mafia: Dispute Settlement and Protection in a New Market Economy*, DPhil thesis. The Faculty of Social Studies, University of Oxford, Oxford, 1996, and F. Varese, 'Is Sicily the Future of Russia? Private Protection and the Rise of the Russian Mafia', *Archives Europeennes de Sociologie*, 35, 1, 1994, pp. 224–258.
[6] A. Konstantinov, *Banditskii Peterburg* (Petersburg, Folio-press, 1997), p. 175.
[7] D. North, *Institutions, Institutional Changes and Economic Performance* (Cambridge, Cambridge University Press, 1990).
[8] No comparative calculations of transaction costs have been made so far. A theoretical argument for the economic efficiency of informal rule-enforcers was advanced by Svetozar Pejovic, 'The Transition Process in an Arbitrary State: The Case for the Mafia', *IB Review*, 1, 1, 1997, pp. 18–23.
[9] See V. Chalidze, *Criminal Russia: Essays on Crime in the Soviet Union* (New York, Random House, 1977); D. Likhachev, 'Cherty pervobytnogo primitivizma vorovskoi rechi', *Yazyk i myshlenie*, Proceedings of the USSR Academy of Science, vol. III–IV (Moscow, Academy of Science, 1935); A. Gurov, *Krasnaya Mafiya* (Moscow, Mico, 1995); A. Gurov & I. Ryabinin, *Ispoved' vora v zakone* (Moscow, Rosagropromizdat, 1991); V. Radzinkin, *Vory v zakone i prestupnye klany* (Moscow, Kriminologicheskaya assotsiatsiya, 1995).
[10] A. Konstantinov & M. Dikselyus, *Banditskaya Rossiya* (Petersburg, Bibliopolis, 1998).
[11] According to MVD data, the number of organised criminal groups increased from 952 in 1991 to 6743 in 1996. Cited in A. Dolgova (ed.), *Prestupnost' i reformy v Rossii* (Moscow, Kriminologicheskaya assotsiatsiya, 1998), p. 254.

754   VADIM VOLKOV

[12] See, for example, G. Dunn, 'The Major Mafia Gangs in Russia', in P. Williams (ed.), *Russian Organised Crime: A New Threat* (London, Frank Cass, 1997).

[13] For an account of trademarks of the Sicilian mafia see D. Gambetta, *The Sicilian Mafia: The Business of Private Protection* (Cambridge, MA, Harvard University Press, 1993).

[14] *Operativnoe prikrytie*, 1997, 2(8), p. 10.

[15] *Obshchaya gazeta*, 20–26 August 1998, p. 4.

[16] Cited in *Economist*, 1994, 19, pp. 57–58.

[17] *Nezavisimaya gazeta*, 21 September 1995.

[18] W. Webster *et al.*, *Russian Organised Crime. Global Organised Crime Project* (Washington; Center for Strategic and International Studies, 1997), p. 2.

[19] J. Blasi *et al.*, *Kremlin Capitalism: Privatizing the Russian Economy* (Ithaca, Cornell University Press, 1997), p. 116.

[20] *Ibid.*, p. 119.

[21] *Zashchita i bezopasnost'*, 1998, 2, pp. 4–5.

[22] Radaev, *Formirovanie novykh rossiiskikh rynkov*, pp. 129, 174, 185.

[23] *Novaya gazeta*, 13–19 July 1998, p. 3.

[24] *Operativnoe prikrytie*, 1997, 3(9), p. 36.

[25] *Bezopasnost' lichnosti i biznesa. Spravochnik' 98* (St Petersburg, Agentstvo AT, 1998), p. 4.

[26] *Ekspert*, 1996, 2, p. 22.

[27] *Operativnoe prikrytie*, 1997, 4–5 (October), p. 61.

[28] *Ekspert*, 1997, 11, p. 40.

[29] *Operativnoe prikrytie*, 1997, 1(7), pp. 8–9.

[30] A. Maksimov, *Rossiiskaya prestupnost': kto est' kto* (Moscow, Eksim-press, 1998), pp. 260–266.

[31] O. Kryshtanovskaya, 'Nelegal'nye struktury v Rossii', *Sotsiologicheskie issledovaniya*, 1995, 8, p. 96.

[32] *Operativnoe prikrytie*, 1997, 1(7), pp. 32–33.

[33] *Operativnoe prikrytie*, 1997, 3(9), pp. 34–36.

[34] *Operativnoe prikrytie*, 1996, 6, p. 9.

[35] *Operativnoe prikrytie*, 1997, 1(7), pp. 32–33.

[36] *Operativnoe prikrytie*, 1997, 2(8), p. 33.

[37] *Ekspert*, 1996, 2, p. 20.

[38] *Ibid.*

[39] For example, D. North & R. Thomas, *The Rise of The Western World* (Cambridge, Cambridge University Press, 1973); F. Lane, *Venice and History* (Baltimore, Johns Hopkins University Press, 1966); C. Tilly, 'War Making and State Making as Organised Crime', in P. Evans *et al.* (eds), *Bringing the State Back in* (Cambridge, Cambridge University Press, 1986).

[40] M. Weber, 'Politics as Vocation', in H. Gerth & C. Wright Mills (eds), *From Max Weber: Essays in Sociology* (London, Routledge, 1970), pp. 77–78.

[41] N. Elias, *The Civilizing Process. Vol. 1–2. The History of Manners and State Formation and Civilization* (Oxford, Basil Blackwell, 1993).

[42] F. Lane, 'Economic Consequences of Organised Violence', *The Journal of Economic History*, 18, 4, 1958, p. 410.

Australian Journal of Politics and History: Volume 44, Number 3, 1998, pp. 415-29.

The *Mafiya* and the New Russia

Mark Galeotti

History, University of Keele

The rise of the Russian *mafiya*, a distinctive form of organised crime, reflects more than just the temporary dislocations and uncertainties of the country's transition from a Soviet state to a free market democracy. Rooted in Russian tradition and Soviet practice, it is also a formidable obstacle to this evolution. This has serious implications for the new Russian polity: weakening central authority, diluting the state's monopoly of coercion, discrediting the market economy and ultimately usurping and distorting the very functions of the state. Any solution will have to come not from tougher policing (which itself would threaten a return to authoritarianism) but from a wider political and cultural response.

Organised crime is a cancer eating at the heart of Russia ... It must and will be destroyed, before it destroys us. Boris Yeltsin, 1996.[1]

The emergence of the Russian *mafiya*, a particularly distinctive, flexible and violent form of organised crime, has been one of the least palatable side-effects of the collapse of the USSR. But it is important to stress that this is a phenomenon rooted in Russian tradition and Soviet practice, not solely a product of the temporary dislocations and uncertainties of the country's transition from a Soviet state to a free market democracy. It is at once shrouded in myth and mystery and the subject of feverish and often alarmist reporting. For example, when former Russian Interior Minister Kulikov presented a progress report to President Yeltsin on the fight against organised crime, in June 1997, he had been drilled by his aides to avoid the popular term *mafiya* in favour of the more neutral "organised criminal groupings", even though his actual report used the term.[2] Furthermore, his statistics appeared contradictory, not least in claiming that the fight against the *mafiya* was being won, even though there were still some 5,000 groupings in the country. In fact, the Russians use a very elastic definition of organised crime, including almost any group of more than three people who committed a premeditated offence. There are probably closer to 350 genuine organised criminal groupings, as Westerners would define them, including perhaps between a dozen

---

[1] *ITAR-TASS*, 17 August 1996.

[2] Inferfax news agency, 13 June 1997, in the BBC *Summary of World Broadcasts: former Soviet Union* (henceforward *SWB*), 14 June 1997.

and twenty major cartels. But such confusion over definitions can be important. That Russians, as well as outsiders, persist in using the term *mafiya* is an interesting starting point in examining this phenomenon. The "original", Sicilian Mafia is not just an organisation, but also a culture, a way of behaving. To put it another way, it is a culture which depends on articulating its values through a type of organisation.[3] Disciplined, hierarchical and patriarchal, it requires its members to conform to certain rules and expectations. These entail "thieves' honour", patronage and clientelism, and competition and demonstrable success, which is increasingly defined in terms of wealth and political connections. Transliterated into Cyrillic as *mafiya*, Russian organised crime is at once reminiscent of but also distinct from its Sicilian counterpart.

On one level, Russian organised crime is a powerful collection of gangs, with its tentacles (the Russians do like the image of the criminal *sprut*, octopus)[4] everywhere, a parasite which may yet strangle its host. Although the Russian Government often lambasts Western "hysteria" about the *mafiya*, its own statistics and representatives seem to encourage such hysteria. Kulikov and his successor, Sergei Stepashin, both regularly cite alarming if largely meaningless statistics, such as the oft-repeated suggestion that it controls forty per cent of the Russian economy.[5] The Russian Central Bank has claimed that $1 billion is being illegally sent out of the country every month by criminals.[6] But who are the *mafiozi*? Once one moves away from the most overt manifestations of organised crime, the thugs and drug-dealers in the streets, then it is often much harder to sort the criminals from the new generations of *biznismeny* ("businessmen"), politicians and movers and shakers of every variety. Is the *mafiya* thus simply a matter of semantics? This very real uncertainty reflects the way that, in the countries of the former Soviet Union in general, and Russia in particular, distinct patterns have emerged. Above all, it is important to place the Russian *mafiya* in its historical and political context and appreciate the extent to which its rise and evolution reflect four key factors:

1 A criminal and terrorist political culture;
2 A sense of political and economic alienation;
3 Links between criminals and rulers that could almost be described as traditional;

---

[3] For a good summary of the recent literature on the Italian Mafia, see J. Chubb, "The Mafia, the Market and the State in Italy and Russia", *Journal of Modern Italian Studies* 1, 2 (1996), pp. 124-31.

[4] Interestingly enough, although hardly surprisingly, the Russians appreciated the Italian TV series *Piovra — potenza della mafia* (Octopus — Power of the Mafia), with its tales of corrupt politicians, isolated police and omnipresent organised crime. The image of the "octopus" (*sprut*) has become synonymous for organised crime.

[5] This figure has become a standard — even though I have not been able to identify a single piece of hard research on which it is based. Given that the Russians can still not quantify their legal economy, though, it is perhaps unsurprising that they have no real notion of the size of its illegal counterpart.

[6] *Daily Telegraph*, 6 June 1997.

4 A deliberate "strategy of tension" on the part of certain political actors.

The Rise of the *Mafiya*

1 A Criminal and Terrorist Political Culture

Russia is a society whose centuries-old tradition has never been characterised by the rule of law. Pushkin's view that "there is no law in Russia: the law is nailed to a stake, and that stake wears a crown" could apply to most periods in Russian history. An absolutist state — whether tsarist or Soviet — reserved to itself absolute power over the lives of its subjects and willingly sacrificed them in its own interests, regardless of the letter or spirit of the law. The gulf between rulers and ruled remained almost unbridged, not least because of the lack of an effective middle class, so that even at the beginning of the twentieth century, social relations could almost be described as feudal. At the same time, Russian society was historically underpoliced and endemically corrupt. In response, citizens replied with banditry, uprisings and widespread criminality.[7] One part of this culture of underground resistance was the rise of a coherent "criminal class" which, while by no means embracing all Russia's professional criminals, nonetheless represented a distinct and vital tradition. By the late nineteenth century, this *vorovskoi mir*, or "Thieves' World", was so structured it had its own language, a visual code of tattoos and a complex hierarchy.[8] It is thus glib, but not too inaccurate, to say that Russians have long been accustomed to being ruled by criminals and butchers and resorting to illegality of their own in response. Alongside insurrection, banditry and passive resistance, organised crime has been a part of this resistance.

2 A Sense of Political and Economic Alienation

In the Soviet period the hidden resistance of the people to their state was as much as anything else a necessary art of survival, especially in the 1960s and 1970s, when the black market increasingly became indispensable. In Lydia Rosner's apt words, "the ordinary Soviet citizen [knew] that to be honest and truthful means to die of hunger."[9] Yet the gap between rich and poor, state and society has widened dramatically since the collapse of the USSR. By 1997, perhaps a fifth of the Russian population was living below the (already artificially low) poverty line, and a similar number between that level and the standard the UN applies.[10]

---

[7] See V. Chalidze, *Criminal Russia* (New York: Random House, 1977), chapter 1.

[8] See S. S. Ostroumov, *Prestupnost' i ee prichiny v dorevolutsionnoi Rossii* (Moscow: MGU, 1980), A. I. Gurov, *Professional'naya prestupnost'* (Moscow: Yuridicheskaya literatura, 1990), chapter 2 and M. Galeotti, "Criminal Russia: The Traditions Behind the Headlines", *History Today* 44, 8 (1994), pp. 12-14.

[9] L. Rosner, *The Soviet Way of Crime* (New York: Bergan & Garvey, 1986) p. 11.

[10] Ekho Moskvy radio, 14 June 1997, in *SWB* 16 June 1997.

Furthermore, democracy does not appear to have led to any public belief that they have any meaningful control over their governance. Indeed, if anything this belief has diminished. In the Soviet era, there were at least widely understood "rules", ranging from the size of bribe needed for a particular service through to knowing the location of real power in any institution. Today's rules are still in a state of flux, beyond most people's ability to predict and thus use. This uncertainty has been exacerbated by the presence of a government which has long since lost the creative energies of its popular mandate of 1991. Boris Yeltsin is, despite his re-election as president in 1996, an ailing and capricious figure. There is no real sense of a rule of law. The new legal codes are only slowly and painfully being issued. The police are under-strength, under-equipped, under-trained and above all, under-motivated.

But above all, this alienation is a social and political problem rooted in the failure of the state to meet many of its obligations to society. The growing power of organised crime is thus a reflection of the absence of credible and legitimate mechanisms to control social interaction and create some sense of common order. Criminals do not (for example) just prey on entrepreneurs. They can also provide funds through banks they own or influence (allegedly, for a ten to twenty per cent cash commission, they can guarantee the involvement of any particular bank in any directed-credit venture). They can match potential partners, expedite business through the maze of bureaucracy and manage the necessary bribery it involves, all the while fending off the demands of other gangs. The police cannot provide the same protection as a private security firm — traditionally a *mafiya* front. An estimated eight per cent of enterprises pay protection money in one form or another, at an average rate of ten to twenty per cent of profits.[11] Over-burdened and tangled in outdated and poorly-framed laws, the courts cannot enforce a contract the way the *mafiya* can.[12]

The gangs do not only have an economic role, but a social one. Membership of a gang can provide an identity, a place in a hierarchy, in a time of anomie and chaos. More importantly, they can offer security, not just for the moment, but also for old age and in case of mishap. Gangs traditionally maintain an *obshchak*, or communal fund to support retired members or their families, for example, at a time when state pensions are almost worthless.[13] In short, the Russian *mafiya* is often seen not so much as a parasite but rather as a vital —- if dangerous and demanding

---

[11] Most of these statistics are based on, or supported by, conversations with Russian law enforcement officers in 1996-97.

[12] Following on from Diego Gambetta's study of Italian crime in his *The Sicilian Mafia* (Cambridge, MA: Harvard University Press, 1993), the role of the *mafiya* as an economic enforcer has been developed by Federico Varese in his "Is Sicily the Future of Russia? Private Protection and the Rise of the Russian Mafia", *Archives europeennes de sociologie* 35 (1994), pp. 224-58 and "What is the Russian Mafia?", *Low Intensity Conflict & Law Enforcement* 5, 2 (1996), pp. 129-38.

[13] J. Serio and A. Razinkin, "Thieves Professing the Code: The Traditional Role of vory v zakone in Russia's Criminal World", *Low Intensity Conflict & Law Enforcement* 4, 1 (1995), pp. 72-88.

— ally in a society in chaos.[14] The rise of the *mafiya* thus reflects the local loyalties and self-help ethos of a polity in collapse. As faith in the Party and the state rapidly crumbled, many communities looked towards defending and furthering their own interests in a form of dog-eat-dog social autarky. In some cases, this could have been anticipated, such as the way local communities and ethnic minorities banded together, often turning to crime as a means of economic survival.

3 Links Between Criminals & Rulers That Could be Described as Traditional

Part of the real reason for the distinctive rise of the *mafiya*, though, has been that while it has developed in opposition to the state and in its absence, it has also been able to act in symbiosis with the state, or at least elements within it. In a corrupt political system, one in which Leninist ideals soon gave way to careerism and cynicism, criminals proved very adept at making political deals. The connection between organised crime and the Communist Party (CPSU) was deeply-rooted. The pre-Revolutionary Bolsheviks robbed banks for funds, and allied themselves with bandits able to provide safe-houses and armed heavies.[15] The first Bolshevik secret police, the Cheka, similarly drew on criminals for informers and executioners. In the 1930s, as Stalin's purges filled the prison camps with "politicals", the criminals were co-opted to keep them in line, leading to the rise of a new kind of criminal with links to the Party and secret police.[16] The 1970s saw a further blossoming of organised crime within and alongside the CPSU, and corruption, embezzlement and black-marketeering became endemic.[17] The apparent explosion of organised crime in recent years has, after all, to a large extent simply reflected its eruption from the shadows, as it could no longer operate behind the scenes within the CPSU.

The *mafiya* is not just a collection of thugs in ill-fitting track suits, or even just the traditional elite of the *vory v zakone* ("thieves-within-the-code"). It is also a

---

[14] Even Aleksandr Gurov, doyen of Russian organised criminal studies, has accepted that "they are fulfilling the role of state agencies". *Moskovskii komsomolets*, 10 November 1996. Federico Varese has examined the extent to which petty entrepreneurs in the city of Perm' voluntarily turn to the *mafiya* in his unpublished DPhil dissertation, The Emergence of the Russian Mafia, Oxford, 1997.

[15] This is discussed in Chalidze, *Criminal Russia*, chapter 2.

[16] This process, and the ensuing war between the traditionalist *blatnye* and the collaborationist *suki* ("bitches") has been comprehensively chronicled in much of the "camp literature", such as Alexander Solzhenitsyn's *Gulag Archipelago* (London: Collins, 1975), Edward Buca's *Vorkuta* (London: Constable, 1976) and Dmitri Panin's *The Notebooks of Sologdin* (London: Hutchinson, 1976). See also Chalidze, *Criminal Russia*, chapter 4.

[17] For discussion of the rise of organised criminality within the CPSU, see J. Millar, "The Little Deal: Brezhnev's Contribution to Acquisitive Socialism", *Slavic Review* 44, 4 (1985), pp. 694-706; K. Simis, *USSR: Secrets of a Corrupt Society* (London: JM Dent, 1982), V. Coulloudon, *La Mafia en Union Sovietique* (Paris: JC Lattes, 1990), A. Vaksberg, *The Soviet Mafia* (London: Weidenfeld & Nicolson, 1991) and W. A. Clark, *Crime and Punishment in Soviet Officialdom* (London: ME Sharpe, 1993).

very powerful economic interest, one which dominates whole economic sectors, and whose "front" banks and companies are among Russia's most powerful. The new Russian elite is a constellation of interest groups and other "clans", many of which at least acknowledge the importance of the *mafiya*.[18] Boris Yeltsin himself sent his condolences to the funeral of the brother of Otari Kvantrishvili, the head of the Georgian mafia in Moscow, who was himself killed during a gang war in 1994.[19] One could as easily look at the close relationship between Moscow's Mayor Luzhkov and popular singer-turned-politician, Iosif Kobzon, a man whom the USA has barred from entry on the grounds of his links with the *mafiya*.[20] Indeed, Luzhkov has even had to strike back at his critics in the parliament, the *Duma*, claiming that 800 deputies' aides are under police investigation for *mafiya* links.[21] For whatever reason, there are many even within the highest echelons of the government who are actually aligned with organised crime and who stand to lose as much from a genuine victory over it, as has been the case for so many within the Italian political class. After all, the *mafiya* makes a useful ally, for reasons I will consider later.

4 A Deliberate "Strategy of Tension" on the Part of Certain Political Actors

Finally, it is clear that there are many individual and institutional interests which benefit from the rise (or perceived rise) of terrorism and organised crime. A sense of anarchy on the streets helps buttress the case for high spending on internal security. It is worth stressing just how much Russia pays for what appears, after all, to be a singularly useless internal security machine. According to my calculations, even in 1996, Russia disposed of eleven separate intelligence and security organisations, and 344,000 paramilitary and security troops.[22] This represents a force twenty per cent the size of the regular military, with one for every 436 citizens. By way of contrast, even the old USSR maintained a proportionately more moderate force about ten per cent as large as the regular military, with one security trooper per 703 citizens.[23] Since then, both forces have

---

[18] For a neat summary of the rise of these "clans", see Olga Kryshtanovskaya, in *Argumenty i fakty* 21 (1997), p. 12.

[19] J. Kampfner, *Inside Yeltsin's Russia* (London: Cassell, 1994), chapter 20.

[20] See, for example, *Moskovskyi komsomolets*, 8 July 1995, and *Kommersant-daily*, 19 August 1995.

[21] *Sunday Times*, 9 March 1997. In fairness, it should be noted that there are 14,000 such "aides", the title often being little more than an honorific granted to a sponsor or fund-raiser.

[22] The services are: the Interior Ministry (MVD), Federal Security Service (FSB), Federal Government Communications and Information Agency (FAPSI), the Foreign Intelligence Service (SVR), the Main Intelligence Directorate (GRU), the Tax Police (NP), the Ministry of Emergency Situations (MChS), Procuracy, the Main Military Procuracy, the Federal Protection Service (FSO) and Presidential Security Service (SBP). The detailed assessments of the security troops are in M. Galeotti. "Russia's Praetorians". Paper distributed by the NATO Special Adviser for Central & Eastern European Affairs, 1996.

[23] *Ibid.*

been cut, but the balance between the regular military and the internal security forces has remained essentially unchanged. This expenditure is a ludicrous drain upon an already overstretched budget, and needs to be justified by a regular parade of "threats". The Chechen war, after all, was stoked into full conflagration by the Interior Ministry and Federal Security Service just at a time when they were making their case for a further budget increase.[24] It is also at times useful to talk up the threat — even as at other times it is worth talking it down.[25] Finally, there are those — such as Kulikov cited earlier — who advocate re-establishing greater state control of the economy. Their interests are often well-served by painting a picture of unchecked *mafiya* penetration of the market economy.

The Political Implications: Destabilising Russia

The *mafiya* are thus both a cause and effect of the central state's lack of authority. Its inability to control terror and organised crime is undermining Moscow's moral and practical authority. The continuing failure, for example, to resolve any of a string of high-profile assassinations, has led to a widespread assumption that those parts of the government not already entirely corrupt are instead mortally stupid. Even according to Kulikov, eighty-six per cent of Russians do not think the MVD can combat crime effectively.[26]

There are entirely practical aspects to this problem. The *mafiya* is at once a loose collection of criminal entrepreneurs, a dominant force behind the new Russian capitalism and a natural response to the failure of the state to carry out various basic social functions. As a result, tax evasion has become widespread, not just because the authorities cannot adequately police the revenue, but because businesses feel evasion is their right given that they are having to pay separately for services the state should provide. The result is a vicious circle, and one which the criminals are happy to encourage. The main implications of the complex role of the *mafiya* are discussed below.

---

[24] See M. Galeotti, "Moscow's Chechen War", *Jane's Intelligence Review* 7, 2 (1995). pp. 50-52.

[25] As a case in point, during 1995 Russia's police and security groups were very interested in developing cooperation with Western agencies; the FSB was also "repackaging" itself as a police rather than a political security arm. As a result, both the FSB and MVD began warning of the apocalyptic threat posed by the *mafiya*. In 1996, as attention shifted towards forestalling NATO enlargement, Russia sought to play down any threat it could pose to the West. In short order, both FSB and MVD suddenly began down-playing the *mafiya* threat and grumbling about Western "hysteria." On the other hand, Interior Minister and then also Deputy Prime Minister Kulikov, developed his conservative position on "economic security" in late 1996/early 1997, warning that the government was losing control over the country's financial and import/export flows.

[26] *ITAR-TASS*, 11 February 1997, in *SWB*, 13 February 1997.

1 It Reflects and Exacerbates the State's Loss of its Monopoly Over Coercion

A key example of the moral and practical implications of the rise of the *mafiya* is that the failure of the police to control crime has led to a proliferation of private security firms.[27] There are now in excess of 6,500 private security agencies, employing more than 800,000, including about seventy per cent of all ex-KGB officers who left the service before retirement age. *Most-Bank* has more than 2,500 armed officers in Moscow alone, equivalent to a regiment of the Kremlin Guard. *Gazprom*'s Security Service has 20,000 staff, headed by a high-flying former KGB and State Tax Service officer.[28] *LUKoil* has an army of its own at its Novorossiisk oil terminal alone. All three have not only hordes of bodyguards, but also commercial intelligence officers, secure communications, indeed the full panoply of state security. Not only does this growth in private security reflect the general helplessness of the police, it also contributes to it: efforts to raise new taxes to support the police have been blocked by the industry, and these private armies can poach the best police officers, leaving the dregs.

Table 1: *Major Mafiya Killings, 1991-96*

1992 December	Vladimir Rovenskii	Chair, *Tekhobank*
1993 September	Ilya Medkov	Chair, *Pragma-Bank*
1993 December	Nikolai Likhachev	Chair, *Rosselkhozbank*
1994 February	Sergei Dubov	Publisher, *Novoe vremya*
1994 August	Anatoly Kuzmin	General Director, *Megionneftgaz*
1994 October	Dmitry Kholodov	Journalist, *Moskovskii komsomolets*
1995 January	Vladislav Listyev	Executive Director, ORT
1995 April	Sergei Kushnarev	Founder, Agrarian People of Russia
1995 July	Oleg Kantor	President, *Yugorskii* Commercial Bank
1995 Augus	Ivan Kivelidi	President, *Rosbiznesbank*
1995 October	Ivan Lushchinskii	Chair, Baltic Shipping Company
1995 October	Andrei Zakharenko	Head, *Primorybprom*
1995 November	Pavel Ratonin	President, *Lesprombank*
1995 November	Mikhail Likhodei	Chair, Afghan Veterans' Fund
1996 November	Paul Tatum	Owner, Radisson-Slavyanskaya Hotel
1997 January	Yury Repin	Chair, *Kutuzovskii Bank*
1997 August	Mikhail Manevich	Deputy Governor, St Petersburg

NB: this excludes killings of criminal figures; for that, see Table 2

What is good enough for *Gazprom* is good enough for ordinary Ivan Ivanov in the street. Even individuals and families seek ways of protecting themselves

---

[27] See M. Galeotti's discussion of this phenomenon in "Boom Time for Russia's Protectors", *Jane's Intelligence Review* 9, 9 (1997), pp. 339-41.

[28] The company's *Sluzhba bezopasnosti* is headed by Vladimir Marushchenko, former department head at the KGB Higher School, Federal Security Agency colonel and head of the Main Directorate of Tax Collection of the State Tax Service. *Nezavisimaya gazeta*, 6 February 1997.

independent of the state. Some will find this "roof" in the local criminals. Others turn to a modern version of the *samosud*, "self-judging" mob law of pre-revolutionary times.[29] Enrolment at martial arts classes and the huge market in legal and illegal personal weapons, from gas pistols to pump-action shotguns, represent alternative responses to the state's obvious failure to maintain an acceptable level of security. In the words of the sociologist Vladimir Shlapentokh, "Now Russians face unrelenting fear, mostly because the evil [*sic*] state machine is so weak that it permits a sort of anarchy whereby unrestrained brute force reigns in the country."[30]

So for some, at the very time when the state's armed forces are being penetrated by organised crime,[31] the failure of the centre necessitates warlordism, the creation of private coercive forces. For others, the answer is to cut deals with the criminals. After all, armed political factions and criminal gangs alike can be very useful, whether policing the streets by eliminating "unofficial" crime or keeping a region alive by breaking strikes, bankrolling economic development and providing employment, even if this is in refining drugs or producing counterfeit goods.

2 It Undermines the Still-Nascent Russian Democracy and Civil Society

Anti-government leaders such as Communist Party leader Gennady Zyuganov, neo-fascist Vladimir Zhirinovskii and maverick nationalist Alexander Lebed have all been able to paint the government as a tool of the *mafiya*. Indeed, none of the main institutions have escaped such allegations, including the prime minister and president, the civil service, armed forces, big business, regional authorities and the Duma. This undermines the respect generally felt for the new order, although it is not entirely unfair. The gangs themselves are a powerful political lobby, often able to develop links to the very heart of Russian politics through such figures as Iosif Kobzon and organisations such as the National Sports Fund.[32] They can also become powerful organisers of machine politics and lobbying, especially further from Moscow and St Petersburg and in regions dependent upon industries they dominate. They can get things done, offering local authorities their services as strike-breakers,[33] middlemen, creditors, even in policing. They have money, they

---

[29] *Samosud* has been ably discussed in C. Frierson, "Crime and Punishment in the Russian Village, *Slavic Review* 46, 1 (1987), pp. 55-69. For a recent case, see *Kommersant-daily*, 6 June 1997.

[30] V. Shlapentokh, "Decentralization of Fears: Life in Post-Communist Society", Paper distributed by the NATO Special Adviser for Central & Eastern European Affairs, 1997.

[31] G. H. Turbiville, "Mafia in Uniform: The Criminalization of the Russian Armed Forces", on the internet @ http://www-leav.army.mil/fmso/geo/pubs/mafia.htm, 20 June 1998.

[32] For a comprehensive exposé of the National Sports Fund, see *Ogonek* 43 (1996), pp. 8-13.

[33] To give one example, Konstantin Pimonov, chair of the Coordinating Council for Miners' Protests at Vorgashurskaya coal mine (Vorkuta), was threatened at gun point to end a month-old strike. *St Petersburg Times*, 10-17 February 1997.

may control or influence the media, and ultimately they can kill.[34] More generally, they begin to represent alternative sources of practical and even moral authority. At times, organised crime actually sees advantage in getting rid of overt or disorganised crime, whether to eliminate rivals or as part of an accord with the state or business elite. One result has been the rise of a myth of the Robin Hood-like "good *vory*": "if there weren't any *vory*, Moscow would be in a bloodbath, resulting in an endless war," goes one commonly-held view.[35] Another way in which criminals seek to maintain a degree of social legitimacy, even if spurious, is by taking it upon themselves to repress those outside the cultural mainstream. In the Russian context, this has manifested itself in several ways. Russian gangs have persecuted their ethnic Caucasian rivals as well as Jews and Asians in the name of Russian ethnic pride, just as non-Russians such as the Chechens can present their criminal activities against the state as a blow struck against imperialism.

The position and power of the *mafiya* is also used to strengthen the case of those who would like to see a return to authoritarianism. As I mentioned before, the heavy-handed invasion of Chechnya was in many ways a case study of the confusion between outright war, the suppression of violent, extra-legal political dissent and a police operation against criminal groupings many in Moscow share. The appointment of Anatoly Kulikov to the additional post of Deputy Prime Minister in charge of economic security in January 1997 was a reminder that — like Gorbachev — Yeltsin must respond to the claims that, in an emergency situation, democracy must be defended undemocratically. We can only hope that he and his eventual successor manage to resist such pressure. One lesson of history worth learning is that emergency measures introduced as a means to an end all too easily become an end in and of themselves. Russia is already a country with all the institutional preconditions for the creation of a police state.[36] A worrying precedent was set on 14 June 1994, with Presidential Decree 1226, "On Urgent Measures to Protect the Population Against Banditry and Other Manifestations of Organised Crime". Security chief Sergei Stepashin cheerfully admitted that it was a return to Soviet-era practices, adding that he was "all for the violation of human rights, if the person is a bandit or criminal".[37] He went on to be appointed Interior Minister in March 1998. When parliamentarians queried some of the more draconian elements of the decree, Yeltsin used his presidential authority to steamroller it through. Paradoxically, such measures do not necessarily worry the *mafiya*. Most groups are well-connected with the police and security agencies or have bought themselves their own "roofs" from politicians or government officials: on average, *mafiya* groups invest about thirty per cent of their funds this

---

[34] One report actually purported to represent the criminals' views — ùsupporting the status quo. *Segodnya*, 7 May 1996.

[35] *Moscow News*, 7 May 1993.

[36] This view has been articulated best by Evgenia Albats: see her *KGB: State Within a State* (London, IB. Tauris, 1995), especially chapter 7.

[37] P. Morvant, "War on Organized Crime and Corruption", *Transition*, 15 February 1996.

way into their own "roofs".[38] The most likely targets of any crack-down would be the smaller gangs and "disorganised" crime — both of which the *mafiya* regards as at best a distraction and at worst competition. The real victims would ultimately prove to be any hopes of establishing a durable democratic civil society and rule of law in Russia.

3 It Undermines the Integrity of National Borders

Organised crime is often an explicitly cross-border phenomenon.[39] The more it can operate in such terms, the more it weakens the moral and practical integrity of national borders which, in the former Soviet Union, were already rather artificial. Large numbers of Chinese citizens, for example, have crossed the border into Maritime Territory and have never returned in what one Russian parliamentarian has characterised as "the silent colonisation of the Russian Far East".[40] Many of these illegal immigrants are forced to join or pay homage to ethnic Chinese gangs. These have (since mid-1994) been developing strategic alliances with Triad gangs in Hong Kong, offering them new markets and opportunities for money laundering, drugs trafficking and the production of counterfeit goods. Criminal links across frontiers are by no means a problem confined to the east. Russia's borders are all dangerously soft, with criminal groups operating freely across them in every direction. Drugs flow east and north, into Russia and also onwards into Europe. Russian expatriates in the other states of the former Soviet Union harbour local allies and branches of Russian gangs. Terrorists and hitmen find refuge across regional and national borders. The exclave of Kaliningrad has become a virtual extra-territorial haven for crime in northern Europe.

4 It Distorts and Strangles the New Market Economy

There is always some hope at the bottom of Pandora's box, and to some this is to be found in the thought that the *mafiya* is a positive phenomenon. Edward Luttwak, for example, has extolled the "Good Bad Guys" who cut through red tape and bureaucratic muddle. In a similar vein, Gavriil Popov, former Mayor of Moscow, has said that "the *mafiya* is necessary given the current situation in Russia ... it fulfils the role of Robin Hood, distributing wealth".[41] While satisfyingly controversial, this view holds little water. After all, while the choice of

---

[38] Conversation with MVD officer, January 1997.

[39] See M. Galeotti, "Cross-Border Crime and the Former Soviet Union", *IBRU Boundary & Territory Briefing* 1, 5 (1995), and C. Ulrich, "The New Red Terror: International Dimensions of Post-Soviet Organized Crime", Low Intensity Conflict & Law Enforcement 5, 1 (1996), pp. 29-44 For a particularly over-dramatic picture of a global *Pax mafiosa*, see Claire Sterling's *Crime Without Frontiers* (London: Little, Brown, 1994).

[40] *ITAR-TASS*, 21 February 1996.

[41] E. Luttwak, "The Good Bad Guys", *Guardian*, 31 July 1995; Popov's comments were during a conference in Moscow, 26 July 1995.

© Departments of Government & History, University of Queensland & Blackwell Publishers 1998.

an entrepreneur to accept or even seek shelter under the "roof" of the *mafiya* may be rational on an individual level, it is not rational in terms of society's overall interests.

In fact, the *mafiya* distorts the market.[42] It creates and protects artificial monopolies (much as the Party and the Plan did during the Soviet era), in defiance of the market. It has abused and manipulated the privatisation process, using its political clout and dirty money to snap up key industries, enterprises and resources. According to a report in *Delovoi mir*, for example, organised crime controls AvtoVAZ, Russia's largest manufacturing plant, while the aluminium industry has become the focus of often-violent struggles for ownership between a variety of legal, paralegal and outright criminal actors.[43] During 1994, for instance, an average of 104 enterprises were privatised every day — and 107 privatisation-related crimes were committed.[44]

The power of the *mafiya* also forces business to spend excessive amounts (thirty-forty per cent of profits, according to one report)[45] on security. Least tangibly, it also perpetuates the dangerous and zero-sum idea that capitalism is merely a matter of buying, selling and, if I can use such an expression, making a killing.[46] In one 1995 opinion poll, only 5.1 per cent of Russians in 1995 thought honesty, ability and hard work were the way to prosperity, while 44.2 per cent cited illegal speculation and 20.4 per cent money-laundering.[47] Thus, in the words of one commentator, "Russia is gradually getting used to living in an atmosphere which is virtually legalised embezzlement ... the ruling [political elite] exploiting their monopoly position of power and making no particular effort to hide it from anyone, are turning themselves and their kith and kin into the new bosses".[48] None of this helps legitimise the new market economy in the eyes of a population which still largely equates it with rent and price rises, unemployment and financial scandals such as the 1993-94 MMM pyramid investment fraud. Even foreign agencies operating within Russia have been forced to accept the *mafiya*'s role and rules. Reportedly, some eighty per cent of all US firms operating in Russia in Spring 1993 had at least once violated the terms of the 1977 Foreign Corrupt Practices Act, which, for example, bars them from paying bribes.[49] Others have

---

[42] There is a growing literature on the economic implications of organised crime — based largely on Italy — which points to its long-term costs. See, in particular, S. Zamagni, ed., *Mercati illegali e mafie* (Bologna: il Mulino, 1993) and G. Fiorentini and S. Peltzman, eds, *The Economics of Organised Crime* (Cambridge: Cambridge UP, 1995).

[43] *Delovoi mir*, 3 April 1997; *Ekspert*, 17 February 1997; *Interfax*, 5 June 1997, in *SWB* 6 June 1997.

[44] S. Lunev, "Russian Organized Crime", *Jamestown Foundation Prism* 3, 8 (1997) (email bull).

[45] Shlapentokh, "Decentralization of Fears".

[46] In the words of the journalist Anna Blundy, "everything is seen as saleable. That is the underlying ideology and it is an ideology." *Guardian*, 27 May 1994.

[47] *Interfax* News Agency, 12 July 1995.

[48] *Komsomol'skaya pravda*, 1 February 1997.

[49] J. Klebnikov, "Joe Stalin's heirs", *Forbes*, 27 September 1993.

been deterred from entering the Russian market, or operate with exaggerated caution. Either way, it limits much-needed inward investment, and slows Russia's integration into the global economy.

Mafiya and Russian Society

This paper has only touched on certain of the issues connected with the political implications of Russian organised crime. The most important point I want to emphasise is that it makes no sense to see the *mafiya* as anything but the most extreme and objectionable symptom of wider problems within the Russian political system. In other words, I am rejecting both the view that the *mafiya is* the political system, as well as the view that it is an entirely separate entity, as it would be in most Western countries. Instead, the political system's perceived lack of responsiveness and social justice, its tolerance for personal clientelism at the expense of law and fairness, its simple practical failings all create fertile soil for the *mafiya*. They must all be addressed before organised crime can be tackled at a systemic level.

In fact, for this generation, the battle against organised crime in Russia has probably been lost. Some gangs will fall, some kingpins will be arrested, but the *sistema* will survive. Of course, there is a great and constant flurry of activity as Russia talks about the need for tough policing; a cynic would note that at one time or another, 1993, 1994, 1996 and 1997 have all been declared the "year of the fight against organised crime". (So what was wrong with 1995?) But the solution is not in policing, because this is a social and political question. What is needed is the satisfaction of most people within the legal ("upperworld") system. Part of the answer lies in establishing a rational and equitable tax code and credible legal systems which bridge the hitherto yawning gap between rulers and ruled, formal and informal constitutions. There is also the need for adequate honest economic opportunities, and a purification of the political system. Yet the *mafiya* will sabotage all these unless something is also done to bring at least the powerful elements into the system. This does not necessarily mean giving them power — but giving them reasons to be legal.

In this respect, the very consolidation of the Russian criminal ecology is encouraging. This is a generational issue. The period 1990-94 saw Russia torn by a series of turf wars, but a relatively stable status quo did begin to emerge. First this happened in Moscow, with the elimination or departure of three over-powerful and thus destabilising figures (Rafik Svo — arrested, died in prison, 1992; Valery Drugach — assassinated, 1993; Otari Kvantrishvili — assassinated, 1994) and then the decline of the Chechens in 1994-96.[50] In St Petersburg, 1995 saw a mob

---

[50] See N. Modestov, *Moskva banditskaya* (Moscow: Tsentropoligraf, 1996): excerpted in *Moskovskaya pravda*, 28 May 1996 and *Segodnya*, 3 April 1996, as well as articles in

war which had a similarly stabilising effect, and in both Moscow and St Petersburg, a rough balance of terror has emerged as the dominant gangs (*Solntsevo* and *Tambovskaya*, respectively) are offset by their wary and numerous rivals. This has still to emerge further east, especially in the country's other "criminal capitals", Ekaterinburg and Vladivostok, but it will probably come.

Table 2: *Selected Killings of Criminal Figures, 1991-96*

1992	Antonov ("Silvestr")	Moscow
1993	Valery Drugach ("Globus")	Moscow
1993	Rafael Bagdasarian ("Rafik Svo")	Moscow
1994 March	Sultan Balashikhinskii ("Sultan")	Moscow's Chechen *Mafiya*
1994 March	Mikhail Kuchin	Ekaterinburg
1994 April	Otari Kvantrishvili ("Otarik")	Moscow's Georgian *Mafiya*
1994 December	Nikolai Suleimanov ("Khoza")	Moscow's Chechen *Mafiya*

The result is that by 1995-96 major *mafiya* bloodletting was largely concentrated on liquidating new threats from the *bespredel'chiki* (literally, "disorderists"), younger generation criminals trying to push their way into the big time. But the new symbol of *mafiya* violence became assassination, a tight, focused attack aimed at clearing political and economic obstacles from their path. What is emerging, though, is a generation of criminals who have benefited from a half decade of chaos and now see increasing advantages in order — albeit an order of their making. The established are in many ways looking to find new status, stability and security, seeking to "launder" themselves and turn the proceeds of racketeering and drug dealing into "respectable" economic power. They are setting up or buying into legitimate businesses, turning *mafiya* enforcers into "private security guards". Kvantrishvili himself, for example, had made much of his charitable work and his role as a patron of the country's sportsmen.

This is the encouraging aspect of the criminals' penetration of the legal economic system. Whereas most business carried out by the *mafiya* is essentially geared towards substantial short-term profits (often through the use of artificial monopolies and economies) rather than long-term and sustainable growth, there are economic but above all social reasons why these "criminal capitalists" may be induced to change their ways. In the words of Aleksandr Gurov, one of the first Russian scholars of the *mafiya*, "from wild, barbaric methods it moves to civilised ones, becomes a part of the state machine and to a certain extent contributes to the country's prosperity".[51] Where once they were hungry predators, now they are rich, established, increasingly middle-aged, possibly married and raising families. They are sponsoring children's hospitals, sending their sons to British public schools and learning golf. Of those businessmen now deemed "licit", forty per cent

Kommersant-daily, 19 July 1995, *Vechernaya Moskva*, 29 November 1996 and *Kommersant-daily*, 1 February 1997.

[51] *Moskovskii komsomolets*, 10 November 1996.

polled by the newspaper *Argumenty i fakty* admitted that they had been engaged in criminal activities in the past.[52] Where once they may have robbed banks, now they own them.

Conclusions

These senior criminals, the *vory v zakone* ("thieves-within-code") and *avtoritety* ("authorities")[53] need to be brought — bought? — into the system and given reasons to create a legal state and surrender the illicit economic multiplier for legal market competition. After all, the dominance of corruption or organised crime need not mean an end to political reform or economic recovery. Britain in the Industrial Revolution, Prohibition-era USA and modern Italy and Japan all managed to reconcile the two. It may stick in the craw to think of them as the new generation of the Great and the Good, the magnates, the charitable patrons, the ones to endow Oxbridge Colleges, but that is the way the world often works: it worked in the USA, albeit in the presence of a much more developed and legitimate political system. There is little reason to believe that the Russian state will not be prepared to reach such an accommodation. Gurov has advocated decriminalising the *mafiya*'s financial base, and joining the forces of the state and the "established" criminals to eliminate the *bespredel'chiki* and those not prepared to accept the new order.[54] Implicit alliances already appear to have arisen, albeit often short-term, geared towards eliminating specific threats to the public order. It is less clear whether the Kremlin will find the right balance, giving "established" criminals incentives to legitimise themselves but without encouraging the *mafiya*.

Leoluca Orlando, mayor of Palermo and a senior expert on and enemy of the Sicilian Mafia, has said that "What is now going on in Russia reminds me of Italy after World War Two ... Democracy and freedom came to [Italy] with the assistance of Mafia kingpins. And as a result they held a conspicuous position in the Italian political landscape for many years." In his view, "Russian gangsters will allow the state to combat organised crime only once they are very, very rich".[55] He is probably right — and it took Italy more than forty years even to begin seriously to combat the Mafia. In the interim, though, the power of the *mafiya* will endure, and Russia will remain trapped in an imperfect and often uncomfortable transitory phase between "state socialism" and market democracy.

---

[52] Fully twenty-five per cent of the sample admitted still to having ties with the criminal world. *Interfax* News Agency, 12 July 1995.

[53] The *vory v zakone* are the traditional leaders, who maintain, interpret and enforce the "Thieves' code", while the *avtoritety* are the more numerous and entrepreneurial gang leaders.

[54] *Moskovskii komsomolets*, 10 November 1996.

[55] *Izvestiya*, 1 March 1997.

Part V
Global Russian Organized Crime?

[20]
The Sexy Russian Mafia

by Lydia S. Rosner

ABSTRACT

This article deals with the perceptions inherent in that phe-
nomenon called the Russian Mafia. It examines a theoretical
problem which lies at the juncture of criminology, sociology
of knowledge, and cultural or cross-cultural studies, and
asks whether significances other than those apparent on the
surface govern perceptions as they concern organized crime
and immigrant illegality. It describes the fascination of the
American press with all newly-emerging criminal enter-
prises and asks several functionalist questions concerning
the possible ramifications of this interest.

Sociologists think of society as denoting a large complex of human relationships, or to put it in more technical language, as referring to a system of interaction. Garfinkel emphasizes that in order to understand behavior, we must train ourselves to see beyond the expected and to resist normalizing behavior or seeing it as rule-governed just because our common sense tells us that it must be so. Further, Garfinkel, in his studies of assumptions and ordinary behavior, cautions that the researcher must look beyond the obviousness of specific viewable circumstances and instead study why specific circumstances occur.

In a study of clinic records, Garfinkel attempted to categorize the collected data. He discovered that a large proportion of the records was incomplete. In the course of his research, he noted that records are given the property of completeness. This expectation of completeness creates the perception that lines and items not filled out on clinic records somehow hampered their analysis. After examining large numbers of clinic records, Garfinkel concluded that in fact clinic records have the property of incompleteness. In fact, when examining clinic folder documents, it became apparent to him that a "prominent and consistent feature" of the records is their poor record-keeping quality. However, it was the reason for such "poor" records which interested him. He concluded that the reason for incomplete or "poor" record keeping was to further the unstated goals of the organization keeping the records, in this case a psychiatric clinic. And not "putting everything down" allowed the various personnel who dealt with the records to use them in different fashions, thus furthering the particular tasks of the various departments within the clinic. Garfinkle's study demonstrated that records have properties beyond those initially imagined, in this case that of recording specific visits to the clinic by various patients.

The crime perception phenomena

As a sociologist, I've begun to examine a theoretical problem which lies at the juncture of criminology, sociology of knowledge, and cultural or cross cultural studies. As with Garfinkel's study, it is worth examining whether significances other than those apparent on the surface govern our perceptions as they concern organized crime, international cartels and immigrant illegality. What I attempt here is to summarize a fifteen-year process and to examine honestly, and without adapting or normalizing the dissemination into the American public consciousness of that phenomenon called the Russian Mafia.

A parallel academic creation of conceptual images existed during the height of the 1950 New York gang explosion that prompted the creation of the Youth Board. Youth Board workers had as their primary responsibility the alleviation of gang violence. This was to be achieved by diverting fighting gangs from their turf during periods of scheduled violence. To accomplish this, Youth Board workers infiltrated the gangs through a variety of methods in order to achieve sufficient rapport with the gang leadership to enable the workers to seduce the gang to leave their own turf rather than to succumb to scheduled violence. This was accomplished by taking the gang "downtown" to movies or other activities that were not part of their life style. Quite often, gang members accepted this seduction as a way of "saving face."

The Youth Board workers became America's experts on youth gangs. They described their gangs to the press, to various funding agencies, and to others whose access to these delinquent youths was limited. During this period, the press, in love with gang stories, prominently featured interviews with gang members who boasted of vast numbers of affiliated youths, a phantom membership reported as accurate because the working press normalized their interview reports. Youth Board workers memorialized various roles of gang leadership, presidents, ministers of war, when in fact they observed gang life through a middle-class-college, educated lens. They, too, normalized the gang into a somewhat abhorrent fraternity, with structured leadership, a clearly defined hierarchy of roles, and a task-oriented and goal-oriented table of organization rather than the pick up-whoever-is-around-structure subsequently defined by Yablonsky as the near group.

Garfinkel would point out that the gang was much more tidy as a group and thus was normalized to fit into the accepted definition of such. The press and the public, the workers and the young gang members themselves found it more convenient to create a rule-governed system, operating on the assumption that if the gang needs definition, the closest definition to reality will suffice. Common sense understandings allow the actor to substitute the understandable when insufficient information is available for other definitions.

Is there a Russian Mafia?

Before returning to the subject of the Russian Mafia I will review some history and then take a chronological look at crime phenomena. By 1984 there were 30,000 new Russian immigrants living in the Brighton Beach area of New York, part of a total population of 75,000 in the United States. In *The Soviet Way of Crime* (Rosner, 1986) I detailed how this population arrived on these shores schooled in crime, an essential ingredient of the way of life of virtually all Soviet citizens. In the former Soviet Union, personal wealth, privilege, dachas, and diamonds rested on control of goods and services illegally diverted from the State and exchanged for other illegally-diverted goods and services in vast and complex patterns of bribery, corruption and blackmail. Immigrants came to America well schooled in bureaucratic circumvention and in the ability to adapt governmental services for private gain.

Unlike previous immigrations, primarily agrarian in nature, this migration was industrial and technological. These new immigrants came with translatable skills. Even without

knowledge of the English language, they were employable. A painter could paint, and sheet metal workers and tool and die makers brought needed skills to the American labor market. This was not the marginal migration depicted in the literature of crime and migration, whose members were depicted as using crime as a way to move "up the ladder" because they had no other way of gaining access to the system.

The immigration from the Soviet Union brought to America's shores many people for whom crime was but ordinary behavior. There, the closer one was to actual product control the more there was to steal. Whereas a doctor could receive "gifts" for quicker appointment privileges, a painter could water down his paint and take some home to sell to friends. A director of a car factory was able to sell preferences to those who were willing to pay for the limited number of cars produced. Control of the rationed gasoline supplies and distribution to favored drivers provided an even better income. Socialized in a milieu where one chose hunger as an alternative to necessary criminality, Soviet migrants came with specific understandings about such behavior.

Émigrés to Brighton Beach brought with them the social and psychological patterns of behavior and expectations learned in their crime-ridden society. They acted out their homeland psychology through behavior that was gratuitous to Brighton Beach. Schooled in bureaucratic circumvention, these urbanites brought sophisticated skills of system beating with them. Some, because of the availability of goods and services in their host country dropped the behavior of their youth. Others, who in their homeland connived to find scarce items by pilferage or payoff had no labor market specialty to sell. They were called the *shabaskniki*. (The term comes from the work *shabashnichestvo*, meaning "self-employed."). They were hard working and provided services as needed. Those who looked upon their activities with disfavor also called them the Mafia.

My early research (1976 through 1980) into the activities of émigrés prior to their departure indicated that there were two types of criminals in the former USSR. One group of criminals was the Survivors. This group manipulated the system in order to feed themselves, to clothe their children and to survive the non-productive, total institution that was the Soviet Union. The second group, the Connivers, operated completely outside the system, creating networks which stole and delivered goods and services to party faithful and to commissars and deputies upon demand. This second group, using private enforcement methods and prison contacts, was the Connivers.

In 1986 I published the results of my study of Soviet crime and its transference to America. In addition to my book, a variety of articles depicting Soviet crime in America began to appear in the urban daily press. Mike Mallow, in *The Philadelphia Inquirer*, sparked further interest in the new phenomena of Soviet crime by a sensational article about a criminal network that he christened the "molina" (the Russian word for both an olive and a not-too-flattering hand gesture), and a variety of police departments began to examine Soviet crime. The New York Police Department assigned a team of detectives to man a Russian desk as part of their Organized Crime Task Force. Thus was the Russian Mafia added to the legends and literature of crime in America.

Daniel Bell described crime as a Coney Island mirror caricaturing the morals and manners of American society. He was describing that dark side of business which provides illicit, illegal goods in a carbon copy of American legal business enterprises. Consumer demand, product distribution, payment and accounting services, and profit redemption are all parallel to those in the legitimate business sector. He recognized that Americans have always found crime "sexy." From Jesse James to Joey Bottufuco, America and the American press have been fascinated by crime and criminals. Thus, word that there was the Russian Mafia provided the press with a new criminal enterprise to discover, elaborate on and sensationalize.

Information dissemination

After publication of my research, I was a featured speaker at conferences about Russian crime, both in this country and in Russia. Even literary groups such as an organization of mystery writers wanted background for their novels about this new crime phenomena. The press, interested in any new immigrant neighborhood, described Brighton Beach as a little piece of Russia, with restaurants and stores unlike any other in America. They looked to Baltimore, Philadelphia, and Los Angeles in order to discover whether criminal enterprises organized by Russian émigrés existed there as well.

By this point, the New York City Police Department had disbanded its Russian desk at the Vesey Street headquarters of their Organized Crime Unit. They felt that there was no significant interest in Russian Organized Crime. A detective who had manned this desk, and who was probably the most knowledgeable person in law enforcement on the subject of Russian Crime, left the department. There was no question in his mind that there was connected crime within the Russian community. He knew of contacts made by Brighton Beach Russians with other émigrés from the former Soviet Union. But it was still questionable as to whether these activities followed the classic organized crime model, or whether this was a network of criminals using prior contacts and imported skills to conduct illegal business.

The press merry-go-round

The press maintained that there was indeed a "Mafia." A count of press phone calls to my office during 1989 alone indicated that over fifteen reporters from a variety of national and international newspapers and press agencies were doing stories on this new Mafia threat. Articles began to appear in *The New York Times, The Nation, Vanity Fair* and even *The Institutional Investor*. Christine Bohlen, on her way to her assignment covering life in Russia, visited my office. Nathan Adams arrived with a former military man in tow, a man who had been the pilot for Brezhnev during his United States visits, to debrief me about my knowledge of these crime phenomena. He later wrote a long polemic article on Russian crime for *The Readers Digest* that was fortunately

later reduced to a few short pages. Reporters from Japan, Holland, several from the United Kingdom, France, and Italy called to ask for background information for stories they were writing for their home newspapers. In 1990, when I began charting the amount of calls received about Russian Mafia crime, I counted approximately twenty-five, some from the working press, others on assignment from the Columbia School of Journalism. Nineteen ninety-one brought thirty-five and over thirty again in 1992.

The networks also came to my door. "Expose" presented a half-hour program on a major gas scam, a solid investigative piece of journalism about a group of connected criminals. ABC took me through the jewelry district in an attempt to identify illegalities, and NBC and CBS all contacted me at one point or another. Even the FBI called requesting information. Certain names kept appearing. Certain individuals, who were running major criminal enterprises were identified; Agron and Belogusa were among them.

In 1992 Craig Copetas published *Bear Hunting with the Politburo*, a well-documented book describing crime as an indigenous factor of life both in the old Soviet State and its new free market economic clone. When he contacted me for background information for his two-part weekend series about specific people and specific criminal enterprises within the US Russian community, we discovered that we were both party to the chain of contacts. Round and round they went. The same reporters, speaking to the same sources, validated the other's conceptual framework of Russian crime and its "Mafia" connections.

Happenings in the CIS

Prior to the breakup of the Soviet Union, private entrepreneurship was illegal. People were sent to prison for what were, and still are, called economic crimes. Due to absolute State ownership of all available goods and services, there was no legitimate open economy in the U.S.S.R. All private enterprise began with the theft of State goods. This was because all goods were State-owned, and the only way to acquire scarce consumer items was to either pilfer them from the source of production or to steal them from the point of distribution.

Shortages created a black market in all goods and services. Thus a State employee (and all were employees of the State) could find work doing private repair jobs for those who could pay him with meat or clothing stolen from their jobs. The employee obtained his supplies from a network of friends whose favors he rewarded with favors of his own. A cement truck driver would exchange some cement, delivered to a private, non-State illicit job for some coats for his children, stolen from a coat factory. A clerk in an automobile licensing agency would barter a driver's license for scarce gasoline for his own use or sale.

Thousands of people got rich at the expense of the central U.S.S.R. budget. Reinforcing the alienation from the central government were the totally corrupt national organizations in the republics. These organizations, which dealt with the central Soviet Government, developed a system in which they were able to expand power politically and economically. People in charge stayed in charge through a combination of power, employment of private procurers for all sorts of goods and services, and acceptance of a totally corrupt system that rewarded this corruption.

Since the ability to gain personal wealth, privilege, dachas and diamonds rested on the control of goods and services that were illegally diverted from the state in exchange for other illegally diverted goods and services, a vast and complex pattern of bribery and corruption existed. Crime was so great that entirely illegal private industries were created outside the system. As with all illegal enterprise, coercion and violence were part of the cost of doing business. This vast network of industries and distributorships resembled those of the capitalist world in everything except their legality, their supply channels and their efficiency. Since the members of the ruling elite were often put in a position of playing hand-in-hand with underground businessmen, they were unable to resist corrupt pressure. Underground millionaires always existed. In Georgia, one such "businessman" was able to get himself appointed as Minster of Light Industry. This millionaire was in the fabric business. His desire to top his career with a public post was aided by the fact that he bribed public figures in the daily operation of his business and thus was able to use blackmail in pressing for his desires. Today these illegal businessmen are part of the newly-rich entrepreneurial class.

This pattern of illegal behavior in a society that did not acknowledge ordinary business was not confined to the elite. At every level, those who could steal or divert official supplies did so. It is hardly surprising then, that with movement toward a market economy, everyone who had watched or been part of the corruption joined in. Believing that the move toward a cooperative movement was legitimate, young entrepreneurs, usually those under the age of 40, tried their hand at "business." At first the old-line Communist bureaucrats did not believe that these entrepreneurs would be successful. Unable to relinquish both ideology and control, the party faithful ignored the moves toward private enterprise and called them black market or illegal. When they finally understood that change was successfully occurring, they tried to regain control. A tug of war ensued between new, young entrepreneurs, who believed that they could become "businessmen," and the old-line Communist bureaucrats and managers of state-operated industries, who had never had to work for their perks.

This fight for control of scarce resources and even scarcer manufacturing capabilities between those who were in power and those former procurers for government officials who were always engaged in thievery and its violent enforcement is what we are now watching. The old-line bureaucrats never believed that capitalism of any sort could be successful in their world. They initially licensed businesses and permitted small enterprises to function. Later they watched the confusion in the market. Often supplies were unavailable because the hobbled and inefficient distribution channels of the prior system were catering to both private

and public enterprises. For example, a privately licensed coat manufacturer was unable to get thread from a publicly held thread mill. Such upheavals are still part of the fact of Russian business.

Russian enforcement agencies, not understanding the difference between entrepreneurship and crime, arrested and imprisoned entrepreneurs for a variety of "crimes." When they discovered that the business system was profitable, they pushed out the struggling young entrepreneurs and took over. Managers entrenched in the Soviet system became "owners." Caretakers acquired their public agencies. Police officials turned to private security. The young entrepreneurs who believed that change had come about were displaced when their success was evident. Everything from nuclear materials to military belt buckles is now for sale. Privatization, although ramshackle, is the ultimate shake-out of this bureaucratically corrupt system.

In the past, attempts to control the kind of behavior now labeled Mafia failed. In large part this was because the very institutions presumed to be upholding the system were engaged in, or had a large percentage of its members engaged in, the very violations they were publicly trying to eradicate. The enforcers were corrupt and paid of to remain so. Force, extortion, imprisonment and banishment were all methods used by poorly-equipped agents of the law enforcement establishment as a way to keep those outside the political chain from participating too largely in the spoils. "Crime" was used as a subjective description indicative of power positions.

Since the dissolution of the U.S.S.R., a society brought up to think that private enterprise was somehow beyond the pale, is trying to adjust to private enterprise. In 1993 the very same Moscow police chief who filled prisons with economic criminals, even after the breakup of the Soviet Union, started his own security business—this while the trials of those he imprisoned had not yet been held.

What is crime and what is free enterprise?

It is thus important to understand the following two points: One, in a bureaucratic society with market shortages, everything has its price. And two, only those who had previously been involved in supposed criminality, both the Survivors for whom beating the system was a way of life and the Connivers, economic criminals known as the Mafia, know anything about business in a country where making money was contrary to Communist ideology. Contract law is in its infancy, and legal recourse for contract violation is non-existent. Thus, since business was considered illegal, we find that as with any corrupt enterprise, enforcement is provided by hired strong men who operate to enforce what a limited and unclear legal system cannot.

Politically-motivated Russians have always labeled some people as Mafia connected. Now both the corrupt former officials engaged in illicit enterprises and those who are participating in the beginnings of a free enterprise structure are labeled Mafia members. Hoarding of goods, distribution of scarce consumer items in exchange for hard currency, movement of scarce items from one republic to another, or selling of privately-acquired imported items on the street, all come under their classification of Mafia activity. Anyone with a Western automobile or the ability to travel internationally also might be called Mafia by a jealous and increasingly-poor pensioned population.

Crime statistics cited by the Interior Ministry, (i.e., KGB) and local police departments throughout the former Soviet Union are inaccurate in a country without computers and with minimum reporting capabilities. Neither a standardized body of laws nor a reporting structure such as the Uniform Crime Reports accurately details criminal activity. Additionally, in the CIS, the very instability of authority structures fosters constant redefinition of what is and what is not criminal. How else can the imprisonment of over tens of thousands of entrepreneurs be explained?

Why is the Russian Mafia sexy?

Accepting the fact that there was a corrupt society in place in the former Soviet Union, and that there are criminals among the immigrant population from there, two questions must be answered in order to understand the phenomenon of interest in the Russian Mafia, as imagined and described. First, is there a function to the Mafia image in the former Soviet Union? And second, is there a function of the Russian Mafia image in this country?

In answer to the first question, there is indeed a function to the Mafia image in the former Soviet Union. The function of defining newly-permitted business activities in the former Soviet Union as Mafia organized crime and lawlessness, while continuing to participate in such activities, determines the social standard of acceptable and unacceptable behavior in a country where beating the system was part of the system. Durkheim stated that the punishment of criminals plays a role in the maintenance of social solidarity and defines boundaries. The criminal, and society's focus on him, sets social guidelines that exert pressures for conformity. For the newly-formed democratic order in the former Soviet Union to begin to examine and set boundaries in a free enterprise system it must define not only legalities in terms of social and business acceptability but also determine who is conducting himself and a business in a socially-acceptable fashion and what is normative behavior.

For over seventy years business was regarded as a Western concept, against the interests of the socialist State. A Soviet businessman had to be doing illegal business and was referred to as being part of the Mafia—a word borrowed from American films. An edict defining the acceptability of free enterprise cannot replace the socialization of three-quarters of a century. Now the term Mafia has became a pejorative term describing anyone making money, having hard currency, or traveling in and out of the country. It serves the purpose of defining the new society's boundaries, however slowly.

In the rapidly-changing social structure of the former Soviet Union, there is still a battle to be played out between the young who desire a business economy with a free enterprise overlay and the old who still maintain their image, enhanced over seventy years, of crime and money as being two faces of the demonic West and part of the corruption of the previously-held ethic.

In answer to the second question, what is the social function of the interest in the Russian Mafia in this country, I suggest that there are many complicated answers. For one, Americans have always been fascinated with crime and criminals. And the Mafia, its godfathers and rituals, have long been myth and reality for the American public. With the fading of the Italian Mafia mythology, the assimilation of the sons and daughters of "made members" into the ranks of lawyers and doctors and stockbrokers, there is a search for a substitute.

The "evil empire" image historically mythologized in novels, movies, and true life spy stories through the decades of the cold war does not die a quiet death with glasnost and peristroika. We have been socialized not to trust the people who swore that they would bury us. We find it sexy to read about immigrants from the former Soviet Union who are involved in criminal activities on a grand scale. Then there is the reality of immigrants from bureaucratically-developed countries expanding their criminal skills by challenging through skillful manipulation the tax structures and other bureaucratic institutions in America.

In this country, scams, forgeries, and other skills acquired under a bureaucratic government flourish as we, too, move to more State-run and organized enterprises. World criminals move freely among venues and take up residences outside the enforcement zones of their activities. They connive to sell the resources of their countries on an open global market. They store their profits in safe havens and create residences far from the criminal enterprise zones. This kind of criminality, previously limited to drug lords and arms dealers, is now available for the price of a discount airline ticket. The global village has legal as well as illegal citizens.

Lastly, the sexy Russian Mafia provides journalists and their readers with a relatively unthreatening, European model of crime—a revisited Marlon Brando world of consigliere, caporegima and soldiers. At least that is the model which is appealingly seductive, although quite inaccurate.

References

Bell, Daniel. (1953). Crime as an American Way of Life. Antioch Review 13, 131-154.

Copetas, A. D. (1991). Bear Hunting with the Politburo. New York: Simon & Shuster.

Garfinkel, H. (1967). Studies in Ethnomethodology: Prentice Hall.

Rosner, L. S. (1986). Crime or Free Enterprise. Odessa Law Herald (Ukraine), 3:94 (189), 39-43.

Rosner, L. S. (1986). The Soviet Way of Crime: Bergin & Garvey.

Yablonsky, L. (1966). The Violent Gang. Baltimore: Penguin.

About the Author

Lydia S. Rosner is a professor at John Jay College of Criminal Justice, CUNY. She has written extensively about Russian migration and Russian crime. Her book, The Soviet Way of Crime, was published in 1986 by Bergin and Garvey.

[21]

POST-SOVIET BUSINESS FORUM ■

THE ROYAL INSTITUTE OF
INTERNATIONAL AFFAIRS
Russia and Eurasia Programme

PSBF BRIEFING   *No. 8   October 1996*

HYSTERIA, COMPLACENCY AND RUSSIAN ORGANIZED CRIME
Phil Williams

Introduction

Assessments of Russian organized crime diverge remarkably. At one end of the spectrum – the worst-case estimate – are those who consider it a dangerous successor to the threat posed to the West by the Soviet Union. At the other end of the spectrum, providing the best-case analysis, are those who contend not only that this threat is usually exaggerated, but that, in the present circumstances, organized crime has positive functions in Russian society and the economy. They claim that it has attained considerable prominence only because of the particular set of economic and political conditions that exist throughout the Commonwealth of Independent States (CIS), and will diminish in importance as these conditions change. In effect, these contrasting assessments are the new variant of the Cold War debate between hawks and doves. Neither is wholly compelling. This paper attempts to crystallize the key elements in these two opposing positions. This is followed by an examination of the scope, the complexities and the limitations of Russian organized crime. The final section uses the empirical analysis to offer a critique of both the worst-case and the best-case positions, and to assess the challenge organized crime poses to Russia.

The worst-case assessment

The worst-case assessment of organized crime in Russia is the direct heir to the conservative assessment of the Soviet threat during the Cold War and emphasizes several features:

- Its highly predatory nature, which is manifested in growing dominance over key sectors of the economy.
- Its high level of cohesion and organization, which is explained in terms of the central role of past KGB operatives as well as some current members of the security services who have transferred their skills for personal profit while retaining their malevolence to the West, and thieves professing the code[1] who are generally portrayed as the Russian equivalent of Mafia godfathers, giving direction and form to Russian criminal activities.
- The ruthlessness, skill and efficiency of the organizations, which surpass Colombian drug cartels, Chinese triads or the Italian Mafia. These characteristics are attributed to long experience in circumventing a totalitarian political system.
- The linkage with nuclear material trafficking, pariah states and terrorist organizations – a linkage that resonates in the public debate by combining familiar Cold War fears with the new red Mafia.
- The close links with criminal organizations from other nations, especially the Italian Mafia and drug-trafficking in Colombia, links that have been facilitated through a series of summit meetings and that are creating global criminal conglomerates which threaten international security.
- The growth of this phenomenon is likely to derail the democratization process and take over the Russian state, leading to the first criminal superpower.

[1]Thieves professing the code were high-status criminals (sometimes called thieves in law) whose status came from strict adherence to the conventions of the criminal world in Russia, including non-cooperation with the authorities of the state, even when they were imprisoned.

While not all those who adhere to the worst-case analysis would necessarily accept every detail of this picture, they all emphasize the seriousness of the threat both domestically and, increasingly, internationally.

The best-case assessment

At the other end of the spectrum are those who, in effect, deny that Russian organized crime poses a real threat. In this view, promulgated by some economists and some criminologists, it is far from the negative phenomenon portrayed in the worst-case assessment. It is possible to identify several central themes:

- Organized crime currently fulfils certain positive functions in Russian economic and social life and has become a substitute for government, particularly in the matter of contract enforcement, protection and debt collection, all of which are critical to the functioning of a market economy. Moreover, rather than organized crime infiltrating business, business often seeks out organized crime to fulfil these functions. This argument is given credence by the precedent of Sicily, where the Mafia developed in response to a weak state and the absence of a legitimate body to enforce business contracts and property rights. With an economy permeated by a basic lack of trust, protection becomes essential. The introduction of private property and private business in Russia has led to a demand for protection that the state has been unable to meet. Organized crime is filling the gap.
- Organized crime simply represents the ultimate form of capitalism, a form that is unregulated by either law or morality, and that is, therefore, particularly efficient at capital accumulation. In this view, criminal organizations are among the most progressive forces in the former

Soviet Union: they are the strongest supporters and are certainly one of the main beneficiaries of privatization; they reinvest criminal profits in the legitimate economy; and they provide considerable entrepreneurial initiative. Every transition is a rough one and what we are seeing is the Russian equivalent of the nineteenth-century robber barons who played such an important role in the industrialization of the United States.

The situation is likely to improve since organized crime is a transient phenomenon that is the product of particular conditions. As conditions change and reform continues, organized crime will dwindle in importance. As the government develops greater capacity to regulate private economic activity while relinquishing its own monopolies, organized crime will find fewer avenues for advancement. And, as the opportunities for organized crime contract, so will its power. Criminal organizations will gradually be assimilated into the legitimate economy and its leaders will become respectable legitimate businessmen, the source of whose wealth is less important than the wealth itself. The power of the market is such that the prevalence of organized crime will diminish as the market becomes free.

Again, while those who adhere to the best-case assessment may not agree with all the details of this summary, they do share the overall thrust of the analysis.

In order to assess the persuasiveness of these competing assessments, it is necessary to explore the reasons for the emergence, as well as the structure and scope, of criminal organizations and their major activities.

The rise of Russian organized crime

The emergence of Russian criminal organizations resulted from the opportunities that arose with the collapse of the Soviet Union and the end of the Cold War, and the incentives and pressures that resulted from the massive social, political and economic upheaval accompanying the transition process. In addition, criminals in Russia had available certain resources and skills that allowed them to exploit both push and pull factors and to become major players in post-communist Russia.

(a) Opportunities

Periods of transition and turmoil generally provide enormous opportunities for criminal activity, not least because of the difficulties of imposing order and enforcing restraint. This underlines one of the most important elements in the best-case assessment: the emphasis on the weakness of the state and, in particular, the inability of the state to provide contract enforcement.

This is only one form of weakness, however. As important as the inability of the state to fulfil certain positive functions necessary for the development of a flourishing market economy is its inability to prevent criminal behaviour. Whereas the first weakness is reflected in the failure to provide a legal and regulatory framework to facilitate the transition to, and management of, the new economic system, the second is manifest in the weaknesses in the legal system itself. Although there is an article in the Criminal Code covering banditry, this has not been used very much against criminal organizations and has generally been regarded as inadequate. Moreover, for a variety of complex reasons ranging from political considerations to genuine concerns about how to incorporate human rights considerations, no comprehensive legislation against organized crime is yet in place. Without this legislation and measures such as witness protection and rules for use of informants, the capacity of law enforcement to contain organized crime is seriously circumscribed. Moreover, as the Main Economic Crime Directorate of the MVD has noted, there are still no criminal penalties for phoney businesses, fictitious bankruptcies and other socially dangerous practices in a market economy.

The legislative vacuum is compounded by weaknesses in law enforcement. The consequences of the paucity of basic equipment, such as cars, telecommunications and computers are compounded by the low pay for law enforcement personnel, something that makes them highly vulnerable to the temptation of corruption. Equally significant, those entrusted with law enforcement lack familiarity with the new financial system and the operations of commercial banks. In short, the learning curve associated with capitalism has proved to be both very steep and very difficult for them to climb.

(b) Incentives and pressures

Organized crime tends to develop amidst political chaos, economic dislocation and social upheaval. Russia has been subject to all three in the 1990s. Hyperinflation, the move away from a full employment economy, and the inapplicability of the old rules and the inadequacies of the new, all created an environment in which criminal organizations could prosper. The collapse of the command economy brought with it the collapse of social and economic safety nets that had distorted Soviet economic life but provided reassurance for the average citizen. Inflation and unemployment meant that new ways had to be found to make a living. Moreover, many high-status groups suddenly found themselves poorly paid and with little prospect of improvement. In such circumstances, organized crime provided an important source of revenue. For a society that had long been used to black markets and evasion of the ostensible norms of behaviour, the new conditions were highly propitious for the emergence of criminal organizations. Moreover, these organizations were able to find a steady stream of recruits as younger men facing unemployment or poor prospects sought to emulate those with Western cars, cellular telephones and considerable money, i.e. those already involved in criminal organizations.

(c) Resources

Even with all the opportunities and the incentives and pressures, however, Russian organized crime would not have attained its current levels without certain skills and capabilities. In this connection, it is hard to disagree with worst-case analysts that it had a very good breeding-ground in the old Soviet system. Patterns of corruption were established, with links between members of the *nomenklatura* and the criminal entrepreneurs who operated the black markets in the Soviet Union providing a launching pad for much criminal activity in post-Soviet Russia. In addition, many people became adept at circumventing state authorities. While the shadow or black economy was much broader than organized crime, the flouting of laws and the accumulation of illegal capital provided a highly congenial environment for the development of criminal organizations.

The Soviet period was also one in which traditions of criminal governance were established and developed. The thieves professing the code were important figures in the Soviet criminal world, and their imprisonment helped to develop the bonding mechanisms that added to their authority both inside and outside prison. The thieves provided arbitration and guidance in the criminal world, offering governance and order in a milieu often thought of as totally disorderly. They subsequently brought their experience and traditions into the new economic and political system, posing a challenge that was all the more serious now that the traditional constraints had been removed. This constellation of circumstances favourable to criminal organizations was evident in the speed with which they developed, the extent of their development, and the scope of their activities.

The dimensions of Russian organized crime

(a) Size and structure
According to the published figures, there has been a constant, inexorable growth in the number of criminal organizations, from 3,000 in 1992 to 5,700 in 1994 and about 8,000 in late 1995/early 1996. At first glance, these figures seem to reveal an ever-increasing threat from an expanding criminal empire. It is equally plausible, however, that the increase reflects other factors: looser criteria for categorizing groups as criminal organizations and in particular the inclusion of small and unimportant street gangs; fissiparous tendencies in many Russian criminal organizations and hence a greater number of smaller groups; exaggeration of the threat on the part of Russian law enforcement authorities anxious for more Western assistance; or simply increased visibility of criminal organizations as a result of more efficient policing and better intelligence analysis. Moreover, the official figures do not reveal the process of consolidation among individual organizations that has led well-informed observers to claim that there are about 200 major criminal organizations with widespread geographical and sectoral influence. According to a detailed analysis by Guy Dunn of Control Risks, there are six large groups in Moscow – three Chechen groups (the Tstentralnaya, Ostankinskaya, and Avtomobilnaya) which have about 1,500 members between them, the Solntsevskaya and Podolskaya organizations, and the 21st Century Association; another four major groups in St Petersburg, two major gangs in Yekaterinburg (the Uralmashkaya and the Tsentralnaya); and nine major gangs in Vladivostok.

Even with the consolidation process, however, organized crime in Russia is highly diverse and fractured, with ethnic divisions, divisions based on territorial and sectoral control and on generational splits, and divisions between those who have established symbiotic links with officials and those who do not enjoy such access. There has been some role specialization, with particular groups dominating specific spheres of activity (e.g. Chechens dominate the petroleum trade, Azeri groups are particularly prominent in the drug business, and Georgians are heavily involved in burglaries and robberies).

This specialization has been helpful in limiting conflicts, at least at times, and has not precluded cooperative arrangements when there were obvious benefits from joint activity, including contributions to a common pool of resources, the *obshak*, which is used to support the families of those in prison, for bribery and corruption, and to generate new enterprises. But there has also been enormous competition among the groups resulting from ethnic divisions, rival territorial claims, and personal animosities among criminal leaders. A major split has emerged between thieves professing the code and the new generation of criminals who do not respect established traditions, are more entrepreneurial and, in some cases, have become authorities because of wealth, rather than status accrued through time in prison. As a result the thieves have suffered considerable attrition.

Overlapping this particular rift is a continuing struggle for dominance between the Russian or Slavic groups and those from the Caucasus. In part these conflicts reflect the powerful internal bonding mechanisms that provide the basis for trust in a milieu without formal laws and rules. These can be based on ethnicity, common experience in the military or security service, or the camaraderie of functionally based groups such as the karate or sportsmen organizations that are a feature of organized crime not only in Russia but elsewhere in the former Soviet bloc. From the perspective of Russian law enforcement this diversity is a weakness: competition is preferable to further consolidation. At the same time, the very diversity and complexity of Russian criminal organizations makes concerted action against them difficult. So does the fact that many of the groups have infiltrated licit business and established inroads in key sectors of the licit economy.

(b) Infiltration of the banking industry
The Russian banking system faces many problems that have little or nothing to do with organized crime. In order to develop into a system appropriate for a market economy, its structure, procedures and underlying norms all have to change. Cosy relationships with state enterprises have to be broken and new practices based on accurate evaluations of credit risks have to be implemented. Yet, so long as criminal organizations exert significant influence in the banking sector, progress will be limited.

The disruptive effect of organized crime was manifest in December 1993, when Russia's major commercial banks closed for the funeral of the Chairman of Rosselkhoz bank, Nikolai Likhachev, whose death was one more in a long series of murders of bank officials. Bank chairmen expressed their alarm and frustration not only at the failure to apprehend the killers but also at the gap between government rhetoric and effective action.

These sentiments were validated by subsequent developments: from 1994 to July 1995 there were thirty assassination attempts against top banking officials, sixteen of whom were killed. These killings, along with the earlier ones, were an important indicator of the efforts by criminal organizations to infiltrate the Russian banking system and take control of particular banks. Criminal ownership of banks is not unprecedented. If the Russians cannot claim responsibility for innovation, however, they have turned this technique into an art form. In August 1995 the MVD All Russia Scientific Research Institute estimated that criminal groups control over 400 banks and 47 exchanges. An even more pessimistic assessment was made by Professor Lydia Krasfavina, head of the Institute for Banking and Financial Managers, who estimated that 70 to 80 per cent of private banks in Russia are controlled by organized crime. What control actually means is not entirely clear. In some cases criminals could have forced their way onto the board of bank officials and become full participants in all key decisions of the bank. Alternatively, they may remain in the background, exercising their power simply through intimidation.

Whatever the precise mechanism, infiltration of the banking system offers significant advantages for criminal organizations. It facilitates money laundering, by both Russian and foreign criminal organizations.

While this is not vital in a system where questions about the origin of money are simply not asked, it is a long-term hedge in the event that serious regulations to counter money laundering are eventually imposed by the Russian government. It is not necessary to worry too much about suspicious transaction reports when one owns the bank. Another benefit is that the organization can use at least part of the capital resources of the bank for its own purposes or, at the very least, obtain preferential credit. Blackmail of business is also facilitated (see below). In cases where businessmen have been engaged in tax evasion, they often find it preferable to pay the criminals than to pay the government. Similarly, access to the banking industry provides resources that facilitate the corruption used by criminal organizations to reduce the risks from law enforcement. Not all the consequences of criminal activity in the banking sector are wholly negative. In the short term laundered money added a high degree of liquidity to an economy desperate for capital investment. Yet these positive effects cannot obscure the negative consequences. It is difficult for the government or the Central Bank to ration credit and control the money supply – two tasks that are essential for effective macroeconomic management – when the banks have their own agendas, in many cases motivated by the desire to facilitate or extend criminal activities.

Not surprisingly, therefore, there have been efforts to clean up the banking sector, with the detection of an increasing number of crimes, more charges being pressed against officials for criminal behaviour, especially in relation to the provision of credits, and a greater willingness to impose sanctions against banks that do not abide by the rules. The effort to impose greater regulation on the banking industry, however, has met considerable resistance. On 18 March 1996, for example, shots were fired into the home of the chairman of the Russian Central Bank, Sergei Dubinin, leading to speculation that this was because the Central Bank had aroused the anger of criminal organizations by revoking the licences of certain commercial banks.

(c) Infiltration of industry

Infiltration of the banking sector has provided access to an excellent source of intelligence for criminal organizations, allowing them to identify targets for extortion, especially businesses that have evaded tax and would find it cheaper to pay a criminal tax than be reported to the authorities. Both domestic and foreign firms have been targets, with the criminals demanding about 10 per cent of the turnover. Although there have been reports that extortion methods have become increasingly sophisticated, with the criminal organizations offering to provide protection in return for a share of the profits, and actually placing their members in key positions in firms, the continued use of violence against businessmen suggests that the notion that businesses seek out criminal organizations for contract enforcement provides only one part of the picture. During 1995, for example, several high officials in the aluminium industry were killed as part of what was clearly an effort by organized crime groups to become major participants in what is a highly lucrative export industry. It followed a pattern whereby criminal organizations have joined with entrepreneurs and corrupt officials to export large segments of Russia's raw-material base.

(d) Contract killings

Events in the aluminium industry have also been part of a wider pattern of criminal activity in Russia, characterized by the increased prevalence of contract killings. According to one estimate there were about 100 of these in 1992, rising to some 250 during 1993. In January 1996, Tass suggested that such killings had now reached around 500 a year. Earlier reports, however, indicated that in Moscow at least, there had been something of a decline from one a week to one a month. Even if the figure of 500 a year is correct, such killings are only a small proportion of the murders in Russia. In 1992, for example, there were 319 murders in Yekaterinburg, but only 20 of them had the characteristics that led law enforcement authorities to classify them as contract killings. Nevertheless, their importance is far greater than their number, largely because the victims of contract killers tend to be bosses of the criminal world who are killed as part of the struggle for power; businessmen or bankers who resist hostile takeovers by criminal organizations; and journalists, law enforcement officers, officials, and politicians who are serious about exposing and eliminating corruption. In effect, the use of contract killing has been extended from an instrument of intergroup warfare to an instrument used to punish or eliminate those who stand up to criminal organizations. The killings themselves are generally done by professionals, many of whom are Afghan veterans or former members of the security services.

(e) Drug-trafficking

Drug-trafficking in Russia has become a major activity, involving not only well-publicized links with Colombian cocaine-traffickers, but also the supply of opium, heroin and marijuana from Central Asia and the Golden Crescent. In addition, there have been several major cases involving large-scale trafficking in synthetic drugs. While much of the trafficking is carried out by individuals or small groups, a great deal of activity is structured and controlled by larger criminal networks. The networks in Russia itself are linked with those in Central Asia and have become adept at both marketing and ensuring a regular supply of narcotics. In 1993/4, 126.74 kilograms of all kinds of drugs were seized in 418 separate incidents; during 1995/6, 457.3 kilograms were seized in 767 incidents. Although the increase can be accounted for in part by greater efficiency in interdiction and continued improvements in law-enforcement techniques, it also reflects what appears to be an expanding market in Russia as well as the growing use of Russian territory for the transshipment of drugs to western Europe. While the problem has been exacerbated by the fact that Nigerian drug-traffickers have also been very active in their effort to exploit what they see as an important new market, the indigenous organized crime groups have found drug-trafficking to be a highly lucrative activity. Whereas some organizations specialize, others combine drug-trafficking with activities such as car theft, prostitution, extortion and fraud. Indeed, one of the strengths of organized crime in Russian is that it has so many different dimensions and engages in such a wide range of activity.

(f) Nuclear material trafficking

The issue that has aroused the greatest trepidation is that of smuggling of nuclear material. Lack of security at some nuclear facilities, and poor inventory management, have provided opportunities for disgruntled workers in the nuclear industry. The possibility that, through either economic need or intimidation, they could offer weapons-grade material to criminal organizations provides the basis for nightmare scenarios ranging from large-scale environmental damage to nuclear terrorism or nuclear extortion. What remains uncertain, however, is the extent to which such trafficking is a core activity of Russian criminal organizations. For the most part it has been the preserve of amateur smugglers. Yet there is some evidence that criminal organizations have been involved on a limited basis. One arrest seems to have involved twelve members of the Solntsevskaya in possession of radioactive material, while in another case, a group of criminals from Yekaterinburg was involved in the smuggling of large amounts of zirconium to the United States and Cyprus. Nuclear material trafficking is not yet a core activity of Russian organized crime, not least because the risks are high and the profits uncertain, but it could become much more important. For groups engaged in trafficking drugs or exporting strategic materials it is not difficult simply to change the product line.

(g) Corruption

Corruption in Russia is extensive; moreover, much of it is self-generated by those in authority and has little to do with organized crime. Yet this contributes to an atmosphere in which principles are less important than profits and which is open to exploitation by criminal groups. Indeed, corruption is used by these organizations to minimize the likelihood of real law-enforcement efforts against them, to obtain counter-intelligence that neutralizes genuine enforcement efforts, or to ensure that enforcement does not result in prosecution or conviction. In a sense, corruption is a way of keeping the state weak and acquiescent. It could be argued, of course, that there is nothing new in all this, and that the old patterns which existed in the Soviet Union are simply being revised to fit the new circumstances. Yet there is a crucial difference: it is increasingly the criminal organizations that determine the rules of the game. In the old Soviet system many government officials used the black market as a safety valve, tacitly acknowledging the role of those who operated in this market. In the new system, much corruption is designed not to overcome the inefficiencies of state control of economic life, but to protect criminal organizations from law enforcement. As some members of the political elite have willingly or unwillingly accommodated those who have the power to hurt

and the wealth to purchase support, a new type of symbiotic relationship with sectors of the state apparatus has emerged in which organized crime is the dominant force. Indeed, systemic corruption as an instrument of organized crime has helped to maintain a safe home base within which criminal organizations can function unhindered and from which they can increasingly engage in transnational activities.

(h) The transnational dimension

Although many Russian criminal organizations are local in character, other groups are heavily engaged in transnational activities and, in some cases, have significant links with criminal organizations elsewhere. Russian criminal organizations are active in Germany, the United States and Israel, as well as in Holland and Belgium. In addition, Cyprus has become a major recipient of the profits of Russian criminal activity, while there is considerable concern in London about money laundering through British financial institutions. In the United States, Russian criminals have been involved in fuel tax evasion schemes, health care and insurance fraud, extortion, car theft, and contract murders. Although Brighton Beach is the main centre of Russian organized crime in the United States, Russian criminal networks are active in Florida, California and the Pacific Northwest. They also have a significant presence in Germany, which has become a source of luxury cars for the Russian market, a major battleground for intergroup rivalries, and an important market both for illicit products and for licit products that have been obtained through illegal means.

Appraisal and analysis

Although this brief survey is far from exhaustive, it allows us to identify the weaknesses of both the worst-case and the best-case assessments. In several areas the worst-case assessment exaggerates by oversimplifying. There is, for example, a real threat from nuclear material trafficking, but to portray it as a major activity of Russian organized crime is to misrepresent what is first and foremost an opportunist activity engaged in by a variety of participants. Similarly, while former KGB operatives are among the more important players in Russian organized crime, especially regarding contract killing, neither they nor the thieves professing the code control what is

a complex, sprawling, multi-dimensional phenomenon that is not subject to simple characterization, let alone central direction. The corollary is that the idea of summit meetings and cooperation between Russian and Italian criminal organizations *per se* also has to be scaled back: it is important to recognize that though some of this does go on, this is far from the establishment of global criminal conglomerates.

For its part, the best-case assessment, fixated on both the virtues and the power of the licit market, ignores the symbiotic links between criminal organizations and members of the political and economic elite, and the resulting capacity of organized crime to perpetuate the weakness and acquiescence of the state even when market conditions change. In other countries organized crime has displayed a remarkable capacity to prosper through economic diversification even when some of the market conditions that contributed so much to its emergence have disappeared. In the United States, for example, it survived the change in market conditions brought about by the end of prohibition. And whereas organized crime in the United States traditionally revolved around the supply of illicit goods and services, in Russia it runs far deeper, partly because, in the transition process, there is no clear demarcation between what is legal and what is not. This has allowed criminal organizations to move beyond the supply of illicit goods and services and extend their activities into what in the West is often characterized as white-collar crime. As a result, organized crime has become a very powerful force in the social, political and economic fabric of post-communist Russia. In such circumstances, respect for the law is likely to be minimal. The symbols of wealth and power displayed by organized crime are very attractive and encourage emulation. Recruitment is easy as illicit routes for advancement promise far greater and more immediate rewards than legitimate avenues.

In short, the problem is unlikely to go away and could get worse. In the meantime, there are several ways in which organized crime can hinder the reform process. Simply because organized crime groups are entrepreneurial capitalists, this does not necessarily mean that they facilitate the transition to a market economy. Far from being a positive force, organized crime threatens the integrity of political and economic institutions and emerging social and commercial norms. Violence against businessmen and bankers can deter at least some foreign investment, while organized crime hampers economic competition and stifles legitimate entrepreneurial activity at the domestic level. It is difficult for legitimate entrepreneurs to compete with those who have ready access to large financial resources obtained through illicit means. Moreover, when organized crime takes over particular sectors of the economy, it proves very difficult to dislodge. In the United States, for example, it still has considerable influence over the construction industry, especially in New York, and over waste disposal. In sum, penetration of the economic system has serious long-term consequences, and is not easily eradicated.

Against this, it is possible to argue, as best-case analysts would, that the licit market will prove irresistible and that there will be a gradual legitimization of criminal capitalists. Although the first generation of capitalists are more concerned with capital accumulation than with the means of achieving it, they will want their sons and daughters to be legitimate, with the result that there will be a gradual transition from illicit to licit business. Support for this thesis can be found in the phenomenon of ethnic succession in organized crime in the United States and the way in which the traditional mafia has declined in importance. Such a process could be assisted by the development of effective rules and regulations to govern the economy. The theory here is that unregulated capitalism in which illicit business looms largest will give way to a more regulated form of capitalism that is dominated by licit business: in short, there will be a gradual cleansing process.

The more gloomy alternative, of course, is one in which the process moves in the opposite direction, with corruption becoming an all-pervasive phenomenon leading ultimately to a collusive relationship between the state and organized crime.

In the final analysis, it may well be the Russian government itself that is the determining factor. The elevation of Lebed during the 1996 election campaign was a promising sign but also suggests that increasingly the major divide in Russian politics is not between reformers and conservatives, but between the corrupt and the non-corrupt. Avoiding the more pessimistic outcome, however, depends not only on the ability and willingness of the political establishment to cleanse itself but also on its capacity to impose a legal framework that allows law enforcement officials to attack organized crime more effectively and that establishes and implements effective regulation for crucial sectors of the economy such as banking. In addition to preventive and control measures, it is also crucial to eliminate incentives such as high levels of taxation for forms of behaviour that allow Russia's nascent capitalists and legitimate entrepreneurs to become easy targets for criminal organizations. The overall task is not impossible, but it is formidable, and requires a far more comprehensive, systematic, and sustained effort than the Russian government has yet developed.

Phil Williams is Director of the Ridgeway Center for International Security Studies.
The author would like to thank Jonathan Harris of the Department of Political Science University of Pittsburgh for his helpful comments on an earlier draft of his paper, Roy Allison and the participants at the seminar he set up on this subject at Chatham House, and Alan Smith for his valuable editorial suggestions. All responsibility for sins of omission and commission remains that of the author alone.

22

Russian Emigré Crime in the United States: Organized Crime or Crime that is Organized?

JAMES FINCKENAUER and ELIN WARING[1]

In recent years there has been a tremendous amount of media, scholarly and law enforcement attention to organized crime involving émigrés from the former Soviet Union (henceforth, Russian émigrés).[2] The Federal Bureau of Investigation, for example, has reflected this concern by issuing reports and establishing a field office in Moscow. Newspaper and magazine headlines trumpet the presence of 'Russian godfathers', and publications have begun to appear in criminological and legal journals.[3] The law enforcement and media attention has mostly occurred in cities and states where there is a concentrated population of Russian émigrés, such as New York City, Philadelphia, and parts of Florida and California.[4]

Despite this increasing attention, there has been little systematic research into the nature of the criminal activities of Russian émigrés in the United States or into how they are organized. As a result, we know relatively little about such issues as:

1. the nature of the organization of Russian émigré 'organized crime'

2. the nature of the harm caused by Russian crime networks

3. the areas of potential development of other types of harm by these networks in the United States.

In fact, there has been little evaluation of whether the use of the term organized crime to describe the criminal activities of Russian émigrés is appropriate. Our purpose here is to begin to address these issues.

Conceptual Framework

The assessment that follows is premised upon a number of assumptions. Three of these assumptions are critical in furnishing the prism through which we will view Russian émigré crime. The first is that criminal organization can be usefully examined both in terms of its structure and in terms of the activities in which it engages. The second is that criminal organization is not synonymous with organized crime. The third assumption is that the nature and extent of harm caused is an essential dimension for characterizing a criminal organization.

Structural approaches have proven particularly useful for the study of traditional organized crime, that is, the *Cosa Nostra*. *Cosa Nostra* maintains continuing hierarchical structures (crime families) which are supported by crime and other ancillary activities and that have a division of labor. When criminal activities extend over time, and when the same individuals are engaging in multiple criminal ventures (as is true for the *Cosa Nostra*), a high degree of interpersonal trust among the co-offenders is demanded. For the *Cosa Nostra*, the code of *omerta* acts to guarantee and enforce this trust. Absent the interpersonal trust that derives from ethnic bonds, rituals, long-standing relationships, being 'men of honor', and the insurance of *omerta*, criminal organization will differ from that of the *Cosa Nostra*. Instead, it is expected that structures which either incorporate market elements or, over time, those which more closely resemble licit 'upperworld' organizations will dominate.[5] In the latter forms, coordination of criminal activities would be focused on short-term criminal ventures and would not incorporate a great deal of repeated-partnering of the same offenders. Instead, *ad hoc* teams come together for specific criminal ventures, forming opportunistic partnerships. This short-term network structure resembles what McIntosh called the 'project type' of criminal organization.[6] Organizational structure is created on an as-needed basis to enable the co-offenders to carry out particular crimes. The criminal opportunities come first, and the organizational arrangements needed to take advantage of these opportunities follow.

There can be organized crimes without there being organized crime. Crime that is organized is characterized by the coordinated activity of a number of actors. A criminal venture may be highly complex and require intricate and sophisticated arrangements, sometime including links between the licit and the illicit spheres.[7] Crime that is organized may also operate for long periods of time, as in the case of monopolization of licit areas of the economy and long-term frauds.[8] Once a venture is completed, however, the organized structure created to carry it out may dissolve. In contrast, organized crime structures continue to exist outside of the specific criminal undertaking or criminal opportunity. Organized crime involves coordination of a number of separate criminal activities in different areas of criminal endeavor, whereas crime that is organized is usually focused on a single area. This contrast is in many ways parallel to that between the ongoing bureaucratic structure of large corporations and the structure of teams which come together for particular projects, such as the production of motion pictures.[9]

Organized crime is characterized by three types of harm: criminal monopoly, violence and corruption. Other forms of criminal organization may involve one or two of these harms, but organized crime is distinctive in engaging in all three and in using each of the three to reinforce the other two. Just as a desire for market monopoly exists in the licit marketplace, it also exists in the illicit marketplace. Monopolization represents total control of a market. Criminal monopolies are attained by eliminating competition. Criminal organizations attain monopoly control through the threat and use of violence and through corruption of the legal and political systems.

Violence as a type of harm committed by organized crime may have both a specific instrumental purpose, as in the case of creating and maintaining criminal monopolies, and a more general intent to create an atmosphere of fear and intimidation. Ultimately, force and violence facilitate community control and undermine the legal system because people are unwilling to report crimes, to be witnesses, or to serve on juries. This type of intimidation is more generalized than that which may exist between an individual victim and an individual victimizer.

Like violence, corruption is instrumental in providing organized crime with insurance against arrest, prosecution, and conviction for crimes. Corruption also facilitates monopoly control by enlisting the authorities in the elimination of criminal competitors. Corruption harms the very integrity of the legal and political systems. Law enforcement becomes distorted, and the rule of law is undermined. The supreme harm is in the minds of citizens who lose respect for the legitimacy of the system and who, as a result, fail to support what they come to believe are corrupted processes.

These assumptions about the structure of organized crime and the nature of the harms it causes will guide our examination of Russian émigré crime in New York, New Jersey, and Pennsylvania. We will first describe the types of crime in which Russian émigrés have been implicated and then examine the extent to which these activities fit definitions and understandings of organized crime.

The Data

In 1992, in response to what was perceived as a growing problem, the New York State Organized Crime Task Force, the New York State Commission of Investigation, the Pennsylvania Crime Commission, and the New Jersey State Commission of Investigation agreed to form the Tri-State Joint Soviet-émigré Organized Crime Project (hereafter TSP). The purpose of the project was 'to identify the nature and extent of Russian-émigré crime within the tri-state region ... in order to assist law enforcement in its ongoing effort to combat the threat of organized crime'.[10] Through a cooperative agreement with the TSP, we were able to examine the law enforcement and other (mainly news media) records assembled by the project team.[11] This enabled us to get a wide view of the types of offending by Russian émigrés who had come to the attention of these agencies. The source materials included 404 separate documents with a variety of formats and lengths. Although this, of course, reflects numerous biases, such as the willingness of other agencies with knowledge of criminal activities of Russian émigrés to cooperate with the project, and the problem of criminal activities that never come to the attention of law enforcement agencies, the project staff made great efforts to collect information from as wide a variety of sources as possible.

Although we are continuing to subject our data to a variety of analyses, a great deal about the nature of the crimes committed by these networks has already been learned by reviewing the crime descriptions in these documents. Following the operational definition used by the TSP, by Russian émigrés we mean individuals in the United States who were born in the region formerly known as the Soviet Union, and their children. These definition includes not only Russians, but others with a variety of ethnic identities including Armenian, Chechen, Ukrainian, Azeri, and Jewish.

Russian Emigré Crime in the Tri-State Region

The most common type of crime disclosed in the TSP investigation is fraud. Although the fuel tax evasion cases are the largest and best known cases of this type, other forms of fraud also appear to be common, and the range of types is quite broad.[12] Many involve typical confidence schemes, and, in these cases, the victims are generally members of the Russian émigré community. For example, there have been several incidents of jewelry switching in which an inexpensive piece is substituted for the real one, while the offender pretends to inspect the item.

More sophisticated frauds are similar to those found elsewhere. A number of incidents involve Medicaid fraud. In these cases, bills for services are submitted when the named services were never provided or were actually non-medical in nature. The services not provided range from medical examinations to the purchase of medical equipment. Another scheme involved the use of ambulettes for transportation that were then billed as medical, and the operation of a prostitution ring through a home health attendant service.

An automobile insurance ring which staged accidents in order to receive insurance payments was operated by Russian émigrés in Pennsylvania. It submitted over 1 million dollars in phony claims in the early 1990s. Here again, the involvement of actors in the legitimate economy – the leader was the owner of a medical clinic and at least one of the doctors employed at the clinic was involved in the scheme – are an essential part of the organization of the crimes. The organization of this scheme is not very different from that used by other insurance scam teams.

Counterfeiting, like fraud, is an area of non-violent criminal activity in which some Russian émigrés have been active. There are numerous incidents involving the production of counterfeit credit cards, and there appears to be a well-established market for such cards that are then used to make purchases to be sold on the stolen goods market. The operation of this ongoing market indicates that this type of offense also involves some level of organization, although individuals who purchase the cards may operate on their own. Counterfeiting of checks, Immigration and Naturalization Service documents, passports, and other documents is another area of activity involving a number of separate individuals who organize the market and supply others with their products.

Russian émigrés are also involved in drug and drug paraphernalia markets. These cases generally involve established networks of individuals and include the importation and street level sales of drugs. There are instances involving cooperation with people from other ethnic backgrounds; most notably there is some evidence of cooperation of Russian émigrés with Colombian drug cartels. There is evidence that former Republics of the Soviet Union are being used as transshipment points for drug importation to the United States.[13] Other Russian émigrés have been charged with the operation of factories producing crack vials in New Jersey and Pennsylvania.

Smuggling incidents involving Russian émigrés range from aluminum to weapons to currency to drugs. There are a number of cases of apparent money laundering involving large cash transactions just below the size that would require the filing of a Currency Transaction Report. Drug marketing, smuggling and money laundering are all activities frequently associated with traditional organized crime. As in the case of stolen goods and counterfeit documents, these are areas in which crime networks composed of individuals from the former Soviet Union are providing illegal goods and services through an organized market.

Russian émigrés have shown both a willingness and a capacity to use violence, including murder, extortion, and assaults. Enforcers work in the extortion of businesses in Brighton Beach, Brooklyn. These specialists work for whomever pays them, and there seems to be little evidence of monopoly control of extortion by any clearly defined group.[14] There are sometimes fights over extortion victims, and those victims who refuse to pay are beaten.

There have been more than 65 murders and attempted murders involving Russians and Russian émigrés since 1981 that have indicia of organized crime. A number of them occurred in the tri-state area, and many remain unsolved or unprosecuted. The murders and attempts that have occurred so far seem, however, to be neither systematic nor designed to protect a criminal enterprise. Instead, they appear to have been motivated mainly by greed or personal vendetta. In some instances one homicide seemed to trigger a long series of murders and attempted murders. In most cases, the offender apparently was paying the victim back for some offense. Russian émigré violence is not random; care seems to be exercised in the choice of victims, avoiding harm to innocent bystanders. The threat of violence is clearly used to intimidate others in the émigré community. In the case of homicides, witnesses have refused to come forward or to cooperate with the police. As has been true in US drug markets involving other criminal groups, Russian émigré violence is also believed to be an aspect of the unregulated competition that exists in their criminal ventures.

Other forms of violence or threatened violence are also common. Kidnapping is one example. Extortion of businesses in exchange for protection is also practiced by Russian émigré criminals. To some extent this may represent the continuation of a practice that operated in the former Soviet Union that allowed legal and illegal businesses to operate without disruption by either the state or criminals. One form of extortion in Russia involves persons called 'roofs'. These extortionists offer protection and security to businessmen and their associates. In return, 'roofs' receive a share of the business profits. The term 'roof' is also used by Russian émigrés in this country. It is not yet known, however, whether the term is being used to describe the US extension of Russian-based criminal organizations, or whether it has simply been appropriated to distinguish a hierarchy among Russian émigré crime groups. Several substantial cases of extortion have been prosecuted in the tri-state region, including the case against Vyacheslav Ivankov, who is charged, in part, with murder in the course of an attempted extortion of two Russian émigré businessmen.

Across a wide variety of types of offenses, these schemes require extensive coordination between actors and infiltration of legitimate areas of the economy. The organization of these offenses is responsive to the specific nature of the criminal opportunity, for example, the need to mimic the operation of legitimate businesses, rather than any existing criminal organization. The crime networks described in the TSP documents are formed by criminal entrepreneurs in response to specific settings rather than by existing structures either continuously operating in a field or branching into a new area.

Of the types of harm that are traditionally associated with the operation of organized crime – violence, monopoly and corruption – the one most clearly evident in these data is violence. The violence is used mainly to intimidate the public, potential competitors, and those who might be seen as disloyal. In this respect, the crime networks described here resemble traditional organized crime. There is, however, no indication that Russian émigrés have established any criminal monopolies; rather the offenses take place in a variety of areas and do not represent the total domination of any markets. Further, at this stage Russian émigré criminals do not appear to be using systematic corruption in order to protect their enterprises in the United States.

Criminal Organization

Licit organizations are shaped by their environments, the actors which inhabit them, the technologies which they use, and the nature of the activities in which they engage.[15] In a comparable way, criminal organizations are shaped by the culture and institutional patterns of criminal organizations in the places of origin of their members, as well as by the nature of criminal opportunities and the institutional patterns of criminal organization in the new location. Thus, Russian émigré criminal organization in the United States is influenced by the institutionalized practices of criminal organization in the former Soviet Union, the nature of the criminal opportunities available in the contemporary United States, and the operation of preexisting organized crime activity in specific markets and locations. We will review the nature of each of these influences and how they have affected the organization of Russian émigré crime.

Influences from the Former Soviet Union

The most obvious influence from the former Soviet Union is the set of cultural practices known as 'conniving and surviving.' As described by Rosner, the particular focus of Soviets on illegal ways of obtaining legal goods and services may be transplanted to the United States.[16] The use of bribery, black markets, and other schemes to survive in Soviet society is well documented.[17] Rosner and others have argued that the attitudes towards everyday fraud and corruption can be expected to be directly transplanted to the United States. In the former Soviet Union organized crime and its accompaniments – corruption, the shadow economy, and the black market – first flourished because of the peculiarities of the Soviet economy and politics. Both the economy and the politics have changed dramatically in recent years, but those patterns had a strong influence on those who have emigrated.

Because of the unique confluence of circumstances and characteristics, the USSR in many ways produced a people uniquely socialized to facilitate their involvement (both as clients and victims) in organized crime. Rosner concluded:

> The new Russian immigrant [to the United States] arrived on these shores already steeped in a criminal system ... and with certain skills already in place. It is the conclusion of this study that these immigrants did not change their behavior to ascend the American social ladder. Rather, they continued patterns of behavior that were ingrained after a lifetime in a social system where extralegal values were stressed .... [18]

Rosner divided Soviet émigrés into survivors and connivers, then further subdivided them into necessary criminals, criminals, and system beaters.[19] Necessary criminals were those who were forced by circumstances in the USSR into criminal behavior there. System beaters were those who violate US law in dealing with bureaucratic agencies here. Ex-Soviets have arrived here steeped in criminal methods and values, and undoubtedly some have used these to continue their criminality and even to become sophisticated, organized criminals.

All the émigrés from the former Soviet Union share a common heritage. It includes the state-run, centrally-planned Soviet command economy which produced product shortages as well as widespread bribery and thievery. No area of life in the Soviet Union was exempt from pervasive, universal corruption. Scarce goods and services which were unavailable through normal channels could usually be gotten through *blat* (connections) or *na levo* (on the left). An illegal second or shadow economy arose to operate in tandem with the official economy.

The notorious Soviet black market was a component of the shadow economy. It marketed a wide variety of products from Western consumer items to stolen goods, drugs, and bootleg liquor and cigarettes. Because goods were priced much higher on the black market, there was also incentive to siphon off goods from the official market for sale on the black market. There is considerable evidence that this practice has not ended with the collapse of the Soviet Union, but, rather, it has expanded. The nature of the goods being marketed has become much more sophisticated, and the consumer market itself has become much more international. The amount of money involved is much greater. The range of illegal goods being marketed today through multi-national links includes antiques, drugs, stolen cars, weapons (including nuclear weapons materials), metals, etc. It has been projected that organized crime in the former USSR may quickly move into such areas as video piracy, crack refining, and computer crime.[20]

The *perestroika* reforms of the late 1980s, and the demise of the USSR itself in 1991, followed by the economic problems of the past several years have all fed an enormous growth of new forms of organized crime in Russia. It is under these conditions that some of the traditional activities of Western organized crime (mostly unknown in the old Soviet Union), such as drug trafficking and prostitution, but especially extortion of new companies, businesses, and restaurants, have become among the more prevalent forms of current criminal enterprises in Moscow and other Russian cities.

The old Soviet political and socioeconomic system bred illegality and corruption on a scale matched by few countries.[21] Simis described the pervasiveness of Soviet corruption and its links to the shadow economy:

> Underground enterprise is a positive tumor of corruption. Like a drop of water, it reflects the whole world of Soviet improbity. Just as the human body cannot live without air; underground enterprise could not survive except for the fact that the Soviet state and society alike are rotten with corruption from the top to bottom.[22]

Although the partocracy of the Communist Party which engendered this kind of corruption is gone, there is every indication that so far at least the crime and corruption have only gotten worse.[23]

Criminal Patterns from the Former Soviet Union

Beyond these cultural explanations, however, lie institutional ones. Those Russian émigrés who are criminally active in the United States will follow patterns and structures similar to those that they are familiar with from their places of origin. This allows us to look at how crime is organized, instead of why people have certain attitudes towards crime and the police, or differing propensities to commit crime. Existing analyses of types of offenders in the former Soviet Union identify four major categories, each of which may have a place among Russian émigrés in the United States. They are professional criminals, criminal entrepreneurs, 'thieves in authority' and the *vory v zakone* or 'thieves in law'. There is some evidence of the operation of each of these types among Russian émigrés in the United States.

Ordinary professional criminals are those who make their living through criminal activity and who specialize in particular crime types.[24] Often, they know each other and either worked with each other or were in jail together in the Soviet Union. These criminal types are of varying levels of criminal sophistication. One of the predominant criminal professions, for example, is pickpocket. There are many examples of professional criminals from the former Soviet Union who are involved in crime in the United States, although in some instances they branched into new areas. For example, David Schuster, who was involved in one of the bootleg gasoline scams in New Jersey, was known as a professional pickpocket back home.

The young entrepreneurs see crime as the easy route to riches.[25] These are young people – in their late 'teens, twenties and thirties – who were not criminals before the collapse of the Soviet Union, but who did of necessity have experience in the black market and the shadow economy. Some are students or graduates of higher education; others were in the military. None has attractive job prospects in the legitimate sector. They are a pool for recruitment by criminal organizations in Russia, or they operate with their own small networks. Unlike that of the professionals, their criminal behavior is not very well entrenched. They are first generation criminals, and their crimes are most often crimes of opportunity.

The 'thieves in authority' (*avtoritety*), labeled comrade criminals by Handelman, emerged largely during the last decades of the Soviet Union, especially during the Brezhnev period. Some were part of the *nomenklatura* of the Communist Party or were Soviet bureaucrats. Some were deputy directors, former administrators of factories or other business enterprises, or ran cooperatives during the Gorbachev era. Some were members of the national security and military establishments. Whatever their specific background, nearly all of them are well educated; they often had international connections before the collapse. Vaksberg called this group the Soviet Mafia.[26] As Handelman points out, these 'gangster-bureaucrats' operate at the intersection of crime, capitalism, and government in the former Soviet Union.[27] They have the knowledge, the experience, the sophistication, and the contacts, to run international banking schemes and major commodities deals. They are also the ones best suited to deal in black market nuclear materials. For these reasons, they have the greatest potential for future harm.

Reputed members of the *vory v zakone* have been said to be the closest thing the ex-Soviets have to being a 'made guy' in the *Cosa Nostra*, and the top members are portrayed as godfather-like figures. The *vory* are the most criminally sophisticated of the professional criminals. Their roots are generally traced to the Soviet prison system, particularly the Stalinist *gulag* of the 1930s. They are characterized by a complete commitment to the criminal life. Following their own laws and rules, they reject any involvement with or obligation to the legitimate world. The *vory* have a relatively non-hierarchical structure, with a low differentiation among the members, and an elite that is considered the first among equals.[28] Afanasyev reports an estimated 600 *vory* in the former Soviet Union, with approximately 200 of them in Russia itself.[29] He says there is a Moscow-based 'politburo'of 10 to 15 *vory* who govern the criminal world through their representatives. Ivankov, arrested with much attention in New York, is believed to be one of the Russian *vory*, and perhaps even among the top leadership group.[30] The FBI estimates that there have been four other *vory v zakone* in the United States at one time or another.[31]

The *vory* share a number of characteristics with other criminal organizations and subcultures, including a set of rules and a code of behavior, nicknames, a slang, and the ability to eject members from the association. They also have a system for mediating and resolving disputes. Whether there is any enforcement mechanism to back-up these resolutions is not clear.

Some challenge the importance of the *vory* both now and as a future threat in the United States.[32] It is alleged that the traditional initiation into the *vory* has been corrupted by the selling of the title of *vor*. If this is so it could mean that there will be increasing difficulty with maintaining internal discipline. The criminal expertise of the *vory* revolves around common crimes like theft, robbery, and extortion. The complex crimes of commodities scams, international banking, dealing in strategic metals, and international money laundering are beyond the scope of criminal expertise for most of them. They may be the most criminally sophisticated at present, but this may change over the long term. Afanasyev and others believe that although the *vory* still dominate the traditional criminal world, especially in prison, the so-called comrade criminals and gangster bureaucrats, with their intertwined links to the government, are growing in dominance of the social, economic, and political structures of the former Soviet Union.[33] Except for money laundering opportunities, the former USSR itself is right now the more ripe location for criminal activities of the comrade criminals, but when that is no longer the case – perhaps 10 or 15 years from now – we can look for them to shift their sights to the United States and elsewhere.

Influence of the Four Types in the United States

Of the four major forms of criminal organizations, the *vory v zakone* may constitute the greatest potential criminal threat currently presented by Russian émigrés in the United States. Whether this threat develops into a reality depends upon a number of contingencies including the presence of a sufficient number of *vory* in the United States, how closely they are linked to the Moscow-based crime leaders, and how successfully they can organize and control the multitude of criminal ventures in which ex-Soviets who are not *vory* are involved in the United States. The potential for harm from the *vory* will depend on how well some semblance of internal discipline can be maintained outside the prison walls where their roots lie. This control will be complicated by the fact that criminal activity is now taking place thousands of miles away from Moscow.

The comrade criminals also pose a potential threat to the United States in the sense that they can interfere with business, trade in dangerous weapons and materials, and interfere with the ability of US authorities to control crime. The threat of Russian émigré criminals seeking to use corruption and collusion to undermine United States law enforcement and other government agencies through the recreation of the comrade criminal status is, as of now, more of a potential than an actual harm. There have been allegations and rumors about police payoffs, for example, but so far no hard evidence has been offered and no corruption cases have been brought. Although they have the knowledge and the money, Russian émigrés do not now have the political contacts and the power to influence the legal and political processes in the United States. However, given that the individuals involved in criminal activity here are products of a system that is used to buying politicians and government officials, and in which corruption is a way of life, it would be naive to believe that American officials cannot be corrupted by these same individuals. At the same time, the pervasive corruption that has been acknowledged to exist throughout governments in the former Soviet republics creates problems for American law enforcement in collaborating with their counterparts in those countries. Thus, for example, attempting to find out whether a suspect now in the United States has a criminal history or is currently under investigation is complicated when there is a substantial risk that the target will be informed about the inquiry. The Immigration and Naturalization Service indicates that it is often impossible to find out if a visa applicant has a criminal background. In these and other ways corruption in the former USSR facilitates Russian émigré crime in the United States.

Although the *vory v zakone* and the comrade criminals may pose the greatest hypothetical threat to the United States, current criminal activity among Russian émigrés much more often takes the form of either professional criminal activity or entrepreneurial crime. Professional criminals carry out confidence schemes, low level thefts, and use of counterfeit credit cards. Entrepreneurial offenders take advantage of specific opportunities, such as those for insurance frauds, tax schemes, long term frauds, and cooperation with other crime groups. At this point there has been no substantial evidence that these activities are operated primarily by individuals with connections to the *vory v zakone* or comrade criminals in the former Soviet Union.

The Influence of Criminal Opportunities in the United States

Criminal organization usually is structured in a way that is thought to be effective for achieving the illegal aims of the organizers. At the same time, the expansion of opportunities for defrauding of government programs, and the ability to take advantage of credit systems that are much more widespread than they were in the past means that organizational forms that are effective in these types of environments may emerge. The frauds of various types, counterfeiting, and marketing of stolen goods that are most frequently found in the TSP files are, regardless of ethnicity, generally committed by small networks of individuals, some of whom may be specialists.[34] In the case of low-level confidence games, this team structure allows the offenders to gain the trust of the victims but to retain the ability to disappear after the deception is revealed. In order to defraud social welfare programs, offenders have to pose as legitimate actors in the system, such as pharmacists, patients, and ambulette companies. It would be very difficult for a single actor to create this appearance successfully. Instead, a network of actors can serve to create the appearance of legitimacy. However, once the scheme is over there is no need or benefit for the exact same set of actors to continue to cooperate. Therefore, a project-oriented network structure is likely to emerge as a consequence of the types of crime being committed.

The Influence of Existing US Patterns of Criminal Organization

DiMaggio and Powell call the tendency for organizations operating in the same areas of endeavor to resemble each other isomorphism.[35] They suggest that three types of forces – mimetic, coercive and normative – operate to create isomorphism. Mimetic isomorphism occurs when one structure is deliberately constructed as an imitation of another. Coercive pressures operate when one organization is forced by another to adopt a particular structure or element of structure, for example by requiring that such a structure be present in order for an organization to receive a resource. Normative pressures operate when individuals in an area of endeavor, who may move from organization to organization, come to expect or prefer a given set of structural arrangements. All of these pressures for similarity to other crime networks may operate on Russian émigré crime networks.

Some authorities have compared the organized crime among Russian émigrés to the American *Cosa Nostra* structure as described by Cressey [36] and others. For example, agents of the Federal Bureau of Investigation have stated that there are between three and five Russian émigré organized crime families in the New York area,[37] and investigators occasionally informally comment that some émigrés try to imitate the 'mob style.' Cooperation between Russian émigrés and individuals associated with the Colombo crime family members in the bootleg gas tax evasion scheme would also seemingly lead to the operation of institutional processes influencing the Russian émigrés to adopt an organizational structure similar to all or part of that of the Colombo family. The reported ties of Russian émigrés to other hierarchical organized crime structures would also seem to support this.[38] Other existing forms of criminal organization, such as those in other communities of recently arrived immigrants, may also be influential if they are seen as successful.[39] The cooperation of Russian émigré criminals with the Cali cartel may, therefore, lead them to adopt a similar structure. Because of the actual nature of the crimes in which Russian émigrés have been involved, it is perhaps more likely that they are influenced by the criminal organization of other groups involved in similar crimes. For example, the auto insurance scheme and some of the Medicaid reimbursement schemes are similar to those operated by other groups.

Actual Russian Emigré Criminal Organization in the United States

Russian émigré criminals operating in the United States have been described by some law enforcement authorities and by some in the media as being structured much like the *Cosa Nostra*. When Vyacheslav Ivankov was arrested in June, 1995, he was labeled the 'capo di tutti capos' of Russian émigré crime in the United States.[40] His arrest was taken as proof of a centralized Russian émigré criminal organization, along the lines of the *Cosa Nostra*.

Another view is that Russian émigré crime networks have no defined organizational structures or hierarchies that look anything like the *Cosa Nostra*.[41] Instead of being organized, according to this view, they operate mostly as individual specialists. As such, they have very fluid groups that occasionally come together to commit a crime. They do not have rigidly authoritarian and hierarchical structures, and the people involved do not answer to anybody in particular.

It is our assessment that neither of these positions is accurate. Our preliminary analyses of the TSP information indicate that there are large ongoing networks of individuals identified by law enforcement as involved or suspected of criminal activities who are directly or indirectly connected to each other. However, there is no evidence of a complex hierarchy or set of hierarchies. Instead, *ad hoc* teams of specialists are mustered for specific criminal ventures in an opportunistic manner. They may move across ventures, and sometimes work on the basis of referrals, vouching for each other. They often create flexible, project-oriented structures, to enable them to carry out particular crimes. In this they do not differ greatly from current trends in licit organizations, where there are indications of a decrease in the amount and degree of hierarchy, increasing reliance on strategic partnerships and task groups, and growing reliance on third party service providers.[42]

The predominant structure is one in which individuals who knew each other in the former Soviet Union, or who know people who know each other, collaborate for some particular criminal opportunity. The backgrounds of these individuals vary, but overall, the non-*vory* professional criminals and the opportunists who currently dominate Russian émigré crime here typically mistrust each other. There are few references to loyalty based on shared ethnicity or culture, despite the fact that some of the players knew each other prior to emigration. With the exception of the gas tax scheme and rare other exceptions, however, Russian émigré criminals seem to associate mainly with each other both criminally and socially.

The use of this type of flexible structure by Russian émigré criminals in the United States is a product of a number of forces. Perhaps most important, it represents a continuation of the patterns and practices that were institutionalized in the former Soviet Union. In particular it reflects the dominance of professional criminals and the young entrepreneurial offenders, rather than the *vory v zakone* or the comrade criminals. Second, it is well-suited to the types of offending in which these criminals are involved. This most often requires team work, flexibility, and the ability to mimic the operation of a legitimate actor or organization. Fraud and confidence schemes, and also certain violent crimes are particularly suited to this type of structure, while control of the gambling in a given area or other similar activities seem not to be. Should any of these situations change, however, for example if the *vory* emerge as important long-term actors in the United States, or if the nature of the crimes in which they are involved should shift, this could all change.

NOTES

1. The writing of this paper was supported by grant No.93–I–CX–0019 from the National Institute of Justice. The views expressed in this paper are those of the authors and may not reflect those of the US Department of Justice, the National Institute of Justice, the Tri-State Soviet-émigré Organized Crime Project or any of its members or cooperating agencies. Emmanual Barthe and Paul T. Haskell provided assistance with the collection and organization of these data. Don Sobocienski of the New York State Organized Crime Task Force provided a number of important insights.

2. We use this general characterization for simplicity's sake, recognizing the distinction between émigrés and immigrants, and also that many émigrés to the United States from the former Soviet Union are not Russians. Virtually all of the émigrés speak Russian.

3. For example, Scott Anderson 'Looking For Mr. Yaponchik', *Harper's*, Dec. 1995, pp.40–51; Traci Anne Attanasio, 'How Russian Organized Crime Took Root in the US', *Organized Crime Digest,* Vol.15, No.19, 12 Oct. 1994, p.1; Robert I. Friedman, 'The Organizatsiya', *New York,* 7 Nov. 1994, pp.50–58; Selwyn Raab, 'New Group of Russian Gangs Gains Foothold in Brooklyn', *The New York Times,* 23 Aug. 1994, p.1; Lydia S. Rosner, 'The Sexy Russian Mafia', *Criminal Organizations,* Vol.10 No.1 (1995); *The Times* (Trenton), 'New Comrades of Crime', *The Times,* 14 Aug. 1995, p.A1.

4. California Department of Justice *Russian Organized Crime: California's Newest Threat* (Sacramento, CA: 1995); authors's interviews with DEA and INS officials, Miami, FL, June 1995.

5. Walter W. Powell, 'Neither Hierarchies nor Markets', *Research in Organizational Behavior* in Barry Shaw and L.L. Cummings (eds.), Vol.12 (Greenwich: JAI Press, 1990), pp. 295–336; Oliver Williamson, *Markets and Hierarchies: Analysis and Antitrust Implications* (New York: The Free Press, 1975).

6. Mary McIntosh, *The Organization of Crime* (London: Macmillan, 1975).

7. See, for example, David Weisburd, Stanton Wheeler, Elin Waring and Nancy Bode, *Crimes of the Middle Classes* (New Haven: Yale University Press, 1991).

8. Ibid.

9. Wayne E. Baker and Robert R. Faulkner 'Role as Resource in the Hollywood Film Industry', *American Journal of Sociology,* Vol.97 (1991), pp.279–309.

10. The Tri-State Joint Soviet-Emigré Organized Crime Project, *An Analysis of Russian-Emigré Crime in the Tri-State Region* (New York, NY: New York State Commission of Investigation, 1996), p.1. See below.

11. We had complete access to investigative reports, memos, information from other agencies and other investigative materials collected by the TSP. However, we did not have access to grand jury transcripts, the identities of confidential informants, and other similar materials.

12. Alan A. Block, 'Racketeering in Fuels: Tax Scamming by Organized Crime', in Alan A. Block (ed.), *Space, Time, and Organized Crime* (2nd ed.) (New Brunswick, NJ:Transaction Books, 1994); Richter H. Moore, Jr., 'Motor Fuel Tax Fraud and Organized Crime: The Russian and the Italian–American Mafia', in Jay Albanese (ed.), *Contemporary Issues in Organized Crime* (Monsey, NY: Criminal Justice Press, 1995), pp.189–200.

13. Louis Freeh, Testimony before the Senate Permanent Subcommittee on Investigation, 25 May 1994, 100 Russell Senate Office Building, Washington, DC.

14. The Tri-State Joint Soviet-Emigré Organized Crime Project, op. cit., p.33.

15. Howard Aldrich, *Organizations and Environments* (Englewood Cliffs: Prentice-Hall, 1979); Paul DiMaggio and Walter W. Powell, 'The Iron Cage Revisited: Institutional Isomorphism and Collective Rationality in Organizational Fields', *American Sociological Review,* Vol.48 (1983), pp.147–160; Richard Scott, *Institutions and Organizations* (Thousand Oaks, CA: Sage Publications, 1995).

16. Lydia S. Rosner, *The Soviet Way of Crime: Beating the System in the Soviet Union and the USA* (South Hadley, MA: Bergin and Garvey Publishers, 1986) .

17. Konstantin M.Simis, *USSR: The Corrupt Society* (New York: Simon and Schuster, 1982).

18. Rosner, op. cit., 132–133.

19. Ibid.

20. Mark Galeotti, 'Organized Crime in Moscow and Russian National Security', *Low Intensity Conflict and Law Enforcement,* Vol.1, No.3 (Winter 1992).

21. Simis, op. cit.

22. Ibid., p.179.

23. See Steven Handelman, *Comrade Criminal* (New Haven: Yale University Press, 1995); Claire Sterling, *Thieves' World* (New York: Simon and Schuster, 1994).

24. Marshall Clinard, and Richard Quinney, *Criminal Behavior Systems: A Typology* (New York:

Holt, Rinehart and Winston, 1967).

25. Handelman, op. cit.
26. Arkady Vaksberg, *The Soviet Mafia* (New York: St. Martins Press, 1991).
27. Handelman, op. cit.
28. Vyacheslav Afanasyev, 'Organized Crime and Society', *Demokratizatsiya,* Vol.II (Summer 1994), pp.426–441.
29. The FBI has reported that there are 279 *vory* in Russia. James Moody, 'Remarks', Fifth Annual Economic Crime Investigation Conference, New York, NY, Sponsored by Utica College of Syracuse University (Oct. 1994).
30. Friedman, 1994, op. cit.
31. Moody, 1994, op. cit.
32. Afanasyev, op. cit.
33. Handelman, op. cit.
34. Elin J. Waring, *Co-Offending in White Collar Crime: A Network Approach* (Ann Arbor, Michigan: University Microfilms International, 1993).
35. DiMaggio and Powell, op. cit.
36. Donald Cressey, *Criminal Organization: Its Elementary Forms* (New York: Harper and Row, 1972).
37. John Stafford, 'Remarks', First International Law Enforcement Sharing Conference on Russian Organized Crime, 19–23 Sept. 1994.
38. Nathan M. Adams, 'Menace of the Russian Mafia', *Reader's Digest* (Aug. 1992), pp.33–40; Robert I. Friedman, 'Brighton Beach Goodfellas', *Vanity Fair* (Jan. 1993), pp.26–41.
39. William Kleinknecht, *The New Ethnic Mobs* (New York: The Free Press, 1996).
40. *The Times* (Trenton), op.cit.
41. Lydia S. Rosner 'The Sexy Russian Mafia', *Criminal Organizations,* Vol.10 No.1 (1995); Roy Surrett, 'Remarks', First International Law Enforcement Sharing Conference on Russian Organized Crime, 19–23 Sept. 1994.
42. Walter W. Powell and Laurel Smith–Doerr, 'Networks and Economic Life', in Neil Smelser and Richard Swedborg (ed.), *The Handbook of Economic Sociology* (Princeton: Princeton University Press, 1994).

23

Inside the Russian Mafiya

The 'mafiya' remains a shadowy force in Russian affairs. Dr Mark Galeotti separates fact from fiction to lay bare how this criminal phenomenon is organised and how it operates.

THE RAW figures about Russian organised crime seem telling enough. Even according to the Kremlin, the mafiya controls 40% of the Russian economy; an estimated 70–80% of businesses pay 10–20% of their profits for protection ('buying a roof' in the local jargon). Russian sources also talk regularly, but mis-

◆ Russian soldiers of the paramilitary police check documents of Caucasian vendors on a Kiyevski food market. Moscow is attempting to reduce the number of illegal visitors from former Soviet countries, of which many are believed to join mafiya groups.

leadingly, of thousands of organised crime, or mafiya, gangs. In part, this reflects the rather less discriminating definition the Russian police adopt of what constitutes 'organised crime', as opposed to any other form of crime involving more than one person and premeditation. More importantly, given the relatively loose and network-based structure of the mafiya, these figures tend to count each component entity rather than only the networks. Instead, Russia has 12 to 15 major mafiya structures, a rather more logical counterpart to China's six Triads or the four to five main criminal organisations in Italy.

Attempts at drawing up formal structures for mafiya groups have tended to represent them as classic pyramids, with godfathers at the top, a larger number

Author

Dr Mark Galeotti is Director of the Organised Russian and Eurasian Crime Research Unit at Keele University, UK.

KEELE
UNIVERSITY

of lieutenants (typically known as brigadiry, 'brigadiers') below and then street operatives. Some even suggest a greater formal compartmentalisation, with liaison, support and security sections. Attempts to apply them in practice, though, simply do not work.

There is no rigid chain of command. There are certainly key figures within the mafiya, including the vory v zakone ('thieves-within-code'), who may have little direct power but great authority and respect, and who often act as mediators and arbitrators, and the avtoritety ('authorities'), who are more conventional criminal leaders. However, even an avtoritet is unlikely to have much of a personal gang of his own. Instead, he is merely a powerful, wealthy and influential member of the network. In the face of an outside challenge to the network, the avtoritet can expect to be obeyed as he masses its forces in response. Otherwise, though, he has authority and influence, but if he treats the others in the network too much as subordinates, he risks alienating them.

Their options range from simply ignoring him to moving towards a rival network all the way to assassination; more usually, though, they will appeal to the other avtoritety of the network or a vor v zakone to uphold their autonomy. This is even visible in gangs named after their leader. While they remain small, then the leader may remain powerful, but as they expand and become, in effect, networks of their own, often within larger networks, then this personal control breaks down.

Most mafiya figures and crews have very broad criminal and even legal interests. There are specialists, ranging from assassins and computer crackers to money launderers and counterfeiters. But they tend to operate largely on the peripheries of the networks, as freelance service providers. The mainstream criminals will seek to establish a wide range of functions within the network and businesses. For a relatively new or unsophisticated criminal, this may be essentially simple, such as collecting protection money from market traders, selling counterfeit goods and running errands for a more established criminal.

Within 10 years, that same individual might be regarded as a 'brigadier' in his own right, with his own clients. He would probably have passed his market 'turf' onto one, in return for a suitable cut, and may now be claiming protection from local factories in the guise of providing private security. Meanwhile, he would probably own a number of seemingly legal

PA News/0070255

◆ A police task force in combat gear lead away a mafiya suspect. Some 12 to 15 major mafiya structures operate in Russia, each with broad criminal interests but no rigid chain of command.

firms and have moved into more lucrative businesses (such as narcotics).

Even the old organising principles of ethnic ties and place of origin are breaking down. Many gang or network names relate to where they first formed or where their original leaders came from, but these often have little bearing on their present location or operation. St Petersburg's dominant Tambov group is named after the city where its first members used to live, just as few members of the Solntsevo grouping still live or work in the Moscow suburb the gang was named after.

As for ethnic ties, even the so-called 'Chechen mafiya' now includes Georgians, Dagestanis, Kazakhs and even slavs. As a result, many of these networks have lost the personal or regional loyalties which held smaller gangs together. They have never acquired the sort of traditions and mythology which plays an important role in criminal cultures such as the Japanese Yakuza or Mafia. With little holding them together beyond self-interest and fear of reprisals in case of disloyalty, they are prone to division and redefinition, as components choose to move into

WHAT'S IN A NAME?

'Russian mafia', 'mafiya', 'Russian-speaking organised crime' or 'East European organised crime' - it is more than just a matter of choice what to call this phenomenon.

'East European organised crime' is blandly uncontroversial, but unhelpful in describing a phenomenon rooted as much in Vladivostok as Moscow.

'Russian-speaking organised crime' is similarly clumsy, as many of these gangs actually speak Ukrainian, or Georgian or any one of a range of other languages. While the criminal phenomenon shares some features with its Sicilian counterpart, it is also different in many key ways, so while 'Russian Mafia' is punchy, it is also misleading.

Hence the transliteration of the Russian borrow-word 'mafiya' has real advantages, underlining both the similarities and also the distinctiveness of this form of organised crime. After all, it is defined primarily by style and mode of organisation. The mafiya is a collection of criminal entrepreneurs, individuals and small 'crews' operating largely autonomously, within loose networks, perhaps coming together on a case-by-case basis to exploit a particular opportunity, which could be as easily be licit as criminal, but then as easily fragmenting.

another network as the balance of opportunities seems to shift. This helps explain the relative instability of the mafiya and its tendency towards internal bloodletting.

Moscow's complex criminal mosaic is still dominated by the Solntsevo grouping, although it and its allies and clients are balanced by the power of Chechen and other North Caucasian gangs and other ethnic Russian groups, forming a (currently) stable triangular balance of terror. There is a similar equilibrium in St Petersburg between the Tambov gang, which is especially dominant in the city's fuel industries and protection rackets, and gangs concentrating on smuggling and narcotics, respectively.

Further east, the capital of Siberian crime is undoubtedly the city of Yekaterinburg, home to the Uralmash gang (named after the factories in which they were first based) and Tsentralnaya (which rose in the city's centre). This is a wild and dangerous region, and while both groups now have their business interests, they are linked to numerous smaller gangs which concentrate on overtly criminal activity. The region's industries, especially aluminium and coal continue to be fought over in struggles which often spill from the financial to the murderous.

The Russian Far East remains dominated by the loose network known grandly as the Far Eastern Association of Thieves (DVAV), overseen by the senior vor v zakone Yevgeny Vasin ('Dzhem'). Nevertheless, this region is characterised by the very number and variety of its gangs, including increasing numbers of ethnic Chinese groupings within the legal and illegal immigrant community. In southern Russia, an uneasy mix of slav and North Caucasian gangs periodically explodes into local conflict. The slavs are largely dominated by gangs based in individual towns and cities, and others within the Cossack community. The North Caucasians include a wide range of nationalities, including, above all, the Chechens, but also with powerful Ingushetian, Dagestani, Ossetian and Azeri gangs. In the face of slav hostility, though, these gangs often co-operate, despite their numerous practical and historical differences.

This is, however, still a very dynamic underworld. While, for example, some degree of stability had been attained in Moscow and St Petersburg by 1995, there is still ample scope for upset and change. Like any competent predator, the mafiya is very sensitive to changes in the political and economic environment. The August 1998 crash of the Russian economy led to a 300% increase in financial crimes in Russia in the following 12 months, and a resurgence in the use of contract killing as a business tactic. Groups may rise and fall, but the spread of the larger networks overseas ensures that they will survive, whatever happens in Russia. The role of the vory may diminish, as tradition takes second place to interest. However, for the next 10-plus years, it is clear that the mafiya will remain a powerful, mercurial and dangerous constant of Russian life. ●

9

Name Index